ELSEWHERE

GUNNAR GARFORS

Elsewhere

The World's Least-Visited Countries

Broken Sleep Books

ISBN: 978-1-916938-96-0

All photos by Gunnar Garfors, with the exception of:
Helena Maria Pestana (45a), Ibrahima N'Gaédé (63d), Claudio Corallo (80a, b, c, e, 81a, b, 82a), Irene Scott (80d), Alessandro Balsamo (166d), Marius Arnesen (210a, c), Justin Jay (248, 259a, b), Wanja Buanes (298c, 299a, b, c), Pierre Selim (298d), Hiba Shalabi (344, 35a, e, 352a, b, 353a, b, c) og Lexie Alford (384-385, 396a, b, c, d, 397a, b, 399a, c, d).

The author has received a grant from Det faglitterære fond.

Graphic design: Øystein Vidnes
Map: Øystein Vidnes, based on map data from freevectormaps.com
Cover designed by Aaron Kent
Edited & typeset by Aaron Kent
Translated by James Ecendance and Aaron Kent

Broken Sleep Books Ltd
PO Box 102
Llandysul
SA44 9BG

To Mrs Garfors

Contents

MAURITANIA

GUINEA-BISSAU
GUINEA

EQUATORIAL-GUINE

SÃO TOMÉ AND PRÍNCIPE

TURKMENISTAN

AFGHANISTAN

BYA

YEMEN

ERITREA

SOUTH SUDAN

SOMALIA

CENTRAL
ICAN
UBLIC

THE COMOROS

FEDERATED STATES
OF MICRONESIA

MARSHALL
ISLANDS

NAURU

KIRIBATI

TUVALU

THE SOLOMON ISLANDS

Foreword:
Everyone wants to find their elsewhere

IT WASN'T ACTUALLY that long ago when I started travelling. In purely evolutionary terms, it has not really been long since anyone started travelling for any reason other than to find food. Nevertheless, I've witnessed substantial changes in travel habits just in the course of my lifetime. In the nineties, it was a big deal to travel to Paris, London, New York, and Hong Kong, not to mention Singapore and Los Angeles or even Rio de Janeiro. By all means, there is nothing wrong with any of these particular cities, apart from them being so far away.

With the continual rise in direct routes between cities, more and more people are trying out new destinations for the first time. It is enticing to experience something new and unique, either alone or with friends and family. For many, the so-called budget airlines have also helped open up the world from within your own country or continent to way beyond either of those. 'Now everyone can travel' according to the adverts, and we have taken the message on board in ever increasing numbers: We will travel. And not only that — both seasoned travellers and newbies are setting out more often on longer and longer trips. Caravans, campers, tents, and shelters have been swapped for a boarding card, and often a print-out as proof of a hotel reservation via one of the numerous online booking platforms.

Finally, we have really taken on the idea of exploring the world. But what has that got to do with those of us who were already doing exactly that at the end of the last century and the beginning of this one? Quite a few people who were travelling before Ryanair took to the skies and before Jet Blue seemingly doubled its fleet every few years, began to feel a little uncomfortable. They were in danger of losing face, or status, in their travel circles, as spending time in Seville, Olbia or Split no longer felt very special at all. Travelling has become a status symbol and therefore you should certainly have been to a more exciting place than your neighbour, boss, and siblings. At the very least you should have stayed at a more expensive, exclusive, or just cooler hotel; you should have found a jealousy-inducing apartment on Airbnb or eaten at restaurants with as many Michelin stars as possible during a way too short, long weekend. If the budget doesn't quite stretch as far as that, your restaurants should at least figure among the chart toppers on TripAdvisor or appear as star-studded suggestions when searching Google Maps. Furthermore, it all should, or must, be documented in real time via Instagram, Twitter, Facebook, TikTok and Snapchat, or a combination of the above. Then comes the essential need of WIFI, or mobile data that isn't going to cost the shirt off your back. Soon not even these elevated accommodation options or restaurants are going to be enough. We want to have something new, ideally as inaccessible as possible and seen by only a mere few. Or to be so obscure and unknown that you can roll your eyes if your audience is in the dark about that particular destination. You also then have the grounds to give a lesson in cultural and geographical facts interjected with social anthropological analysis of the people who live there. The locals.

Paris is by and large an exception. Most of us are so familiar with the place that locals are not a requirement. The city itself still passes as a romantic destination, even if it is amongst the most visited and touristy places in the world, and, as a result, not exactly very original, exciting, or even that romantic.

For more and more travellers who, of course, have been to both Paris and London numerous times, elsewhere is what it's all about. That means off the beaten track, far out in the sticks, or where nobody would think it is possible to live — or could even bother travelling to. Elsewhere is fashionable. Elsewhere is out of this world. Elsewhere is the new thing. Yes, even, a curious bar close to home full of locals speaking in dialect. Or 'elsewhere is the new black' as one would put it on the semi-world wide web. The exception being North Korea, where they just have intranet, although it does include dating services.

Elsewhere is also where you say you have been if you do not want your interviewer to know the coordinates of the destination travelled the previous day, like when I was in Afghanistan with two friends: Both of them had told their mothers that they were in Iran, a laudable endeavour to reduce anxiety and insomnia at home, but the reality was a place that could not, just could not, be known about — they were off the beaten track in a place deemed so dangerous that they were in danger of being put up for adoption had their mamas known.

As an umbrella term for dream destinations, elsewhere is a relative notion. For some people it would mean a village in their own backcountry, for others a mountain in Armenia, or maybe a carefully chosen vineyard in Portugal, Italy, or Chile.

There is just one remaining question: Where is the best place for you to feel off the beaten track? Almost no matter who you are, I think the world's least visited countries should be taken into consideration. Both geographically and culturally, they are rather unfamiliar and distant. And they are, needless to say, places that virtually no one travels to. Some call it the ultimate travel bucket list. But it is not enough to just travel to a place, take a few pictures and return home or onwards to the next location. Travelling without speaking to those who actually live there is essentially of no greater value than watching a clip on the Internet. Personally, I believe that a traveller who hunts out other cultures without allowing themselves to be in a way influenced by the experience, without pondering over social differences or challenging themselves over the arrogance of the developed world, is not much of a traveller at all. One can successfully navigate from A to B without scarcely having travelled anywhere. But of course, the fact that people take trips to other countries at all is a good start, nonetheless.

Travel is a bit like an important football match. There are very few who are not at all interested, having never played it in any way, shape, or form. Others are happy to be spectators, some in a rather more active and enthusiastic way than others. And then there are those that actually play themselves. Perhaps it is only these who can really grasp what football is about at any given time and how it is played in different places, as they fundamentally understand the game.

The same also goes for travelling. Unless one is open to listening, to be able to find out why things are different than they are at home, or even try other ways of doing things then the chance is lost to understand yourself or see yourself in the light of humility. We really are fortunate, as we can travel. Living in Norway, the UK, or other developed democratic nations, we have the opportunities that arise from excellent infrastructure, countless air routes to other countries, as well as respectable income and passports that open up the world.

Then this can also be taken advantage of — we travel as if it were an Olympic sport. We are travelling as much as we possibly can, but doing so while on holiday to relax from an overdose of overtime is not always the most desirable time to properly get to know a country. But just as long as we can big ourselves up through photo-sharing of our real experiences from exotic locations, then we are content with receiving the affable comments and likes from those stuck at home. We tend to stay in developed countries, without a need to overly relate to the issues that must be endured and overcome for those beyond the Western bubble. The odds are not exactly low of meeting someone from there either. All in all, it is quite ironic that many of us travel primarily with other likeminded people from the Western world — exploring destinations, eating at restaurants, and staying in hotels together. Many of the best-travelled among us rarely even talk to a single local. Maybe with the exception of the waiting staff that is. And then a little reluctantly with the occasional highly sociable guide.

I was no exception. But by travelling to many different countries, I have forced myself to think about the established truths. People in other places of the world are not doing things incorrectly, they are just doing those things differently. And who is to know — perhaps different is also good, or perhaps a different way of things is even better than what is 'normal' in our culture. Even in Norway, like many other places, we don't have just one culture, but multiples: What works within the steep inclines of Sunnmøre is not necessarily right for the inhabitants of near-Arctic Helgeland, or Sørlandet bathed by sun and sea. Not to mention the differences abound in Oslo from plush neighbourhoods home to ambassadors, districts of high-rise blocks to swanky café living. Intercultural couples often have few complaints concerning challenges and misunderstandings when compared to couples from different regions across diverse Norway.

No matter where it is that we call home, we view our neighbourhood, village, town, city, island, or country as the centre of the world. And this goes for everyone else too, including those whose home address is off the beaten track, the places we consider Elsewhere.

In stark contrast to us, the vast majority outside of the Western bubble cannot travel. First of all, they are unlikely to have money to spare and that includes for a passport as well, if they are even fortunate enough to live in a country where passports are available to all. Most are living in undemocratic countries where just getting a passport in your hand usually demands approval from the powers that be, and such approval will often only be granted for official business. Incomes are often so low that buying tickets for a single travel or multiple connections can be unthinkable or demand years' worth of savings. Not to even mention the stigma they soon encounter if they actually get to travel in the end and arrive in another country, if that is a Western one, in any case.

Things are rarely as they seem. But those that do not dare to dive into the depths will be left with a surface level impression. And that can be dangerous — just ask the Trojans. After they allowed the giant wooden horse behind their city walls, their travelling days were over. The horse was full of Greek soldiers, and the battle was already lost by the next morning.

Top politicians from every country should be mandated to travel widely to countries with challenges other than their own. Not by private jets and presidential limousines, but by walking into ordinary homes and being among those that live there. Nothing creates a better understanding of people, cultures, faiths, history, nostalgia, and peculiarities than travelling in such a way.

"The only thing we have to fear is fear itself," US President Franklin D. Roosevelt said in his inaugural address in 1933. I would assert that the same applies for when we travel to unusual destinations too. We are all going to die sometime, and the risk of that happening due to a heart attack at home in your living room or from being hit by local fireworks is far greater than something happening in Yemen or on the Solomon Islands. Why let a fear of the unknown stop us from exploring the world, seeking out experiences and learning to like, understand, and grasp cultures other than our own? Travelling and really meeting each other creates a common understanding between people on a level that no other practice can reach — bridging viewpoints, cultures, nations, religions, beliefs, and favourite football teams. I really believe that this world would be a better place to live in if more of us travelled, got to know one another and were open to other mindsets than our own. It cannot lead to anything else than increased respect, greater friendships, and an abundance of smiles. And maybe this would also be a cause for diminishing conflict the world over and reducing the number of wars.

There is, of course, the environmental dilemma. Everyone understands that planes emit exhaust gases and leave a trail of misery. The fact that the pollution is released high up in the sky makes its effects worse according to most experts. That should not be ignored, as air traffic and travel in general creates emissions, but it would still be wrong to just automatically blame passengers, who actually already pay carbon taxes as part of the ticket price, without wider criticism. Because, after all, our society has been geared towards aviation being essential for so much more than just getting people from A to B. We expect speedy deliveries of seafood, car parts, letters, parcels, and flowers, by which going by air is a fast, efficient way.

In addition, there are also many other culprits dirtying our atmosphere and it is important to look at the whole. Stopping air travel without also changing other habits would have little effect on the big picture. For example, our Internet use pollutes just as much as the aviation industry, thanks largely to gigantic sever centres requiring electricity and cooling all over the world. The development of new sensors, gadgets and gizmos that are all connected to the Internet means that the power needed for all that connectivity is also rapidly increasing. If The Guardian's prognosis is right, the Internet will account for 3.5 percent of the world's greenhouse gas emissions within eight years, and as much as 14 percent by 2040.

2.2 percent of global CO_2 emissions are produced by the aviation industry. Together with meat produced for human consumption, accounting for 8.6 percent of emissions, the aviation industry largely shoulders the blame for climate change, if one is to believe politicians and mass media far and wide.

"When people think about what they can do on a daily basis to be more environmentally friendly, the first thing that comes to mind is recycling waste and avoiding plastic bags. These are of course important, every little helps, but what really helps is to eat less meat, drive less and fly less," Karen Richardsen Moberg told me, a scientist at the Western Norwegian Research Institute. In my opinion, this is a simplification. People in most Western countries get the opportunity to vote in democratic elections and can cast their ballot in favour of political parties whose platforms set a strong climate agenda and can really make a difference concerning emissions.

To focus on the 11 percent of emissions that are caused by aviation and the meat industry is better than only focusing on the 2.8 percent derived from waste management but is still an oversimplification that is not of significant help towards achieving the 1.5-degree goal outlined in The Paris Agreement. If we are to reach this goal, then both governments and consumers need a plenary way of thinking, unabridged by tabloidization.

Let us try to have a closer look into the numbers. I say 'try' because no one has access to exact figures, and they are continually changing, in all circumstances. Everything presented from various surveys, reports and articles are therefore estimates, often varying wildly even within the same emission categories. I have used different sources to try to present as accurate and representative data as possible. The problem is that no matter what one does, the numbers just do not add up. By adding together all the different types of emissions one comes to a figure that is over 100 percent, which obviously is not correct. I have therefore been forced to tweak and estimate based partly on the conflicting information from the various sources.

But first: How much pollution can be attributed to wars and military activity? It is important to recognise that global defence, or military operations, are actually not reported within the data on emissions. And this is by no means because they are not producing any emissions. They have however managed to pull the wool over prying eyes with the argument that their emissions are military secrets, and that they therefore must be kept away from the public gaze. We have to say that we do not know exactly how extensive these emissions are, but estimates show that the US Military alone is responsible for 5 percent of all emissions, according to Barry Sanders, author of *The Green Zone: The Environmental Cost of Militarism*. This includes all activities performed by US defence forces, but it is notable that emissions increase dramatically whenever conflicts begin or escalate. The US Military is the largest in the world and uses 37 percent of the entire global defence budget. The US Military's budget is as large as the next seven countries on the list combined (China, Saudi Arabia, Russia, UK, India, France, and Japan), equating to over a third of the world's combined defence and war budgets. This is in the region of over 1.6 trillion USD per year (or put another way: 1.6 million million or 1,600,000,000,000).

As if that spending was not bad enough, the world's largest military superpower — the US Military — has enjoyed a universal exemption from all world climate treaties. A comfortable position for the worst environmental culprit in the world. If we also include defence related emissions globally, they amount to 13.5 percent of the world's emissions, and that is a conservative estimate. In addition, all new wars will substantially increase emissions. By any account, these 'secret' emissions mean that the total percentages per industry in civilian reports are inflated and must be reduced accordingly when emissions from the world's armed forces are taken into account. I have done this in the following table. In the left-hand column 'Without Defence' I have included the various types of emissions that can be found in civilian reports. But since military emissions are very much a reality, though kept secret, they need to be included as well. This is shown in the right-hand column, 'With Defence' where other sources of emission have been reduced by percentage, while leading to a corresponding increase in total emissions.

Another brain teaser is the fact that higher temperatures lead to less fresh water, and a lack of this ever so vital liquid has repeatedly shown to increase levels of conflict or cause

Sectors	Without Defence	With Defence
INDUSTRY	26.0 %	22.5 %
Cement	8.0 %	6.9 %
Steel	8.0 %	6.9 %
Textile	4.0 %	3.5 %
Aluminium	1.0 %	0.9 %
Other industries	5.0 %	4.3 %
TRANSPORT	21.7 %	18.8 %
Private Cars	11.0 %	9.5 %
Trucks	4.0 %	3.5 %
Cans and Lorries	2.0 %	1.7 %
Shipping	2.5 %	2.2 %
Aviation	2.2 %	1.9 %
FOOD PRODUCTION & AGRICULTURE	23.2 %	20.1 %
Fish and meat-based food for humans	8.6 %	7.4 %
Pet food (Factory made)	3.2 %	2.8 %
Other agriculture	11.4 %	9.9 %
HOUSEHOLDS & BUILDINGS	12.2 %	10.5 %
Private and commerical buildings	7.4 %	6.4 %
Internet	2.0 %	1.7 %
Waste Management	2.8 %	2.4 %
Unspecified energy production (estimate)	16.9 %	14.6 %
The defence sector	No data	13.5 %
Total	100 %	100 %

Emissions caused by oil, coal and gas are included in the relevant emission categories.

Further oil, coal and gas emissions are found under 'Unspecified energy production'.

wars. This leads again to militarisation and yet more emissions and dwindling water reserves. A vicious circle.

I am often confronted with my own carbon footprint which some journalists assert as gigantic with the amount of flying I do. With a job in the Norwegian Broadcasting Corporation (NRK), I have a pretty standard income. Almost all of my income goes on kerosene, so there is little left to spend on other ways of creating pollution. We can look in more detail at the emissions from the aviation industry:

The total global emissions per year amount to 35.8 billion tonnes of CO_2 (without the defence sector, or 41.3 billion tonnes with it). Aviation accounts for 781 million tonnes, or 2.2 percent (1.9 percent if we count military activities). There were 4.3 billion passengers on 38.1 million flights worldwide in 2018. That means 104,000 flights per day, on average, undertaken by approximately 25,000 passenger planes, 17 percent of which operate long distance. Each plane transported 113 passengers, on average. Which means that each passenger was then responsible for 0.18 tonnes of CO_2 per flight. There is naturally a difference between a one-hour long flight and one that takes 18 hours, whether there are 10 or 400 passengers on board and whether we are considering a new propeller plane with two engines or an old jet with four, but because all planes need to reach cruising altitude — which requires the most fuel — and since many of us fly both short and long-distance flights, then utilising such an average is not completely off the mark.

It is also not fair to divide emissions between only the passengers on board each plane. Such as the world is now, people in the Western world expect to have fresh fish from Lofoten, in the far north of Norway, served in the restaurants of Oslo, Dubai and New York. If your car breaks down, you want it repaired straight away. To reduce warehousing costs, it is necessary to employ logistics to deliver most spare parts directly to the garages. And not forgetting postal deliveries that are expected to arrive the next or even same day. The customers of today do not find it acceptable to have to wait for trains, ships, or lorries. According to the Norwegian newspaper, Aftenposten, 20 percent of revenues on commercial passenger flights are derived from freight; meaning that particular restaurant guests, car owners or recipients of parcels indirectly contribute to aviation emissions even if they have never taken a flight. Local politics also plays a part. If there hadn't been any flight routes to the far north of Norway, Finnmark, or further south among the mountains and fjords of Sogn og Fjordane, then Norway would have been more urbanised around the big cities than it is today. At the same time, those living in regional cities from the north to the south, have the expectation of direct international connections on their doorstep.

People demand that the big cities and the world beyond are quickly in reach. This doesn't necessarily mean that they will actually ever take any flights, but the fact that they exist at all, makes people feel more comfortable and generally safe in this knowledge to not have the need to move away from their local district. It is therefore not that illogical to subtract 20 percent of the aviation emissions for freight and the same for maintaining the attractiveness of settlements in more remote areas of Norway, or the back of beyond in Turkmenistan for that matter. Calculating things in such a way means each flight is no longer responsible for 0.18 tonnes of CO_2 per passenger, but 0.11 tonnes instead. Climate change scientists are largely in agreement that releasing greenhouse gases at 10,000 metres can be even more harmful, so permit me to double the emissions to 0.36 and 0.22 tonnes per flight respectively, to give a more realistic picture of the environmental damage.

Another example that is rarely mentioned is the food for our pets. The production of food for cats and dogs has become a huge industry which now accounts for more than a quarter of the emissions caused by all food derived from animals. There are approximately 450 million pet dogs and similarly pet cats in the world, totalling 900 million four-legged creatures. Producing their food emits 3.2 percent of the annual global CO_2 emissions, which means 1.1 billion tonnes (1,144,000,000). Since the average dog weighs 22 kilos and the average cat only 4, there is a big difference in the environmental damage attributed to these two animals. The average dog is responsible for 2.1 tonnes of CO_2 emissions each year, compared to 0.4 for a comparable cat. I am not saying that people shouldn't have pets, but utilise our own leftovers to a greater extent, just like people did before these pet food producers arrived to bombard us with commercials.

But let me also touch upon another issue: Reproduction. To raise a child in the Western world causes a dizzying environmental footprint, according to a 2017 study published in Environmental Research Letters. Having one less child would save each parent as much as 58.6 tonnes of CO_2 per year for the rest of their lives. That is as much as between 163 and 532 flights per year (depending on which of the four figures are used). Of course, I am not suggesting that people should stop having children, but it is just worth being aware that having a child actually contributes substantially to emissions, and that more prospective parents may in the light of this look at other options. There are many unwanted children in the world, an alternative to consider can be adoption.

Having a car is also well known to have an impact on climate, both because of the production of the vehicle and due to the emissions during its lifecycle. A small petrol car or an electric one adds on average 3 tonnes of CO_2 per year to the planet, while a large petrol driven BMW emits twice as much. The reason why a Tesla isn't necessarily better for the environment than a small petrol car is the huge emissions associated with the production of such a powerful battery. Transporting people over 1,000 kilometres by plane would typically require 25 litres of fuel per passenger, given an average load, although it also depends on plane type and weather. The EU average for private cars with a driver and one passenger is actually exactly the same: 25 litres of fuel per person. Emissions from the production of the car also come in addition to this. Emissions from the production of an aircraft is divided by so many millions of kilometres travelled by passengers that the true figure is marginal.

But back to flying. As a case in point, what if we changed our holiday habits from travelling within the Western bubble to rather exploring other cultures. If we travel differently and use our trips to exchange knowledge and establish friendships with people who live where we travel to, then travel can be a part of the green climate shift as opposed to being part of the problem. Increased mutual understanding across borders and cultures reduces the risk of war and conflicts. This in turn can lead to a reduction in military budgets and in the long run also reduce military operations the world over, consequently also reducing the need to maintain the related substantial emissions.

A reduction of 14 percent in defence activities across the world would reduce greenhouse gas emissions as much as the entire combined effect of aviation. But we have to be realistic with there being deep short-term resistance to any reduction in military operations within the current political climate. NATO, with USA at the head, are rather demanding that members increase forces, something which will also lead to 'enemies' following suit, aiding a vicious circle. An increase in military forces comes with an exceptionally high cost to the climate, quickly eating up any emission savings people otherwise manage to achieve through eating less meat, building in timber instead of concrete and steel, and knitting their own clothes from wool instead of buying polyester. To maintain the current strength of, not to increase, military forces, is in other words probably the most positive climate measure we can dream about in the short term.

Increased militarisation would in fact be catastrophic for the climate. The US has the world's largest economy, in part from being the world's largest weapons manufacturer by far: The USA already sells over 40 percent more weapons than Russia, who come in second place, and these two countries together account for more sales than all other countries combined. That Donald Trump, who does not believe that people contribute to global warming, is no longer president may pave the way for policies that are more environmentally friendly. That is way overdue.

Because, to just lay it on bluntly: If we increase the world's defence budget, that is already responsible for 13.5 percent of emissions, instead of decreasing it, then the Paris Agreement does not stand a chance, almost regardless of our actions. More travel between cultures can contribute to mutual understanding and insight at the same time as potentially reducing the need for weapons.

But who is going to say that to the likes of even a small Norwegian manufacturer, such as Kongsberg Defence Systems? Even an unassuming country like Norway knows full well how to protect jobs and incomes, at whatever the cost to the environment. Just don't mention that to anyone. The governing powers are very creative with their accounting to make Norway on paper look like an environmentally friendly nation. That I'm going to come to very soon.

I find it fascinating to learn who is the most critical of travel being a polluting activity. In the summer of 2018, I got in a conversation with a guy around my age. He was of the opinion that my travels were reprehensible. He was good at recycling everything himself, bought almost solely organically produced food and took public transport whenever he could. A little later into the conversation it turned out that during his lifetime he had bought four brand new cars, he did not like seafood, almost only eating beef when at a restaurant, he had a dog and a cat and lived with his wife and three kids in a relatively new detached house they had built themselves. The construction industry is accountable for substantial emissions, and cement is a little-known major culprit. Admittedly, new homes use less energy over their lifetime. Further revealed was the fact that there could possibly be a couple of trips to New York a year as well. "Well, and at least once to a bit of European sun, of course. Anything else just doesn't work with the lack of sun in Norway," he said, but by this time he had begun to speak a little more quietly than when we started our conversation.

According to official statistics, that omit military activities, Norway is accountable for 0.12 percent of global emissions. That means that every citizen in Norway emits 8.3 tonnes of CO_2 per year. That is almost double that of the average world citizen (4.8 tonnes) and a quarter more than the average EU citizen (6.75 tonnes). Qatar is the worst in the world with 38.5 tonnes per citizen, according to Our World in Data. This Gulf State, along with Kuwait, are the only countries that produce more oil and gas per citizen when compared to Norway.

But we have to have a closer look at this. Norway does not include emissions that are related to our oil and gas production, in stark contrast to Qatar where the emission figures for oil and gas production are included in their yearly totals. Since Norway's production actually occurs offshore, it is therefore not counted as part of the country's emissions, even though Norway controls the economic area in question. Most statistics put the blame upon the end consumer. Oil that is exported to Canada, for example, and used there, will have negative consequences for Canada's emissions, not on Norway's statistics despite them having produced the oil.

Norway is responsible for 2 percent of global oil production and 3.1 percent of global natural gas production. A James Bond reminiscent 0.07 percent of the world's population produce 2-3 percent of all the oil and gas. When oil and gas are directly linked to over 54 percent of all global emissions, according to Norway's Minister of Oil and Energy, Kjell-Børge Freiberg, this means that Norway is responsible for 1.36 percent of all accountable global emissions! Another way of putting it would be that 1/1426 of the people living on earth cause 1/73 of all the pollution. Or, to sum it up using a third digest: Each Norwegian emits 90.2 tonnes of CO_2 per year. That is a far cry from the more palatable official figure of 8.3 tonnes, which does not take into account the production of oil and gas. With a lofty

90 tonnes of emissions attributed to each and every person in Norway, this is twice as much as the official worst offender of Qatar.

That statistics are just statistics and can be used for pretty much any cause is well-known, but this does not help the world's climate save the slightest gramme of CO_2. Only by changing the attitudes of those in charge can emissions be reduced so that it actually makes a difference. Then it is a matter of using substantial resources on the research and development of environmentally friendly substitutes so that we can secure the provision of incomes and employment for future generations. As a paradox, Norway actually has the resources to become a frontrunner in such research focused on our future, as a direct result of its oil-derived Sovereign Wealth Fund, commonly known as The Oil Fund.

It is just so much more demanding to do that when the oil is just sitting there and can be pumped out. At least according to the lobbyists that are paid to squeeze out every last possible ounce, from the oil, before something else takes over. A little bit like trying to sell 'broadband' over dial-up long after fibre optics have connected even the fjords and mountains.

My point is not to glorify one cause of emission over another, but to show the various types of pollution side by side in such a manner that the whole picture is clearer. Still, the reality is such that unless we as consumers, especially in the Western world, don't act on all causes of emissions, not just on two or three, then things will change by too small a degree to ever achieve what The Paris Agreement has mandated — in any case not before there is so much global pollution that humankind goes extinct from the lack of oxygen with no one then left to pollute any more. It is not such a wild accusation that that is leaving it a little too late.

It is a mightily good thing that Elon Musk is planning colonies on Mars. Whether you are planning a trip to space or would rather stay on earth, I would gladly receive a postcard. As Augustin of Hippo once said: "The world is a book, and those who do not travel read only a page." Or, not travelling is like insulating your own mind and intellect.

Wishing you a great many eminent trips!

About this book

TO BE ABLE to inspire you to find your Elsewhere, or perhaps contribute to the case against, I have undertaken the journey on your behalf and gone to the 20 least visited countries in the world. I have travelled to each country at least twice, whenever possible to other places than those I explored the first time, in order to discover alternate perspectives, try out new things and meet new people. With each country I have included the official statistics for toursists per year. To put the figures of toursim into perspective, Norway is the 47th most visited country in the world with over 6 million registered visits a year. Or the 153rd least visited country if we make use of this book's angle. I am concentrating on the least visited countries, hence the countries with less than 50,000 tourists per year, all located in Africa, Asia, and Oceania.

It is worth noting that no official consolidated statistics exist for the number of tourists for all the countries in the world. Among tourism departments and other bodies that count tourists, there is no unified definition of what a tourist is or how they should be counted. The UN's tourism organisation, World Tourism Organization (UNWTO) publishes an annual overview, but I have discovered that the numbers provided by the various countries can vary enormously, as it is up to each country to report as they please, or what they see as beneficial. The figures from UNWTO, for example, show 2,000 tourists for Tuvalu, but the tiny island nation is only served by three or four propeller planes each week, with a total of approximately 10,000 seats a year. It is highly unlikely that 20 percent of all passengers are tourists, based on my trips there and conversations with both locals and visitors. The figures also include the few individuals that arrive by sea. A visit to the Tuvalu Bureau of Statistics showed that the figure of 2,000 tourists had been rounded down from 2,300 and that it included every foreigner that arrived in the country, whether for work or pleasure. By going down into the numbers, I found out that only 800 people had visited on holiday, as a 'tourist'. Saudi Arabia is another outlier that didn't start issuing tourism visas until early in 2018. Nonetheless, they have included for many years every pilgrim going to Mecca in their tourist statistics, thereby in many ways turning religion into a hobby. Perhaps not such a bad idea. Few wars have ever been started owing to disputes over recreational activities.

Some countries operate under the guise of clearly inflated numbers, presumably under the mistaken assumption that doing so will fool or inspire more people to travel there on holiday. I first put together an overview of the least visited countries in 2013 in an article for my travel website, *The Garfors Globe*, garfors.com, with an updated version two years later. The articles have now had millions of hits from around the world and are still read by hundreds, if not thousands of people every day. Most people will naturally never visit the least visited countries, but are seemingly curious about them, wishing inspiration for unusual travel destinations.

UNWTO is also lacking tourist numbers from the very least visited countries. Somalia was not even a member until autumn 2017, and others, for salient reasons, do not have anyone working with tourism or delivering in numbers. In many cases, I have had to collect information from other sources than from UNWTO. Where the official numbers have evidently been wrong (reported by the members themselves), I have also sought alternative sources for more credible information. It is doubtful that I have discovered all misreporting, but I dare to claim that this is the most accurate and the only complete overview that exists.

However, such statistics can never be completely accurate. Some countries only count tourists arriving by plane, others are concerned with arrivals by ship or base their numbers on reports from hotels. Many countries use the information travellers themselves have provided on immigration forms as a starter. Others have no other choice than to estimate. Within the Schengen area, for example, there are no immigration forms to base European numbers on. And then there are the people who are actually travelling on business, but say they are tourists to avoid bureaucracy, or intrusive questions from border police. Not to mention journalists that quite often travel to 'difficult' areas as tourists, despite being there for work as an employee or freelance journalist. Some might call that immoral and short-sighted, but as a reporter the alternative might actual mean permission is not granted for entry. For a freelance journalist that could be the difference between receiving an income that month, or not.

This book is no guidebook. With regards such information I have been content with including brief descriptions on how to get visas for the various countries, in its own alphabetised chapter at the back of the book. In terms of more apt travel information, I recommend that you search the Internet for the country, city, or island, or better yet — that you use social media and get in contact with locals or immigrants who know things inside out as they live there. The exception is information on hotels, with them rarely needing to use these, or never, unless they have overbooked the Christmas party. Most hotel rooms can now be booked via various websites where former guests have left comments and ratings. In my experience, these give a good picture of how things are, but to double check service and equivalent ratings, you can check Google Maps. If the place is really at the edge of the world and without a single review on the Internet, I then use travel forums on social media or just go from hotel to hotel asking to look at the room on arrival. Then you can likely get to bargain a bit as well, to hinder you going right out of the door to the competitor. The latter method is not recommended if you turn up late in the evening.

A web search on the airport or seaport you plan to arrive at may often give you valuable information, particularly with regards which transport companies can take you there, how you best get to the centre and what it ought to cost.

I returned to these 20 countries between August 2017 and October 2018. I have taken the freedom in choosing to start with the most visited of the least visited countries, thereby concluding with the absolute least visited country in the world.

The book is otherwise much more than a potential travel list. The goal is to deeply explore these relatively unknown countries from new angles. To be able to understand. To be able to convey meaning. And to show the bubble that we from the Western world live within, as seen from the outside. Because in many ways we are living in a pretty safe incubator with well-functioning infrastructure, low unemployment rates, relatively high incomes, good education and health systems, freedom of speech and free elections. In addition, there is relatively good gender equality and people are not persecuted for having the wrong religion or not believing in anything at all. We are quite exceptionally privileged.

That is not the case everywhere off the beaten track. It is rare that positive stories reach beyond these places and there are two main reasons why: Quite a few of the countries are plagued by war, terror, hunger and misery or a combination of these, and that is unfortunately what is newsworthy. Articles on war crimes and famines are not spiced up with insight or glimpses of daily life either — that would likely be wrong with regards to the context the storyteller and audience find themselves in. The rest of the countries are so small, unknown, remote, or poor at marketing themselves that there has never been any particular reason why you would ever have heard about them.

I have tried to share stories from the people I have met, from those that actually live there. The most adventurous among you may be inspired to visit at least one of the places. Others may be very content by having me travel on your behalf, so that the trips can be undertaken at your own pace from soft armchairs next to fireplaces within the safe and cosy surroundings of home.

Perhaps I can contribute with a more in-depth insight of these unknown and often underestimated countries. Through conversations and dealings with people from these countries, I have tried to explore different aspects of society and daily life. The goal has been to convey experiences and meetings with cultures most people know very little about.

I hope that the book will open eyes. Elsewhere is found a long way away geographically, emotionally, and culturally. It is outside of our comfort zone. Few of the countries have been mentioned in Western media, at least not about things other than war, terror, disease, and wickedness. One-sided information and a lack of extensive knowledge about many countries is a problem for democracy and broader public awareness. My writings can hopefully contribute to changing a little of this, provide background information and reveal countries with various reasons for why you most probably have never been to them. The least visited countries in the world may also be said to be the most exotic. The definition of exotic various enormously, but often includes characteristics of being something unusual, unique, or different.

Do note that the list has naturally changed due to the pandemic, but that it is still both relevant and useful as a picture of former normality and that it is likely to remain relatively accurate also in the future. Countries like Turkmenistan, China and Japan were for instance closed for tourists throughout 2022 but opened in early 2023. North Korea is still closed for tourists as of June 2023. These four countries were as such tied as the very least-visited country in the world in 2022. Neither of them are expected to be so in 2025.

But enough beating around the bush. Let's travel far away instead. Somewhere that is Elsewhere. I hope you will experience an open literary journey, and that it might sometimes be of inspiration to you to see one of these places with your own eyes, or at least contemplate travelling to a country, or a place, you still haven't been to.

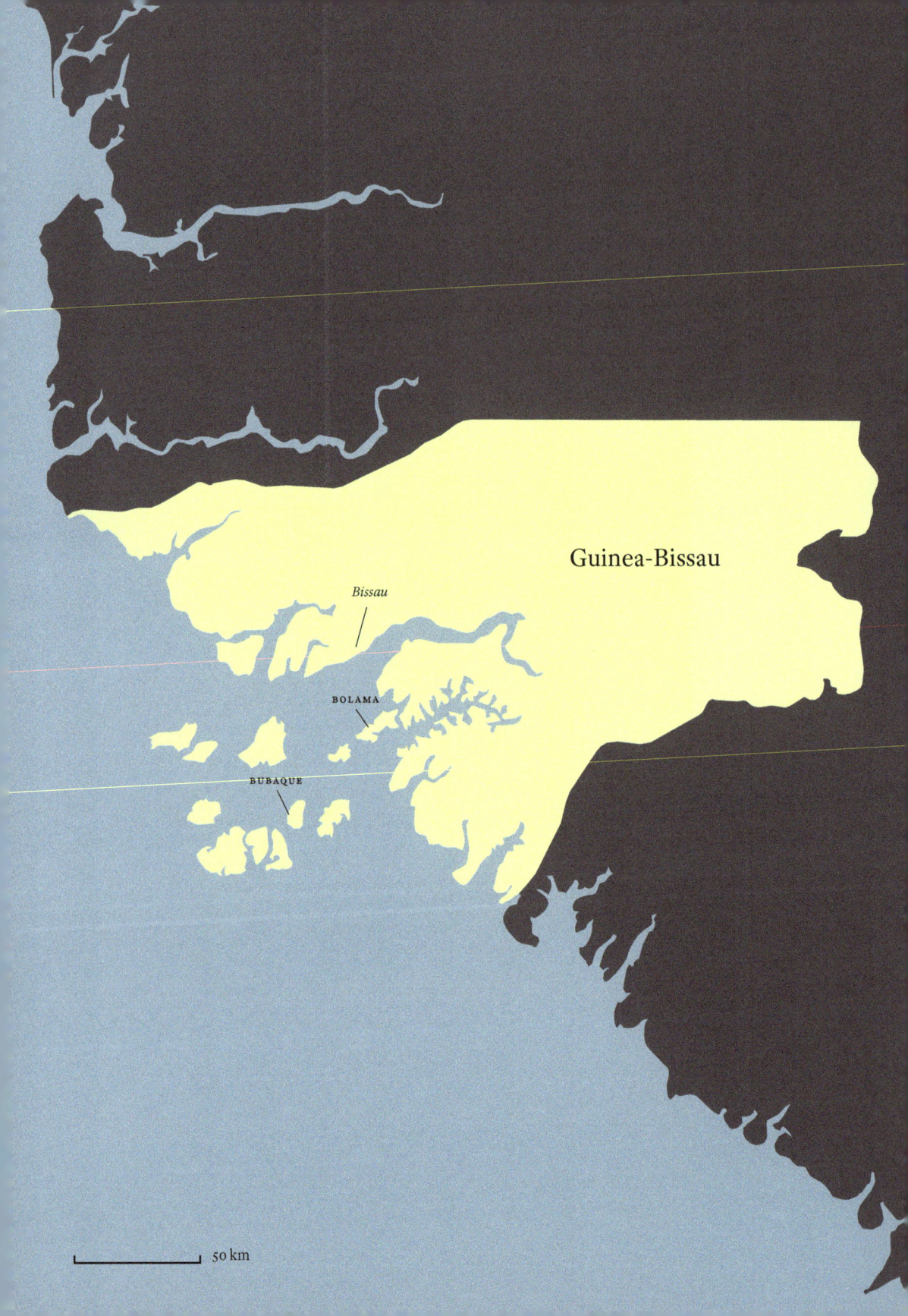

Guinea-Bissau

Bissau

BOLAMA

BUBAQUE

50 km

Guinea-Bissau, Africa

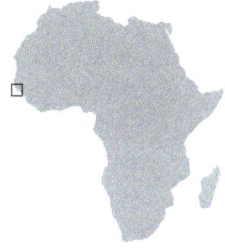

INHABITANTS: 1,800,000 (Wikipedia)
TOURISTS PER YEAR: 44,000 (UNWTO)
AREA: 36,125 square kilometres

THE HUNT for the least visited country in the world starts out in what should be, and in many ways actually is, a paradise. And an extra exotic start on the journey to the world's 20 most exotic countries is not exactly loathsome. Guinea-Bissau is a maritime jungle oasis with incredibly beautiful islands, the biggest archipelago of the continent and a surprisingly diverse animal kingdom both on land and in the ocean. In addition, there are all the party loving locals, that know how to appreciate restaurants and an active nightlife. The atmosphere peaks during the carnival in the capital, Bissau, during February and March. This is when people are invited to dance to music played on bamboo instruments, dressing up using plant-based face paint and clothes woven from local foliage. The dance competition among the streets is legendary, thanks in large part to the audience that also dress up and flock together to cheer along the participants. The dancers belong to numerous ethnic groups and have specialised themselves in ceremonial dances from their home villages. Two ladies gave me a local shirt in red, green, and yellow, the colours of one of the tribes, and invited me to join in. But alas my dance skills do little more than offend those looking on, so I declined in the politest way I could. It seemed to work, at least I didn't detect any resentment, and a few seconds later a bottle of beer was put in my hand.

"No problem, I don't like to dance either," said the beer-donor, a smiling man around thirty years old, wearing jeans and a very bright yellow shirt, before he jogged on together with the dancers while turning to me and toasting the air. The theme of the dances reflected various subcultures from the many ethnic groups and their interaction with nature, which is of great importance to them. Expect an absurd blend of very different dance styles, not to mention an imaginative mixture of trendy clothes and bizarre combinations that are not in fashion anywhere. But my goodness, how fun and colourful.

It is not quite as funny that coups seem to be almost a national hobby in the country just north of the 'bend' on the West Coast of Africa. No president has completed their five-year term since the poverty-stricken country gained independence in 1974. As recent as 2009, both the president and the leader of the coup attempt were killed in a shootout. Guinea-Bissau is a reliably unstable country. The area's been like that long before independence. It was once a part of the kingdoms of Gabu and Mali, until the Portuguese started getting involved in the late 15th century. The territory was given the name Portuguese Guinea, although its nickname said a lot more about what went on there, The Slave Coast. The Portuguese remained on the coast, with the interior not being explored for another 400 years. Slaves were in plentiful supply on the coast, and more slaves from here were transported to Europe than from anywhere else in Africa. Some other African countries exported even more slaves overall, but primarily to North America.

In 1956 the fight for independence started in earnest. The political party PAIGC (African Party for the Independence of Guinea and Cape Verde), or the guerrilla organisation as it was referred to by the Portuguese, quickly seized control over a large area. That the European colonists hadn't properly explored the jungle gave the locals the upper hand since they had the local knowledge. They also received support from local allies in neighbouring countries and weapons from the Soviet Union, Cuba, China, and African countries on the far left of the political landscape. PAIGC governed most of the country in 1973 and declared independence. Guinea Bissau was recognised as a sovereign nation the following year. Perhaps just in the nick of time, as only 11 African countries have since become independent. It was nevertheless the first Portuguese colony to gain independence, coincidentally just after the Portuguese dictator Marcelo Caetano was overthrown in the Carnation Revolution in April 1974. Portugal's other four colonies also gained independence within the next 14 months: Mozambique, Cape Verde, São Tomé and Príncipe, and Angola.

There were 11 coups or coup attempts between 1980 and the double killing in 2009 mentioned earlier. And another four coups, or at least attempts, after that. It was in fact so chaotic that the country was governed by the military for five years until 2014. Only then it was felt that the country was stable enough to pave the way for a more structured civilian government. Eight prime ministers tried to lead the country through the five-year period from July 2014. Five of these governed through 18 eventful months, and all eight were from the PAIGC party. The mess stemmed from a power struggle between the president and the political elite, but also due to the constitutional requirement that states that the president is the head of state, while the prime minister leads the government. The prime minister also needs a majority in parliament. President José Mário Vaz, popularly known as Jomav, had not quite understood this principle and exceeded his jurisdiction on two occasions, and was reprimanded by the Supreme Court. The punishment was no more than three days in prison. As in many places in the world, having good contacts in high places has a lot to say. Vaz was the first president since independence to finish a five-year term, despite a never welcome corruption charge that was never proven. He was replaced in 2020 by former prime minister Umaro Sissoco Embaló who he himself appointed four years prior. It is rarely particularly peaceful in Guinea-Bissau.

But oh, how idyllic it can be in the lush green country with a myriad of small inviting islands, cashew farms and plantations everywhere, surrounded by untouched forest. The country is the sixth largest producer of cashew nuts in the world and earns a reasonable amount from fishing or fishing licences. But not enough. Poverty is widespread.

The desire for more tourist dollars and euros has been a factor in the government making it easier to visit the country as a tourist. Not that it has been particularly difficult, but the lack of embassies abroad has made it more impractical than problematic. These days you can easily apply for an electronic visa online. Fill in your personal information, attach copies of scanned plane tickets, passport and passport photographs and pay by credit card. All done in your web browser. In no time at all you will receive an email stating that your application has been authorised. And then all you need to do is just travel. Or so one would think.

The end-to-end electronic application process is unfortunately not as complete as it seems. To get passed the police checks at the airport a printout of the email is required, something that was not stated anywhere the last time I checked. If you don't have this, then you are going to have a memorable stay at Costa del Aeroport. In reality this means an unpleasant chat with a semi-senior police officer lacking primary school English capability, inside a small windowless bluish office. Eventually an interpreter will convey the message that you will have to go to your hotel and printout the email and then return to the claustrophobic blue room. Merely showing the email on your smartphone will not suffice and the printer on the desk by the policeman's side is not for your use. It is also not satisfactory to let the officer take a photo of the email on your phone or to transfer it via Bluetooth or email. But do not despair. In the meantime, the officer will look after your passport in a black computer case secured by a miniature brass padlock.

On the way to my hotel, I passed many buildings from colonial times, most of which had fallen into a state of disrepair. Maintenance has apparently never really been high on the agenda in large parts of Africa, particularly not when it comes to buildings constructed by more or less arrogant colonists, and that is understandable. Former colonists should also take responsibility for the lack of creativity. Because the country name isn't particularly original and may be one of the reasons for relatively few tourists. By that I mean it doesn't exactly stand out. Guinea-Bissau does after all compete with a cluster of other countries with similar names, such as Equatorial Guinea, Guinea, Guyana, and Papua New Guinea. And also, the French territory of French Guyana in South America.

For marketing purposes, several of these countries should change their name. Not only because there are many of them, but also because the word guinea long ago was the name for something as plain as a British coin, worth one pound and five pence. Although, the

country name is probably derived from the Portuguese word Guiné, which in the 15th century was used for the area where the Guineans lived. Guineans were people living south of the Senegal River in what is now Senegal, Gambia, Guinea, and Guinea-Bissau. Most of the latter consist of low-lying sumps and mangrove forests. Exotic enough, but not exceptionally exciting.

It is fortunately not mainland Guinea-Bissau that is the most fascinating part, but the Bijagós Islands that are among the most underestimated, wild, and enticing in all of Africa. The 90 islands and islets actually make up what is apparently the only archipelago in the continent. That impressed the British as well, and for a short period in the 1790s they challenged the Portuguese ownership of the colony, based out of these islands. The Bijagós Islands are now the tourist machine of Guinea-Bissau. Thanks largely to Portuguese and French couples that run everything from guesthouses to hotels in a fashion that tends to be described as luxurious, depending on what you compare with. Foreign tourists have western demands and expectations that local hotel owners so far have not been able to live up to, but they are in the process of learning. A tourist machine in one of the least visited countries in the world is inevitably less well-oiled than in for instance Mallorca or Las Vegas, but you are likely to meet Europeans here, particularly the Portuguese, French, and the odd Spaniard. The option to stay in one of a rising number of foreign-owned hotels might make it feel safer to travel here. One of them, Dakosta, has even introduced its own slogan: 'Privacy is the new luxury. Unknown is the new security'. And they are onto something — there is something that feels off the beaten track about the first sentence. The second answers rhetorically that who is going to bother to carry out terror in a country no one has heard of. The accommodation offering on the 23 inhabited islands is satisfactory for most people, and the fact that several of the restaurants serve gourmet food also contributes to a trickle of tourists. The two best known islands, with the most impressive service levels and the most visitors are the main island of Bubaque and the most populous, Bolama. Both are covered by palm trees and patches of jungle. Electricity is unheard of on some of the less modernised islands. Expect local kids to tug on you if you make the trip there — they want to feel if you are actually real with your unusual skin tone or whether you are merely a ghost. Or a hologram — if they had only known what that was.

But there is more to these islands than guest houses and eateries, other senses are also catered for. If you familiarise yourself with the styles of visual art, necklaces, and masks from the different islands, you will discover small regional differences, similar to the differences seen in the artistic expression of traditional dress from various areas of Norway. The natural scenery consists of coastal savannahs, sand banks, mangrove forests and palm trees in abundance providing the perfect sanctuary for both saltwater hippos and crocodiles, as well as monkeys and antelopes. But I shouldn't just quickly pass by hippos.

The saltwater species is rare and is only found on and around the island of Orango. Make a note of the name. Dolphins and giant turtles will also keep those with scuba gear company. For those who don't like getting wet, there is no shortage of spectacular beaches. They are usually at your disposal and at your disposal alone, but don't be surprised if you are affected by snow blindness. That is how white the sand is. Just don't expect an ice-cream seller or beach volleyball net.

Fortunately, according to most tourist-shy tourists, the archipelago is too far from Bissau. Not in distance, but in travel time. The boats do not run every day and take many hours. How long exactly naturally depends on which island you are going to, as well as weather and wind conditions playing a role. You should account for anywhere between five and ten hours, unless you contact your hotel, who can fix rapid sea transport. Small boats with large outboard engines can then take you to your destination in less than two hours, but they will set you back accordingly. Unless lengthy sea journeys are one of your favourite activities, it may still be worth the money, despite the lack of comfort.

It had taken me many hours to get there, thanks to theoretical time schedules that were not adhered to. My strategy was therefore uncertain. I decided the best thing to do was to sit down at a café near the port and check with the crew hourly for any news. Eventually there was something.

The preferred form of transport in between the islands are pirogues — small open boats with or without a sail. They can carry a dozen or so passengers and are a great way of getting in touch with locals and receiving advice on restaurants, activities, and accommodation possibilities. It was on one such pirogue that I had gotten to know about Luke's bungalow. The most important thing when depending on pirogues for transport is to have plenty of time. Waiting for high tide, a corresponding pirogue, better weather conditions, the engine to be fixed, the pilot eating his lunch or a combination of these is usually the rule, not the exception. I had brought with me more fruit, biscuits and drinking water than I had thought necessary, thanks to previous experience. A few years earlier I had taken only a few oranges and some water onto a boat that ended up taking 40 hours, not eight. I also received plentiful advice about not to go on any pirogues under heavy winds as there were numerous examples of pirogues having gone down in big waves and strong winds. Should the wind pick up too much, one should only hope of being stuck on Bubaque. Otherwise, supplies may run out after a few days, even though a speedboat can almost always be summoned. Just be prepared for a sky-high price should the captain be capable of detecting your hard-to-hide desperation.

I stayed in a wonky, small bungalow, without any lights other than an oil lamp. Electricity poles and wires were something unknown, the same for diesel generators. The cabin had been built with various types of wood and the floor was just sand, like the beach it had been built on. A couple of palm trees fortunately provided shade, and a constant breeze made it quite comfortable. The food was served by my host, Luke.

"You know, as in Lucky Luke, the cowboy," he smiled. The 50-year-old wouldn't give me his actual name, but it hardly mattered. The similarity to the cartoon character was certainly evident. The ambling man wasn't much taller than me but had black hair and pretty much constantly had a cigarette in his mouth. His mangy mongrel could possibly pass for Rantanplan, so only the horse Jolly Jumper was missing. And of course, the Dalton brothers. I should have brought my brothers Øystein, Åsmund and Håkon and the story could have made it into the comic books. Åsmund is the tallest, Håkon is the shortest.

But looking from another angle, oysters were hard to come by in the Wild West. The ones that I was served in Guinea-Bissau had been fetched from the sea floor less than an hour earlier by local kids, according to Luke. They tasted perfect. Not too salty, and with the long-lasting, characteristic aftertaste that emerges when one slowly chews the oyster meat. Vinegar, onion, or lemon as condiments were nowhere to be found, but I prefer oysters without mixers anyway.

The Bijagós Islands didn't come under Portuguese control until 1936, and some of them are still off-limits to outsiders. For instance, Rubane and Enu, are considered sacred and used for private ceremonies. Furthermore, some islands are nature reserves and are therefore 'closed'. The inhabitants believe in 'another world' that is difficult to attain. To get there one must behave well towards fellow humans behave nicely to fellow humans in this world, as well as to be in harmony with one's own soul and nature. This can be influenced through ancestors by the help of prayers and sacrificial gifts. They also believe that some people, in particular priests (oronhôis) and village chiefs, have the ability to mobilise invisible forces, and rituals have an important place in their culture. The same for respect towards nature. But it isn't only their faith that means the 30,000 inhabitants take on looking after their islands seriously. Rules for the treatment and conservation of land and water systems on the islands have evolved in an excellent way through several centuries of political, social, and economic changes. The handling of resources is further integrated with culture, social norms, and religion. The result is perhaps the best functioning and diverse ecosystem in West Africa.

As a male traveller, having some freedoms restricted may not be all bad. The island of Orango, where the saltwater hippos are found, is governed by women. There is of course nothing wrong with that, but it might be a good idea to know that they are traditionally the ones who pick a spouse, with the male having very little say on the matter. This is less applicable to male travellers, but it may be wise to bring the wife along - or suddenly you could have two.

There is far more to Orango than just hippos and female leaders. The beaches alone are worth the visit. The vegetation is also quite different to that of the neighbouring islands, with the middle resembling more of a savannah than a jungle with its high yellow grass and wide-open plains and the occasional patch of white sand far from the sea.

To travel to Guinea-Bissau without paying these islands a visit is a bit like spending a night in a hotel next to Oslo Airport and then boasting about having seen Norway. (There are actually more people who do this than you would have believed, and even with their limited knowledge of Norway claim that the area around the airport is 'amazingly and totally stunning', without having seen a single fjord, mountain, or island.) Don't fall into the same trap in Guinea-Bissau. Leave Bissau or stay at home.

Back on the quayside in Bissau I met two very nice brothers. Lémus Lama managed to get to Europe via Cape Verde eight years ago. The 36-year-old now lives in Madrid where he works as an electrician. Their mother had died a few weeks before we met each other, and he had only just returned because of the funeral.

"And there will be a little time for holiday as well. I will spend three weeks here now and get to visit my three brothers and most of my five sisters."

His younger brother nodded proudly in his white T-shirt. His English was not top-notch, but good enough to understand that he was being talked about. Lémus told me that life here was hard, and that he had decided to head for Europe to try his luck there. He now pays taxes with a happy heart and can send money to his family in Africa.

"Did you know that hospitals are free in Spain? And that you don't have to pay a bribe to see a doctor?" he almost shouted at me. I smiled. He didn't expect an answer but further asked what I was doing here.

"I am on holiday," I answered.

A broad smile crossed his face.

"You mean you are here for the ladies?" he laughed. I smiled.

"No, I have a girlfriend at home."

"But you are not married?"

I shook my head.

"Then you can just as well have a girl down here? The women here are exceptionally beautiful! And you, as a white man, can have your pick!" he promised me.

It wasn't really on my agenda to pick up some babes in Bissau. My partner, Caroline, was waiting for me back home. But Lémus was right. It wasn't at all difficult to be noticed by the women. It was actually difficult to not draw their attention.

One night I had sat myself down at a bar counter after having walked around in the sun all day, breathing in the sights and sounds. I was thirsty. Since the country is a former Portuguese colony, Super Bock was the main beer on offer. I ordered a chilled lager. Almost before I had even been served the little brown bottle, an exceptionally pretty lady had sat down in my company. She was in her twenties, slender, sexy and with fake dreadlocks. I am not particularly skilled at recognising who has had hair-extensions,

but in this case, it was obvious; they were bright blue. They were however not the only reason she seemingly demanded attention wherever she walked. Her heels were so high one would struggle to measure them, and her outfit had been designed to crane necks all around. Her large breasts stood straight out from underneath the dark blue dress with glitter woven into the fabric and a surprisingly small neckline. Her breasts worked like a magnet to all eyes, likely independent of gender and orientation of the beholder. The concentration of silicone breasts across Guinea-Bissau is in all probability low — in this instance I assumed that a powerful push up bra was working its magic. She was clearly working.

"Hi!" she said. "What are you doing here?"

"I am on holiday," I responded.

"In that case I am sure you can stretch to buying me a drink," she suggested.

"That I can probably manage, but I don't pay for love," I said.

She laughed. It was a playful and charming laugh, but at that moment I felt it almost scornfully.

"I'll leave the love to your wife, but I can give you sex that you can only dream of," she said, before staying silent while keeping her dark red and fulsome lips open enough so that I could see her exceptionally white teeth. It was likely for the best that I hadn't taken a big sip of Portuguese beer.

"So, most of your customers have a wife at home?" I continued.

"Yes, the single ones are usually too young to be able to afford to pay what I demand," she nodded, offering me her hand while looking straight into my eyes. I don't think I have ever seen so dazzling, yet deep and beautiful eyes. They were large and seemed mild mannered.

"My name is Tiffany."

I took her hand and introduced myself before I started to tell my story. The idea was to tell her that I was writing a book, and that I was not interested in paying for sex, but that I would be happy to pay her some francs for an interview, since I would potentially be taking up some of her paid work time.

I didn't get any further than my writing of a book before I was interrupted.

"Ha! And you think that I haven't had authors, politicians, businessmen or actors as customers before? You won't impress me with a fancy title."

Her temperament made me smile. She was blessed with good looks, a smile and wit, and I told her that I didn't doubt an impressive resume of customers. That made her calm down a bit. I was able to finish what I had planned to say.

She shook her head.

"That would ruin my reputation."

"How come?"

"If it comes out that I charge for interviews, I will scare away customers and destroy my whole business model. They will firstly not believe I am any good in bed since you prefer to spend your time talking to me. Secondly, they may fear that I will tell you who they are, what I do to them, and that their wife or employer might then find out. Unless we go to your hotel room, that is, there I'll do whatever you want, and that includes answering your questions."

"That would ruin my reputation," I countered.

"How come?"

"Some of my friends would be disappointed that I took you to my room without having sex with you, and my girlfriend would hardly believe that I took you to my room without having sex with you. It's a lose, lose, situation."

We reached a compromise.

I bought her a drink from the bar, and she promised that she would answer my questions if I didn't take out my notebook. But only until she finished her drink.

"You mean that you'll sit with me longer if I buy you more drinks?" I tested the water.

"Dream on! I cannot be drunk when I pick up a customer or two later today."

She was smart. Street smart, in any case.

The bartender gave her a gin & tonic, with lime, after just a nod from her. I guessed this was her local place. I got another Super Bock. The 20 centilitre bottles didn't last very long in the heat.

"A customer or two, you said? At the same time?" I wondered.

"Gladly, but then I'll charge triple."

"Triple? For two guys?"

"Two men or usually a man and a colleague of mine. You have no idea how many guys dream about having a threesome. Most of them with two girls. And the willingness to pay accordingly. It's all about knowing what your services are worth," she explained.

"You have clearly thought this through."

"Of course! Do you want to see my business plan or something?» she asked and took a long slow sip through the black plastic straw.

I was in no doubt that she actually had one.

"So, how long do you intend to stay in this...well...job?"

"I am halfway there. I am saving for an apartment. When it has been bought and paid for, I'll start working as a hairdresser. You see my dreadlocks? I made those myself,» she said, quite proudly. "But being a hairdresser doesn't pay enough to get any kind of place, so I do this."

"Isn't it pretty awful having to sleep with just about anybody?"

"I don't fucking sleep with just anybody. Firstly, I consider every potential customer. I, for instance, come over to you. You look pretty decent, aren't so old that it will take forever, and white enough to have money. Besides, I love sex. And I never do anything if the guy or guys don't use a condom."

Suddenly, she drank more of her G&T. I understood why. A few handsome guys had entered the bar, not surprisingly they were far more attractive as potential customers than I was. They had also noticed her. I could feel the long glances from my right. I thought I had time for one more question.

"What about a boyfriend or husband?"

«I am only 28 and have plenty of time. But I don't want him to read about me in your book, so don't write that I am called Tiffany, OK?»

That wasn't a question. It was an order. She then sucked up the remaining drops from her drink, pushed it aside and gave me a silent farewell by raising her eyebrows, before getting up and graciously walking over to the table of newly arrived bar guests. I turned my head as she left. Tiffany knew the trick of how to walk in those high heels.

She didn't look back during the change of pasture. The woman was a complete professional. But whether her night was a success or not, I don't know. I made my way home to my hotel. And just for the record, her name isn't Tiffany. Unless she originally gave me a fake name and is actually called Tiffany. To have made completely sure, I should have perhaps given her the rarer pseudonym of Åsbjørg.

Prostitution in many forms is widespread in Africa, and visiting westerners know how to take advantage of what is on offer. Although they do not always pay with cash. It is not unusual that the 'payment' comes in the form of all sorts of pampering during the week, or weeks the man is there. She, or even they, yes, I have seen plenty of middle aged and old white guys going around with a woman on each arm — they get to stay with this man in a luxury hotel, with all meals included and often gifts such as clothing or jewellery as part of the arrangement. The man then has free reign to 'love' all the time they are on holiday, without paying directly for it.

"Yes, and then at home I can say that I haven't paid for sex," a dutchman told me. The tall blonde man in his fifties often travelled to West Africa on holiday.

"It is like an unwritten rule. The women never ask for money, but mostly get whatever they want," said Bas, not his real name.

"Around here I can just go into a bar, or even just stand outside one and gaze into the air, and just like that, I have the company of beautiful young women. Then I can just pick whoever I want," continued Bas with a grin. He added that he hadn't experienced such easy access to women back home in Amsterdam since the late 1970s. It is worth mentioning that the same form of prostitution is also going on in Gambia, a bit further north, but there, Western women are equally making the trip.

People in Guinea-Bissau are rather stationary, but it has nothing to do with laziness. Norway is almost exactly nine times bigger than the West African country, and we have, for instance, 30 times as much road. The standard of infrastructure is poor here. Even in the capital only a few roads are paved, and even in the centre most residential areas are located next to bumpy unpaved roads. The red sand they are made of creates vast amounts of dust, although not as much as in the Middle East. The exception is in the old town next to the port in Bissau. It is paved pretty much everywhere there, in between the partly dilapidated buildings that were constructed and painted by the Portuguese in the early 20th century and that have hardly seen any maintenance since. The colour combinations are magical and make walking in the streets a pure pleasure for photographers and those in search of likes.

The restaurants in Bissau serve excellent Portuguese cuisine for a low price. One still doesn't come here in search of Michelin stars, but maybe to party. That is something they certainly have mastered here, late into the night within the dark city districts. Streetlights have never been a budgeting priority, but there is no reason to be afraid of the dark. Bissau is mostly a safe town, and it also feels like it too. It is mostly like that in this little country of just over a million people. At least the country is safe, just as long as you are not the one leading it. There were all those coups, you know.

As is usual before leaving my Norwegian home, I had made a note of all the exchange rates for any currency I could end up needing, including those of countries where I would only have a stopover. Delays or cancellations can suddenly mean a stay for a day or two in a country I had not planned on visiting. If possible, I withdraw money from ATMs, but they had been few and far in between on my first trip to Guinea-Bissau in 2012. I was then able to exchange cash with money men on the street, or in more official looking locales. American dollars were most sought after then and are still favoured in most countries, although the Euro is seemingly more popular now both in Guinea-Bissau and a number of other African countries. Unless you know the exchange rates, it is virtually guaranteed that you will get a worse rate that you should have received. There are many ready to take advantage among the world's currency sharks.

In 2018 the situation was different. More restaurants accepted credit cards and almost half the ATMs I tried worked fine with my Norwegian Visa card. That usually gives you a better rate than exchanging foreign currency. However, the very worst thing you can do is to choose your own home currency for the transaction if this is offered by the machine. This applies to everyone and every currency. Always pick dinars, nafka or dong instead of a set exchange rate in the cases you get the option to choose on the card machine at the hotel, restaurant, or shop. As usual when on the road, it pays to keep it local.

Although exactly that may be difficult and perhaps not desirable when it comes to air travel. There are six 'airports' in the country, albeit five of them can hardly be called anything other than a patch of ground, or at best, an airstrip. None of these provide scheduled flights, and the runways consist of grass or gravel. The only international airport is just a few kilometres north of the centre of Bissau and the few airlines that fly to and from Osvaldo Viera International Airport are all from abroad. Dakar in Senegal located 400 kilometres to the northwest is the only scheduled regional destination. Several foreign airlines fly there. That then suits very well with the 19th least visited country in the world lying just north of Senegal.

"Can you take a picture of us?" these children in Bissau wondered. "Only if you stand still," I replied.

I met lémus lama (left) and his younger brother on the quayside in the capital. The former had emigrated to France, but came back for his mother's funeral.

The Portuguese building style persists even long after the colonists relinquished control of the country.

Maintenance is in short supply here, especially when it comes to buildings erected by colonial masters.

Such pirogues are widespread in West Africa. They are used as fishing boats and for transporting both goods and people. They often have seals.

Minibuses are a common mode of transport here. You'll be more cramped than on the bus back home.

The catholic church came along for the ride when Portugal colonised Africa and has remained since.

Street markets abound in Bissau. As a bonus, there are so few tourists here that you don't have to haggle.

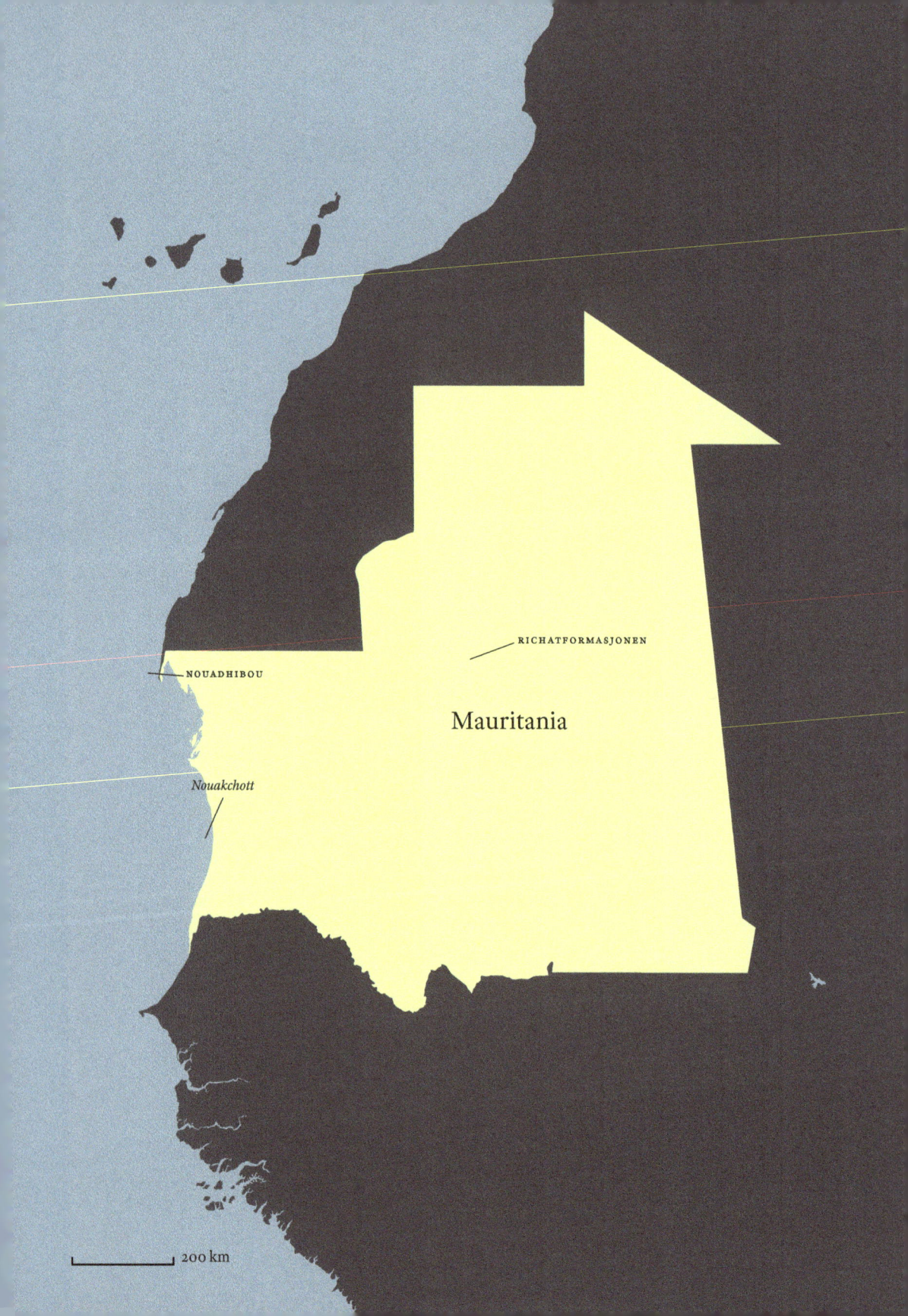

RICHATFORMASJONEN

NOUADHIBOU

Mauritania

Nouakchott

200 km

19

Mauritania, Africa

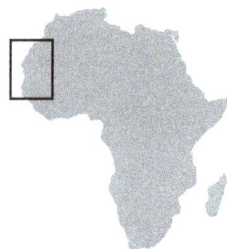

INHABITANTS: 4,300,000 (Wikipedia)
TOURISTS PER YEAR: 39,000 (UNWTO)
AREA: 1,030,000 square kilometres

WE REMAIN on the west coast of Africa still. The journey north to Mauritania from Guinea-Bissau took us through Senegal, which encircles the whole of Gambia, and is where middle-aged men and women from the West help themselves to young, beautiful, but otherwise poor locals. Mauritania, by the way, is a country that you really shouldn't get confused with the southern paradise of Mauritius, east of Madagascar. Mauritania is 'everything' Mauritius is not. Firstly, the country is primarily desert — 90 percent of the land is comprised of sand. Bone-dry Saharan sand. Muslim rule means that the country is also dry when it comes to a choice of drinks. The same cannot be said for Mauritius with all its numerous bars. Both countries can boast about their beaches, with almost Mauritania's entire 600-kilometre-long coastline consisting of beaches that are rarely, if ever, used. Swimming in a burka has somehow never really taken off. Mauritius, on the other hand, is a mecca for swimming, snorkelling, diving, and honeymoons.

There is also a gulf in the difference in size. Comprising 1,030,000 square kilometres, Mauritania is enormous. It is almost three times as large as Norway, and 505 times larger than little Mauritius, with its paltry 2,040 square kilometres.

Mauritius was named after Prince Maurice van Nassau by a Dutch admiral in 1598, while Mauritania got its name from the ancient kingdom of Mauretania, which existed from 300 BC and lasted a thousand years. The name means 'land to the west' and for a period was led by King Atlas, who is credited with inventing the model globe. It is perhaps not so strange that he saw the need for such an invention — the country back then was even greater in size than it is today, encompassing what is now Morocco and Algeria — the largest country in Africa.

Today the Mauritanian coastline is almost uninhabited. On the beaches of its few coastal towns there is still a lot of life, but almost all of it is related to fishing, including in the capital.

"Do you want to buy fish for dinner? Buy your fish from me, mine's the freshest!" yelled several of the colourful salesmen after me as I walked through the fish market, which lies just ten metres from the beach itself, on the outskirts of the million-strong city of Nouakchott. It was like a scene from the comic Asterix, minus the fighting using fish as the weapon of choice. Mauritania's geographical location means that one sees an ethnically mixed population, with many of North African descent and a relatively light skin tone, while others have darker features from southern and Central African forefathers. Geographically, the country forms a bridge between Arabian North Africa and the more 'traditional' Africa. Roughly speaking, the inhabitants of Mauritania are divided into three groups: Half of the population is Bidhan — an ethnic group with Arab ancestry — while one-third are Haratin — descendants of slaves from all over the continent. The last ethnic group comprising one-sixth of the population can trace their family tree to West Africa. It is perhaps a little unusual for Westerners to think about people in categories, but in Mauritania the differences between these groups are at the root of a caste system that is out of the ordinary — more on that later.

The most colourful thing about the fish salesmen is nevertheless the clothes they wear. Some have an optimistic belief that brilliant, disparate, and sometimes gaudy colours will attract buyers. Colour theory is presumably on the school curriculum in Mauritania, with a vivid spectrum on display from fish, lobsters, crabs, and shellfish. The choice is flawless. Some sold over countertops, others had their wares in cooler boxes full of ice — there was no electricity available in the covered fish hall without walls.

A little down from the yellow, sun-bleached building, now almost ochre, the traditional long, narrow fishing boats in a multitude of colours lay shoulder to shoulder. Fishermen, porters, and mechanics jumped between them. All were men. There were women there as well, but they were on the beach relaxing, selling fish or finding someone to buy fish from — fish that they could sell on with sufficient margins to defend the raid on the chaotic strip of beach. Five or six well-covered teenage girls were delving around the water's edge, braving a few steps out into the waves before they suddenly turned and raced back, giggling, and laughing behind the black scarves concealing their faces. The clothes were a clear sign of religion they belonged to. With the exception of a small group of Christians, more or less everyone in the country is Muslim. The breaching of Muslim values is punished by fines or imprisonment, while atheism is so strictly forbidden that those found guilty of it are sentenced to death. The same applies to the crime of blasphemy.

I was standing a few metres away in the shadow of an upturned wooden boat perched on trestles, following the blue-green waves as they smashed into the sand, shore, and the girls, with a steady rhythm and intense power. It made it difficult for boats to launch off the shallow sand flats, also hindered by other boats on their way in. Even though the beach is long, it was very cramped for space. It was all about being as close to the fish market as possible, since under this blazing sun the catch can soon lose its value. For the fishermen and salesmen, it's a question of getting the seafood delivered quickly to their customers, who can then put it in the fridge or on ice, or at least fillet the fish as swiftly as possible, with the hope of selling most of it before the flies spoil the fish. Ice is expensive; not everyone can afford such a luxury, and I could smell that as I walked away from the beach and back through the open fish hall. Fortunately, a fresh breeze somewhat improved the situation. I was doing an inspection before lunch, conditions likely changed for the worse through the day.

Nouakchott has only been the capital since 1960, the same year that the former French colony gained independence. In the Afroasiatic language Tamazight, spoken in northern parts of Africa, the name means 'the place where the wind blows'. With breezes coming in off the Atlantic Ocean, it's quite an appropriate name. Unfortunately, the city is completely flat, so in the centre, several kilometres inland from the coast, you barely notice the wind. It's just hot. Scorching hot.

Just like in Guinea-Bissau, Mauritania is ruled by a leader who took power in a coup. Under General Mohamed Ould Abdel Aziz, the military toppled the president in 2008. Aziz later resigned as general in order to be able to 'legitimately' run for presidency the following year. He won. Few were surprised about that.

Something less well known is that Mauritania was the last country in the world to ban slavery, officially as late as in 1981, but it wasn't until 2007 that the law was introduced to criminalise the trafficking of slaves. This meant that for 26 years slavery was illegal, but there was no way for it to be enforced. Things take time, and bad habits can be hard to break. Five per cent of the population still live as slaves., Especially amongst certain tribes in the north, being a slave owner conveys status, but slavery has not been eradicated completely in the southern region of the country either, which we will look into later.

Certain terror groups have their base in the desert, and it is not advised for Western tourists to travel inland alone. Two terrorist attacks in particular gained a lot of attention in the international press, and still play a part today in keeping visitor numbers so low for this vast West African country. The most gruesome attack took place near Aleg on Christmas Eve in 2007. Four French tourists were killed, and one seriously injured. Masked men attacked a family who had stopped for a picnic by the side of the road. Police later arrested nine men with links to Al-Qaeda and referred to them as members of an isolated sleeper cell. In the West the attack received massive press coverage, and the international community failed to be convinced that this was a one-off event. Among other things, The Dakar Rally of 2008 was cancelled as a result of the attack. Two years later a suicide bomber from the same terror group took the life of an American teacher and injured two Frenchmen just three days after the Mauritanian presidential elections. Compared to many other countries, two attacks is not a great number, but for one reason or another the fear has never gone away. The explanation I was given is that much of blame lies largely on the nomadic lifestyle and proliferation of gangs in inland regions of the country. People

know that shady groups persist within unknown regions of the desert and fear that they can strike at any time, at any place. It is difficult to get rid of the sense of fear — something that means we still associate Mauritania with terrorism, even today.

I kept mostly to the coast. In Nouakchott I had arranged a meeting with Ibrahima N'Gaédé, an engineer who works for the Ministry of the Interior and, among other things, is responsible for the servers and software that mean that visitors can get a visa on arrival, or VOA. The expression visa on arrival is music to the ears of many a traveller. It means that you avoid wasting time having to frequent an embassy, like the first time I visited and had to stop by the diplomatic consulates in both Berlin and Dakar before eventually obtaining a visa.

I am thankful to the 36-year-old for the work he has done. Any country without unnecessary bureaucracy is a friend of mine. Far too many places ask for needless information before they issue visas. Just what are they going to do with information about flights or hotels at the moment of application? If I don't get the visa, I've wasted time and money to no avail. And if I'm coming, then I'm coming, and they'll find out about it at the border. Then they are free to ask me where I'll be staying — which is exactly what they do in Mauritania. It has to be said that there is a great level of creativity and time wasting in the diplomatic world of visas. Certain countries require, for example, a print-out of your bank statement, letters from employers, information about how many wives you have (and how many you are planning to bring along with you on the trip), a copy of every page in your passport, a criminal record check from the police, details of the religion of your parents and spouse(s), medical certificate, a copy of your vaccination card, proof of negative HIV test, and/or a list of every country you have visited in the last ten years, the latter with the provision of five lines on the application form. I just wrote 'all of them'.

Ibrahima, or Biba among friends, reached for his can of Sprite. It is possible to find restaurants that serve alcohol under the counter in Mauritania if you know who to ask, but very few locals actually drink in this Muslim country. I kept to juicy, perfectly sweet orange juice, freshly squeezed of course. A desert country or not, there is good access to familiar and unfamiliar varieties of fresh fruit. For the most part this is down to trade with their neighbours. We ate dinner at San Francisco, one of the city's most popular restaurants. Ibrahima had suggested for us to meet there.

"I don't eat out very much, so I'm the wrong person for restaurant recommendations, but I asked several colleagues and they all suggested San Francisco," he explained as we entered the dim premises. His tone was almost trying to vindicate himself of responsibility just in case the meal turned out to be catastrophically bad. I could understand why. Inviting foreign guests to a restaurant and ending up with unhappy friends is bad enough in Norway, a country that sits high up on the bucket list of many a fussy gourmet traveller the world over. I could only imagine how awkward it would be in a country that almost no one visits in the first place, a country with so few recommendations on travel sites that a single ruinous portrayal from a visiting westerner would have many potential tourists avoiding San Francisco like the plague. There wasn't a great deal of light penetrating the restaurant, primarily due to its small and partially covered windows. On the walls hung large TV screens showing international football, and as we know, sunshine and flatscreen TVs have never been the best of friends. In spite of the darkness, I liked the atmosphere. Laughter floated freely around the tables, almost all of which were occupied and around some of them people were extra tightly packed together in order to make room for everyone. Biba had been given good advice. We hit it off and discussed everything from football, surfing to Mauritanian city planning, before the subject turned more serious.

"I've also heard about this thing with slavery, but have never seen it with my own eyes," he replied to a direct question from me.

"As far as I understand it's not a question of slavery in the traditional sense. It's more like the class system in England or the caste system in India. In any case, many people outside the cities work for almost nothing, so if you look at it that way, strictly speaking you can call it slavery," he chuckled, taking a slurp of soda. We were waiting for our main course of king prawns. My mouth had been watering ever since being at the fish market earlier in the day and I hadn't been able to stop myself when I saw them on the menu. I had likely walked past the prawns that very morning and took it for granted that they were fresh.

"Many families see themselves as nobles and claim that they have blue blood. They would never permit their children to marry someone from a lower position, people who they see as almost slaves. And at any rate, slavery was widespread here for a long time, and now it's still there at the back of people's minds, in their psyche," Biba continued with an air of gravity. As we are aware of, making something illegal doesn't necessarily mean you're going to stop anything, and the same can be said about the ban on slavery, which was so ingrained in this country. Photojournalist Seif Kousmate visited Mauritania in 2018 to write a piece about modern slavery and was able to verify that tens of thousands of people still live as slaves here. The vast majority come from the two African minority groups mentioned earlier. As many as half of the Harantin people live as slaves or in slave-like conditions. Much of this goes far back in history and applies to the whole of North Africa. The Arabs raided villages and introduced a strict caste system that is still in use today. To put it briefly, the lighter-skinned act as the masters, and so much higher in terms of hierarchy than those with darker skin that it equates to a master-slave relationship. Since the status of the slave is passed on from mother to child, 'recruitment' is guaranteed. The lack of education among the slaves further contributes towards maintaining and legitimising the practice.

"When I was younger my mother told me each and every night that we had to respect our 'masters' because their caste was higher than ours and because they were 'saints'," a young man, Moctar, told Kousmate. He managed to escape, but his mother refused to join him and even later criticised him for having fled his 'owner'. It is not unusual for freed slaves to return to their 'owners' under their own free will because they have a sense of loyalty and think that it's wrong for the master concerned to have lost his 'property'. We can view it as a different dimension of Stockholm syndrome. Moctar has no plans to return to his life as a slave and has now gotten a place at school. His dream is to become a lawyer in order to fight slavery in Mauritania.

Fortunately, he's not the only one, despite a good deal of opposition. Activists working against slavery have often been harassed or even tortured. At the same time, the ruling powers deny that there is any problem with slavery. And for some of them, there certainly is not a problem — their slaves are a benefit, not a drawback. In the 2019 election there was a hope that the most important anti-slavery organisation in Mauritania could actually gain power. Initiative for the Resurgence of the Abolitionist Movement (IRA) was led by Biram Ould Abeid, who came second in the 2014 presidential elections. But yet again he finished as the runner-up, this time around with 18.6 percent of the votes. The time was clearly still not right to beat the sitting president and former coup-maker Aziz who was succeeded by his ally Mohamed Ould Ghazouani. The incumbent president is also an Arab and, in many ways, personifies reality in Mauritania — the light-skinned Arabs have better jobs, more leadership positions and higher salaries than those with more pigment in their skin.

I had spent a few days exploring the capital on foot and it was striking just how reserved people were. Almost nobody said hello or smiled — just like being back at home in Norway, I thought. Neither Norwegians nor Scandinavians in general have an especially good reputation of being friendly out in the wider world. We are seen as arrogant and dismissive, something I have often faced. My theory is that we are shy, but this hardly excuses the fact that we barely smile at people we meet — unless we've got alcohol in us, then we suddenly become a lot more Mediterranean in nature. It was as though Biba was reading my thoughts.

"Maybe you've noticed that we're not the easiest to get to know. In contrast to Senegal to the south and Morocco to the north, we are quite simply a bit dull. And that's a shame, because then we don't get to meet others. I don't really know why it's like this, but I think it's because many of us have got it too good. We have too much money," he claimed.

It wasn't quite the angle I was expecting. Maybe in Norway, but not here. Sure, the airport is brand new, and I was surprised by a modern four-lane highway with streetlights stretching all the thirty kilometres to Nouakchott. But a glut of money is something else — was I really in Africa?

"Too much money? How so?" I wondered. Officially, forty percent of the population live below the poverty line. A high concentration of donkeys is a sure sign of low income.

When you can't afford a vehicle powered by petrol or diesel, you resort to one that runs on grass. Nouakchott is swarming with donkeys, and men of all ages sit on their carts behind the donkey and steer. Sometimes the cart is empty, at other times there are two full oil drums or as many possessions as can be carried. In any case, the animals walk at their own pace. I can quite understand why they've gained a reputation for being stubborn. Who volunteers to just move mountains, barrels full of oil, or all worldly possessions?

"I'm mostly talking now about Nouakchott. We've discovered oil, so there's some corruption here. People have enough, and that means that they aren't so keen to approach other people. They don't need to sell you anything," Biba explained.

With the exception of the fishermen and a woman on the street selling coffee and baguettes, he was right. Nobody had approached me, which I perceived as highly unusual considering this was Africa. People on the streets of the capital deliberately avoided my gaze and did not smile. A few had yelled warnings to me when they saw me taking pictures, which they clearly did not like.

"Do you think this is contributing to the lack of tourists?" I wondered.

"Sure. In addition to the fear of terror attacks," he said, under his breath. He had heard this before, including from his brother who lives and works in France. Especially there, many saw Mauritania almost as a synonym for terrorism after the doomed family picnic that had made terrible headlines in France and elsewhere in the West.

It does not exactly help our stereotyping that most men in Mauritania often cover their faces with a kind of scarf. It is actually a type of turban, most often called cheche or haouli. The rectangular cloth is between three and five metres long and is wound around the head. When it is being put on, it starts and ends at the top. The turban is essential, and by no means only decorative. Desert dwellers need to take measures to stop the body being constantly hammered by the elements. The headscarf protects its owner against sunlight and heat, not to mention dust and sandstorms. The eyes, respiratory system, and skin all benefit from a little protection in this tough climate of hot winds and cold nights. But the traditional dress does not just cover the head. Over their bodies they wear a boubou, which has been perfected to withstand the sun and wind. The bold white robe is personalised using gold embroidery and over the generations, it has evolved as an answer to the forces of nature. It consists of a robe with a hole in the middle for the head and two large open sleeves. When it gets exceptionally warm in the summer, the sleeves can be rolled up to the shoulders. Pockets are sewn on each side with space for personal possessions. In wintertime, long undergarments can also be worn. That might mean just a broad pair of trousers called saroual or an additional long shirt with short or long sleeves called tunic that can be made of different materials such as cotton, sheep's wool, or camel hair. Some versions stop below the waist, while others go all the way to the ankles. On their feet people wear sandals, typically made of gazelle hide. Just as in Norway, the temperature influences the choice of underwear, and temperature variations in the desert can be extreme. And just like in Norway as well, there is a big difference between the clothes worn by the coast and those on the plains. The long, colourful garments in use on and by the sea would be of little use in the desert.

No matter the temperature, you will not see female legs in Mauritania. It is quite simply unacceptable. Outsiders should not even be able to see the contours of women's legs through their dresses, which are called melahfa and are often made of a colourful fabric in creative patterns. The dress consists of a long piece of fabric that a woman wraps around herself in a carefully rehearsed and particularly elegant manner; getting dressed is not child's play. They usually wear at least two layers, amongst other reasons to stop the gazes of men other than their husband. But there were also exceptions to the rules. In sports arenas even the forces of conservatism have given up. There, Mauritanian women wear shorts too.

In their traditional dress, only the eyes and hands of the men are visible. At long last, a country where men wear burka-like clothes, even if they can quite easily be removed with no repercussions. To the untrained eye everyone looks anonymous and almost the same, but there can be great differences in colour combinations, technique, and embroidery if one takes a closer look.

For thousands of years, trains of camels have crossed the country on established routes with well-covered Bedouins as their eminent escorts. The bold, traditional style of clothing is effective and lifesaving in a land of almost only desert.

But well-covered Muslims are not the same as terrorists, recounting historical attacks or not. Biba, in any case, did not think that the fear of terrorist attacks and obscured men alone were keeping people away from the country.

"The most important reason behind the lack of tourists can be blamed on the total absence of a focus on creativity at school. Here it's the losers, those who have failed the traditional education, who go on to become artists, singers, designers, or writers. And it shouldn't be like that! It's one thing that we don't have anything exciting to offer tourists, but what about ourselves?" he asked rhetorically. He wasn't exactly selling his country, and I thought he might benefit from seeing the potential in surfing, kiting and ancient monuments.

At long last a waiter arrived. He was balancing two portions of king prawns on one unusually long arm. On the other he had found room for salt and pepper shakers as well as vegetables, rice, and French fries. He had covered all bases with the side dishes. Ibrahima barely noticed the food. As someone who was not an artist himself, he was surprising passionate about the subject.

"In Mauritania you're seen as a success if you find a well-paid job and can sit in an air-conditioned office all day long. It might be extremely tedious, but then you're living a

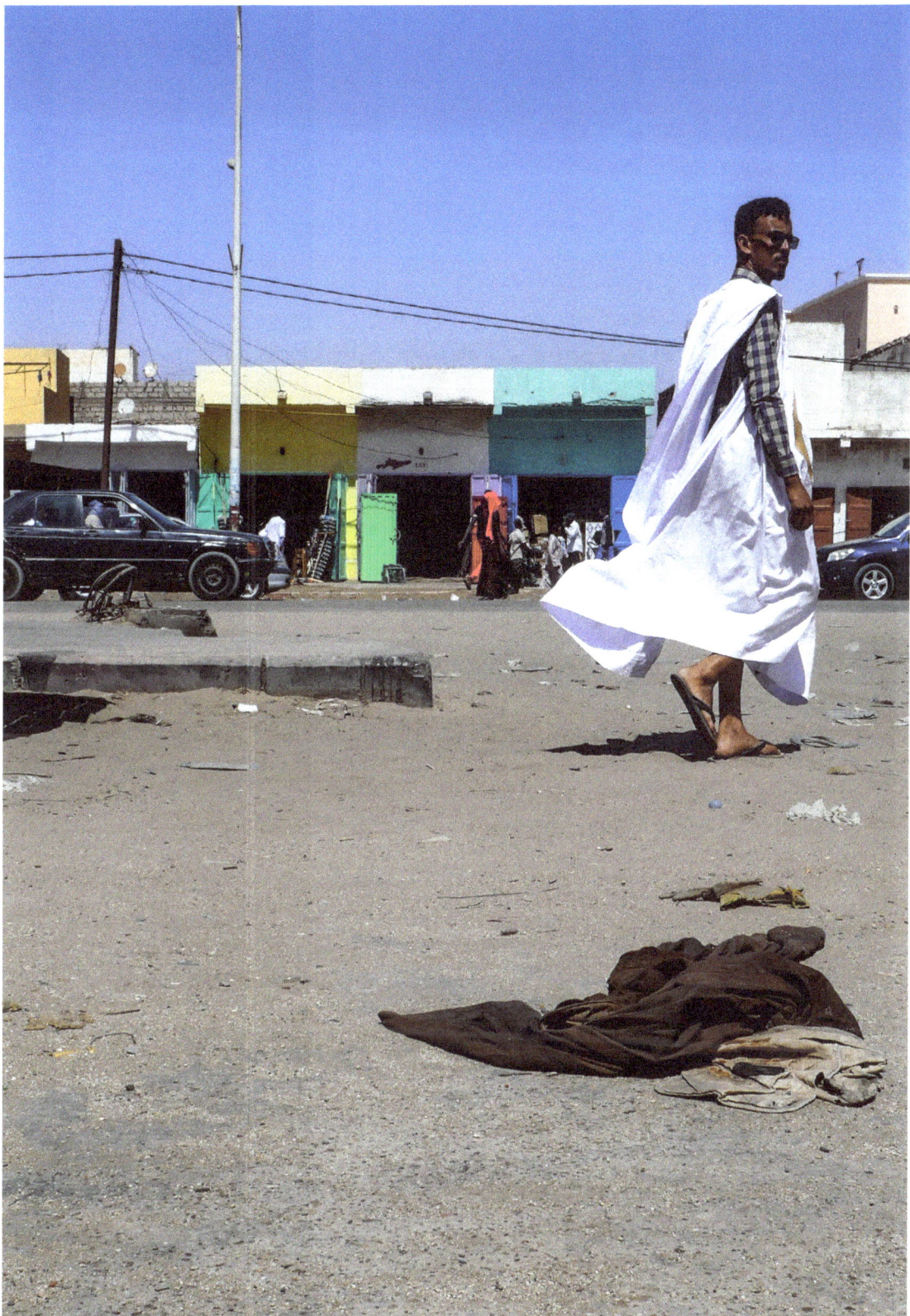

good life and have a high standing. And you can often leave work early without anyone complaining. While creative people who spread ideas, opinions, and joy, we're not interested in them. It shouldn't be like that!"

He worked in an office as well and he was the first to admit that he was not particularly artistic, or creative. But he wished he was like that.

"Then maybe I could help bring more tourists here, by marketing our wonderful country. Here in Mauritania we're terrible at promoting ourselves as a country and a tourist destination. Nearly everyone mistakes us for the little island of Mauritius." He spluttered. He was obviously sick of being on the wrong side of Africa. If nothing else, he has made it much easier to get into the country thanks to the new visa system.

Mauritania is perhaps best known for having one of the world's largest ship graveyards, all the way up in the north, just outside of Nouadhibou — a city of around 100,000 inhabitants. At its peak there were said to have been three hundred shipwrecks along its beaches. That I had to see with my own eyes. I took a domestic flight from Nouakchott and in three-quarters of an hour I was at the only gate at Nouadhibou's tiny airport. Since the occasional international flight from the Canary Islands or Morocco goes off course and lands here, everyone has to go through passport control, even from domestic flights. The hacked off official checked my visa and whether I had an entry stamp before nodding me through. I walked out of the microscopic terminal building. The highway runs straight past it, just a few metres from the entrance doors. There was nowhere to be dropped off or picked up; to get to a car you first have to cross the busy road to a gravel car park. There was no pedestrian crossing.

In Nouadhibou you cannot simply flag down a taxi. Taxi drivers flag you down if they like the look of you. The government has recently introduced a rule stating that only holders of Mauritanian passports can drive taxis. This is reportedly to protect the profession, and perhaps it does, but it has led to an acute lack of taxis, and the few taxi drivers that you will find are appropriately expensive. What can be positive about this is if they get the impression that you are the right customer for them, they will almost propel you into the back seat of their car — at least until they realise that you cannot speak French. Then you are swiftly manhandled back out again. It took me three rapid rounds of being shoved in and out of as many back seats before I got one who was tolerant enough of my deficient language skills to be willing to make an attempt at driving me to the ship graveyard. It is located some kilometres out towards the southern tip of a narrow peninsula shared by Western Sahara and Mauritania. Nobody lives just north of the border in Western Sahara, but nonetheless, surly Mauritanian border guards make sure that nobody is able to visit the ghost town of La Güera in the neighbouring country. The city was established by the Spanish colonial master Francisco Berns as recently as 1920. In its golden age it even featured an airport, but by the early 2000s sand had reclaimed most of the city and there were just a few fishermen left. Now even they, too, have given in to the Sahara. But the city never really had a realistic chance. Even its name is pretty unfortunate, coming from the Spanish word agüera, meaning 'drainage ditch'.

If you want to go there you first need to travel legally to Western Sahara, and thereafter rent a boat or just begin walking across the desert. My taxi driver actually tried to drive me over the border on the narrow road from Mauritania after I insisted and tempted him with an extra payment. The border guards were not impressed and put a quick stop to it. The driver received orders to make an immediate about turn and we drove pretty dejectedly towards the ship graveyard just over a kilometre away. He missed out on his bonus, and I missed out on exploring a ghost town. Once there, I jumped out of the taxi and began heading for the beach. The taxi driver nodded when I asked him to wait in exchange for a double fare. Having to hike back to the centre of town in the heat of the sun was not especially alluring.

"What do you think you're doing?" yelled someone from behind me.

I turned around and waited for a man in military uniform to make his way over to me. Fortunately, he was smiling.

"I was thinking of going to look at the impressive ship graveyard you have here," I answered the guard, who must have emerged from a gate in a wall that concealed the industrial activities from the outside world. It looked like some kind of engineering works.

"You're not allowed to. We're not proud of the ugly, rusty wrecks here. This is not what we want to be known for," he said.

"But I've travelled all the way from Norway to see this," I said, a never exactly innocent white lie.

"Where is Norway?" he asked inquisitively, before catching himself. "Anyway, it makes no difference. We don't want you showing this."

He had seen my camera.

"Can I just take a quick look, just for a few minutes?" I proposed and began walking gingerly back down towards the beach. Against all odds he came along quietly. Perhaps I represented a welcome change in the otherwise monotonous day of a guard.

"All right, but then I'll have to come with you. And no pictures," he replied.

"Not even from here?" I asked from the water's edge. Rusty pieces of iron, empty oil drums and a great deal of plastic were lying all around. It wasn't very appealing.

"Especially not from here! But nice try," he smiled.

"Can't I take a selfie, then?" I hinted, as a final attempt at a photo, on the verge of desperation. His answer goes to show how it often pays not to take no for an answer.

"Yeah, that's OK."

I pulled out my phone, switching to the front camera, and instantly saw that the only real wreck this kind of picture would be able to show would be me.

"Could you take the selfie for me?" I asked, well aware that it wouldn't be a selfie anymore. He confounded all the odds once again. He agreed. The compact camera was placed in his hand, and he took three pictures, before passing the camera back to me. He then proceeded to walk back towards the gate from which he had emerged. He didn't look back and I took the opportunity to snap a few more pictures. Quite a security guard.

Those few minutes were nonetheless enough. There were only a dozen ships left of what was once the world's largest collection of shipwrecks. Now there were just a few workers remaining to cut up the ones that were left. The wrecks used to be deliberately run aground in order to be dismantled and sold as scrap, but eventually there weren't enough workers willing to take on the job for the money they were being offered, and Mauritania stopped receiving the ships that had barely gotten there under their own steam. Therefore, a backlog of some iron and steel hulls are still lying there, but hopefully the clean-up process will be complete in not too long. The fact that they have cleaned up at all ought to be a positive, and not in the least disappointing, but I have to admit that I had been looking forward to photographing more spectacular rusty ghost-ships in Nouadhibou Bay. But money talks. There used to be money to be made from salvaging the metal; now penny-pinching shipowners send scrapped vessels to Bangladesh instead. There the pay is lower and the workforce far more plentiful. Almost forty times as many people live in Bangladesh than in Mauritania, which has just over four million inhabitants. As the journalist Seif Kousmate has demonstrated, Biba's portrayal of things is relatively rose-tinted, but it might be worth asking yourself where are there more 'slaves' — in Bangladesh or in Mauritania?

It was soon about time to leave Mauritania, but first eastwards on a 600-kilometre detour. A distinctive 100-million-year-old circular mountain formation is located there, made up of five ring-shaped eighty-metre-deep channels, one after the other. At the outer edge of the thousand-year-old town of Ouadane lies the Richat Structure, nicknamed the Eye of the Sahara or the Blue Eye of Africa. At fifty kilometres across, you need to get high up in order to get a decent perspective. For those of us struggling to find a budget-friendly and safe travel route to Ouadane with an all-inclusive hot-air balloon trip, the satellite image on Google Maps is a good second best. Personally, I found nobody who was both willing to drive me to the formation and who actually knew how to get there, but I was told by the proprietor of a café that from ground level the eye is quite simply too big to be particularly exciting to look at or take pictures of. It's just sand and rocks in somewhat difficult terrain. The very few who actually make the trip rent a four-wheel drive with a driver, but with the exception of certain enthusiastic archaeologists, all end up being disappointed even if they are standing virtually in the centre of the formation. At such close quarters, nothing seems especially exciting. If nothing else, one is maybe a tiny little dot in the direct eyeline of an astronaut. The innermost ring is twenty metres wide and six kilometres across, while the outermost is a whole fifty metres wide and between seven and eight kilometres from the centre.

It was originally believed that an asteroid or a volcanic eruption caused the circles. Now scientists think that it was a symmetrical stone cupola that has collapsed, followed by 100 million years of erosion. None of them, however, can quite account for how all of the almost perfect rings are at the exact same distance from the centre. This has opened itself up to all kinds of speculation. Plato himself thought that the Richat Structure was the remains of Atlantis and that the channels were dikes that the inhabitants navigated with boats. Of the five rings, two were said to be filled with water while three were tracts of land. In Greek, Atlantis means 'The Island of Atlas' and Plato believed that it referred to the island in the middle of the structure.

We shouldn't knock Plato, even if he probably never saw the formation with his own eyes. The legend of Atlantis was, in any case, barely a footnote in his works, but something that in retrospect has stirred the most interest. However, the odds of Atlantis actually having been located in the Sahara Desert, six hundred kilometres from the nearest ocean, would be extremely remote.

There are several islands in the Atlantic that are more likely candidates.

The beach is busy most of the day. Most of the activities are related to boat and fishing logistics.

This guy invited me to share valuable shade with him.

Pale blonde men from rural Norway struggle to stand out on the beach in Nouakchott.

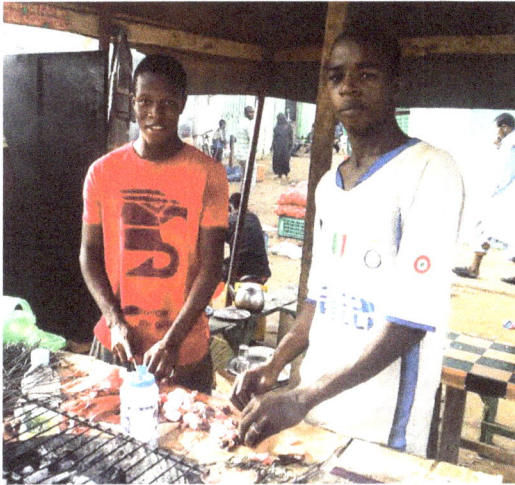
The barbecue spit comes with pieces of goat meat and lumps of fat.

This donkey is enjoying an ever-so-slight break. There are usually hundreds of kilos on the cart.

In Mauritania, small fish are unusually transported in sacks.

Ibrahima N'gaédé has created a system for issuing visas at border crossings.

The shipyard will soon be history. Local labor is expensive compared to that in Bangladesh.

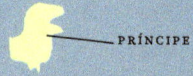

PRÍNCIPE

São Tomé and Príncipe

São Tomé

ROLAS

50 km

18

São Tomé and Príncipe, Africa

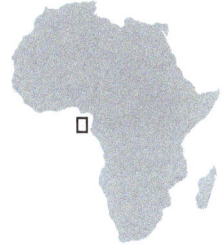

INHABITANTS: 200,000 (Wikipedia)
TOURISTS PER YEAR: 29,000 (UNWTO)
AREA: 1001 square kilometres

THE AFRICAN ISLAND STATE of São Tomé and Príncipe is located to the south of Ghana and to the west of Gabon in the Gulf of Guinea, and includes a large island called São Tomé, and a smaller one called Príncipe. The Italian professor, scientist, and pyramid expert, Livio Catullo Stecchini, worked on the manuscript for the book Sahara, in which he claimed it was in fact São Tomé that had been the true Atlantis, but he did not manage to get his work published before he died in 1979.

Atlantis or not, São Tomé and Príncipe, based on its nature, has the foundations to become a future tourist favourite, although there are not that many who can actually work as tourist guides yet. Only the Seychelles has fewer inhabitants among the 55 countries found in Africa. The country has an exciting history, unique nature, numerous beaches with sand in different colours, diverse rainforest, distinctive mountains, and many activities to offer, both sea-based and on land. So far, there is only one reputable Western airline which can take you there, but out of the world's least visited countries, it may still be the one with the greatest short-term potential. It is a mystery why there aren't more tourists here.

To put it one way, travelling on my own here was just not on the agenda. My brother Øystein and friends Asbjørn Havnen and Torgeir Halvorsen insisted on coming as well. It was clear they weren't joking. They bought tickets 6 months before I did.

The plane from Accra in Ghana landed on schedule just in time for dinner. Here that usually means seafood, and you will not be running a successful restaurant for long in the middle of the Atlantic unless the goods are fresh. Over the course of a week, we tried out all the best restaurants in the capital São Tomé, which has the same name as the island it is on, and we concluded that there was one that buried all the others in terms of quality and service. 5entidos-Restaurante is run out of a residential building on a construction site about one kilometre from the centre. That is to say, you go there, and definitely leave, in pitch-black. Streetlights are not very widespread here, just like elsewhere in Africa, but there isn't really crime either, so we never felt unsafe or threatened.

In any case, Asbjørn was with us. He is called Doctor Vodka among friends, owing greatly to his drinking skills. He has somewhat trained his drinking in various Stan countries and a couple of war zones, but he gets a head start anyway from his muscular and large body that burns away alcohol relatively quickly. Another advantage is that we are never bothered by tiresome salesmen, pickpockets, street gangs or thieves, when we are together with him. Doctor Vodka might as well have 'don't mess with my friends' tattooed on his forehead, but few outsiders would have dared to come close enough to be able to read it. In São Tomé and Príncipe, as in Guinea-Bissau and other former Portuguese colonies, Super Bock is one of the most popular beer brands. In hot countries, the beer is often served in 200ml bottles, or shot glasses, as Doctor Vodka calls them. Neither Torgeir, Øystein nor I were especially anxious strolling back home in the dark.

The chef, João at 5entidos, also lives in the building housing the restaurant and showed hospitality as if it were an Olympic discipline. The most impressive thing, however, was the eminent quality of the food. Most of it came from the sea just a stone's throw away, including the tuna he cooked, pretty much in a gourmet way. The only thing missing was the small portions. The second time we ate there, we arrived early. We knew we would need time to digest the food. And once again, we were very well received.

"Norwegian friends! Today I have don't have much tuna, but if you like, I will put to one side what I have for you, as you appreciated the dish so much the last time. In a quarter of an hour, a group of food-loving wealthy people will be coming here, but I would rather serve the finest delicacies from Neptune to you," said João.

"That sounds like a brilliant plan. We'll take everything you have," said Torgeir.

"Are you sure? Then you may not have room for the chocolate mousse," quipped the chef.

Torgeir grinned. "You know, Norwegians always have room for dessert! At least when it contains local chocolate."

Cocoa beans have been grown here for half a millennium. The first town on São Tomé was founded by the Portuguese in 1493. Seven years later, the first settlement on Príncipe was founded, 150 kilometres to the northeast. Thereafter, the islands were gradually colonised, especially once the new inhabitants realised how good the soil was for growing sugar, cocoa, and coffee. Being located a little out in the Atlantic meant that it also became a natural hub for the slave trade, at least for the slaves who did not remain to work on the plantations. The owners needed a large labour force there, and it was convenient that this was free. Unlike in Mauritania, there are no more slaves on the islands.

São Tomé and Príncipe became independent in July 1975, and only 15 years later the country held democratic elections, completely without violence. They were among the first in Africa to do so, but then the official country name is The Democratic Republic of São Tomé and Príncipe. Though, having 'democratic' in the name is usually a sign of the opposite, if we compare North Korea, Congo, Ethiopia, Algeria, and Laos. And let's also not forget the 'good, old' GDR, even though the country no longer exists.

As well as democracy, chocolate and coffee, the attractions here include something very familiar to Norwegians — a road tunnel. But attractions often come about by having just the one. The hole in the boulder that juts out into the sea is so famous, that you can take it with you on your travels on postcards. The tunnel is probably no longer than about 50 metres, and has beaches on either side, but the locals are proud of every tunnel centimetre they have space for: With just 1001 square kilometres to spare, the country as a whole is a similar size to a Norwegian borough in the Arctic north, and the road 'around' the main island is a measly 125 kilometres. Well, kind of around — 30 kilometres of road to the southwest are missing to form a complete circle. And there are no plans for a road there right now because right in the middle of these two dead-end roads is a national park. The solution, of course, could be a second tunnel, albeit somewhat longer than the first, but there are both too few people living on each side and too few tourists coming here for there to be such plans in the years to come.

The day after the gourmet dinner I was to meet a man to carry out an interview. Its roots stem from a pleasant Estonian who was travelling from Tallinn to Lisbon via Norway in 2014. He had seven hours between flights and invited me for coffee to exchange travel tips. We have kept in touch since, and he is now engaged to a Santomean lady. Before leaving for São Tomé, I made contact, and he told me about someone who would turn out to be a colourful guy. I had not received any other information than 'you have to meet him', and for me that was interesting enough to make an appointment — at his workplace, which turned out to be a sterile and drab office building in the centre. I knocked on the white office door on the second floor and got a loud 'Enter, please!' as an immediate response.

The man sat with his back to me in a modern office chair. The large black leather seat looked soft. After finishing off a sentence on a laptop, he turned around. Henrique was 170cm tall and had short, curly, and mostly black hair. There were a few grey hairs, but all in all pretty good for a man of 65.

"Have you been to this country before?" he wondered.

"Yes, a few years ago. Then I took a boat from Libreville. It took 40 hours," I answered.

"40 hours? Was the canoe made from a hollowed-out tree trunk?" he grinned, before asking me to sit down on an office chair like his own. I explained how I had hitched a ride with a low-speed cargo boat a few years earlier. I'd been told that the trip was going to take eight hours, but it had taken three times as long as that. He kept chuckling until I joked that it wasn't a surprise that they had so few tourists in the country. Tourists,

or the lack of them, was a topic he took seriously.

Henrique Pinto da Costa has qualified opinions about people like me. Tourists, that is. He has studied ecology, with a focus on tropical islands, and not just his own. He has spent a long time in the Caribbean, and from time to time he teaches at several educational institutions in the United States, including the prestigious Yale University.

"Tourism is a very special industry. If you are not well organised to handle tourists, you have lost before you start. We have so few tourists here, that I would rather call them guests than tourists. We don't get more visitors through putting people up in hotels and then calling them tourists," he pointed out.

He went on to highlight the role of the authorities, which he thought needed to be more active. The professor asserted that tourism ought to be part of an active and dynamic strategy. In São Tomé and Príncipe, tourism has hardly been on the agenda of the politicians, and most of it has been left up to the private business community.

"The principal things are infrastructure and facilities. We have the airport, but our roads cannot accommodate any more traffic than there is today. And let me just add that infrastructure includes satisfactory healthcare. Who on earth dares to travel here if we do not have good hospitals that can offer help in the event of an accident?" he asked. The man spoke like a waterfall — this clearly got him going.

And he had a point, especially when it comes to more mature tourists who often have active or latent ailments that make this an important consideration. There are quite a few high-quality resort hotels here, but they are a long way off being as large as those in the Caribbean or Turkey, where they often have their own doctors.

"Last but not least, we must involve the local people. They must be able to be a part of the industry, be a part of creating economic value," proclaimed Henrique.

In addition to teaching, Henrique leads a small organisation that specialises in consulting within biological variation, development, and diversity. He thinks that tourism must be a natural part of society and its extent proportionally aligned to population. He made a comparison of tourism with cocoa and chocolate. That is not as unusual as it sounds. São Tomé and Príncipe has some of the best cocoa plants in the world, and chocolate factories from the world over select cocoa beans from here. But it has led to overexploitation of the rainforest and a short-term pursuit of this raw material that earns people money. The rainforest has suffered, and hundreds of plant and animal species have disappeared. Without doubt, Henrique is passionate about his country and wants more people to experience it. But not at any price.

"Nature is number one! If we do not look after it, we cannot make a living from tourism. People come to have real experiences, to understand history. Nature is a mirror for the country. And who will care about the beaches if they are surrounded by weeds, by wasteland?" he asked, without waiting for an answer, as he turned off the laptop on the desk at the same time. I figured I had taken up enough of his time. Henrique sounded like an environmentalist but did not want to be seen as one. He considers the need for growth and the interplay between the authorities, landowners, and workers, in stimulating the economy. Just as long as it happens on nature's terms. And that is not necessarily a contradiction.

"Cocoa beans are just a raw material here in Africa, while chocolate is made in Europe. The only exception is Claudio Corrallo," he continued. I had already agreed to meet this world-famous chocolatier later on, and now I became even more expectant. While we had been talking, Carlos came in — the son, a guy of about 190cm with curly hair and a big warm smile. We had just happened to have met each other at a bar the night before. It's a small world — São Tomé and Príncipe — even smaller.

"Now we have to show you what we work with," he said, smiling. We walked out of the office, down a flight of stairs and across to a large four-wheel drive vehicle. Carlos asked me to take the front seat.

"There is a lot to see along the road, and I have seen it before," Carlos explained.

Father and son were going to take me to their rainforest.

Henrique and Carlos Costa had together established, a new — if ever so small — rainforest. They bought 70 acres of forest a few years ago, planted it and made the conditions right, so that diverse plants native to these latitudes and soil, could thrive. They claim to have made it a success: In a few years, they have taken what was part of a cocoa plantation and turned it into a rainforest. Over a thousand plant species now grow here, at an impressive pace.

"The climate means that some trees can grow several meters a month. Our approach must be ecological," Henrique stated. Completely calmly, but without room for discussion.

"The interaction with nature is crucial, we must let the environment and those who live here, interact together. Only in such a way can we let the history of this country carry on," he said, and struck his hand carefully on the dashboard for effect.

For Henrique, it is all about taking the best that nature has to offer and help facilitate biodiversity. His warm eyes lit up as he talked about it. He actually lives in a wooden house less than a kilometre from his mini rainforest. Inside he has masks, paintings, rugs, and other artifacts from all over the world. The house itself is built upon sustainable principles, and the bywords are recycling and power production without emissions. The latter is solved by means of a mini hydroelectric power plant by a stream. Numerous green plants grow around the house, and he uses many of them in his cooking.

Our eventual destination of the rainforest was located almost in the middle of the island at an altitude of 500 metres. From the asphalt road we turned off and continued onwards on a gravel road. A few hundred metres further on, we turned left again and suddenly drove on two almost hidden tyre-ruts that showed the way into the rainforest. Two minutes later we stopped and left the artificial climate in the car. The humidity hit us. Fortunately, the temperature was a little lower than in the lowlands. We were quite a height above sea-level after all, and it seemed as if all the plants protected us against the heat.

Grasshoppers sang from the trees. They were accompanied by birds of many varieties that formed an orchestra. But I could not see a single bird. There were too many trees and plants — it was green everywhere. Large leaves, small leaves, oblong leaves, and round leaves. Straight and crooked tree trunks. The musical tones were so varied that there had to be a plethora of avian species. A symphony orchestra. Totally incredible! But I did not get to enjoy the concert without interruption for very long.

"São Tomé and Príncipe should be the chocolate country of the world. If we do things right, it will be, and then the tourists really have a reason to come here," said the energetic man, enthusiastically, before gathering a breath and continuing. It was never quiet for long.

"Father Christmas lives in your neighbouring country, Finland. Everybody wants to visit him and that has a great ripple effect. And I had thought that Father Christmas lived in Norway," he said and grinned. "The Finns really undercut you there! And if I am not mistaken, the Icelanders are about to do the same with the midnight sun," he laughed, and pointed out that we must raise our game in Norway. I was impressed with the level of knowledge about my home country. And he was not done.

"You have oil and seem to have been so content with it that you gave away both Father Christmas and the midnight sun. We can make the same mistake. It's not enough to just deliver perfect cocoa beans — we have to take ownership of the chocolate, which is the product that everybody wants," smiled Henrique and pointed at his stomach. The man was in good shape, so he could not have eaten too much of the brown gold.

Henrique was silent for a minute or two, but he wasn't finished with the country comparison.

"But you have gotten it figured out with the salmon!" he resounded and launched into a proposal for the ultimate gourmet meal for the future: Norwegian salmon and chocolate from the island state for dessert.

"And did you know that our economy in the 1950s was largely based on Norwegian whaling?"

I was not aware of that. Norwegian whalers in their time constantly travelled south in search of new prey after having mostly driven whales in the north to extinction. Over several years they raided the area around these islands, until the whales were almost extinct here and they travelled further south to find new prey. As is well-known, the whalers ended up in Antarctica and almost made the whales extinct there as well, before

they pointed their ship's bows homeward.

In São Tomé and Príncipe, father and son convey a future tourist idyll with eminent beaches, unique mountains, and as fresh seafood as it is possible to have. You cannot deny there is potential.

"We must turn our country into a paradise. And I'm not talking about a biblical version. But nature alone is not enough, we must be able to offer both activities and stimuli. To achieve this, we need an overarching strategy. And we need educated people. Practical people, not politicians."

While the father was talking, the son took me from tree to tree and from one bush to the next. Occasionally there was silence from the senior party, and junior was able to tell me how fast the specific plant grew, what the Latin name was, and when the first one had been planted.

"Look!" Carlos shouted abruptly in the middle of the Latin lesson. "Look at the bird!" A crane with an impressive wingspan glided into our field of vision and manoeuvred between tall trees without making a single stroke of a wing. Majestic.

Carlos said that people who wanted to live in harmony with nature were welcome to build a home in the rainforest without having to pay anything for the plot of land. I was tempted to sign up as a resident but decided to let the thought go. It would have hardly gone down so well back home.

"But we have to be sure that they have the same mindset as us, and that they want the best for the animals and plants," Carlos said enthusiastically. His father nodded in the background.

We drove back to São Tomé. I asked questions about the villages we drove through, but otherwise it was quiet in the four-wheel drive. There was much to take in. Father and son were in agreement and were clearly very serious. The only question was whether most of the countrymen and women were of the same mindset. We were back down in the capital just after normal time for lunch.

"We should have taken you to a restaurant, but unfortunately we have to go on," said Carlos. "We'll drop you off here instead. At this café they have coffee and chocolate from Claudio Corallo. And say hello from us when you meet him!" I jumped out and waved to the enthusiasts.

Inside the café, the worn-out beige ceiling fans were on max, and on maximum racket mode, likely not having been oiled since a distant memory. But it was okay, the false breeze helped a little in the high humidity. It was much warmer by the sea than up at altitude. At the counter I ordered a sandwich and juice, in addition to coffee and chocolate, which I asked them to serve for 'dessert'.

The chocolate melted slowly on my tongue, and the complex flavours were supreme and hardly possible to describe. It was not sweet, just full-bodied, and intense. The dark pieces seemed to intensify in my mouth and made me just want more. I was already looking forward to meeting the man behind the first-class product. Then Øystein, Asbjørn and Torgeir appeared.

"Are you ready for surfing?" asked Øystein. His eyes were glistening. My brother has a lot of surfing experience from Stad on the northwest coast of Norway, but the temperatures are lower there. Much lower. There was no need here for either a wet or dry suit. The water temperature is absolutely perfect all year round — the same for the waves. Even my west of Norway-loving brother saw the temperature-related advantages of surfing closer to the equator than the Arctic Circle. Far closer! The equator actually runs through the country, on the small island of Rolas two kilometres south of the southern tip of São Tomé. You can even celebrate crossing the invisible line with a sneaky little cup of something. Bar Equador is located just 70 metres from the equator.

Rolas is only two square kilometres and has nice beaches. The options are nonetheless far better in São Tomé, where there are many surfing beaches, suitable for all from experts to beginners. Out of us, only Øystein could surf, so we went for the latter category. And I was already looking forward to seeing Asbjørn on a surfboard. One can say a lot about Doctor Vodka, but the word graceful is seldom used, even though throughout the 1990s he showed top class acrobatic skills as a goalkeeper for Førde IL football club.

"Get the biggest surfboard you have," Asbjørn told the instructor, Pedro. The Portuguese man in his thirties looked like the parody of a surfer and was popular with the ladies both back home in Portugal and in the former colony further to the southeast.

A large board was handed out with a smile, and soon after, the novice was in the water. Seeing Asbjørn on a surfboard should have been like watching a hippopotamus with ballet shoes.

So, I had believed, anyhow.

But how wrong I was. On the oil tanker of a board, Asbjørn miraculously surfed the second wave he tried. And from then on it only went from strength to strength. A natural talent had been discovered. Pedro refused to believe that Asbjørn had never surfed before.

"Bandits! You tried to trick me into betting money on the lack of surfing skills of your friend. Like in King Pin, only on boards and not in a bowling alley!" he joked. Before Torgeir and I were put down.

"I think it's best if you go and play in the sand or something like that. Before you drown," he said. As subtle as if the tax inspector had arrived in an aircraft carrier on a tiny lake. Torgeir and I slinked off to the other side of the beach with the surfboard between our legs. It was perhaps best not to get in the way of the professionals. But we sneaked into the team picture, so as not to lose face. In this country, you don't need to be able to surf anyway. There are so many beaches that you will rarely have an audience to impress. You can find white sand, black sand, or yellow sand. Or rocky beaches if you prefer that. The sand on the former is so fine that paddling and swimming are good options. Many of the beaches are flanked by rough rocks and green vegetation, which make for perfect backgrounds for Christmas postcards, primarily going out to family and friends to show what a lovely holiday one has had. A few are notably closed to people. The turtles are allowed to lay their eggs there in the warm sand in peace. For this is the tropics after all, and the water is pleasant. The distance to the mainland also guarantees clean and clear water. Here, there is minimal pollution. And when the beaches are as deserted as they appear to be in an authentic holiday catalogue, the question is just how long it will last. All in all, we are talking about some of the best beaches in Africa. And as such, in the world. And then I'm not including the beaches on Príncipe. They are even more spectacular, receiving even fewer visitors.

The next day, both Asbjørn and Øystein wanted to do some more surfing. Torgeir and I had discovered that it wasn't really on to wear out the waves too much, and that it was probably much more rewarding to learn about chocolate. In São Tomé and Príncipe, there is only one way to do this: by visiting Claudio Corallo, the chocolate man and legend, who is seemingly the only one processing the cocoa beans from São Tomé and Príncipe in São Tomé and Príncipe.

Torgeir and I met him in his whitewashed detached house, located behind a metal gate right next to the beach in the middle of São Tomé. His assistant, Christina, opened the gate and let us in with a big smile. For the two guard dogs, the smile was good enough proof that we were friends, not enemies, and they just sniffed around lightly interested in us.

"Isn't it safe here, then?" asked Torgeir, looking a little nervously at the dogs. Rarely has he received such a direct and disparaging answer from a lady, and that says quite a bit.

"Friend, no place is safe when you produce the world's best chocolate!" We could almost hear Christina rolling her eyes before she showed us to the front door and knocked. A few seconds later, Claudio opened up. In slippers and jogging bottoms.

"Welcome," he said with a shy smile. The man in his sixties pointed towards a wooden table surrounded by four chairs inside the kitchen, and we took the invitation.

"Do you want hot cocoa?" asked the chocolate celebrity. When the world's best chocolate maker asks you such, the answer goes without saying. With skilled movements, he heated hot chocolate on the gas-fired stove. Torgeir and I sat like expectant children sitting at the dinner table on Christmas Eve, waiting for the adults to finish eating so that the presents could be opened. We were to taste the world's best cocoa, made by the very Corallo himself.

After a few minutes, the smell of cocoa had taken over the small and rudimentary equipped kitchen. He said nothing else while preparing the cocoa. It was quiet, but we felt welcome. Then he poured the viscous drink into two brown ceramic cups. Torgeir and I almost raced each other to the first taste.

"It's just cocoa and a little sugar. Absolutely no milk," said Claudio, just in case we thought we were drinking milk chocolate-based cocoa. But then he has had journalists from the world over visiting. Some of them have obviously concluded that there was milk in the cocoa he served. We weren't given time to arrive at any such assumptions.

What a taste. Clean, and not bitter in the slightest. The viscous liquid was surprisingly light and easy to drink. A tad sweet, but not markedly, and heavenly good.

"How does it taste?" asked Christina.

"Wow! Absolutely fantastic!"

Torgeir came out with 'wow', I said 'absolutely fantastic'. When intoxicated by chocolate, anyone can complete each other's sentences in the best Huey, Dewey, and Louie style. Claudio was clearly content with the response, and finally began to speak.

"I'm no chocolatier. I'm a farmer. I grow coffee and cocoa beans," he explained with a cautious smile. This was not a boastful man, even with the reputation of being the world's best chocolatier.

He had started with coffee and cocoa in Zaire and Congo but moved here because of war. The fact that he likes diving is a bonus, with sea on all sides. But he has spent most of his time in far greener surroundings.

"I liked the cocoa plant and wanted to learn all about it. I have never liked chocolate, but I wanted to find out new things about cocoa. It went badly in the beginning — everything I planted was bitter. The bitter taste was like a defect and was the last thing you want when looking for quality. It took years of cultivation, watering, trials, experimenting and failing before I got rid of it," he said, and took a sip of water. He likely needed variety from only chocolate-based drinks. Afterwards, he came out with indirect criticism of other chocolate producers who he believes do not know the beans they use. That may be in order - after all, they just buy the beans and have them delivered.

"They have no knowledge of history, of the soil or what the climate has been like while the beans have ripened. It's like making a chair without knowing where the wood comes from. For me, it is important to be present throughout the whole process, including on the plantation. I know the soil and the whole process the beans have gone through, including the transformation. That is why I'm a farmer, not a chocolatier."

"You could become a really big farmer within cocoa. Are you thinking of expanding production?" hinted Torgeir, a little pushily. Hopeful Halvorsen was hooked and wanted to secure reliable deliveries home to Florø in Norway. Claudio smiled, before he dashed Torgeir's hope of being able to buy the world's best chocolate at the local shopping centre in Norway's westernmost city. The chocolatier told of how he has never intended or had the interest in becoming a major producer. Largely due to it being difficult to follow the development of all the various beans as the owner of a large plantation.

"And you're quickly forced to use fertiliser or insecticide. I do not use any chemicals. My plantation is not a cancerous growth in the forest — it must be a natural element of both the forest and the ecosystem that it is a part of. If the beans do not grow in balance and harmony with the rest of the forest, then it is the first step in destroying it all. Both the forest and the soil."

The man undoubtedly had full control over what he was doing, and in a highly competitive market to boot. Chocolate is available in a multitude of varieties all over the world. But Claudio cares little about the competition. He does it his way.

It was a natural point to ask him about his competitors. The answer was immediate and brief.

"I have no competitors," he said spontaneously, without being arrogant in any way. He answered as if he really meant it and believed it.

His secret lies in good work, but minimal actual work. If the conditions are good, the bean plants do the job themselves, he explained to the chocolate novices from Western Norway.

"And now I eat the chocolate I make myself."

It took him years to do that. Paradoxically, he had never been a big chocolate fan. But the chocolate cannot be for everyone: there is simply not enough of it. The production is only one and a half tonnes a month. The chocolate and coffee Claudio produces is sold under his own name. In shops, cafés, and bars across the country there are Claudio Corallo packages in silver or white packaging. The white ones are the luxury variant and somewhat more expensive. The regular products are sold in characteristic silver bags that also look quite exclusive.

Depending on the season, between 120 and 200 people work on the plantations and 13 at the factory. It is located on his property, in its own building behind the whitewashed house. Torgeir and I were invited in. Øystein and Asbjørn on their surfing jaunt missed out on a trip that would have made Charlie and the Chocolate Factory seem like an excursion for nursery children to a textile museum in deepest Tajikistan.

We had to take off our shoes outside. Inside it smelled just like we expected. Only more intense and hallucinatory wonderful. Workers in white coats stood by different benches and finished different types of chocolate product, by hand. With 70 percent cocoa. With 73.5 percent cocoa. With 80 percent cocoa. And the ultimate product: Small glazed balls of ginger covered in 100 percent cocoa. Those did not even taste bitter, despite the total absence of sugar. And I am the one who gets stomach acid in my throat as soon as I taste chocolate with more than 70 percent cocoa; it is always bitter. There is clearly chocolate and there is chocolate.

No, Claudio does not need to worry about his competitors. But under two tonnes a month?

A scandal! Or a good reason to move to the island in the Atlantic, if only for guaranteed deliveries.

As Norwegians, we have descendants here. Spirited Norwegian whalers have certainly made sure of that. There is supposedly documented evidence in the national archives of the country, but I never managed to get there.

It doesn't look good for Norwegian genes in the next country, because neither whalers nor Vikings ever got as far as the other side of mainland Africa.

The old buildings on this cocoa plantation are still in use.

Claudio Corallo inspects every single bush he collects cocoa beans from.

There are 13 employees at Claudio's chocolate factory. All the chocolate is handmade.

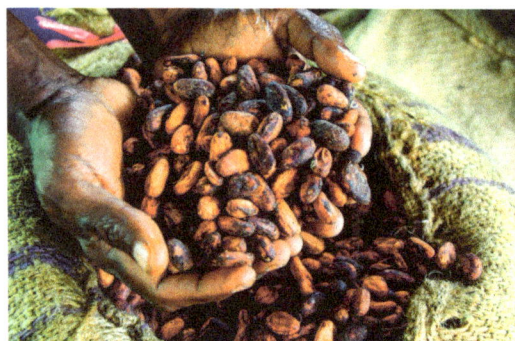

The aroma of cocoa beans is intense and, if you take a handful of beans, your hands continue to smell for some time after.

The cocoa fruit is bright yellow before it is harvested. The kernels in the fruit are the cocoa beans.

Even the things that look like machines in the chocolate factory are hand-powered.

It smells heavenly inside the chocolate factory! The samples we got didn't last long.

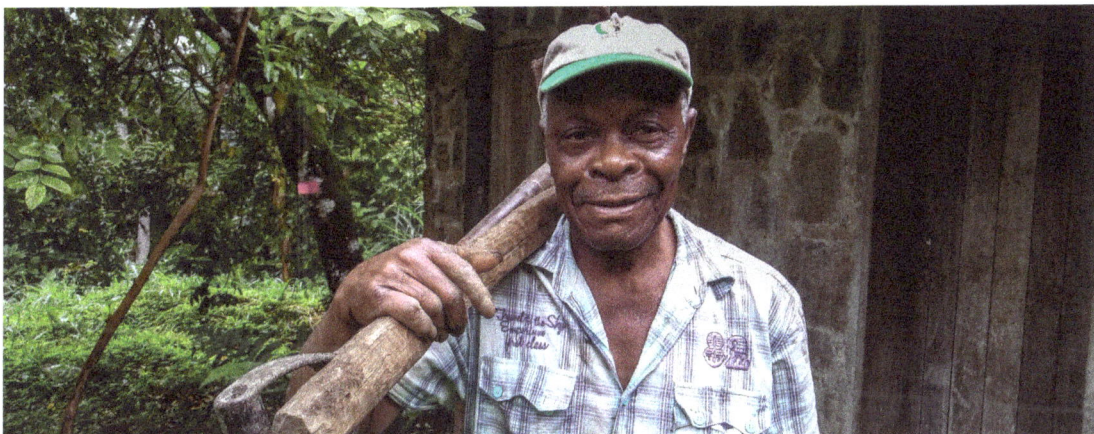
Henrique Pinto da Costa's handyman helps out in the rainforest in the centre of São Tomé.

Asbjørn (left), Øystein, and Torgeir at Hovud beach, near the centre of São Tomé.

Showing kids pictures of themselves is a guaranteed success. Øystein puts on a show in a small coastal village.

Of the world's 20 least visited countries, São Tomé and Príncipe is perhaps the one with the greatest appeal. Here you get everything: Good food, golden beaches, beautiful mountains, and very welcoming people.

Carlos Costa (right) with a friend in the rainforest.

The forestry worker has cleared the forest with a chainsaw, which he takes with him in the simplest way possible.

There is always a lot of life and bright colours near the market in São Tomé.

Two photobombers sneaked into the photo of the two extreme surfers on the right.

As long as there is only one, even a road tunnel can become a tourist attraction.

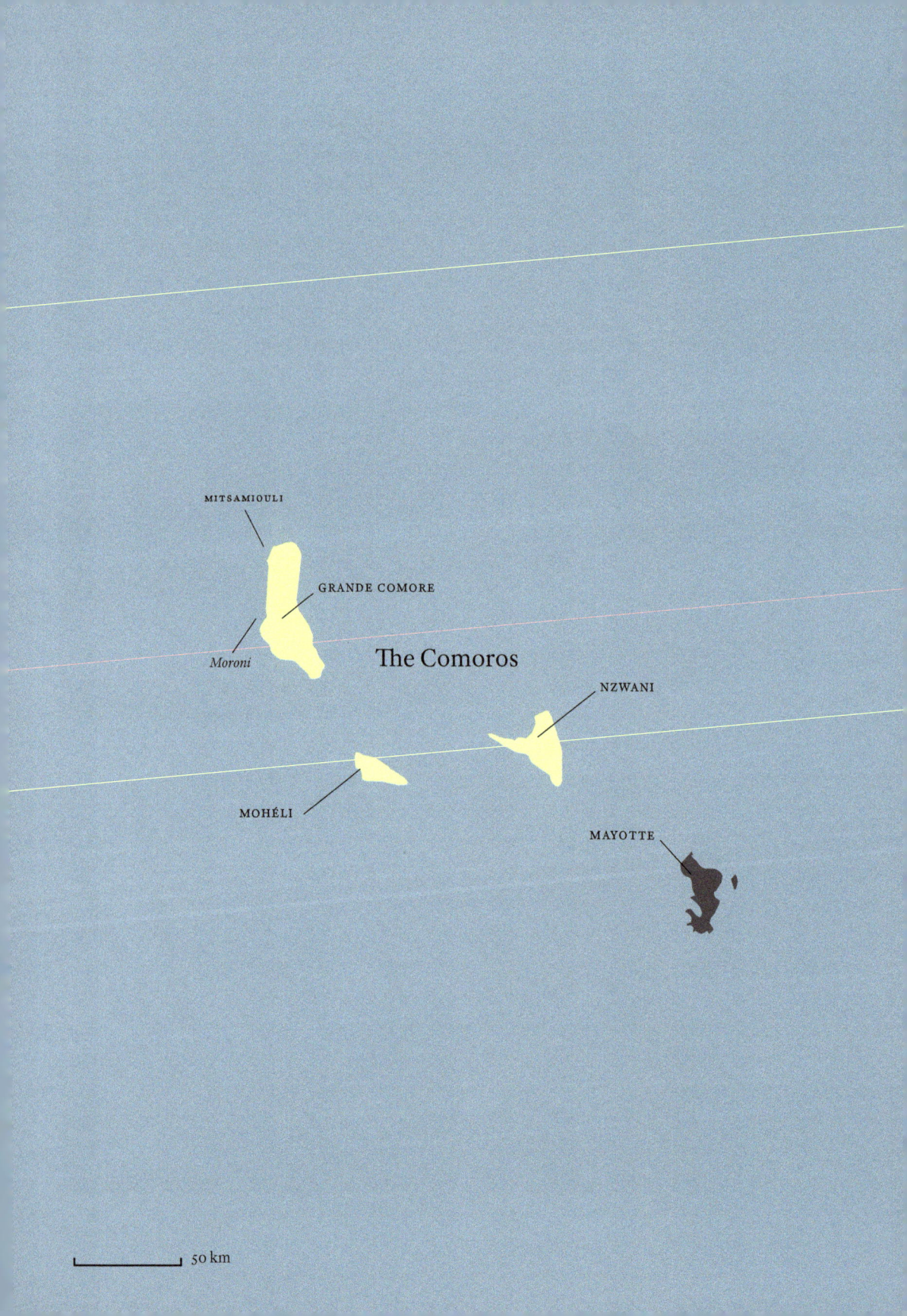

MITSAMIOULI

GRANDE COMORE

Moroni

The Comoros

NZWANI

MOHÉLI

MAYOTTE

⊢————⊣ 50 km

17

The Comoros, Africa

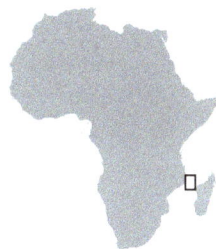

INHABITANTS: 800,000 (Wikipedia)
TOURISTS PER YEAR: 28,000 (UNWTO)
AREA: 1862 square kilometres

THE COMOROS is one of the most underrated holiday destinations in the world. Not only is the nature fantastic, with abundant green forest growing around rugged volcanoes and colourful lakes, but there are also countless chalk-white beaches almost screaming out for fearless bathers with a snorkel and diving mask. The playful dolphins are also interested in company, while the numerous turtles should preferably be observed from a distance.

The island paradise is located in the Indian Ocean between Mozambique to the west and Madagascar to the east and south. Compared to São Tomé and Príncipe, the country is 60 percent larger, bust still only of comparable size to a backcountry borough in central Norway. Both countries became independent in 1975, separated by just six days. The Comoros was first to go it alone, after the parliament declared independence from France. Less than one month later, the government was overthrown in a coup. Since then, there have been over 20 coups or attempts here. Like in Guinea-Bissau, it is almost a tradition, although, it has likely come to a stop with the last coup now in 2001. Since that time, the country has been reasonably stable in a political sense, even though they have been in a long-lasting discussion with France about who owns the island of Mayotte. This island is the one that has been prosperous in the area and is home to many French people. The island has been French since 1841, although the Comoros has never relinquished its claim to ownership, despite the fact the inhabitants voted to remain as part of France in two referendums. The last time they went out to vote was in 2009. Then, over 95 percent voiced a yes for France, and two years later the island became the 101st department in France, the only one with a Muslim majority. To formally become a part of France, they had to change some laws. Mayotte went from Islamic to French law, and among other things, the minimum age for marriage was raised from 15 to 18 years, and women were given the same right to receive inheritance as men. Taxes also went up, and over a period of 20 years, the inhabitants will gain the same social rights as in mainland France. In 2014, Mayotte was further consolidated into the EU, and it seems very unlikely that the island will ever become a part of The Comoros. Should that be the case, The Comoros would immediately move out the list of the world's least visited countries, due to the abundance of visitors with berets on their heads and baguettes under their arms.

The Comoros has been settled since around the 7th century. Historians believe that Polynesian emigrants from what is now Indonesia were the ones who first discovered the islands, and that they settled on Nzwani, the second largest island. Some are of the opinion, however, that there have been people here since Christ left the earth, but nothing has been proved.

First impressions are surprisingly positive when you land on the airstrip north of the capital Moroni. The relatively modern airport made from concrete, glass, and metal, fits in on the African island like Oslo's futuristic Opera House would fit in among a centuries-old rural village. It is clear that the politicians, in any case, dream of attracting more tourists — there is just an immense lack of infrastructure in almost all other parts of the country, other than the airport. Well, the 15 kilometres of road to Moroni is of a suitably modern standard, that is, as long as you drive at night and are completely alone on the road in a car with well-functioning headlights projecting a thousand metres ahead. And have a chauffeur. I had one.

José worked as a handyman at the hotel I had made a reservation for, and this evening his job description included being a driver. He took the task seriously, with a driver's hat and so on. I asked him what I just could not miss seeing in his country.

"Nothing! There is nothing you should miss out on. This is the world's most beautiful island, and we have the world's best seafood and the world's nicest turtles and the world's finest women and the world's best coconuts," he reeled off enthusiastically as he kept his gaze fixed on the road. Maybe a little too enthusiastically. It sounded like something he'd practiced, even though he saved it a little with a charming smile right at the end.

"How can the turtles be nicer here than they are in Cape Verde?" I wondered.

"They never bite you, always pose for a picture and taste absolutely fantastic," he said.

"I think they do in Cape Verde too," I grinned back and began to wonder what defined a 'nice' turtle, compared to other turtles, and whether meat from nice turtles sells better than meat from those who are nasty to each other.

"That may be, but I have not been there," José replied.

"It's unbelievably nice there! I can really recommend travelling there, especially to Santo Antão. By the way, where have you been beyond The Comoros?" I wondered.

"Nowhere," was the reply.

His entire pitch for The Comoros suddenly carried less weight due to a lack of any comparison, but he got top points for effort.

Early the next day I woke up to chirping from hundreds of different bird species. It turned out that the hotel was surrounded by one of the greenest views I have ever seen.

There is no shortage of experiences of nature in The Comoros — you just need plenty of time and a great four-wheel drive or good hiking shoes to reach the sight-seeing encounter. I wanted to see as much of this paradise as possible and decided to explore the main island, Grand Comore. The Comoros also consists of Nzurani and Mohéli, two islands of similar size, and at least 20 smaller islands, various islets and skerries. Not including Mayotte.

On this trip I wanted to explore the whole of Grande Comore. Or at least as much as it is possible to reach with a car. Then there are not exactly many options. I had to experience the island ring.

The coastal road — the main artery — encircling the main island has been paved. At one time or another at least. Now there is little of the top layer remaining, and you cannot expect to maintain an average speed any higher than 20-25 kilometres per hour. In principle, this is great as you can then take your time, with a clear conscience, exploring the volcanic island of Grande Comore, or Ngazidja, as it is known locally, and follow the obligatory detours. But, as there is hardly a hotel to be found outside of Moroni, you are almost pushed to drive at the maximum of what the chassis and tyres can tolerate, in order to do the 160 kilometres around the island in a single day — that is if you do not think it is perfectly acceptable to stay in a tent by one of the eminent beaches or settle for bungalows that have not been maintained since the early 1970s. And yes, you should consider settling for one of those options, because here it really is an island paradise with capital letters. From the beautiful beaches you can see up to the 2361 metres high Karthala, the highest point on the island and a very active volcano. In the context of volcanoes, this means that it has had eruptions more than 20 times since the 1800s. But I would maintain that the crystal-clear blue water, the pale white beaches and coral reefs with hundreds of fish species, molluscs and shellfish compensate for any possible eruptions. Besides there is an alert before an eruption. Usually.

I have never seen as many hikers as in The Comoros. Few people have their own car or motorcycle. When public transport is also completely non-existent, and only a few minibuses run on the very busiest stretches of road, then this is how it is. When a car passes by, people simply raise their hand and shout at you if you do not stop. There is no sophisticated use of the hitchhiker's thumb in the air evident here. As a rule, cars stop if there is available space, most drivers have themselves experienced not having a car and know how hard it is waiting still for hours. Unless they are just going a kilometre or two, and don't have any items to carry, then it is usually too hot to walk in the sun. My rental car was a black Toyota Hilux with a rear seat and cargo bed. The large vehicle was seen as suitable hitchhiking material hundreds of times — as soon as I was within sight or hearing distance. I had seven hikers with me at the peak, three inside the car and four on the cargo bed. The first one I picked up turned out to be a tourist from South Africa. Alan and I quickly connected, and he made it clear that he wanted to join me travelling around the whole island. It was no wonder, as the first man onboard, he had gotten the most comfortable hitchhiker seat in the car: the front seat. Alan comes from Soweto outside Johannesburg - like Nelson Mandela and Desmond Tutu, without any intention of making additional comparisons with the Peace Prize winners. Previous visits to South Africa have shown that people there generally do not know the term TIA, or 'This Is Africa', perhaps not wanting to acknowledge its existence as they see themselves as enormously well-developed compared to the rest of this part of the world. The three letters are useful for just about anything, when something does not go according to plan in most of Africa. It might be something that does not work, a bus that isn't running, or food that is not served until hours after the order was put in.

South Africans like to present themselves as the leaders in their part of the world in absolutely all areas, something that is often the case. Therefore, it is perhaps completely legitimate that they do not associate themselves with TIA, at the same time as being insulted when the term is used about their continent. Elsewhere in Africa, most people seem to have such an awareness that they recognise that things do not always, or better said almost never, go according to plan, and enough irony to use TIA just about anywhere.

I told Alan about this, and the whole thing almost became a joke. Whenever the road was unusually bad, even for The Comoros, I readily threw out TIA. Alan would then sigh and felt insulted. The same thing happened when we ordered lunch at the only restaurant / shed in Foumbouni on the east coast. It took almost an hour for the chef to bring out the smallest fish I have ever seen on a plate — the goldfish of one of my cousins seemed like a whale in comparison. We were the only guests. A new sigh emerged when we had to pay.

"TIA," I whispered in a suitably discreet fashion. That wasn't necessary, as the restaurant owner spoke only French.

"What now?" snapped Alan back. I showed him the receipt. The price was higher than the cost of a whole lobster at the best hotel in Moroni. The opportunistic owner had clearly taken advantage of the monopoly situation. Fortunately, I did not experience the same thing at other places on the island.

Hikers came and went around the island, but Alan stayed. I had started in Moroni, picking up Alan a few kilometres further along, and then had driven south. It turned into an anticlockwise island detour. In the evening we had gotten about as far north as it is possible to get, close to the small town of Mitsamiouli. We decided to check out some bungalows that were supposed to be about one kilometre from the main road, along a cattle track of a drive that could only dream of becoming a road. The standard of the first bungalow choice could have made any arbitrary hundred-year-old hunting cabin on desolate Norwegian Arctic Island of Jan Mayen seem like Caesars Palace Hotel & Casino in Las Vegas.

"TIA," croaked Alan, a little worried.

A nice guy with braided hair invited us into a kind of white house with a large green garden. The standard was basic, if non-existent, to say the least. The same was true of beds, toilet facilities, running water and windowpanes. And he did not serve food. If nothing else, the view was good — the hut was within a perfect stone's throw from the sea.

We drove onwards to our plan B. A few kilometres later, the bungalow hunt had suddenly taken us to one of the world's finest beaches. A wiry man of about 30 was working with coconuts there. He climbed up the palm trees with a long-handled knife, chopped off the nuts that promptly fell to the ground with characteristic thumps, climbed back down and then sold them. The price depended very much on who was buying, with foreigners apparently gladly paying 20 times more than the locals. He introduced himself as Ishmael.

"There used to be a luxurious hotel right in the middle between two white beaches that stretched out in an almost identical pattern on each side," he could tell us in crystal-perfect English, as opposed to most of the others we met, where French, Arabic and Shikomori, a kind of mixture of Swahili and Arabic, are spoken in The Comoros. Few people can speak English, but with one of the two luxury hotels on the island as a former neighbour, he had made the effort to learn language number four. And it may not have been in vain.

"With the hotel in the middle, the beaches looked like an angel from the sea. Absolutely magical! And it probably looked even more wonderful from the air," Ismael speculated. The hotel has been demolished now, and the plot has been bought by a huge company from the Emirates. It is only a matter of time before a new luxury five-star hotel appears like a new saviour. The main question is just whether the road from the airport will be good enough to make the project possible. A collaborative road improvement project between Taiwan and The Comoros has recently started, and here and there several kilometres have already been improved, but the time schedule is uncertain. Perhaps the sheikhs need to throw more money in than just for the hotel itself to get some impetus behind the road improvements.

I bought a coconut from Ishmael and gave him a dollar.

"Is it 20 times more than you would get from the locals?" I asked with a smile.

"No, you bargain well," he replied. "Only 3-4 times more," he laughed. If nothing else, I am directly supporting the local economy. He wondered where the next trip would take me before he told us about a mysterious drama that happened by the beach.

"Over 20 years ago, an Ethiopian Airlines plane crashed into the sea just 500 metres from land. Both the hotel guests and I were shocked witnesses. Fortunately, there was a medical convention happening, so 20 French doctors were among the first who managed to get to the wreckage and got many out alive," said Ismael. According to news articles, the Boeing 767 aircraft had been hijacked and was trying to land at the airport a little further south when it ran out of fuel. 125 people died in the crash, including Mohammed Amin, who was one of the leading photojournalists in Africa. Several of his videos were central

in putting the 1982-83 famine in Ethiopia on the international agenda, something which led to Bob Geldof and Band Aid making 'Do They Know It's Christmas' into one of the best-known Christmas songs in the world. It also inspired 'We Are the World' by USA For Africa. Divers can still find remains of the wreckage from the plane on the seabed, if they are not disturbed too much by the numerous playful dolphins that jump for joy in the area. Here, the beaches are partly used by those who live nearby, and by the occasional fortuitous visitor. The accommodation available in the area is so far not good enough to enable more people to take the trip.

After the first bungalow, we were sceptical of the two other places that rented out bungalows near the beach where we had met Ishmael. The cabin standard on other forays was also low, thanks to a complete lack of maintenance since the bungalows had been built. The age-old receptionist wore a spacious hyper-modern green and red dress with a psychedelic pattern. In Norway she would have been forced to retire.

"Working keeps me healthy, in a good mood and keeps my wits about me. I have nothing else to do. My husband died many years ago, and my children live in Europe," she explained when I asked if it wasn't more tempting to just enjoy life on the beach in her latter days. She went ahead of us at a surprisingly fast pace on the path between the palm trees. I had asked her to show us a bungalow before we decided, learning from previous experiences. The woman unlocked the green and crooked wooden door to one of the bungalows. We inspected the hut.

"There is no running water?" asked Alan.

"No, but every morning one of our employees will come with water and fill the tub on the bathroom floor so you can shower," said the lady.

Well, a shower of sorts. With the help of a scoop, one can both 'shower' and flush the toilet. The two single beds were like something out of a high-risk prison. Curtains were non-existent. The four cockroaches that ran across the floor did not exactly add to the positive impression either. If nothing else, there was at least electricity to charge mobile phones, but no light bulbs in the lamps. I usually always ask to see the hotel room before I decide. It is not always very popular, but it has saved me from a few hotel dumps over the years.

We politely declined and got back into the car to drive on. Accommodation option number three, just a few hundred metres away, was a notch better. I did not see any cockroaches in the bungalow we were shown, but the bedsheets had hardly been washed since the previous Norwegian EU referendum in 1994. There were mosquito nets over the beds, but with larger and innumerably more holes than a van full of Emmental cheese. The owner welcomed us with a smile. She was half the age of the previous receptionist. And twice as big.

"Do you have Internet here?" I said hopefully.

The round woman began to laugh, before pointing to a path that went to some cabins. "No, but we have an incredibly beautiful beach. What do you then need the Internet for?" she philosophised while she led us. The question was in fact a real one, not rhetorical. Fortunately, there are still places to be found where people ask such questions. It is a massage for the soul to use one's energy to extract the maximum out of the uniqueness of a destination. That should not be able to compete with the fastest Internet access in the world. But I have taken it upon myself to be more concerned with conveying an experience than enjoying it. Sometimes I have hardly finished something exciting before I spend more time figuring out how I can best express the wording to a picture of the whole experience. I may have experienced periodic Internet addiction. It makes me wonder, and not just because of potentially stomach ulcer-causing stress factors and abstinence, but just as much because of the need to speak of what I have been so lucky to do, as quickly as possible, giving rise to not really experiencing what I wanted to share about in the first place.

Some good things come along the third time of asking. After seeing two cabins which were a fiasco, we let ourselves be persuaded and accepted the least shabby beach cabin she had. The shower solution was identical to the one we had seen before, but at least here one of the electric lamps worked. We said yes to the bungalow. Regardless, the only other option was to return to alternative number two anyway, skulking back with our tail between our legs, or to drive an hour and a half further around to Moroni. All in the dark.

"TIA," said Alan again, almost without shame, this time. Apart from a quick trip to Mozambique, the 36-year-old had never been to Africa, with the exception of his home country. The Comoros became his baptism of fire. And he learned fast.

The next day, it was Alan who had taken over as the TIA officer. On the way south, he delivered more TIA quips than I had done the day before. Maybe not such a surprise, because there was plenty of worthy material. Road works that led to a half-hour wait without any understandable reason, a two-kilometre detour over washboard-like tyre ruts, the driver who parked in the middle of the road that went through a village when he had to deliver eggs to a shop, and the lunch café that did not serve lunch, coffee, or anything similar. I dropped Alan off at the airport and said goodbye. Things did not get any better. The flight by an African airline turned out to be quite some time behind schedule.

"Four hours late. Totally TIA!!!" it said in the text message I received from him later.

The Comoros is far more than just the main island. Nzwani is half the size of Grand Comore and lies 80 kilometres southeast, halfway to Mayotte. The island is also called Anjouan and is the world's perfume capital. The country is therefore often called the Perfume Islands. It comes from the fact that most of the ylang-ylang plants in the world grow here, and they are widely used in the production of pleasant fragrances around the world. Thanks to this island state, the world smells a little better. This also applies if cooking is your thing: The Comoros are among the leading vanilla producers in the world, but true to tradition, they only supply the plants. Others process them.

This is Africa. Or TIA, as Alan would have said.

The smallest of the three large islands is called Mohéli, or Mwali. It is located about 40 kilometres from the other two main islands and likely boasts the most beautiful beaches of all. It would be quite a job in this country, if it is at all possible, to pitch one indescribably beautiful beach up against another indescribably beautiful beach and choose a winner. The turtles really thrive throughout Mohéli, something the few snorkelling and diving tourists know to appreciate. Diving centres do not exist outside of Grand Comore, so you must bring your own equipment. From the main island there are speedboats to Mohéli, but as a foreigner you need a permit from the police to be allowed to get your sea legs. That means a trip to the police station, with your passport in your pocket. An alternative is domestic flights, but they have such a poor reputation when considering regularity that it will usually be faster by boat. And wetter. The boats have space for nine passengers, and all will receive a good measure of salt water both in their hair and on their clothes. If nothing else, the luggage is well covered with tarpaulins, so it usually arrives at the destination just as dry. It must be mentioned that the boats also do not operate with any regard to a timetable, so it is a high-risk sport to take the boat on the same day, for example, as catching a plane.

The giant marlin fish and whale shark complete this paradise and make it a must to have diving masks in your luggage. It helps that the temperature on the land never goes above 34 degrees and very rarely below 20. The annual average is a comfortable 26 degrees, but the humidity may be on the high side for the average European in the rainy season between November and April. I was last there in January, with the exception of some especially heavy downpours I had little to complain about.

Basically, Madagascar has the exclusive rights to the lemur, the exceptionally cute animal that lives in and jumps between trees at lightning speed. It became even better known due to the animation of the same name, as the fourth largest island in the world, but the mungomaki lemur, which originates from there, is found on only two of the islands in the Comoros today. As if people needed even more of a reason to travel here.

The Comoros has much to offer, but most of the islands are covered with vegetation, so the one million inhabitants live packed quite densely together in a relatively small area. In theory, there are about 500 people per square kilometre, in reality this is many times more. By comparison in Norway, there are hardly 14, but that too is only in theory due to various mountain ranges, forests, and Svalbard. Norway also has a somewhat larger defence. Without definitive enemies around the Comoros, a military of only 500 soldiers is seemingly enough, and there are just as few jobs in the police. Perhaps the poor quality of roads and a lack of tourists help keep the country mostly law-abiding: There are few rich people to steal anything from and it is impossible to make a quick getaway. However, this does not seem to have had much effect when it comes to corruption. 150 countries are less corrupt than the Comoros. African countries are consistent offenders, if not amongst the worst, on the lists of corruption.

This applies, to a much smaller degree, if we travel to Oceania and almost all the countries there. But almost 12,000 kilometres to the east, headhunting is the main story. The only question then is which is worse.

The beaches in and around the capital Moroni are not particularly clean.

While elsewhere it is paradise, here there will probably be a new luxury hotel. This means the beach will be closed off to most people.

The play of colours in the Comoros is worth the trip alone.

At the vintage petrol pumps in Moroni, the petrol must be pumped by hand.

The hotel was surrounded by greens of different shades. The forest is home to myriad chatty bird species: the world's best alarm clocks.

The standard of some of the bungalows was not up to par, but the view was somehing to write home about.

BOUGAINVILLE

Honaria

The Solomon
Islands

NGGELA SULE

GUADALCANAL

100 km

16

The Solomon Islands, Oceania

INHABITANTS: 600,000 (Wikipedia)
TOURISTS PER YEAR: 26,000 (UNWTO)
AREA: 28,400 square kilometres

WHAT IS NOW KNOWN as the Solomon Islands, was in its time a heartland for head-hunters, literally speaking. Cannibalism was widespread and was not gotten rid of until long after the Spaniard Álvaro de Mendaña de Neira 'discovered' the archipelago in 1568. He had sailed from Peru, and named the islands after King Solomon, known from the Old Testament. After a while, missionaries came here in the 19th century, but they had limited success with conversion despite the name of the country. The fact that Neira received the honour of both discovering and naming the country is unjust as it happens, because there have been settlements here for at least 6,000 years, maybe as far back as 30,000 BC. But as always, the winner writes history, and it is difficult to write history when you lack written language.

The Solomon Islands are located northeast of Brisbane in Australia, directly east of Papua New Guinea and west of Tuvalu. The fact that the country name is plural is understandable. In addition to the 13 main islands, there are over 900 smaller islands, together forming an area of 28,400 square kilometres, the same size as the agricultural heartland of Norway. The islands maybe seem quite isolated on the map, but if you look carefully, it is only 3-4 kilometres from the archipelago of Shortland in the northwest to Bougainville to the east in Papua New Guinea. As a little digression, the inhabitants of Bougainville voted for independence in a referendum in June 2019. There was a large majority for independence, 97.7 percent of voters wanted to make Bougainville yet another country in the world. In July 2021 authorities in Papua New Guinea and Bougainville signed an agreement. It says that Bougainville will gain independence between 2025 and 2027, given that the parliament in Port Moresby ratifies the deal. The pandemic in combination with national resistance to concede control of any part of Papua New Guinea still makes it anything but certain that Bougainville becomes the 199th country on the planet. As if that wasn't enough of a caveat, the referendum was advisory, not binding.

The Solomon Islands have been owned by, or at least ruled by, Spain, Germany and lastly

Great Britain. The country did not become independent until as late as 1978. Therefore, it is not so strange that there are some people here with both Scottish and Welsh genes, or that I saw some inhabitants with blond hair.

"My cousin has the same colour in her eyes as you," I even got to hear from a lady I bought coconut from. "Your blue-green colour is not greatly different from the sea that the white beaches frame," she continued.

I love the way she worded it, about what must be the world's most beautiful frame. And when a country has a top-class beach and that beach is called Dolphin View Beach, then we are pretty much done talking. The country must be visited. Let me also add that when this stretch of sand of just under 200 meters, is located three quarters of an hour by car from the capital, boasts a small hotel that is totally off the cosiness charts, and is in a country that is a mere three-hour plane ride from Brisbane in Australia, one can safely start packing the suitcase. Only the main island of Guadacanal, where the capital Honiara is located, has an international airport. From there, propeller planes and cargo boats with passenger dispensation reach the rest of the island kingdom.

It can seem like one of the most peaceful places on earth, and it is just that. But this has not always been the case, not even long after the head-hunters had put down their knives. We don't have to go any further back than the Second World War to be able to talk about bloodshed and hell on earth. So many great warships from both sides were sunk here that the strait between the main island of Guadalcanal and the neighbouring island of Nggela Sule is called Iron Bottom Sound. It is mostly down to the battle of Guadalcanal, where things really went awry.

The Battle, or Guadalcanal campaign, was the first major revenge attack against Japan in the Second World War by the Allied Forces, and in six months from August 1942 to February 1943, 67 ships were sunk, and between 1300 and 1580 planes crashed or were shot down. 19,200 Japanese died, while the Allies 'only' lost 7,000 tops, and therefore emerged as victors from the bloodbath. The so-called Scout, who was actually a local policeman called Jacob C. Vouza, received much credit for the Allied victory, and is well-known in the Solomon Islands. On a scouting mission behind enemy lines, he was discovered and taken prisoner. The Japanese tied him to a tree and tortured him for several hours to obtain information about American and Solomon positions, but Vouza refused to speak, and he was eventually stabbed several times and left for dead. This did not stop someone of such hardy standing. He managed to bite through the rope tied around him and miraculously returned to the American forces several kilometres away. He was able to relay what the Japanese were up to, and that they were planning an attack. An emergency telegram was sent to the military leadership, who then had ten minutes to prepare for the Japanese attack on Alligator Creek, the river that flows into the sea near the airport that is in use today. That was just enough time for the Allies to get in position, and they took a definitive victory. There is a statue now of Vouza near the harbour in the capital Honiara. Something well-deserved.

"Guadalcanal is no longer just a name of an island in Japanese military history. It is the name of Japan's military cemetery," said Major General Kiyotake Kawaguchi, who led an infantry brigade for Japan during the battle.

Still, the biggest winner was perhaps a psychological one. Japan had been seen as almost inhuman on the battlefield, with fearless, highly trained, and world-leading soldiers in the navy, army, and air force. That it was suddenly possible to beat them became a mental boost for the Allies. Japan was no longer invincible.

As mentioned, the Solomon Islands first became independent in 1978, when Great Britain was compelled to give up yet another colony. So, the main language is English, but with a twist. Visiting foreigners get to hear mostly English, which is spoken well enough for them to be able to follow and participate in the dialogue, at least until the locals up the ante and speak even more broadly than they usually do. Then you might as well take the hint and stroll onwards. Either they are tired of conversing with you, or they are simply talking among themselves, in pinjin. It sounds a bit like a made-up language but is based on English. An example will be given soon.

The archipelago goes by the nickname of The Happy Isles, or Hapi Isles in pinjin. I can understand why. Smiles sit easily here, and one does not take things so seriously. Along the roads and on the beaches, most people said hello, and some stopped to have a chat.

But I found the biggest smile a couple of hundred metres from Dolphin View Beach. The wonderful Edith Chottu lives there with her extended family. She rents out four bungalows on the beach on the northwest coast. The bungalow business is called B-17, named after a type of aircraft of the same name that crashed into the sea just off the coast. The American plane was one of many that were shot down during the Second World War. History does not tell if the pilot survived. However, the fact that they are named after a wreck, says nothing about the standard of Edith's bungalows. Two of them, in any case, have a kitchen, but no bathroom or running water and are made to a very simple standard with walls and floors of bamboo poles. Two of the others are similar to Western standards, with elegant wooden floors and modern bathrooms. The main problem is the roads here, of a standard that only allows for an average speed of about 20 kilometres per hour. So even though the B-17 is only 25 kilometres from the centre of Honiara, it is a lot more remote than it would otherwise sound, and without particularly many people who would happen to just drive past. The road reaches only 50-60 kilometres to either side of Honiara, while there are villages positioned around the whole of Guadalcanal, so Edith has far from the worst location. Many on the south coast are dependent upon boats. I was there out of season, and with the sparse customer base, she haggled herself down to half the price per night for the nicest bungalow. Fair enough without electricity and internet, but with a sandy beach just ten metres from the large and pleasant terrace in front of the cabin. As well as an almost 80-year-old American aircraft wreck to entice those with a diving mask.

Edith is a colourful host. She is missing her left hand, and chews betel nut, like so many of her countrymen. She is one of the few women who do, but this is some of her depth of colour in several ways. The fruit comes from the palm tree species Areca and is used by many in large swathes of Southeast Asia. Betel nut is a stimulant like coffee, but with an extra unique side effect due to the powerful red dye. Chewing the nut causes both teeth and lips to turn dark red. Among hardy and experienced betel nut chewers, the teeth are so discoloured that they are almost black. Smiles are not particularly attractive, and the breath is a chapter entirely on its own requiring dental expertise to describe in detail. But Edith shows some betel nut moderation and is not quite there. Not yet anyhow.

In 1988 she took a minibus to Honiara, and as usual the driver drove like a madman. There is great competition for passengers, so getting to the next stop or pick-up point first is essential. On the Solomon Islands, drivers stop exactly where that is, including in the middle of the road, if there is an extra paying passenger or two. It seems that no one has ever considered the inflated diesel costs by driving so fast and so wildly. Edith sat on the left side and held her hand out of the open window. Then things went awry, the driver could not keep the wheels on the road, and he flipped over several times. Her hand was pinned down and almost crushed.

"Unfortunately, this happened on a day the doctors in the whole country were on strike, and no one nearby had the competence to help me. So, the bleeding, dirty and crushed hand was just wrapped in a piece of cloth, and before the doctor's strike had ended, the wounds became infected and amputation was then the only solution," she said, before getting rid of the betel nut in a large saliva blob that landed in the sand, making a big red mark.

A missing hand wasn't a catastrophe for Edith, and she later married and had five children with her husband. They lived back then just as she does now, on the beach, in a large and delightful bamboo house. But then things started to go wrong. First came the divorce. The man found a younger woman, with two hands. Fortunately, she lost neither the beach plot nor the house. Not then.

In the Solomon Islands, there were ethnic conflicts between 1998 and 2003. It started as civil disobedience and fighting between different ethnic groups. Militant rebels began harassing immigrants from the island of Malaitan, which is also part of the Solomon Islands. Thousands travelled back to their home island, but some stayed and set up a militia in response to the oppressive and sometimes violent conduct. In the years that followed, there were kidnappings, looting, coercion from both sides and impartial elections. By 2003, things were so crazy that over 2,000 international soldiers came to the country to try to help calm the situation. They gradually succeeded. Some commentators called the Solomon Islands a non-state, others meant that the country had never managed to consolidate the different ethnic groups after having been an independent country for more than 20 years. No one disagreed that there had been unrest, a lot of unchecked unrest.

By all counts, the chaos was unrivalled cover for evildoing, and a group of Edith's jealous neighbours seized their chance to destroy her house in 2005.

"They carried out what was outright vandalism, destroying almost everything and taking the rest. In the beginning I sat down on a tree trunk on the beach and started crying. But that did not exactly help. So, I got myself together and started collecting bits of this and that, things that could become building materials," said Edith. It evoked bad memories. A tear was shed from her left eye. And this was a tough woman who I could not really see crying often, or even at all. Anyway, she was not the kind to give up.

Just two weeks later she had built a hut.

"Well, it was more of a kind of shed. I'm no construction worker. But I now had a place to live. And after a while I built more huts. Me and the five kids needed a little space."

After the unrest in the country, there were many orphaned children in the area, and children of parents who did not have the capacity to take care of both themselves and children. But enterprising Edith took it in hand and invited the children to dinner on a home-made long table on the beach, built of driftwood.

"A complete mishmash of children just came by, and I knew of nothing else than to do the best I could to support them. We fished in the sea, we picked coconuts from the palm trees, and after a while I managed to establish a garden patch where I grew some vegetables."

The kids kept coming to dinner, day in and day out. At its height the single mother supported 13 children. In addition to the five of her own. But it did not end there. In 2010, her ex-husband died of diabetes, just 56 years old. In 2013, the new wife became ill and died. They had had four children together. During the funeral, Edith took things into her own hands again.

"No bother! I will take them all," said Edith and quite simply took her ex-husband's kids, so now she is a mother of nine.

"No, they are not formally adopted. They only do it like that in Australia. Here in the Solomon Islands, they just live with me and look at me as mother."

There are ever more grandchildren, and she knows how to get them working. The kids ran errands, kept the bungalows clean, or made food. And served breakfast, lunch, and dinner to me. There were not many restaurant options in the neighbourhood. Absolutely none, actually.

"What do you want for dinner?" asked Edith.

"Well, now then. Do you have a menu?" I replied.

"No. Just say what you want, and we'll fix it."

"Lobster?" I said, almost joking.

"No problem. How many do you want?"

And there was me thinking that staying at Dolphin View Beach could not get better.

When Edith heard that I was writing a book, only a few minutes passed before the adopted son and a neighbour-boy had made an outdoor office for me on the terrace, equipped with a good chair and desk.

"If your book is bad, you at least cannot blame me," she grinned, spitting betel nut juice on the sand in front of the cabin. The red spots were there three days later when I set course back towards the capital.

Something I like best about the Solomon Islands is the abundance of coconut juice. It is served straight from the nut for breakfast, lunch, dinner and in most of the bars. It is extremely refreshing in the heat, though it rarely gets too hot here. We are normally seeing a maximum temperature of between 25 and 32 degrees, and the sea is never far away for the possibility of cooling off.

During recent years, some luxury hotels have been built in Honiara. In addition, so-called eco-lodges have arrived around the country. You will find Western standard facilities here and luxury bordering the beach, but then it comes at a price. A few hundred dollars a day is not uncommon, something that blows most backpackers' budgets, and which is way beyond what the locals earn in a month. If nothing else, the bars and restaurants in luxury hotels are good alternatives when the Internet is non-existent at the more budget-friendly options. I usually got the password without any trouble at all after ordering a full dinner, and somewhat more reluctantly when I stuck to a latte.

One day I decided to rent a car, and I found a local car rental office. Ilyn was behind the counter and tempted me with a Mazda for 50 dollars a day, without even a deposit. The choice was between white and grey. The temperature was the deciding factor, I chose the white one, which would usually be a little cooler. I showed my driver's license and paid in cash. Credit cards were not essential, but with such limited roads, it would be difficult to steal the car with any success anyway. After I signed the rental paper, the rental agent took me outside to the backyard. There were three or four mechanics working away on very worn-out cars, most of them South Korean and Japanese. It turned out that the white car was missing a wheel, and Ilyn dashed back into the office and fetched a new key, before I speedily headed off in the grey car, which had done 200,000 kilometres - according to the speedometer, at least. It felt as if it had done three times as much. The steering slipped worse than a dirt-cheap first car bought when 17 years of age; the shock absorbers were gone, and the car made noises that would make any feathered creature jealous.

But the car got me to and fro and everywhere I wanted to go. Far up in the north on Guadalcanal, Francis was trying to hitchhike on the roadside. I call it road, but it resembled more of an enhanced sheep track. My rental car, which the designer had mysteriously managed to place four doors on, was well out of its depth. But in the Solomon Islands, no one batted an eyelid because of the car. Almost everyone I passed shouted 'hi' or waved, but that was obviously because of the foreign driver clearly at the wheel. I cannot remember having encountered more friendly people, not even in Ireland. Francis had also waved first, before the waving turned into a hitchhiker's thumbs up. I was alone in the car and did not mind company. He had dropped his nephew off at school, he said. I had passed by Selwyn College in the village of Verenaaso a few kilometres earlier, he was going a further twenty kilometres and was dreading the long walk.

"There is only a minibus in the morning and evening," he said apologetically.

"No problem, I'm going the same way. How far does this road go?" I answered.

"That depends on three things: your car, your car insurance, and how foolhardy you are. When I saw the car, I thought of ditching the hiking, but when I saw you, I changed my mind," he replied, and smiled. I took it as kind of a compliment.

The road only got worse and worse, and after a while the automatic gearbox complained ever more as I strained over mounds of stones, large ponds, and moderate rivers. At a river I considered giving up — it just looked too deep. But suddenly a four-wheel drive came and drove straight through it. It did not look so disastrously deep, so I took the chance and put my foot down. The river water flooded halfway over the bonnet, but fortunately the engine did not stop, and after a few seconds we were over onto the other side.

"Not once did I think you would have driven over here, but thank you very much," said Francis. "You saved me 3-4 hours of walking."

The hiker asked me about Norway and among other things wondered about the standard of the roads.

"You surely have better roads there than here?"

Yes, except for some bumpy roads in Western Norway. There are probably a few stretches that could be worse in a couple of places deep within Åsedalen and up in Naustdalslia, I thought, thinking of home. My home borough, Naustdal, is full of good examples when it comes to bad roads, though our mountain tracks are not as bad as the road I drove on in the Pacific. I tried hard to keep the level of detail down when replying.

"Yeah, pretty much. But I come from a more rural part of Norway, and there it can often be similar to here."

I guessed he didn't have local knowledge of rural parts of Norway — Sunnfjord. It turned out that he had never been outside of the Solomon Islands but wanted to try to get a job on a farm in Australia next year.

"My brother-in-law has worked there for three years, and he is very happy. Besides, I want to experience another culture, another country and see some other faces than I do here."

The man had really grasped it.

A few kilometres later I had no other choice but to turn around. In the middle of the road, about a hundred metres ahead, there were rocks protruding far too far up for Mr. Mazda to negotiate them, and a sea of mud on each side made it impossible for me to drive around on one side or the other. So, I missed seeing Lambi, the hometown of Francis, with about 100 inhabitants living around what he described as incredibly beautiful bay — with a white sandy beach lying deep within it.

On the way to back, I stopped in Mangakiki instead. I met Onorato Bell there and his wife Miteresia. As the oldest in the village of just over 100 inhabitants, they lived in the middle, surrounded by younger inhabitants, many of them their children, grandchildren, and great-grandchildren. But they did not speak English, except for 'Welcome, welcome!'. The wide, relatively toothless smiles were reassuring so the reception was genuine.

Four of the descendants, boys aged 6-10, wanted to show me the beach. I understood immediately the reason why as we sneaked past the last bushes and saw the sight that had only been waiting for me. The bay was covered with green trees on both sides, and at its heart was a stereotypical Pacific Ocean beach, with a small river that flowed out in the middle. And apart from this group of friends, there was no one else on the sand.

Paradise.

Francis was disqualified by living there himself, but he had said that his village was far more beautiful. The next time it's going to be a four-wheel drive for me and a trip to Lambi. The Solomon Islands are an undiscovered destination for most, but especially those who enjoy diving, snorkelling, fishing, and surfing, are on the cusp of discovering the country, and they likely have a great tourism future ahead. The luxury hotels that are being built will also probably speed up tourism, but the country should perhaps primarily focus on infrastructure, and especially the roads. Although, when wonders like Mangakiki and Lambi become far easier to visit, what was idyllic can quickly vanish.

The car was driven through ponds of unknown depth, over rivers and on gravel, sand, and mud roads until I returned it two days later. The car needed a wash. It was still Ilyn Kuong who stood at the counter. She had a mechanic with her who I recognised from when I had picked up the car.

"You are back!" she said, breaking out into a big smile. I grinned.

"Are you surprised?" I wondered.

"Well, I had hoped you had crashed so we could buy a newer car," she joked. I think so, anyway.

She introduced me to the mechanic. Peter Bobbey was seemingly a shy guy, but he had a firm grip when I was greeted.

"We're closing in an hour. Do you want to join us and have a beer at Coconut Café?" asked the rental agent. I knew no one in Honiara and wasn't exactly hard to ask along. We agreed to meet at the café which was more of a bar. The location was idyllic right by the sea, with several wooden tables placed along a small pier that extended out between two beaches. The bar counter was under cover. The selection was sparse, and they served neither tea nor coffee — not even coconuts, despite the name — but the location was completely perfect. A cooling breeze swept over the tables on the pier outside, feeling incomparably good in the unduly high humidity.

With every beer Peter drank, he became a little more talkative. After number four, we were talking football.

"I love the way Norway plays football," he said, raising his glass for a toast.

"What? Now I'm not completely with you. Norway is completely useless on the football pitch. Do you mean a Norwegian football player?" I replied. But I clinked my glass next to his, for the sake of it.

"Come on, man! They beat Brazil. I am never going to forget that."

I raised my glass for a slightly more forceful toast. This was a good man. And there was me thinking it was only Norwegians who still lived on that victory over the world's best football team, back in 1998.

After a while, as the evening drew on, we talked about all kinds of things. From football we went over to cars, politics, travel, and the nightlife in Honiara. And suddenly Peter came out with:

"This is the first time I've talked to a white man. I love you!" Then he gave me a big hug. As a car mechanic in the middle of a capital city, he had certainly seen many Western people, and exchanged niceties, but had never had conversations with anyone before. I bought a new round of beers. It's not every day I get a good man-hug.

"Where did you come from before the Solomon Islands?" asked Ilyn.

"Australia," I replied abruptly.

"No wonder you came here instead!" she laughed. "What were you doing there?"

There was no way out of it other than telling them what I had done in Sydney. Together with Ronald Haanstra and Erik de Zwart, two friends from the Netherlands, I had set a Guinness world record for being the fastest to fly around the world via the six inhabited continents using scheduled flights.

"Crazy fuck!" Ilyn cried, before she laughed uncontrollably. "You crazy, crazy fuck!"

And Peter would not let it slip, he wanted to follow up. They said something or other in broad pinjin, stood up, then climbed up onto the wooden table, raising a toast and did a small dance for the world record.

We managed to fly around the world in 56 hours and 56 minutes, and it was without doubt total madness. With an average speed of over 750 kilometres an hour, we had been on planes and at airports for almost two and a half days after travelling from Sydney to Sydney, via Santiago, Panama, Madrid, Algiers, and Dubai. To set the record, one must start and end at the same airport.

They simply could not stop grinning because of the world record and continued talking in pinjin. I hinted strongly towards them possibly translating so I could follow what was said.

"Just give a few sentences to me in English, and I'll translate them into pinjin," challenged Ilyn. After getting such a tempting invitation from someone who rented out cars, I could not help myself. One sentence turned into several in my head:

"I really love driving here in the Happy Isles, especially as long as I do not crash my boss' car. But sometimes I do, and then I usually get sacked. I might as well just party the night away," I joked.

Ilyn and Peter grinned in unison. I had to promise that I was not in the habit of predicting the future for real. Ilyn thought for 30 seconds before rising to the challenge:

"Mi lavem tumas fo draev lo hia lo Hapi Isles, mek sua nomoa mi no brekem car blo boss blo mi. Bat samtaems mi sawe accident wetem car blo boss blo me so hem sakim mi. Ating hem gud fo mi drink en pati full nait ya nomoa."

What an almost made-up language.

It turned out that one of Peter's friends was sitting and drinking at one of the other tables, and he came over to us late into the evening. The emaciated guy was clearly drunk. Despite them speaking in bandit-language, even I realised that he was slurring his words. He had driven to Coconut Café and was planning to drive back home.

"Should I drive you to your hotel?" he offered. Firstly, the hotel was less than a kilometre away, and I like to walk. Secondly, I was not exactly keen on being driven by a drunk driver.

"Well, I think it'll be OK. You are not exactly completely sober," I smiled, in an attempt to be convincing. He was not offended and just laughed back.

"No worries. It's Thursday today. The police never have checks on Thursdays," he promised. Nevertheless, I still politely turned down his offer, and asked if I could give him a little money, so that he could take a taxi home.

"Didn't you hear what I said? No checks!" he said loudly, a little irritated.

My point that there were other reasons why one should not drink and drive, fell on deaf ears. He said goodbye to us all and sped off in a red, old Ford. I did just the same in blue, half-worn-out Adidas.

The relaxed lifestyle here is perfect for chilled-out holiday trips, detox stays, convalescence from burnout and honeymoons — perhaps a combination of these. You will find 'secret' beaches, coral reefs with colourful life forms in all shapes and sizes, and lagoons where you can rest completely in peace in your sailboat or dive until you get the bends. You just have to find an island where it is just you and your chosen travel partner in a luxurious bungalow, surrounded by palm trees, orchids, and well-kept garden beds, with the beach only metres away. Chalk white, of course. And on the roadless south side of Guadalcanal there are good surfing possibilities — the challenge is just getting there. Ever more foreigners who are looking out for unique surfing beaches, and who can afford to pay for the boat rides, are making the trip there.

Incidentally, on the smaller islands, you don't need to be completely alone with your chosen companion if you don't want to. A butler can be ordered, even answering to any name, where he stays in his own discreetly located bungalow. Though, they are close enough to show up within three minutes if you whistle. Via a walkie talkie.

If such luxury blows the budget, there are resort hotels where children are not allowed; screaming kids are not going to destroy the idyll. These are not exactly cheap either, but then everything is included. You do not unfortunately get your own island, but a picnic in front of the sunset on your own beach is also very amiable. Then you just have to live with 3-4 other private beaches on the same island. And a complete shortage of butlers.

The Solomon Islands are still so unknown that the price of such luxury is a good notch below the equivalent in one of the more well-known resort destinations starting with M: Maldives, Mauritius, Malaysia, and Madagascar.

Ecotourism is expanding here too, but not on the main island. Solomon Airlines has several small propeller planes that transport tourists to small boutique hotels or rental bungalows on the other islands. Just be aware that the airline's reputation for being punctual is terrible. The locals usually bring along a thick book and an even larger bottle of spirits. If you can think ahead, then buy tax-free size.

It is far further between comfortable hotels in West Africa. Widespread corruption in most of the countries in the region means there is a shortage of most things, including in Guinea.

These proud beach lions were eager to show me their favourite beach, just a hundred metres from Mangakik village.

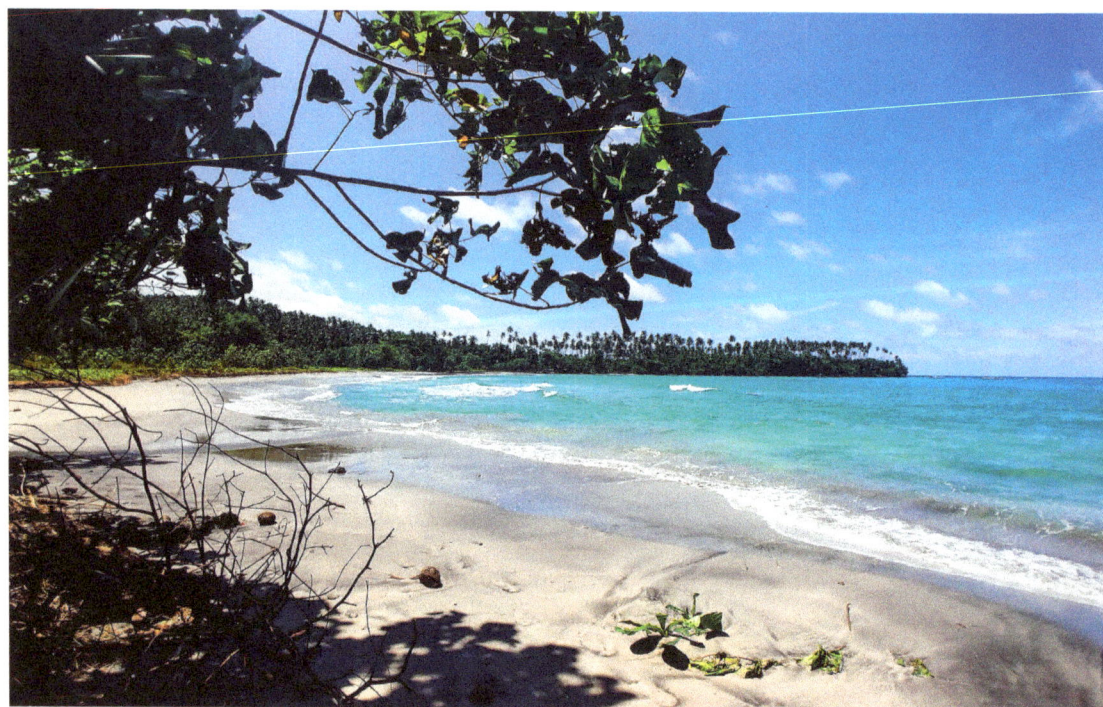

A river runs through the middle of the stereotypical pacific beach. Absolutely magical!

A local Linselus (left), Ilyn Kuong, Peter and I at Coconut Cafe. People are curious, and tend to come over and chat.

Soda bottles are just so 2018. Coconut water is healthy, tastes fantastic and costs little.

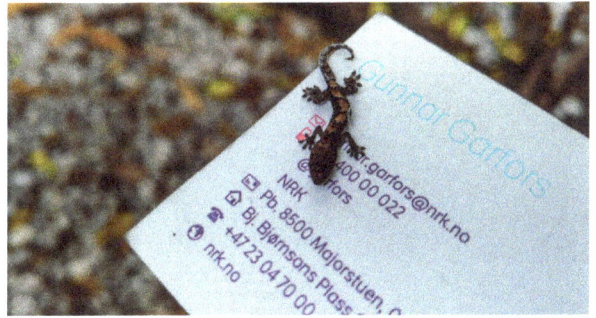

And I thought I wouldn't be visited by anyone in the hotel room.

The food you can't find on the market in Honiara is unlikely to be of any use to you anyway.

It's quite common to wash clothes and bed linen in one of the many rivers here. They don't need a tumble dryer either, with hot stones close by.

Three friends meet in separate canoes outside b-17. I wave to them and try to strike up a conversation without success. Edith explained that her neighbours were typically shy.

A proud Edith Chottu beside the finest bungalow she rents out.

In the Solomon Islands, cargo ships also carry passengers.

There was a fierce competition to be a guide in Mangakiki village.

Miteresia Bell and her husband Onorato Bell are supposedly the oldest inhabitants of Mangakiki. I don't know how old, though, as they didn't speak understandable English, and the kids who showed me the beach only said they were "very old".

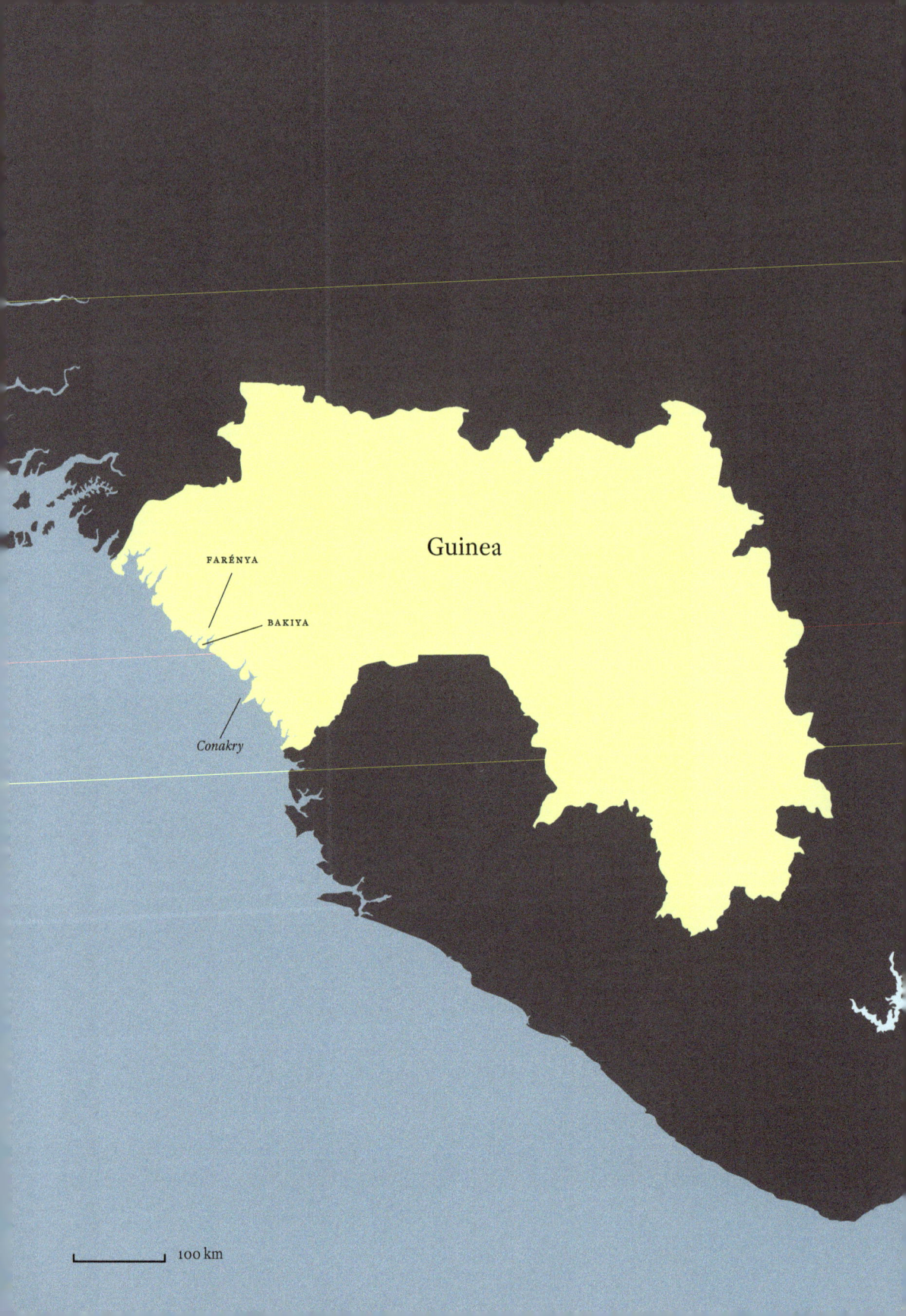

Guinea

FARÉNYA

BAKIYA

Conakry

100 km

15

Guinea, Africa

INHABITANTS: 12,400,000 (Wikipedia)
TOURISTS PER YEAR: 24,500 (UNWTO)
AREA: 245,836 square kilometre

IT IS DIFFICULT to name the world's most corrupt country. Transparency International is now doing just that, but it appears as if most emphasis is then placed on top-level corruption, with politicians and national and multinational companies at the forefront. North Korea, Somalia, Syria, or South Sudan usually head this list. Corruption at the top of course also affects the woman on the street and the man with the backpack, but it might not be felt so directly on the skin of most people. Guinea is the size of the United Kingdom and is in West Africa, just southeast of Guinea-Bissau and directly north of Sierra Leone. Here, it seems corruption has permeated almost everywhere to a greater or lesser degree, even though Transparency International's list for 2017 reveals 31 more corrupt countries, including the Comoros.

Purely on a personal level, I experienced minor corruption from a couple of insalubrious guys. I was out walking on the street northwest of the city, not too far away from the Sheraton Hotel, which is a landmark right next to the sea. There were small sheds in different colours and in different states of repair on both sides of the street, which functioned as shops or small bars. I had ambled along a few hundred metres from my small hotel, which was well below the standard and price of the Sheraton. In my right hand I held my black compact camera. An idiotic thing to do.

Exactly as I was about to pass a blue booth of little more than a square metre, where a man under its roof was selling scratch cards, one of the customers outside took my hand and held on. The man was a little older than me and fittingly overweight. Seemingly a policeman in a uniform and a police hat, but the cloth 'Police' sign hung upside down over his left chest. It could have meant a fake policeman, a drunk policeman or a dyslexic policeman.

"Wait here!" he commanded, moving his hand up and grabbing my shoulder.

"You are not allowed to take photographs here!" the man shouted. He had not brushed his teeth that day. Or that week.

"I have not taken any pictures, I can show you," I offered.

"You have a camera, it's not allowed!" he continued. "You must come with me."

But first we had to wait. The reason was that the man had already bought scratch cards, and he wanted to check to see if he had won anything.

"Stand still here," he said, releasing his hold. He needed both hands to scrape at the card. I considered running away — it would have taken me four calories to run from the fat man with short legs. He did not have a gun either, but I was a little too curious, and wanted to find out what he had in store for me. There were a lot of people on the street in the sun, so I felt relatively safe. Even though I did not know what he was going to do, I was sure that he was after money. TIA.

"Fuck!" he said. Or at least something similar, in his language.

There had obviously been no winnings. But that could quickly change. Now he had a Western 'hostage' who probably had pockets full of money. He grabbed my shoulder again and led me across the street, over the hard-packed sand near the asphalt that did not cover the entire width of the road. It was plausible to believe that the contractor had paved less of the road than he had been paid for, and then stuck the money he had saved into his own pocket.

Fifty metres further on, there was a real policeman. At least he looked like one. The man was in good shape and the uniform both fitted better and looked more professional. But the scratch-card-man knew exactly what he was doing and explained something to the younger guy with a blue police hat on. The new policeman demanded to be given my camera. I turned it on, showing that none of the pictures were from the capital Conakry. It did not make any difference, and the policeman took the camera from me.

"You are not allowed to have a camera here," he said, referring to a non-existent rule. I have experienced something similar before, from corrupt police officers in other countries.

"You have to pay to get the camera back," he said. The scratch-card-man sniggered. This was going his way.

"I do not have money on me," I lied.

He took the camera behind his back as a demonstration.

"Then I suggest you get hold of some money."

"How much is the fine?" I asked, suitably unimpressed.

"$100!" The answer came back immediately. I did not even bother to ask if I would get a receipt, as I knew that this was total bullshit. I was not thinking about giving him $100, even though the camera was worth seven times as much.

"I do not have as much money as that. I'm just a poor tourist," I said. I knew that the word poor was not compatible with a Western person in Guinea, but everything is relative.

"Let me go to my hotel," I said. I had to get hold of some lower value notes than the 50 dollar notes I had in my pocket.

My hotel was just 400 metres away, and I knew they were not interested in my camera. They were corrupt, but hardly had immediate criminal contacts. I walked from there, confident that they would not do a runner. In my backpack I found a 20 dollar note that folded and held in my hand. In addition, I found three single dollar notes that I put in one of my pockets. They should, if nothing else, end up arguing about an amount they could not just split in two.

Little and large were not impressed with my twenty dollars, even though it was several days wages and would be able to pay for a whole pile of scratch cards. But I realised from their body language that they were far more interested in getting some American currency than in a Japanese camera. I handed the folded note to the thinnest man.

"This is not enough," he said.

"That's absolutely everything I have," I said. And waited, seeing the grip on my camera begin to loosen.

"Let me just check my pocket," I said, and after a couple of seconds of fumbling, I pulled out three more notes from my left pocket and handed them to him, at the same time as I grabbed my camera with my right hand. 15 percent extra was enough to let the camera go without a protest.

"Have a nice rest of the day," I replied, before turning and walking back towards the hotel. They were not going to get the time to find more reasons to give me twisted fines. They were too busy with splitting the spoils in two and did not follow me.

The rest of the week my camera stayed in my shorts pocket when I was not using it. I do not like to contribute to corruption, and in this case, I could have gone to the police station to try to get them to come to my rescue. By chance, it happened to be located across the road from my hotel. Nonetheless, there were at least two problems with that idea: They speak French in Guinea, and I cannot. In addition, I would have likely had to wait at least a couple of hours, based on the queue outside the police station. Then it would not have been a given that the camera buddies, who spoke a little English, would have still been where I had left them.

I could have of course also reported it stolen — that would not have been far off the truth — and gotten myself a new one paid by the travel insurance. But I like best to fix my own problems. Moreover, experiencing corrupt people directly is an experience in itself, although not necessarily a good enough reason to travel to Guinea. And then one should perhaps ask why people act in this way. Many do not own a jot, often combined with the fact that they are already affected by corruption coming from above. Then in many ways, one is forced to further carry on the chain. A vicious circle.

The meeting with Momo Zayatte was far more positive. He worked for his father who owned the hotel and was helping out while I was staying there. He sees a bright future for Guinea before him, despite some challenges with corruption.

"There are enormous opportunities for those who want to invest. There is nothing more to do in Europe — people with money should make use of the need here in Guinea instead. This is the next Eldorado. But we need help to develop the country, we need help with money, and we need help from people who can show us how to do things."

The tall man in his late thirties was combative and perhaps a little too young to see or worry about all the challenges the country was facing. Or maybe his age was a blessing. If you think you can do something or think you cannot, then so it will be. And it did not seem like just young, naïve, and over-optimistic activism either. The country has gold, diamonds, and coffee, not to mention that they are the world's second largest producer of bauxite, which is the main ingredient in aluminium. On top of that, Guinea has a fantastic shoreline, beneath all the rubbish.

In other words, Guinea has all the prerequisites to be a wealthy country. But thanks to years of corruption, it is only politicians who have piles of money here. Most of the money disappears out of the country in any case, to owners of foreign companies, thanks to shady and lucrative agreements signed by unscrupulous politicians who have failed their people.

"The president is now in his second term, and he wants to change the constitution to be able to be in power longer," said Momo. Presidents who have been in office for a while tend to want to remain even longer. It is seldom wise and seldom popular. As if that matters in various dictatorships around the world.

The current President Alpha Condé got what he wanted and managed through a referendum to get the voters to agree to a nullification of his presidential terms. That meant that he could run yet again in 2020. Not surprisingly he won the election. But not everyone was pleased. There was a coup in September 2021 and 41-year-old colonel Mamady Doumbouta took over. The military claimed that this was not a traditional coup but a liberation of the people and that new elections would be held as soon as possible. Doumbouta vowed not to run for election, but laws, rules and promises are known to be changed suddenly by those with power in hand.

Momo was hopeful for a brighter future.

"We Guineans don't want to be laughed at any longer. Ever more young people travel abroad and study in Europe and North America. They are educated on a completely different level than the previous generation. New people and new blood are what we need. I do not care who, as long as the person concerned can change my country in a positive direction, is willing to change course and think anew," he stated.

But even Alpha Condé was innovative and revolutionary when he first came to power in 2010. Unfortunately, power does something to politicians in positions of leadership, so it is no surprise that Momo questions the intentions of an old politician carrying a lot of ballast.

"He wanted to have power. Now he wants to have even more power, without having the law on his side. He has gone too far and outlived his role. He was also born in the 1930s."

Unfortunately, such a mentality is the rule rather than the exception in Africa. It is not at all unusual to extend the number of terms a president can serve. Mugabe in Zimbabwe, Museveni in Uganda and Kagame in Rwanda are just three examples. All managed to change the constitution in their country.

Momo was perhaps impassioned a little above what was normal. He evidently wanted more than just working at his father's hotel. On top of that, he had been inspired by his brother Kamil, who had previously played professional football for Hull City in England, and who had also been the captain of the Guinean national team.

"We have to get our own country out of the pit first. People are suffering. We are rich in natural resources and have good initiative. We have the best coffee in the world in Guinea, but no one knows that. We can manage it, but then we must put our country first and love our own. Everyone has to work together," he almost shouted.

There was no denying his desire to act. Momo had suddenly gotten a stage, and he had to use it the best he could.

"I am not afraid of going to jail for telling the truth. We need more people to speak up, but the lack of education among the masses suppresses us. People do not think for themselves. They forget that Guinea is both one of the richest and poorest countries in the world."

He said the last sentence while he got up and pointed to the door. Momo politely explained that he was running late for a meeting, and we shook each other by the hand. But he was not quite finished yet and laid down the gauntlet as he showed me to the door in the air-conditioned room. I was happy for the break; it was 35 degrees outside and scorching sunshine.

"Western people must stop giving us money! Even to well-meaning organisations, most of it ends up in the corrupt food chain here anyway. If you want to help, come here, and invest. Together, let's create jobs and establish Guinea as a tourist destination. And do not contribute money to our corrupt politicians!"

"Or the corrupt police guys," I thought.

The capital Conakry is constantly growing, and that is not only a positive thing. The city is located on a peninsula, accessed by only one main road. There is therefore slow-moving traffic in one, the other or both directions for large parts of the day. The locals just call it an everlasting traffic jam. I had had quite enough of that the last time I visited. This time I walked into town. Well, I took a motorcycle taxi on the way back — in the afternoon it is usually too hot to walk — kind of back anyhow. On the way, it was tempting to cool off in the breeze on one of the beaches. The magic of beaches is irresistible, even though the beaches in the capital are so littered with rubbish. There is something about the water, the sand, and the atmosphere. Despite all the rubbish, people hang out here for hours around dusk. At a kind of fortuitous bar built of tarpaulins and dried tree trunks, I bought freshly squeezed pineapple juice. Most of the others drank beer that likely to cooled them better in the West African heat. Kids ran around and played or played football on the dark sand. Around them lay plastic in the form of

every conceivable and unimaginable product in colours that likely once screamed out on busy supermarket shelves to be plucked and bought.

Rubbish is a big problem in Guinea. The ports are almost covered by plastic, paper and rubber that floats around the boats scurrying in and out with passengers and freight, with often more plastic that will most likely end up on a beach here, on Cape Verde or in Norway. But no one seemed to mind the waste that lay everywhere. The rubbish has been here for so long that it seems natural, no matter how damn awful that sounds. How much more difficult will it be if we do not teach the kids and convert the adults to stop throwing rubbish into nature themselves, when that's all they know?

On Saturday night I met Momo again. He was in high spirits.

"Are you going to join us going out? We have the best nightlife in Africa, with incredible DJs. Not to mention the club culture here, you cannot find any better place," he proclaimed. There was certainly no shortage of enthusiasm. I needed to get up early but joined for a couple of glasses at a pub before Momo went on to the nightclub. Well into the first drink he noticed an acquaintance.

"You must greet Ohmed! He is working on an incredibly exciting project," he said to me, before he headed off to grab his friend. Two minutes later we were introduced, and Ohmed Camara began to tell me about his Road of Slavery project. The 35-year-old has delved deep into the history of Guinea.

"The US Navy was involved directly and coerced many people into slavery," he began. Saving the climax for the end, wasn't his thing. Sufficiently aghast, he took that as a sign to hop back to the beginning.

Ohmed had become interested in the slave history of Guinea through his father, Naby Camara, who died of an illness in 2013. The ophthalmologist ran several clinics and worked as a consultant in the Guinean Health Department. This had made access easy for him for contacts high up in the system. Father and son had gotten to know two American professors in the early 2000s. A friendship had developed, and the Americans had encouraged the Africans to start digging together into the slave history.

The approximately 40-kilometer-long Ponga River, which flows into the Atlantic Ocean at the town of Boffa about 100 kilometres north of Conakry, was central in the slave trade with Europe and North America. This can be substantially attributed to the British-American merchant and sea captain Styles Lightbourne, and his wife, who later took over the slave trade after her husband. On his first trip to Guinea, Lightbourne saw the most beautiful woman he had ever seen on the edge of the village of Bakia in Guinea. Ohmed showed me the book, In Memory of a Dear Friend, which one of the American professors had written. Naby Camara was mentioned several times. The research for this book led them to discover what Lightbourne is supposed to have written in his logbook:

"I anchored my vessel in the bay and went ashore in a rowboat. A light breeze eased the intense heat which rose from the white sand on the beach. A short distance away, by the end of the avenue, I could see the slave village towards which I was heading to do business. I noticed a few people strolling but none of them approached me. Some banana plants grew on the side of the avenue facing the river, where a young woman bathed. She was tall with bronze coloured skin and wore only a sarong around her waist. Using half a coconut she poured water over her head. I was astonished by her sheer beauty, to the extent that I even dropped my sword and pistol to the ground. That's when the girl noticed me and ran between some trees and disappeared."

The woman the captain had seen was Elizabeth Bailey, the daughter of Portuguese Emmanuel Gomez, who had come to Guinea several decades earlier. He had found a local beauty there who as it happens was the daughter of a local chief, and he married her. Captain Lightbourne wanted to buy slaves from Emmanuel Gomez who was the chief in Bakia. But Gomez insisted that they first got to know each other through agreeable African festivities with music, dance, food and drink and everything else that goes along with that.

"When Lightbourne discovered how much Gomez wanted for a slave, he asked to marry the chief's daughter as well, likely in the hope of paying less for the slaves, but also because the daughter turned out to be the beautiful girl he had fallen for down at the beach," said Ohmed, taking a sip of Fanta.

In 1809, the year after the US Congress officially abolished slavery in the United States, Lightbourne and the girl married. Something as insignificant as an American slave ban was not going to stop slave owners in the American southern states or the supreme couple. Mr. and Mrs. Lightbourne had long-term ambitions for large-scale export of slaves, and just a few months later they had established their own little slave trade in the village of Farenya some 30 kilometres further up the river. A human store that included a so-called slave factory where the slaves lived. A factory! That says something about the total lack of empathy, not to mention disdain for human dignity. But the business went well, and they kept having to expand. There was a great demand for slaves in North America, and not much time passed before Lightbourne himself became the chief. Lightbourne's traits were said to be charismatic, intelligent, and very ambitious. As the wife of a chief, she was given the title of queen. Queen Niara Bely.

The couple collaborated with caravan owners who transported slaves from all over Africa. In exchange for gold and ivory, they managed to get many slaves to the factories, at its height there were 6,000. While they were waiting to be shipped north or west, they worked on the farm. Despite the formal slave ban, which only applied to the northern states, the slaves were sold between South Carolina and the Caribbean islands. The ban also meant an increase in price. As captain of several of the sailing ships, Styles Lightbourne was himself away from Farenya quite a lot. He always made the return journey with a somewhat less suspicious cargo onboard the ship, everything from sugar, tobacco, firearms, and knives to beads, textiles, and metal tools.

Queen Niara Bely ran the affairs at home, and she became known as a very tough and successful businesswoman. Lightbourne disappeared in 1833, most likely in an accident out at sea, after which Niara Bely ran both the factory and most of the village with an iron fist until she herself died in 1879, almost 90 years old. During the last thirty years of her life, she and her sons went over to the production and sale of coffee and peanuts — not coming from piousness, but fear. Constant new attacks by British and American warships trying to enforce the slave ban had made the trade too risky. The Queen eventually yielded to be baptised by English missionaries the year before she died. And it was only then she really became known, almost as a legend. People still sing songs about the mythical powers she supposedly had. During her lifetime, there were not many women with power, not in Africa in any case.

Otherwise, it was not just Styles Lightbourne and the Queen who traded slaves in Guinea until the mid-19th century. There were many slave factories along the Pongo River, and the stories are often surprisingly similar. The descendants often lived for a long time on the power and the money derived from the slave trade, and several of them later secured lucrative positions in both politics and business in Guinea and other West African countries. Several leaders today in Africa have former slave traders in their family tree.

Today, the eight villages along the slave route from Farenya to Bakia have almost become a tourist attraction. There are still many ruins from the palaces and the villas of the chiefs — or correctly named, the slave traders — and the factories. In addition, we can see the churches where the missionaries operated from. The slave route has developed into an important tourist initiative in Guinea, and nearby you will find almost deserted and relatively clean beaches. Residents from the United States and the Caribbean especially travel along the slave route to get an insight into history. For some it is coming back to their own roots and understanding how their ancestors were treated as trade objects can be difficult. Visitors want a guide for such trips, something Ohmed has managed to create a business out of. After working together with his father, he is a knowledgeable guide.

During the conversation, it came out that Ohmed could not present indisputable evidence that the US Navy had actively supported the slave trade in the early 19th century, even though numerous signs indicated such.

"The navy of course wanted big, strong, robust, and fit men. When one shipload after another passed with ideal men, the temptation must have been too great, and some high-ranking officers must have begun to place orders for slaves themselves," he said.

Even if the story was true, the US Navy would never admit it. The claim for compensation alone would make it impossible. That much money does not exist.

And there is far more to do in this underrated country. The best way to get acquainted with it is a pretty typical Norwegian thing — to go for a walk. I walked through dense rainforest and saw impressive waterfalls, steep slopes, rugged cliffs, charming villages, and views that are really in the top echelon when it comes to the colour green.

Because this country is lush! There are several companies that now offer guided tours. Many of them put a lot of effort into showing an authentic experience and gladly offer accommodation in the villages. The most impressive thing, however, is that they send some of the profits to the villages. Guinea has an impressive offering within ecotourism, but paradoxically, the main challenge is the lack of tourists. There are many well intentioned Western holiday makers who are looking for increasingly more sustainable destinations, but then it is far easier and more practical of course being an ecotourist a little closer to home.

Incidentally, Momo was right about what he said regarding the nightlife. There are several impressive music festivals and a generally underrated nightlife in Conakry. Guinea has some of the best kora players in the world. A kora is a sort of guitar-inspired harp, and in the capital, there are many places with live music — few of them are without a kora band. Both Ohmed and Momo are optimists and believe that both the nightlife and music festivals can meet the challenge with competing events in Europe and North America. But then many measures are required, like improving infrastructure and replacing top politicians. All the smaller initiatives are privately run, and none receive government support. Corrupt governments do little if they do not get a slice of a future cake themselves.

"We must start from scratch and think anew. The government does not help us with tourism," said Ohmed, who is involved himself in several music festivals and is trying to make Conakry more attractive in terms of music and nightlife.

"We are well away! People here may not have much, but we can party," he said and ordered a new Fanta.

"Just not today," he said, excusing himself with a slightly embarrassed smile: "I'm a little drunk."

He had been in town to celebrate having a group of American tourists book a trip to experience the slave route. They had clearly paid well for the untraditional tourist attraction.

Traditional slavery was not common on the islands in the Pacific, but in recent times there have been several trials involving 'modern' human trafficking. Women have been lured from their homes on paradise islands with promises of well-paid jobs and subsequently forced into prostitution on the island of Guam, three hours by plane due east of Manila in the Philippines.

Fortunately, we are not going to Guam, despite this small American island being in Micronesia. The 14th least visited country in the world is also in this region —the Federated States of Micronesia.

Unfortunately, no one is picking litter on the beaches around Conakry, and then it quickly looks like this.

This guy sat for a long time and looked out to sea.

Amateur football on the beach.

Even professional footballers prefer to train on the beach.

That kids grow up with such beaches being the norm, commonplace, is frightening for the future.

So do the sheep.

A few hundred metres away from my hotel balcony, I almost lost my camera to two corrupt police officers.

Momo Zayatte has faith in a bright future for guinea.

Federated States of Micronesia

YAP

CHUUK

Palikir

POHNPEI

KOSRAE

200 km

14

Federated States of Micronesia, Oceania

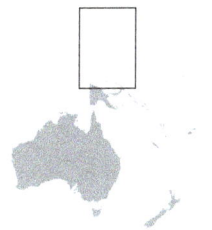

INHABITANTS: 105,000 (Wikipedia)
TOURISTS PER YEAR: 24,000 (UNWTO)
AREA: 702 square kilometre

TRAVELLING AROUND the Pacific Ocean can be more annoying than a tone-deaf busker with ear defenders and bodyguards, right outside your door. You cannot escape it. It is not just a matter of disappearing on the next plane in a couple of hours. There are usually several days to the next departure, and the planes are often full. And here there is no such thing as cheap tickets because it is not exactly double-decker aircraft like the A380 or 747 that operate the routes across the Pacific Ocean. Therefore, a single delay can often trigger a domino effect within your entire itinerary. There is a lack of daily flights in what is a huge area of ocean with the occasional, almost invisible, island. Just try to find the various islands by randomly zooming in on Google Maps. Due to the limited transportation on offer, there are also very few visitors who travel here, something that makes the journey here even more exotic than it already is. It isn't exactly helpful that almost no one has heard of the various countries here either, except for Fiji.

Micronesia is a gigantic ocean area of seven and a half million square kilometres — almost as large as Australia — and includes thousands of islands, including five island nations. Micronesia is often used as a short version of the Federated States of Micronesia when speaking, but it is only one of the five countries. The other four are Palau, Nauru, Kiribati, and the Marshall Islands. Most of them you will read more about later in the book.

The Federated States of Micronesia is comprised of four well-dispersed provinces, or states, with each having their own main island. All lie roughly in a straight line. The three easternmost states are, starting from the west, the wreck diving paradise of Chuuk, Pohnpei, where the capital is located, and little Kosrae of 100 square kilometres with just under 8000 inhabitants. It takes almost an hour to fly from Pohnpei to the rest. The fourth state is called Yap, the main island has the same name, and the state is located 1500 kilometres northwest of Chuuk, which is not an island, but a lagoon. Not only is Yap more isolated due to the sheer distance, but there are no flights departing from here to the other states in the country, only small planes to a few of the small islands in the vicinity.

If you're planning on going from Yap to other parts of the Federated States of Micronesia, the fastest way is via the aforementioned Guam, with passport control hell awaiting you there as Guam is part of the United States. And with a monopoly for United Airlines, the costs are a good deal higher than flying even the monopolised domestic routes in Norway. And that isn't a joke when considering the high cost of living in Norway.

Altogether, the Federated States of Micronesia is comprised of over 600 islands and atolls covering a total of 702 square kilometres, which is almost the same area as a small borough in inland Norway. But statistics are only statistics. Due to the large distances between the islands, the country controls an area of ocean of over 2.6 million square kilometres. Had the ocean been defined as land we would be looking at the tenth largest country in the world. Any way you look at it, this is though the 14th largest exclusive economic zone in the world, with the Lilliputian state having substantial and exclusive rights to the economic utilisation of all resources, both in the sea and on the seabed.

In Yap one will find the largest coins in the world, in the form of large round stones that are called rai. The very largest are as much as four metres in diameter, and the smallest only 30 centimetres, which is still very large for a coin. And like many other coins, most here have a hole in the middle. There are around 6,500 stone coins, or rai stones, all over Yap. When they were in use about a thousand years ago, they remained in their permanent places even though their owners changed as a result of trade transactions. The monetary system was based on oral transfer of ownership. The buyer and seller were simply in agreement about exchanging a stone lying in a certain place for a commodity or service. Therefore, there was never a need to move the giant coins.

Micronesia was 'discovered' by Spaniards in the 16th century. Most believe that it was Álvaro de Saavedra Cerón who was the first man to discover it in 1528, when he sailed across the Pacific Ocean. Fellow countryman Alfonso de Arellano, who arrived on the ship 'San Lucas', concluded that this was not a place to idle. First, the ship was attacked by men in canoes with spears. They demanded that he sailed onwards, and he heeded the not exactly subtle hint. But on Pulap Atoll 300 kilometres further west, in the present-day state of Chuuk, two sailors went ashore to fetch water. They were clubbed to death while the rest of the crew watched on from the ship, and their violent reputation came into being. In the 1600s and early 1900s, many Westerners came here, but neither Britons, Spaniards, Russians, French nor Americans ventured deeper into the islands and kept their sporadic settlements beyond the Chuuk Lagoon itself. That may not be such a surprise after the clubbing episode. And it was far from a one-off. People who went ashore without consent were usually killed, so the fact that the inhabitants gained a reputation as wicked hunters and killers, was not so strange. Since the 1800s, they have calmed down quite a bit, but to this day the inhabitants of Chuuk are far less accommodating than those living in the other three states, and in older guidebooks you can read about it possibly being dangerous to stay outdoors after darkness has fallen.

I intended to find out if that was true. I took the first flight to Chuuk. Or maybe I should call it an air cocktail. It took me seven flights to get there. Fans of airplane food would have given a little toe or two to repeat my route: Oslo-Berlin-Beijing-Seoul-Taiwan-Palau-Guam-Chuuk. One gets many meals during 30 hours of travel.

I confronted the Micronesian, Aliven, with the poor reputation of his fellow citizens while we sat and watched the majestic sunset over small atolls far away. He grinned. Aliven made a living from various small jobs and had introduced himself as a gardener when I was about to go through the gateway to my hotel on the main island of Weno. We chatted and I realised that he could have added a chef, sailor, driver, fisherman, security guard and shop assistant as titles if he had had a business card.

"Dangerous, no!" Not for you foreigners. There can be quite a bit of fighting, and sometimes someone that pulls out a knife, but then that is always between gangs from different islands. With as foreign as you look, nothing will ever happen to you," he comforted.

After checking in, I strolled along a dirt road of a route to Blue Lagoon, a hotel and diving centre south on the main island. On the way back I took another route of a similar standard. After a couple of kilometres, I came to a volleyball net that hung right across the road while 12 youths played. A car came right after me. Then the game stopped while one of the youths held up the net so that the car could pass before the match resumed. One must be solution-oriented on a small island where there is limited traffic. I exchanged some polite phrases with those playing. None of them were particularly talkative, and I ambled on. Shortly after, a car came up from behind and stopped right next to me.

"You look tired, jump in!" said a 35-year-old with sunglasses, cap, and an otherwise traditionally rough appearance. He was alone in the car, so I got the front seat.

"It's Saturday today, aren't you going to have some beers at the hotel?" he wondered. "You cannot waste time with walking."

The driver's name was Romeo, and as he dropped me off, I invited him to join me at the best pub. He brightened up and said he would come back later. The bar is connected to a hotel where I knew many young Americans were staying. The US military has in fact a project where an engineering squad is improving and expanding a school. They are electricians, carpenters, and plumbers, but they still go around in military uniforms during working hours, not to mention when they travel, as the airline, United, gives uniformed personnel the right to board the plane before the rest of us, including those with business class tickets. Outside of working hours, I reckoned that the odds were pretty good that they would have some drinks, and that they would likely attract other people with a thirst with more of a local connection. It probably helped that a diving centre was located right next to the hotel.

"Few drink beer more often than divers," my diving instructor said to me in 1995. But he was from Scotland and perhaps not entirely representative. Maybe divers drink beer often, but not in large amounts every time. Diving when drunk is apparently not the done thing, so I have heard. In Chuuk, there is a 50 percent tax on all alcohol that is sold, and all alcohol is imported except home-made varieties. The high fees and the lack of microbreweries is also not a great help for increasing the number of tourists. On the other hand, food in restaurants is so cheap that it is compensation enough.

The first time I was in the Federated States of Micronesia, I chose to visit Pohnpei. On the largest island in the country one can find the ancient city of Nan Madol. It is called the Venice of the Pacific, and with good reason. The city is made up of 92 man-made small islands that are surrounded by — or connected by — canals. The city was the capital of the Saudeleur dynasty from around 1200 to about 1628. The 18 square kilometre area contained bathhouses, swimming pools, caves, dwellings and enormous temples and cemeteries. They believed in the tore god Nahn Sapwe, sometimes called Daukatau, to whom they sacrificed food and animals. The impressive Nan Madol should be on many more people's destination lists. But then there is still the issue of accessibility. Ten flights and 34 hours from Oslo is not tempting for many, although this city is also on the list of candidates for Atlantis, including, Mauritania and São Tomé, among others. Nan Madol is called the eighth wonder of the world by some. Being worth a visit is not something that needs to be discussed — just remember to bring chili sauce to spice up all the plane food you have to endure.

I had sat myself down at a table on the outside terrace, with a view over the lagoon. It made the American lager a little more appetising. At first it was just me and a local loved-up couple there. They hardly minded me, and I enjoyed the stillness of the Pacific Ocean. One by one, the American builders arrived. In the end we were eight, and we chatted about this and that. Romeo showed up a couple of hours later.

"Pardon me for being late, but I had to dump the car and eat dinner with my wife and my eight kids."

"You have eight kids?" I wondered. I have none myself, only six siblings. And a half-sister.

"Yes, I am the youngest of 17 siblings, and then I got the idea that I should beat my dad and have 18 kids," he laughed and took a sip from the imported Heineken bottle. "Now I'm almost halfway."

"And each one is with the same wife?" fired in Bud. One of the Americans.

"Yes, I told her about my plan with 18 kids before we got married and said I could have some of the kids with other ladies. She was having none of that. 'That you can fucking forget, I'll give you all the kids you want,' she had replied," he chuckled.

"And she's ready for ten more?" Bud asked doubtfully.

"Yes, sure, else I have to find someone who is," smiled the serial father and made a toast.

Maybe there is something in the rumour that people from Chuuk are made a little wilder than in Pohnpei. A bit like Norwegians in the old days, you know. The Vikings were not exactly completely tame either.

Not until 1886, after the locals had stopped clubbing each other and visitors to death, did the Spaniards establish a settlement here. After that the Germans took over, or better said, bought the area from Spain in 1899, before the islands became Japanese following the alliance between Germany and Japan. And after the Second World War, the United States as victor, became the owner of the islands here. It is broadly similar to what happened to one of the island states further east. More on that later.

The war, seen indirectly, has had a tourist-promoting effect. As many as 24,000 visitors a year to the Federated States of Micronesia has a lot to do with diving. But it is not just the clear water in the Chuuk lagoon, or the many idyllic small islands without human settlements around the lagoon, that provides a magnetic attraction. It is also to do with bombs and grenades — or better said cannons and torpedoes. The lagoon was pretty much perfectly suited as an anchorage for large parts of the Japanese fleet during the Second World War. Not only is the lagoon deep enough, but there are few suitable points of entry, and all of these were well guarded by soldiers with cannons, anti-aircraft guns and other artillery deterrents. Just not enough of a deterrent.

On 17th and 18th February 1944, the Americans carried out Operation Hailstone, a relatively long lightning strike with aircraft, submarines, and ships. This resulted in 250 Japanese planes, 44 ships and one submarine now lying at the bottom of the sea. There they function as a unique and gigantic underwater museum for divers from all over the world. The best known of all is the cargo ship Fujikawa Maru, which was built in 1938, and sank in this February six years later. Both dive magazines and the renowned British newspaper The Times believe it is one of the world's best wrecks to dive on. The top is located just nine meters underwater, a 152-millimetre cannon sits in the bow, and in one of the cargo holds there are four fighter jets produced by Mitsubishi. The wings were disassembled so that there was enough space for everything in the cargo ship. In the Chuuk Lagoon, there is something for everyone's liking and skill level: Some wrecks are so deep that taking a closer look is defined as compression diving. Not something for me, but my brother Øystein can hold his breath for five minutes and had a smooth free dive down to 59 meters. I think.

Chuuk is now the most populous state with 50,000 inhabitants, but it still cannot boast luxury hotel complexes, hostels, or other particularly tourist-friendly infrastructure. The potential for a non-violent invasion inspired by tourists is therefore not totally in place.

I invaded on my own. When the United plane landed on the way from Pohnpei, I was among a dozen foreigners who disembarked and passed through the immigration counter here. With only one hatch for foreigners and one for residents, it still took some time to stamp us through. As usual in this part of the world, I was the tourist — the others were businesspeople. The airport is located on Weno, which is the second largest island in the lagoon. And what a green jewel. Teroken, a small peak of 364 metres, rises to the south, while Tonachau — at just over 200 metres — lies directly east of the airport. The little hill and a distinctive mound at the top are completely covered with leaves — there is not a single trunk visible. The vegetation, of unknown origin to me, consists of many different varieties of trees, plants, and flora in abundant shades of green. If you counted all the green and turquoise colours in the water around the island, you would be completely overwhelmed. It is heavenly beautiful — a heathen can become religious from less.

To mention tribes, there have been people living in the Federated States of Micronesia for 4,000 years. In the beginning, tribal chiefs and deputy chiefs ruled through a decentralised system with religious and economic headquarters in Yap — the island with the stone coins. Until around 1990, Chuuk was called Truk, something one still partially sees in the airport code TTK. The whole thing apparently comes from a Western misunderstanding, like Bombay, which is now called Mumbai. But the hotel where the American military-clad stay has perhaps the most innovative name in the country. Truk Stop. A pun on the American Truck Stop. Having to explain jokes, or attempts at jokes, has never been successfully achieved by anyone. It does not help at all that the hotel bar is called Hard Wreck Café.

Starting from the terrace outside there is a long narrow wooden jetty over the long shallows of the beach. Furthest along are the diving boats. One day when I was on my way there to take a picture, I met Neison. He stood on the jetty, halfway out, watching tens or hundreds of thousands of small fish swimming in shoals, seemingly without purpose or meaning, in the shallow water. It was just before sunset and about to become dusk due to some clouds covering the fireball sun. He smiled cautiously, but there was no sparkle in his eyes. Not until he started talking about fish that is.

"Just wait a bit longer, then the bigger fish will come to hunt. And then you are going to see chaos among the small fish," he said, and went on to say that he was building a house on one of the other islands, but that he lacked machinery, so he had to mix the cement himself, by hand. It was no wonder that the 29-year-old was not bursting of joy.

"I'm completely exhausted and just had to head to Truk Stop to get a good night's sleep. I was coming here to buy more cement, but I realised that I needed to rest, so my friends took the bags with them to the island," he said. And chuckled.

"But first I'm just watching some fish action," he said, pointing to the small fish beneath us.

"Look, here comes the beast!" he shouted.

I could see the dark shadows of four or five fish, a few kilos each, swimming inwards at a devilish pace, and the entire water surface, as far as a radius of 20-30 metres around us, boiled from petrified small fish desperately trying to survive the attack. The sound was intense, like someone constantly throwing sand into the water, while the black shadows ate what they could. And suddenly it was completely quiet again. The small fish went back to swimming nice and calmly in shoals, while the much larger predators withdrew to plan their next raid. And it continued like that until it became too dark to see anything else. It is a good thing that the small fish only have two seconds of memory, otherwise the survivors would have been completely traumatised.

"Enough entertainment for today," said Neison, before he said goodbye and went to his room. We met each other again the next day. He smiled with his whole body and had clearly had a good long sleep. I was going to eat lunch and he was going to have breakfast. I asked when he thought he would have the house finished.

"In a few weeks, I hope."

"Do you need any help?" I offered. The smile quickly turned into a broad smirk.

"With that little body there?" he said in a loud voice and slapped me on the shoulder with a big smile. He could stretch easily across the table with his long and powerful arms. The Micronesian was a whole head taller than me and apparently far stronger.

Neison thanked me for the offer, but said he was building the house alone. At least the shell, then he would get help with the electrics and plumbing. Traditionally, a Micronesian man should be able to build a house from the ground up, and that was his thinking. Without Norwegian help.

"You also need to know about farming, fishing and boat building to be able to take care of the wife and family," Neison explained. "And when all this is in place, I can inform my parents that I am ready, and they have the task of finding an acceptable wife."

"Right? Won't you rather find her yourself?" I interrupted. He smiled.

"It is possible to give the parents a prod in the right direction," he replied wisely.

Once suitable wife material has been pinpointed, it is time for a family visit, where the two families will try to come to an agreement. In that case, the young couple can live together with the man's parents until the wedding day. Simple and straight-forward. And being practical is a real deal breaker. Historically, it is all about how well the man works which is the most important thing — not how well-built and good-looking he is, or how he performs in the bedroom. And it is evidently still like this to a degree.

Up to 70 percent of people live in Chuuk and on the islands off Weno, like Neison and his six siblings. This means that they are completely dependent on a boat with an outboard engine — by Yamaha. In one of the harbours in the centre, I counted 46 outboard engines. All were Yamaha. I asked Neison why and expected a monopoly-derived response. I did not get that.

"Yamaha is the best. And here we are extremely dependent upon the engines just going and going and going. We do not have the time, will or money to be fixing engines all the time."

I saw two Yamaha outlets, but I don't know if it is in fact a complete outboard motor

monopoly. Out of the hundreds of boats, I counted one non-Yamaha engine of an unknown make. It wasn't a good old 'Norwegian' Evinrude either — recalling that it was Ole Evinrude who emigrated from Oppland, Norway to the USA in 1882 and invented the outboard engine.

As long as there is daylight, there is a lot of hustle and bustle in the harbours. Sometimes there is a family member around, looking after the boat, talking to acquaintances, or having a cigarette. Other times, whole families are out on a shopping excursion. Afterwards, they help each other with what they have bought on board the boat. Then it has to be tightly secured, as it can be a bit windy out in the lagoon, often with whitecapped waves. It is fascinating to see all the open boats in many different colours. One of the harbours is positioned within a bay and goes almost completely all the way around. From above, the tightly packed bright boats look like a symmetrical flower. The grey outboard engines resemble small bees while the ropes protrude like long, thin dandelion seeds.

Whole families go on shopping excursions at least once a week with the open boats. There are 3-4 marinas right in the centre of Weno, and supermarkets, food markets, various stalls and a couple of restaurants are very close by. The same, of course, goes for Truk Stop. Everything is setup for this kind of living on small islands, with a shopping centre and airport approximately in the middle. But apart from the road between the airport and the centre, the roads are in a terrible state here too. The Pacific Islands were near the back of the queue when asphalt was shared out.

I decided to go for a run on the useless roads. Eastwards from the airport it is in such a bad state of repair that I jogged past nine cars that slowly tried to negotiate all the holes in the road without damaging their chassis or wheels. When I travel, I always pack ultralight trainers, football shorts and an extra T-shirt, as well as Biotex hand washing powder, because in my opinion, there are several reasons why jogging is especially undervalued when travelling:

1.   Jogging is an excellent way to get to know a new place and discover, for example, restaurants, nightclubs, parks, beaches, and hidden paths which you may wish to come back to. You would otherwise never find many of these places.

2.   As a foreigner, you almost always stand out when you jog, and you can strike up conversations with local people more easily. At least if one smiles at the people you meet and pass by.

3.   On holiday, one is accustomed to sitting stiller than usual, both in airplane seats and on beaches. It's easy to get out of shape. Being in good shape makes you feel better, and you are more able to travel a long way.

4.   On holiday, one tends to eat and drink more and of a better standard than usual. Again, it can quickly influence the waistline and force the purchase of new and larger clothes.

5.   Untrained people often have a greater struggle with jet lag than those who train.

6.   Having a good sweat occasionally, makes one sleep better.

7.   If you take your smartphone with you, you will likely use the camera function since you are almost guaranteed to jog past something of interest you would otherwise never have seen. Several of the photographs I am most pleased about are from runs. There are also maps on the phone in case you should jog off the beaten track.

8.   Studies show that getting out on a run is good for your own mental health.

9.   I personally notice that running increases my creativity. I usually get several new ideas during a run.

10.   One doesn't need to worry about starting from zero when it comes to training after you return home.

11.   In more and more cities, you can join organised jogging-sightseeing excursions. It's an excellent way to discover a place. As a bonus, you get to know others. And in some places, there are marked trails or maps, so you can run the routes alone.

12.   Through social media, on a sports field or at the local sports shop, you will usually be able to find a running partner or someone who knows about a jogging club, if jogging-sightseeing hasn't completely taken off exactly where you are.

After I had passed the airport in Chuuk and jogged some kilometres east, I came to Akoyikoyi children's school with about 100 pupils. This school was started in the 1990s by the American — Clark Graham — who moved here a long time ago.

"In 1966, I travelled here because of the Peace Corps, without other intentions than doing a good job. I had no plans about staying on or travelling. But what can one do when one meets a fabulous lady?"

The man from Illinois has lived here ever since. With a clean-shaven head, the white man was not difficult to spot. Together with one of the sons, Clark saw the need to establish a better education provision for children, and he has never looked back. Now his students are among those who score the best on joint tests throughout the Pacific. Almost all the students come from poor families in the northeast of the island. There, an average family is of seven people, and only a minority have a fixed income.

"We do not take payment from parents, because we want to offer a good provision for everyone regardless of background. But it also means that we have to constantly work hard with financing and apply for stipends and support from both programmes and private individuals," said Clark while he drank his iced coffee with a straw.

Before he started running the school, he ran a diving centre. But there was little in the way of support from the government.

"Palau has done a lot right and has more than 100,000 tourists a year [actually 123,000]. They have marketed themselves well, started with shark diving and put in place infrastructure. It has not happened here, despite the fantastic wreck diving opportunities," sighed the 75-year-old.

There is also constant wreck looting going on. Parts of the wrecks disappear, something that makes them less attractive to dive on.

"Don't they have laws against such things?" I asked.

"Yes, lots. But... but... but..." he said, with two-second-long breaks between each 'but' for artistic effect. "Enforcement of rules is not something one is particularly good at here in Micronesia," he explained, smiling resigned to the fact.

Add into the mix the natural decay of the wrecks and Chuuk can hardly base its income on diving tourists forever. Many people are happy to see the fish, but then the government needs to crack down on too widespread dynamite fishing that kills large quantities of fish and damages coral reefs.

"Besides, we have nothing to offer divers when they are not diving. What are they then going to do? A major investment is needed here if we are to bring in more tourists and therefore be able to employ more people. Almost no one here has a job or education, despite the enormous opportunities we have when considering fishing, diving, and nature," said the teacher, before he spoke about how difficult it was to find well-qualified teachers for the school. Even proactive visits to eight universities across the Pacific had produced no results. And only three out of seven teachers are local. The other four are Americans.

"We do not find qualified teachers here, and we do not pay enough to attract foreigners. Furthermore, I want teachers who have travelled, who have seen the world. How can a person who has not been outside his own country otherwise prepare children for an increasingly international and global future in a good way?" he wondered, and I nodded. I very much agree.

"Now we are looking at bringing in people for a year or two at a time, almost as volunteers, but that takes a lot of time. Especially since I refuse to let it affect the quality of the teachers. It is the teachers who are important, essential even. The syllabus has far less of a say."

"By the way, what is the minimum wage here?" I fired in.

The man began to laugh, yes, really laugh. I understood that the question belonged at home in the Western world, and I went a little red. Clark excused himself and said that someone without education was lucky if they received 75 cents an hour.

"And a director receives $25,000 a year. It isn't surprising then that many travel to the United States and are content to flip burgers at McDonald's for the rest of their lives on the same salary, if not better." The Federated States of Micronesia became independent from the United States in 1986. As part of an agreement with the United States, the inhabitants were allowed to retain the right to live and work in one of the 50 states. Over a quarter of the people here have taken advantage of this offer.

We did not have much time before he had to go to a teacher meeting, but he managed to tell me where the best diving was. Once a diving instructor, always a diving instructor.

Clark is not the only one who is engaged with education and the future of the children of the Federated States of Micronesia. Túúttúnnap, or storytelling, is completely essential when it comes to the culture, history, and life of those who live here. It is also used in teaching, to communicate, and to share knowledge. But with large-scale and rapid social change, parts of this tradition are in danger, and the same goes for being Wesetan Aramasen Chuuk, or a native of Chuuk, asserts L.J. Rayphand in his doctoral dissertation. He comes from the village of Inaka, which means countryside, on the little island of Udot right in the middle of the Chuuk lagoon. The 38-year-old has children of his own and wanted to dig into the history of his own people and find out how the storytelling tradition could progress in a digital world. There are not many in the country who take a doctorate, but thanks to a strong interest, impressive willpower and financial support from family, friends, and colleagues, he managed to complete his doctorate. The most important support though was likely from his wife who made it possible to combine an exhaustive study while having children.

"I will always remember everything you have done for me," he wrote in the introduction to his dissertation. Or 'Ai kapong, ai tong, ai pwos, fiti ai kinisow', as it is written in Chuukese.

Chuuk is often looked at as the home of the wretched, a peculiar place where strange people live. It can be about the violent history, but also the state being the poorest in the country. What it originates form, I never really got a good answer to, even though wagging tongues point to incompetence among the leaders, especially when it comes to usage of financial resources.

Young men in the state also have a reputation for high alcohol abuse with subsequent uninhibited conduct towards themselves or others in the form of drink driving, knife juggling or fighting. It is not especially uplifting even though Romeo believes that it is only about internal conflict. And the dubious rumour is, as mentioned, not exactly something new. Photography from the middle of the last century shows local men who look angry and peer almost wickedly at the camera without a smile, but with earrings of shell, tattoos and long hair pushed up in a kind of tuft on top that is held in place by a wooden comb — not exactly helpful men in hula skirts, kids playing and running barefoot in the sand or attractive smiling ladies barely covered by a thread, like the sailors had dreamed about for months at sea.

The barbaric reputation they had before, has fortunately been replaced now by a far more benevolent one. They go along with most things, argue as little as possible and are willing to discuss compromise. It is almost as if they do not care, instead, following the path of least resistance, the first and best alternative or the last thing suggested to them. They received their dose of confrontation in the 16th century.

It is said that they are now masterful at finding amicable solutions. One theory is that it comes from the lack of chiefs. There was no one to go to when they needed advice or resolution, so they had to think for themselves. Conflict, as is well known, seldom leads to anything good, and the lack of war-mongering figureheads taught them instead to work together.

"It requires a whole village to raise a child," goes a saying here in Micronesia. It revolves around the inhabitants of the village cooperating: No one knows everything, but everyone knows a little. And when different people with different strengths teach the little ones, they grow into people too. Often good people.

"Before contact with foreigners, túúttúnnap was the instrument we had to depict the world and the universe. The navigators and travellers used it to share their experiences of distant lands and of ideas and newly learned crafts and techniques," writes Rayphand.

Túúttúnnap as a method is fundamental to the island community, and some fear that Western influence will lead to this storytelling disappearing and at the same time robbing Micronesia of important parts of its identity.

"What children say, is the fruit of a coconut palm," is another local saying. What children say is the actual coconut, the foremost raw material in the whole of Micronesia. Just as the coconut is a cornerstone of local culture, of equal importance are children and what they seek. Children here will learn the art of thinking, communicating, and speaking. Túúttúnnap should be the curriculum far beyond the Pacific Ocean.

And one doesn't have to head far before storytelling is of least concern. In the 13th least visited country in the world, it is all about survival. Perhaps not surprising for a country known for violent and brutal conflicts.

utan eigen båt kjem ein seg ikkje langt i chuuk.

det undra meg at dei spela vegvolleyball med så store mogelegheiter for strandvolleyball rett i nærleiken. truleg blei dei to kilometrane til sjøen litt for langt å gå.

jentene trefte eg på joggetur. dei bad meg ta bilete av dei. «då kjem vi oss til europa på kameraet ditt.»

neison held på å byggje hus. først når det er ferdig startar jakta på kone.

på hard wreck cafe skriv ein helsingar på eindollar-setlar. tek du bilete av denne skuldar eg deg ei øl.

desse joggeskoa heng så vidt i hop etter at eg har brukt dei i nesten 100 land.

Federated States of Micronesia tilbyr dykking i verdsklasse, sjølv for vestlege landkrabbar.

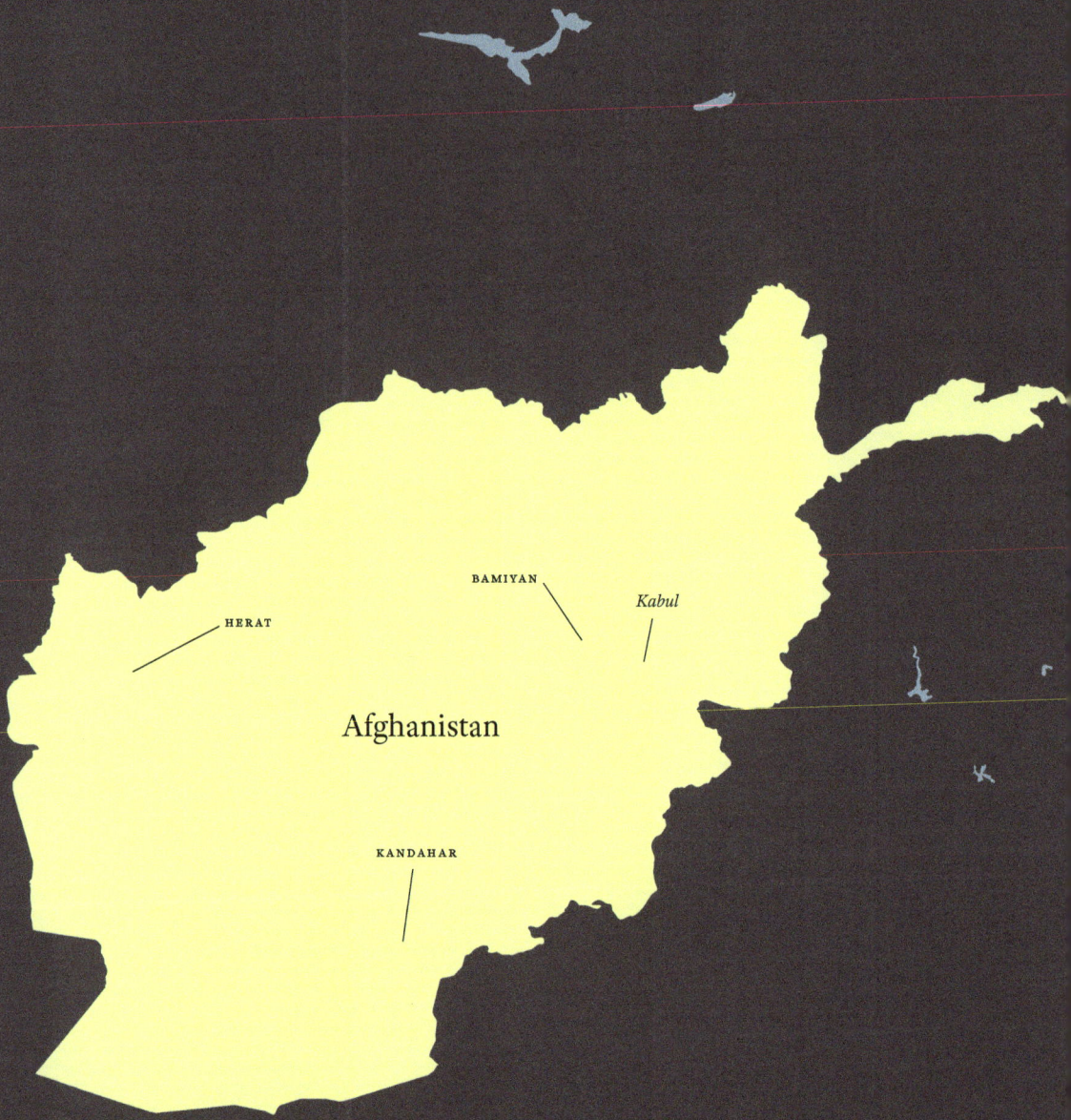

HERAT

BAMIYAN

Kabul

Afghanistan

KANDAHAR

200 km

13
Afghanistan, Asia

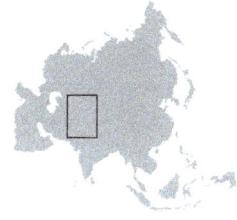

IHABITANTS: 34,700,000 (Wikipedia)
TOURISTS PER YEAR: 13.400 (New York Times og UNWTO)
AREA: 652,864 square kilometres

WHO EXACTLY NEEDS luxury when one can rather enjoy world-class hospitality? I am so lucky to have a good friend from one of the most hospitable countries in the world, Afghanistan. Nathkai Safi lives in Oslo and works as a surgeon. She came to Norway in 1990 and has not been to her homeland more than four times since then, even though some of her family still live in Afghanistan. Due to rumours of a certain risk of kidnapping and a generally unstable security situation, I asked for advice from people who should know a little about the lie of the land in Kabul before my journey there. Nathkai's relatives were not strangers to helping a guest visit the country, one which is almost exactly twice the size of mainland Norway, but much more compact and completely lacking any coastline. They had numerous acquaintances who also had acquaintances and were sure that they would be able to find me a good guide. From Nathkai in St. Hanshaugen, Oslo, I was put in contact over the Internet with a cousin in Kunar, east of Kabul, and subsequently Mehdi Yari, who of all places lives with his Afghan wife in Drammen, Norway. They moved there several years ago due to work. I did not quite know how an Afghan in the Norwegian city of Drammen was going to be able to help me, but I heard back from him quickly. It turned out that he had an enormous network.

"A friend of Nathkai is a friend of mine," said Mehdi.

"And an enemy of Nathkai?" I said jokingly.

"Hahaha... don't you try," he sniggered over the telephone network.

I told him that I was interested in getting in touch with someone who lived in Kabul, who had a car I could rent, and who could get hold of contacts at the Ministry of Tourism for me.

"You should talk to Bilal," Medhi replied, without a moment's delay. "The people who Bilal doesn't know; you will not be able to contact either. He is a fantastic guy who lives right in the centre of Kabul."

He sent me the contact information for Bilal Sarwary. Four phone numbers and one email address. And a tip:

"Use WhatsApp, he always answers quickly there."

There was a bit of toing and froing to get a visa, to the extent that I had to abruptly turn myself around and buy a ticket with less than a day's notice. I would have thought that such impulse purchases to 'unusual' or suspicious destinations were typically picked up by both Norwegian secret service and foreign sister organisations, without me thinking much more about it. The impulse ticket was from London. I took the opportunity to pick up a couple of other visas while I was already there: To Libya and Uzbekistan. The capital of Great Britain is without doubt the best European city when it comes to obtaining visas for numerous countries.

From Gatwick I was going to fly with Turkish Airlines via Istanbul and onwards to Kabul. At gate 22 there was a queue — the staff checked all boarding passes and passports.

"What is your final destination?" asked the blonde and brown-eyed woman, almost 40 years of age. She looked English.

"Kabul."

"What?"

"Kabul. In Afghanistan."

"And you do not have any luggage?"

"Only hand luggage. I like to travel light."

Whether it was the destination, lack of luggage, my age, or a discreet tip-off from a counterpart in Oslo, I'm not sure, but right after I had been allowed into the waiting area, a dark-blonde woman in her late forties approached me. She was suitably attired in denim trousers and a tight-fitting suit jacket that fit perfectly — probably tailored.

"I have to check your passport," she said. Firmly, not in any way rude, but without any frills or the almost obligatory 'please' tagged on. After all, we were in Great Britain. I gave her my passport.

"Come here," she said, and walked a few metres further before sitting down. It made her suit jacket open on the side, and I saw a pair of handcuffs.

"So, you're police?" I asked, rather unnecessarily. Clearly in civilian clothes, but not just anybody manages to get handcuffs through security at Gatwick. They are almost seen as weapons because one can quickly injure someone by using the metal chains. I once tried to take handcuffs with me in my hand luggage from Dublin — they were quickly seized. And I was given a definitive warning from security.

"That's right," she replied curtly. "What are you going to do in Kabul?" she asked in a sharp manner.

"I'm a tourist and I'm going on holiday."

If just a glance could undress someone, then it happened at that moment.

"Do you want me to laugh, or what? No one goes on holiday to Afghanistan without luggage. What are you really going to do?" she followed up. Without smiling.

I discovered that I might as well tell the whole story, and she found out that I was travelling as a tourist and going on a holiday of sorts.

"Look, I'm travelling on a tourist visa," I said, pointing to the visa sticker in my passport. She was still holding it in her right hand, with the Afghanistan page open. The passport was brand new and there were no other visas or stamps in it. I kept going.

"But then I am also writing a book about the world's least visited countries. And Afghanistan is one of them. To do it in the best possible way, I travel as a tourist myself."

It is the first time I have told the truth and nothing but the truth, but still realised that my audience did not believe a single word that I said. Usually, I would have bluffed my way out, had it not been for the fact that this person had the power to prevent me from travelling.

It did not help the situation much when she asked where I was travelling to afterwards.

"Libya," I replied. She could have likely figured that out herself anyway, with a couple of phone calls.

The interrogation lasted for 25 minutes, and I had to show her both my security card from NRK Norwegian broadcasting, my press card and find some news articles on the Internet where I was mentioned as a writer before she even began to consider believing what I said.

"Do you have your old passport?"

"No, it's completely full and is at home. But I have another passport which you can look at." I travel so much that I must have two passports. In Norway, it is possible to get a so-called duplicate passport if you travel a lot with work. It is often the case that one passport is with an embassy pending a visa, and then I need another passport to travel with. The disadvantage for most people is that a duplicate passport is only valid for two years, not for the usual ten, but it makes little difference for me as I usually fill up a passport after about a year.

The policewoman had likely stopped me on the suspicion that I belonged to at least one of two categories: Either, I had no idea what I was doing and would probably get myself killed by travelling to Kabul, or I was looking for a meaning in life and was considering joining a terrorist organisation. My book history was likely the only thing I could tell of that convinced her that the suspicions did not hold any ground. The second passport had visa stamps from, among others, Yemen, Mauritania, Guinea-Bissau, Djibouti, Iraq, Equatorial Guinea, and Algeria. Also, the next destination on the agenda, Libya. In addition, there were some more innocent stamps from Fiji, Vanuatu, and the United States.

I had to talk about each of the countries I had a stamp from, and if it was one of those I was writing about.

"Are you going to steal my book idea, or what?" I said flippantly. The lady had not even once come close to a smile, so I had to try to do something about that.

"Yes, why not. I can just lock you up for a few months so that you cannot publish any books in the meantime," she said, before I saw something reminiscent of a tiny twinkle in her eye and a microscopic smile of macroscopic proportions. She only actually had a sense of humour, after all.

I grinned.

"Yes, good luck finding out which country is the least visited," I said. "That stamp is in my old passport at home."

"Syria," she guessed. Without hesitation. She was not one to hesitate.

"Good guess, but Syria is not actually on the list. Too many tourists enter from neighbouring countries. And before the war, they received more than five million tourists a year," I said.

"Final call to Istanbul!" said a male voice over the loudspeakers.

"Well, if I cannot write your book, then you might as well do it yourself," said the policewoman. She had shown me an ID card with a picture on it, but no name.

"With my job, I do not want people like you to know who I am," she said when I asked about it. And then smiled, almost normally. She gave me a double-sided A4 sheet of paper that told me a little about what I had been through. I put it in my pocket.

"Can't I have your first name at least?" I asked.

"No. You can give me a nice name if I end up in your book. Now jump on the plane."

I took my backpack, checking that I had two passports, telephone, and wallet before I said goodbye.

"And you," she said. "Good luck!" She likely meant that I needed it.

The next thing I heard was 60 seconds later.

"Boarding completed."

At 34,000 feet up in the air, I read the handout I had received from the policewoman. It said that I had been stopped on suspicion of terrorism, and that the police had the authority to do more or less what they wanted with me. That included stopping me, questioning me, searching all my belongings and, if necessary, imprisoning or deporting me. In other words, I had no rights other than to ask mercifully for a lawyer if I were to be arrested. If they thought that a lawyer would stop me from talking about what they were after, they could nonetheless reject my request for a lawyer.

I landed in Kabul early the next morning, after a stopover in Istanbul. I had arrived at one of the world's most vigilant airports. As usual, without luggage, I was first through the passport control, the baggage hall and into the country. I expected to see someone with a 'Garfors' sign, that Bilal would possibly come over and say hello. None of the 12 men outside the terminal building showed any interest in me. It was chilly, and I was travelling without an outer jacket. I took off my suit jacket, putting on a blue hiking sweater, and put the suit jacket back on. Outer jackets are awful to travel with — my pet hate! If it is too hot to wear them, then they take up a lot of space and are always in the way. In Kabul, according to the Internet, it had been well over 30 degrees a few days earlier, so I did not think I needed an extra layer. It was only 10 degrees at seven in the morning, but the hiking sweater did the trick. I looked at my phone and was surprised to see that the Norwegian mobile company — Telia — had a roaming agreement in Afghanistan. The phone had coverage.

At the other end I heard a very tired 'hello'.

"Hi, it's Gunnar."

"Fuck, are you here already? What time is it? Sorry, I must have fallen asleep," said Bilal. A brilliant first impression. But he quickly gathered himself and asked me to go to car park C, which was 500 metres away, and to wait there.

"I'll send a man. He will find you."

Someone sending a man can be somewhat ambiguous, and in Afghanistan it can have a far broader significance. There are military men with weapons everywhere. There are civilian men with weapons everywhere. Not to mention tanks, trucks with machine guns mounted above the cab and roadblocks, bomb-proof barriers, ten-metre-high concrete walls, barbed wire, and sandbags stacked in every imaginable and unimaginable place. There is barely a single logo or a single national flag anywhere, apart from the Afghan flag, which flies in the wind over the whole city. With one exception, none of the embassies for example have any signs or flags that are visible from the outside. They do not want to make it any easier than necessary for people to be able to identify who is operating out of the premises, but everyone in the city knows at least where the most prominent embassies are. The United States, Japan and Great Britain operate from the largest premises. Iran also doesn't hide-away in a wash-closet and is the only embassy with the country name on a sign outside an extremely well-guarded entrance.

I sat down on the curb side and waited. I was far from alone in car park C. Waiting with me were many friends and family members of others who had travelled on the same plane as me, a packed A330 with around 300 passengers. People without a ticket cannot get close to the terminal building. And one by one, my former passenger colleagues came along, wheeling packed baggage trolleys. If you travel from overseas to Afghanistan, orders obviously come raining in from far and wide. The product range available here is not quite on a par with that offered in Istanbul. Or in Delhi, Dubai or Drammen, Norway, for that matter.

It took three quarters of an hour, but then my man arrived.

"Are you Gunnar?" he wondered. Mohammad worked for a taxi company that drove in unmarked cars.

"Sorry I'm late, but it's chaos here! You should be happy you don't live here — there are roadblocks and detours everywhere. We specialise in important people and foreigners, so people with devious intentions must not find out what cars we are driving," he said. After barely driving for a quarter of an hour we had arrived at our destination, with Mohammad stopping in front of a dark red metal gate. It was the only opening in a 4-5-metre-high wall that encircled a white house with a couple of parking spaces and a garden plot. In the sunshine, outside of the house, Bilal was sitting on a braided chair. A

small wooden table was positioned in front of him. There were six mobile phones lying on it, several of them were charging up, connected to a branch socket with a long cable that went into the house. On a smaller table there was a thermos, instant coffee, and tea.

"Welcome to Afghanistan!" said Bilal, warmly, before getting up and greeting me. I was given a big and long-lasting hug. If I had received a hug like that in Norway, it would have been from a family member after many months away from each other, but long-lasting hugs are commonplace here. Men hug each other, and then they usually exchange a handshake.

Hospitality in Afghanistan is not eclipsed by what I have experienced in any other country. It is simply among the very best in the world, perhaps without competition.

"If Afghanistan was a bank, then people would be the currency," smiled Bilal, as I told him how grateful I was that he had welcomed me, as well as giving me a bed in the guest room.

Bilal was wearing a black perahan tunban, a traditional Afghan dress consisting of wide trousers and a kind of tunic. With a black beard, balding and a few kilos over the ideal weight, he looked 10-12 years older than his 36 years. People age quickly here, perhaps not surprising with the harsh climate, large temperature differences and generally so many ghastly happenings under the guise of terror and other mishaps. But things are compensated in a way in professional life, with people being able to rise quickly through the ranks. Ministers, top managers, and others in senior positions are far younger here than I am used to at home. Bilal has worked as a reporter for the BBC for ten years. When I visited in the spring of 2018, he was working freelance for international media houses as well as gearing up for the election a few months later. He had decided to stand as a parliamentary candidate for Kunar province, where both he and Nathkai come from.

Bilal is a very smart and incredibly welcoming man with an extensive network. Every night at his home, friends and acquaintances were invited for dinner, tea, Cuban cigars or just a chat. He continually received cigars from friends on overseas trips.

"It's the only thing I want as a present. It was dead-stupid that I forgot to ask you as well for some tax-free cigars, because now I will soon be empty," he explained after I asked where the nearest cigar shop was.

His guests included ministers, deputy ministers, top executives, and former politicians. Bilal cultivates friendship with them all, but seemingly not just for his own political ends. Relations seemed genuine and warm. I asked about Bilal's ambitions.

"There are so many challenges in my country that I will do what I can to contribute to solving them or reducing them," he replied.

"And in time, do you want the presidency?" I wondered. As if any potential future presidential candidate would reveal such a thing before they had even been elected to parliament.

"Absolutely not," he replied instantly. "Right now, it's all about getting into parliament.

And if I do a good job there, then we'll see what comes of it," said Bilal, in a politically correct way.

In Kunar province, four representatives were going to be elected — three of them men and one woman. Quotas, but it has to be this way in a country like Afghanistan. Nine years earlier I had barely seen a woman without a burqa. Now the majority wore the hijab, while some had thrown away their headgear all together. The women were most liberal in Kabul, but it seemed to me that the burqa-wall had come down outside of the capital as well. It was perhaps a small sign of significant progress.

"The women do what they want," said Bilal. And it is about time after a long period of conservative rule, especially since the country was once at the foremost in women's liberation in the 1960s and 1970s. At that time, miniskirts were more common in Kabul than in London and New York.

"We are modernising ourselves in many ways. In Kabul, you will now find more and more cafés and restaurants with a western feel, attracting the youth and the new generation. This then leads to the elderly moving here — they want to follow what is going on, and at the same time can feel a little younger than they are," continued the 36-year-old.

Slice is one of these cafés. It is run by Ahmad Farid Amiri, an acquaintance of Bilal. When I hinted about coffee one day, he took me to Slice straight-away.

"We started in 2016, and it was an immediate success with espresso-based coffee, a range of western baked goods and free Internet. And then we are in the best street in the city," he said. The 29-year-old economist is a natural business talent and is also used as an adviser in the Ministry of Foreign Affairs in Afghanistan.

"I have travelled quite a lot, and they thought I had some good ideas and something or other to contribute," he said, without it appearing pretentious. When he opened, he had not had a single barista or baker who could make what he thought was necessary to be successful. The solution was to get in a baker from South Africa. After a while it happened that the baker was not only seeking adventure but was also unemployed and desperate enough for money that he had set course towards the conflict area in Asia. I had a coffee inside the actual café, while Ahmad spoke. He did not want coffee himself.

"I have already drunk seven cups today," he laughed.

The café could just as easily have been in Berlin, Buenos Aires, or Seoul. The atmosphere inside was calm, and young coffee-thirsty people sat at their own tables. Some sat alone, others talked about this and that.

"Bringing in a foreigner turned out to be a winning chess move. Not only did he train a dozen locals, but just the fact that people knew the main baker was from South Africa, meant that we gained many new customers. He became the talk of the town, and therefore so did the café too. But after 14 months, we agreed to end the collaboration. It was expensive for us, and he had started to have enough of the security situation here in Kabul," said Ahmed.

The security situation. The words, or a paraphrase of it, is often used here in Kabul. It is the explanation for everything that does not go well. For the unemployed. For economic stagnation. For missing visitors. And of course, for what is on full show — the bombs. The security situation is almost like TIA in Africa.

Bilal had already considered the future possibilities in getting more visitors from abroad.

"Afghanistan could become a tourist magnet in the future. The only thing we lack is satisfactory security. We have everything else. Mountains, lakes, islands, rivers, food, and culture. The nature here is monumental and magnificent, and you can really experience four seasons in a day," he said, just a little bit proud.

But then there was this security situation. I had felt safe myself since I had arrived, and there was by no means any oppressive atmosphere in the city, the like of which I have experienced in other war zones, so I had to ask.

"Is it really so bad?"

"We are a long way from being Syria, Libya, or Iraq. But we are not exactly Sri Lanka, Maldives, or Seychelles either," Bilal replied. Absolutely serious. Before he grinned.

"We do not have enough beaches. And, you know, the security situation," he said with a twinkle in his eye. If you do not have a morbid sense of humour in Afghanistan, you should not work as a journalist or politician. Or even stay here.

The security situation also means that the UN staff working in the country never actually see anything other than what is inside the high and very well-guarded walls that encircle them. I had been told of a Frenchman who worked at the base, a few kilometres from the airport, and he invited me to visit. It took me 15 minutes just to get through the various checkpoints, and I had to leave my camera outside. He stood waiting for me behind the innermost security fence. We exchanged handshakes.

"Welcome to Afghanistan!" he said, with a wide smile, before we went to the restaurant / bar / dance floor / karaoke club / billiard room. It is the meeting point of the camp, and you can buy good food at a reasonable price, as well as western alcohol, which is otherwise unthinkable in Afghanistan. We ordered sparkling water, and I picked up my notepad. He did not like that.

"I am not allowed to comment on anything, so I would appreciate it if you do not take notes. Or use my name," he almost whispered as he leaned forward. Not because he was especially secretive, but because of the extreme security measures put in place by the UN in one of the most dangerous countries in the world. Earlier, I have always been impressed by those who work for the UN in Afghanistan and thought of them as tough and bold. But it is even safer to work here than in a little Norwegian factory on a far-flung sedate farm. UN personnel are forbidden to go outside of the camp, and if they are attending an external meeting, they are driven from door to door in a guarded UN vehicle. The only special case is to be able to shop at three approved supermarkets, but even there they are not allowed to stay any longer than 20 minutes.

As ironic as it sounds, since I was in Afghanistan after all, I got to hear that the most dangerous thing they experienced was Saturday nights in the bar, within the UN base.

"We can have some pretty heavy nights here. We work an awful lot, so it doesn't always take many drinks before one gets quite drunk. With the high pressure of work, there have been some fights. Because here you talk, drink, party, work and hang out with the same people — there is no one else to visit. And suddenly two colleagues can end up in the same bed. I believe that can be quite awkward the following day." Smiling, he denied that it had happened to him as the main culprit.

UN employees have basically two years in each place they are stationed, but every six weeks they get one week off, with a free ticket to exactly where they wish to travel. This is in addition to usual holiday. The Frenchman mostly took the opportunity to go on diving holidays.

"But for the first two days, I do largely nothing except lying down and relaxing. The job here really takes it out of you. We do not see much horror ourselves, but we hear a lot through the families and friends of our local colleagues," said the man in his forties. About half of the staff at the base are local, so the foreign UN staff get, if nothing else, a certain impression about how it is to really live here.

I thanked him, and we walked back towards the gate. I had to be escorted out of course. We passed several people who were jogging around the base area, and others who were going for a walk.

"Yeah, we have to put in many circuits if we are to get a training session out of it," said the Frenchman.

Outside of the base I was picked up by Aziz Hewad, who is one of Bilal's best friends. The next day he came to Bilal's home, said hello, and had a green tea with us before he asked if I wanted to go on a trip around the city. The currently unemployed IT engineer drove a white Korean-made saloon car. Bilal had quite a bit of work to do and waved us off. It was clear that I did not need to rent a car — Aziz drove me exactly where I wanted and refused to accept payment for it. Dubiously, I was allowed to fill up the petrol tank on a couple of occasions.

I was a tourist in Kabul. There are not many who are, or even want to be. We saw various monuments, the cricket field, a gigantic clearing that was used as a football pitch by many teams simultaneously, and one of the largest flags in the world, which hung from a giant flagpole on a hill above the city. Then we stopped by a plumbing shop, of course. That came about as one of Aziz's friends produces pipes at a factory outside of the city centre and delivers to this very plumber, and others, in the middle of Kabul. Factory manager Mohammad was currently on a visit to check the stock levels at the plumber.

'Made in Afghanistan' was written on the white plastic pipes. Mohammad employed 55 people at the factory and is currently waiting for a visa for Canada to be able to buy new production equipment that would replace 'some Chinese rubbish', in his words.

We sat in plastic chairs on the street right in front of the store, and the store manager served us tea. I had borrowed traditional Afghan garments so I would stand out a little less. There are blonde men here too, and I was mistaken as Mohammad's brother. He has blond hair and green eyes. Western people are worth a lot as hostages, and if I walked around in western clothes, the wrong people could quickly take an interest, and then it's easy to ascertain where I'm from. The risk is low, but if some clothes can help reduce it, then I'm not against that.

"Do you want to see the tomb of the last king of the country?" asked Aziz. I wasn't exactly hard to ask along. Neither was Mohammad. He had a couple of hours off before the next meeting. As the guest, there was simply nothing to be discussed — I was to sit in the front. The factory manager insisted.

"Which airline did you fly with?" he asked.

"Turkish Airlines," I replied.

"That's really good! I flew with them for the first time a few months ago when I was on a business trip. You must choose row 24 — there is an emergency exit, so you get plenty of space for your legs," he said enthusiastically. "And with the food you even get wine!" nearly shouted Mohammad.

"What? You get wine on the plane?" asked Aziz. "That's a luxury! Do you get just one bottle, or can you have more?"

"As many as you want, but you have to drink them on board," smiled Mohammad. Aziz was in total awe. He had not travelled internationally by plane before, and Afghan airlines do not serve alcohol.

We arrived at the tomb. King Mohammed Zahir Shah ruled from 1933 and managed the feat of keeping the country peaceful, respected, and stable until he was deposed in a coup in 1973. There have been varying degrees of conflict in the country ever since. He died at the age of 93 in 2007 and is now laid to rest in a beautiful marble mausoleum on Maranjan Hill with an expansive view over a large swathe of Kabul. Two soldiers stood guard, but we were allowed to enter. They said they had not seen tourists for many months. I was not surprised.

The next day I woke up before Bilal and went out into the garden. His teenager was digging away in the ground to plant various vegetables. He was using what they had — a good old iron shovel with a handmade handle — and I took my turn when the teenager had a breather. Suddenly someone rang, and he went to open the metal gate. It was Aziz. I thought Bilal was still asleep, but a few minutes later he came down from the upstairs bedroom while he was talking on four phones at the same time. The man should have performed at the circus. He was clearly stressed.

"We have to go to a TV station. I'm going to be interviewed. Do you want to come?"

"Of course," I replied spontaneously and jumped into the back seat of Aziz's car. Bilal was still talking on a couple of phones while Aziz reversed out. After a while, I found out what was going on. A suicide bomber had blown himself up in the queue at an ID registration centre in Western Kabul. The largely Sunni Muslims who live there, are especially vulnerable to IS attacks.

"At least 18 have been killed and more than 50 have been injured," said Bilal. As one of the few English-speaking journalists in the city, he was a sought-after interview subject within international media. On the way to the studio, we met many ambulances on their way. They drove nearly in relay between the site of the explosion and the hospital, which is earmarked for all the war-injuries. We stopped outside the hospital entrance. Many relatives had begun to gather on the pavement, to the extent that they blocked-off parts of the road. They were trying to find out the latest news about their loved ones, who might not have been alive anymore. Men in camouflage clothes with machine guns hanging on their arms kept control of the crowd. Many hugged each other. Some were crying loudly. The final death toll after the bombing was later raised to 57, with well over 100 injured. Many of them were women and children who had been queuing to receive ID cards, which people need to be able to register themselves for the election. Therefore, it was seen as an attack against democracy. IS, who have since taken responsibility, wanted to scare people away from bringing legitimisation to the next government.

"What do you think about the explosions and terrorist attacks you are constantly experiencing?" I asked Aziz after we had dropped Bilal off outside the TV station. After the election, I heard back from Bilal — he had unfortunately not received enough votes to be elected and had returned to journalism. That was a pity because he had a positive drive that the country needed. With his will to just keep going, my guess is that he will try again. The premises of the TV station, like the embassies and nearly every other office in Kabul, were anonymous and without any signs outside. No one wants to attract unnecessary attention.

"This is how it is. It's normal," replied Aziz.

"Aren't you afraid, or at least afraid to move around outside?"

"No, not at all. If we give in to the fear they are trying to sow, we have lost. It's not like I've just stubbornly decided not to be afraid — I take the usual precautions and keep myself well updated. And I'm also good at statistics."

"What do statistics have to do with fear?"

"We are more than five million people in Kabul. The risk of being struck is low, especially if you stay away from certain areas of the city and crowds. Almost all the attacks are related to politics," said Aziz.

He believed that social media contributed to the reputation of Afghanistan being worse than other places that encounter terrorism.

"The news of terrorist attacks now reaches far more people, much faster, thanks to Facebook and Twitter and 4G coverage everywhere. Everyone knows someone who knows someone in Afghanistan, and particularly information about major terrorist attacks is quickly shared. And because of our history with a lot of war and adversity, people notice terrorism here more. Both the media and most people are expecting attacks; therefore, every single attack is thoroughly covered in the media. It is self-reinforcing and makes my country seem to be even more violent than it is," sighed Aziz.

And he is onto something, even though terror strikes down innocent people in a growing number of countries. Afghanistan and Iraq share the top spot in the statistics of the countries that are hardest hit by terrorism, measured in deaths. But the number of deaths has gone down since 2014 — the deadliest year of terrorism with almost 33,000 killed worldwide. Terrorist attacks, no matter where they are, usually lead to a reduction in visitor numbers. I think it would be too easy to blame terrorism, and I refuse to let attacks prevent me from travelling around the world, looking for experiences and learning, understanding, and enjoying other cultures. This may perhaps sound strange, but if I take everyday precautions, I can also feel at home on the streets of Kabul. It is dangerous to be alive, no matter what — I could suddenly be snuffed out after being hit by a tram in Oslo or a falling roof tile out in the country. I can of course hide in the wardrobe at home, but then suddenly the house could burn down.

It is also entirely possible to be a tourist within a safe sphere in Afghanistan, but it is perhaps best to be outside of Kabul. You have to fly there no matter what, but if you do not have local contacts in the city, I advise you to stay at the airport and wait for the next internal flight to Bamiyan. It is one of the 34 provinces and is located almost in the middle of the country. The Silk Road has travelled through the province earlier, and this has resulted in cultural influence from both the west and the east. But Bamiyan is best known for snow-capped mountain peaks, a fertile valley, colourful lakes, and not least, what were once the two largest Buddha statues in the world. They were carved out of a mountainside in the 6th century but destroyed by the Taliban in 2001 because they were viewed as 'non-Muslim'. There are mountain caves here that were previously used as dwellings, and in other parts of Bamiyan people still live in such caves. At an altitude of around 2,500 metres, it is cooler here than you would otherwise experience in the scorching hot Afghan summer; something that draws almost 200,000 Afghans here on holiday every year. There are tourists even in winter — most of them come to ski in the one and only ski centre in Afghanistan. The conditions are amazing, something that more and more Europeans are discovering. Out of the foreign tourists, it is especially ski enthusiasts from Switzerland and France who occasionally venture here to test out the powder on the numerous slopes. This is a contributing factor to why the standard of the hotels is surprisingly high. Bamiyan is also the only province in Afghanistan with its own tourist office, something that on its own can be seen as a sign of security.

Every spring, the local ski club organises The Afghan Ski Challenge, a race that is open to all, regardless of whether one skis or snowboards. Everyone starts at the same time, and the winner is the one who passes all checkpoints on the way down and subsequently crosses the finish line first. Otherwise, there is just one rule that serves as a reminder to participants of which country they are in: 'No weapons allowed'. It is only likely when such rules as these are no longer needed that Afghanistan will truly be able to dream of a distinct increase in tourist numbers.

Back in Kabul, the security situation is far more unstable, but even there you can find small park areas with signs telling of the existing weapons ban. I walked around Kabul on my own, in local dress, and I felt safe. The atmosphere was almost like at home, and daily life continued as normal. I could have been anywhere in Central Asia, aside from the plethora of armed men, both on the streets and behind pickups. And we are not just talking about handguns — Kalashnikovs thrive here.

"Terrorism is unfortunately not uncommon in Brussels, Madrid, or Paris either. So, we are not alone, even though we likely have the worst reputation when it comes to bombings and terrorist attacks," said Aziz. We had lunch together at a restaurant not far away from Slice. On the menu were various meat dishes: Grilled lamb, chicken, and beef on skewers, accompanied by fresh vegetables. The chefs had real flair.

Suddenly my phone rang. It was the main Norwegian news desk. The death toll from the explosion was now over 30. Enough for it to have become a news item in Norway as well. NRK broadcasting had no correspondent in Afghanistan at the time, so I was able to serve as a witness. I told about what I had heard, and what I had seen outside of the hospital. Neither Aziz nor I wanted to travel to the site of the explosion. Terrorist groups like to wait for journalists to come to the scene, and then they detonate another bomb or two. Journalists being killed are a good guarantee of even more coverage in the press.

The terrorist attack was the lead issue several times on the Norwegian bulletins that afternoon, with a quote from me. My parents did not know I was in Afghanistan. My dad heard it first on the news bulletin while my mum was called up by a friend who had heard the broadcast. I do not think the friend tried to scare my mother, but you maybe don't want to find out your son is in Afghanistan coincidentally through a friend. On the other hand, I'm a little unsure of how to exactly tell my mum that I'm in war-torn country. The first time I was in Afghanistan, in 2009, I told her about the itinerary a few days before departure by phone, after our normal chat about weather, wind and local village gossip.

"By the way, I'm going to Afghanistan for my Easter holiday," I said.

"Alright," she replied calmly.

"Alright? Aren't you going to be a little worried?"

"Gunnar. I have six other kids."

I'm not totally sure, but I think she was joking. In any case, I have now neglected to inform her about when I am going to countries in the same league, including Somalia.

P.S. Promising developments with regards to democracy and equal rights have both been stopped and heavily reversed since Taliban took power in Afghanistan in 2021. Few countries acknowledge the fundamentalist, militant, and jihadistic Islamic organization as a legitimate government, but that doesn't stop them from being a de facto power. The world community has withdrawn almost entirely and stopped essential funding to the poor country that may crumble and implode as a result. Imposed sanctions are hurting the weakest. Some tourists still visit the country, but doing so helps legitimize the Taliban and tourist numbers are expected to decline in the foreseeable future.

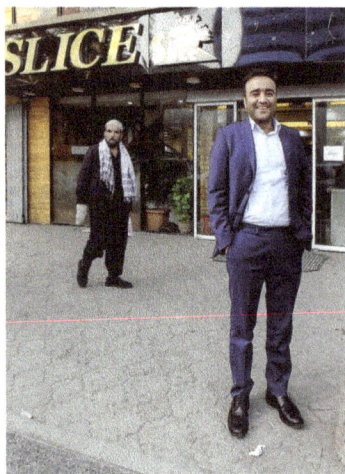
Ahmad Farid Amiri runs the slice café in Kabul.

Military personnel are everywhere in Kabul.

I was strictly instructed to wear localised clothing to reduce the risk of kidnapping.

The world's largest buddha statues in Bamiyan were destroyed by the Taliban. the province has now reopened to tourists.

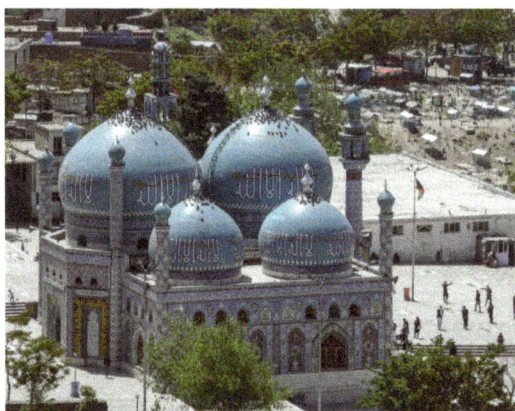
The blue Karte Sakhi Mosque in Kabul has fortunately not been damaged despite years of conflict.

Even in Afghanistan, people need to unwind with carousels and cotton candy. Around the Qargha reservoir, 15 kilometres from Kabul, it's crowded on Fridays for the big picnic day.

It is not uncommon to see goats with their herd even in the centre of Kabul. The goats go wherever there is food to be had.

The marble mausoleum where King Mohammed Zahir Shah lies. Note the surveillance balloon above the building, on board is a remote-controlled camera with extreme zoom.

Bilal Sarwary has a good selection of mobile phones.

Bilal in his living room, where he entertains friends almost every night. People traditionally sit on the floor in Afghanistan.

There are about as many people in Kabul as in the whole of Norway.

Most of the trolleys here are simple, but people use what's available to make ends meet.

i was invited to lunch by some pipe layers in Kabul, they didn't have much food, but were happy to share.

Most women still wear headgear, but it seems to be more liberal now than nine years ago.

there was chaos outside the hospital after an explosion that took 57 lives.

SEYLAC

SOMALILAND

PUNTLAND

Somalia

Mogadishu

200 km

12

Somalia, Africa

INHABITANTS: 14,300,000 (Wikipedia)
TOURISTS PER YEAR: 12,200 (garfors.com)
AREA: 637,657 square kilometres

THE MOST CORRUPT country in the world also has the lowest gross domestic product per capita. Somalia is positioned like a number 7 around the east coast of Africa and is slightly smaller than Afghanistan. The two countries are also probably the most famous among those least visited in the world. Unfortunately, that comes about from war, terror, bombs, and famine. But it hasn't always been like this in Somalia. After liberation from Great Britain in 1960, it developed into one of the pioneering countries of Africa in the 1970s and 80s, forged by stability and economic progress. It was the jewel of the continent. Several of the current presidents of Africa even studied in Mogadishu.

"We were the lion of Africa," said my guide Omar proudly, with a slight dreamy smile. He paused before continuing, with the smile now wiped away.

"Now we are the hyena."

There are many terrible reasons why the country located in the Horn of Africa has been in the news more often than most of the other 54 African countries. Civil war broke out in the mid-1980s, when various clans gradually entered into an alliance to stand-up against the central government, and in 1992, the UN entered with US-led military forces. The objective of the various clans has always been political influence. Almost 25 years without a functioning government followed, and Somalia became a non-functioning nation. Various factions fought for power within what, after a while, became an ever-larger power vacuum where nothing functioned except lawlessness. Different fractions repeatedly had blood on their hands. Since a transitional government was established in 2004 — and especially since support was provided by military forces from other African countries in 2006 — things have gradually improved. Slowly, but not entirely assuredly. At long last, a certain amount of optimism has the upper hand once again in Mogadishu, where the government has managed to gain a reasonable level of control over the terrorist group Al Shabaab.

"We have been ruled by weapons for many years. Now we are increasingly governed by the law. It feels good," said Omar.

This has contributed to more and more Somalis in exile moving home to help rebuild the country, but after many years of extremely poor PR, tourists however still shun most of Somalia. But money talks. Turkish Airlines has flown daily to the Somali capital for several years. They are not doing it out of kindness — a contributing factor has likely been the Turkish President Recep Tayyip Erdoğan's charm offensive, laying the grounds for significant Turkish investments in Somalia. There is more construction activity in Mogadishu than in most other cities in Africa. New business operations require more employees and more goods, and negotiation must be undertaken for those goods. There are also several other lesser-known airlines flying in and out of Mogadishu daily, or several times a week, and in November 2018, renowned Ethiopian Airlines started flights from Addis Ababa for the first time since the late 1970s.

And Somalia wants that — the reason why the central government never gave up control of the airport in Mogadishu, even when Al Shabaab was at its strongest and created fear in almost the whole capital and large swathes of the country. But then the area around the airport also looks like a fort from a war zone, and that is not very far off the truth.

I thought that the airport in Kabul was impenetrable, but here it truly gives it a run for its money. This must be the best military guarded airport in the world, with soldiers, armoured tanks and firearms and cannons of all calibres. Just getting into the airport area when I was going to leave the country, meant I had to go through seven security checks. The outermost check, outside the actual airport, was the most difficult, and I also had to go through it on my way into the country. The slight, but machine-gun-equipped soldier in his twenties thought I was a terrorist threat, and at first refused to let through the Toyota pickup with me, a driver, a guide and two armed Somali guards on the pickup bed. Bodyguards are a requirement to be allowed into the country at all, and I should have preferably had as many as six machine-gun-equipped guards.

Despite countless warnings about how dangerous Mogadishu was going to be, it went surprisingly well in the city that must have a far higher density of guns per inhabitant than a settlement in Wyoming. Though, that might be stretching it a bit far. The state has more firearms per inhabitant than any other US state. And that is in the country with the most firearms per citizen.

We passed through well over a hundred roadblocks during the days I was in Somalia, and I wasn't allowed to cross between districts on foot. The car had blacked-out windows and four armed soldiers sat on the pickup bed at all times — double the number since the trip from the airport. These were hired through the local tourist office I used to get into Somalia. When we stopped, they quickly jumped out, secured the area, and signalled that I could get out. At a couple of junctures, I jumped out to take a picture without telling anyone. That did not go down well and in hindsight was hardly the cleverest thing I've ever done.

"This is a very dangerous area — didn't you see how the neighbours were looking at you?" reprimanded Omar. I had only noticed that they returned my smile when I nodded at them, but I wasn't looking for danger signals either. And Omar would perhaps make it appear more dangerous than it was. He does run a business after all that depends on visitors believing it is dangerous. How else can he demand $600 a day? This includes accommodation, food, drink, transport, and guards, but steep nonetheless. Gross domestic product per capita in Somalia is unequivocally the lowest in the world and only one third as much as the next country on the list. The level of wages in Somalia is not high either, but with the few tourists he guides every year, even the big dollar notes will not make it a successful business. It is not of great help either that only a tiny minority of the tourists stay longer than two or three days.

I stayed at Sahafi Hotel International in Mogadishu. It turned out that it was one of the most popular places to stay for national politicians and businesspeople and was therefore an unsurpassed terrorist target. Omar had told me about Jazeera, the hotel closest to the airport, which had been bombed multiple times. The hotel owners wanted an end to that of course. We drove past the hotel on two occasions. It was surrounded by enormous bombproof walls that were constructed of concrete slabs, sandbags, and barbed wire. The dual carriageway that goes passed it has even been split in two to make room for safety measures. The two lanes closest to the hotel are now used just as a buffer surrounded by walls and a gate that was well protected by machine-gun equipped guards. All traffic other than the hotel traffic must share the two lanes that are left.

"There have been many explosions here," explained Omar.

To begin with I was completely content that I was not staying at Jazeera, but I began giving it a thought after I had greeted three former ministers, several members of parliament and a couple of high-ranking officials at my city centre hotel. If nothing else at least, there were three roadblocks between the hotel and the nearest public road. Getting into the actual hotel was possible only through a metal gate guarded by 3-4 soldiers with machine guns.

"This is very safe," said Omar. Then he showed me the way, through cheerless and dim corridors, up cement stairs and finally out of a door. We were on the roof of the hotel. On the way up, it was impossible not to notice the armed guards in each stairwell. They were bored and were listening to the radio and occupied by their phones. There is never much to do for a security guard before there is too much, and then the guard should have ideally been much more vigilant than they were just before it all kicked off. It was plausible that they would get a warning well in advance from gunshots or loud bangs at the gate of the hotel itself before it really went south. From the roof there was a reasonable view of one of the main streets. It was scorching hot up there. The sun was high in the sky — shade was non-existent. The exception was inside a small shed with holes for windows, but without glass or frames. Two snipers lay in the narrow strip of shade under the eaves on one side of the shed. They were asleep. That inspired confidence.

"They do not sleep when they are needed," said Omar. I was not won over. How could they possibly know when they were really needed?

Two more guards were sitting inside the actual shed. They had fled from the scorching sun, and if nothing else, they were awake. Both had a machine gun on a strap across their backs, smoked American cigarettes and greeted us drowsily without showing much interest in the incumbent potential terrorist threat.

In one way or another, most of what goes on in Mogadishu is about security, and it became the topic once again in the evening.

"Never let anyone enter your room, even if they knock. You are only safe in there," said Omar, completely out of the blue.

I did not make a comment about the window over the door to my room. If someone wanted to get in, it was not especially difficult to break the pane of glass. Double glazing has not exactly taken off in Somalia. A prospective intruder had to pass a whole heap of guards first in any case, so I was relatively calm about it.

"But the hotel here is safe, far safer than Jazeera, right?" I asked, mostly to keep the conversation going.

"Of course!" promised Omar, before stopping to think. Likely to work out how he should best follow this up.

"Though a BBC journalist was shot right outside the hotel in 2006. Yes, and two French journalists were kidnapped from here a few years after that. And well, then the previous owner was shot and killed in 2015. But you know, it really is completely safe. Now."

It wasn't even an attempt at black humour. If I had had sleeping pills, Valium, glue, anything, I would have taken it to get to sleep that night. The strongest thing available was fluoride tablets. I doubled my daily dose and took two. It didn't help very much. The first night, however, was without incident. I can testify to that because I did not sleep for even a moment. But at breakfast things began to unfold. Just after we had sat ourselves down in the restaurant and been served tea, there was an explosion some place outside. A bomb was the first thing I thought of.

"Another terrorist attack?" I asked.

"No, no, no, it was not terrorism, it was just an assassination," Omar replied calmly. And took a sip of tea. One long slurp. He really savoured the tea. But then of course, every sip could always be his last.

"You could tell from the explosion. It was an assault rifle, not a bomb. Someone likely took out a carefully planned target."

"Oh, just an assassination? Very relaxing," I replied. The sarcasm was not noticed. But I was impressed with his competence differentiating noises and the precise and seemingly professional way he conveyed himself.

Took out a target.

Not to mention how important it was for him to categorically reject the possibility of terrorism. But as the head of a tourist agency, with an author in his company, I could largely understand it. Later I got to know that there hadn't been as assassination, moreover, an assassination attempt. The designated victim, whose identity I never got to find out, had survived. The shooter had missed. So, presumably the shooter was dead — killed by either police, military, fortuitous armed passers-by or by displeased terrorist bosses.

A year after I had stayed at Sahafi Hotel International, things went wrong again. In November 2018, Al Shabaab attacked the hotel with three bombs and killed at least 20 people, including the hotel owner Abdifatah Abdirashid. The terrorist group later said that the target had been to 'take out' government employees who residing, or just staying, at the hotel. On the hotel website uniqhotels.com, the hotel is described quite truthfully, in a straightforward manner and without a marketing filter. Let me summarise:

'We are known as the most dangerous city in the world, and it is largely well-deserved as most other luxury hotels do not otherwise come with an increased risk of death and kidnapping. But there have only been two serious incidents that have involved our guests, and that's not too bad for a war zone. Our staff will give you a warm welcome, and you can choose rooms from four largely empty floors. There is air conditioning throughout the hotel and that is impressive when considering the lack of fuel and electricity in Mogadishu. To be able to visit the city at all, you must first convince the border police that you are not crazy. If you manage that, Sahafi is a good hotel to stay at.'

Incidentally, Omar is also part owner of Visit Mogadishu. It is perhaps the absolute worst name in the world for a travel operator because who in their right mind wants to visit a city with a name so terrifying that it causes sweats, depression, and sleep deprivation? On the other hand, the company does organise trips to Mogadishu, so it is not any kind of misleading marketing. They have also now broadened their range quite a bit and offer trips to other parts of Somalia. One evening he told me more about his country and his business. I was the only tourist at the hotel.

"Most of the tourists are from Germany, the United States, Ireland, Australia, and China. You are the first Norwegian. The first lady is coming in September. She is American," said Omar. He perhaps exaggerated a little. It later emerged that when he had said most of them, and highlighted the German visitors, he had meant no more than twelve people in total. There are not many people who take this trip to the war-torn country.

It is worth mentioning that Somalia has six states which are subsequently divided into a further 18 regions. Roughly speaking, the country is divided into three. The state of Somaliland in the north is self-governing and is a safe and exciting nation to visit. There are many cave paintings that are thousands of years old and a wild and varied nature. Recently, no pirates have operated from Somaliland either. Consequently, the state gets several thousand tourists per year, and it is only thanks to this that Somalia is higher up on the list of the least visited countries in the world than it otherwise would be.

In the middle is the state of Puntland, also operating with a degree of self-governance, but is less stable, has fewer flights, is less well known and therefore also gets far fewer tourists than Somaliland. Both Somaliland and Puntland want independence, but neither of them is recognised by any other country. Farthest south are the last four states, which in reality is Somalia, and which includes the capital Mogadishu. The most positive thing many people believe they can say about Mogadishu is that they have seen a film from there, but Black Hawk Down was filmed in Morocco.

"How many customers have you had for the other destinations in Somalia?" I asked, as we sat in the well secluded and fenced-off rear garden of the hotel.

"Er... we've had some questions here and there, but so far it is actually none."

"None? As in absolute zero?" I could not help but ask. Having destinations in a portfolio ought to point to experience of those destinations. Such as a minimum of one visit with a minimum of one customer or at least someone who pretended to be a customer on a first test trip. My scepticism was ignored. If you are a tour guide in Mogadishu, you can hardly afford to take things too much in. A year later I received an e-mail from Omar — a proud guide was able to tell me about the first two tourist groups he had taken beyond Mogadishu, to Kismayo in the state of Jubaland, 400 kilometres southwest.

"We have the oldest culture in Africa, two rivers and incredible beaches. Guaranteed to be deserted," smiled Omar, shyly. He was perhaps expecting a joke or a snide comment about a beach visit in Somalia, but I did not say anything. So, he carried on, with a little more self-confidence.

"Have you been to Somalia before?"

"Well, once before. Although, that was only Somaliland," I replied, knowing too well that very few people here are especially pleased that Somaliland wants independence. I had hitchhiked in from Djibouti in 2010 and was dropped off in the small town of

Seylac. There I almost got into a fight over something as banal as who was to sit in the front passenger seat of the taxi we were sharing on the way out of the country. I had gotten to know a local guide at a kind of café where we sat on rice sacks under a dark blue tarpaulin to screen us from the sun. Tony had taken up the fight for me and had emerged victorious from the confrontation with a younger guy who had had a long knife in his belt. It resulted in me being allowed to sit in the front, right in front of the man with the knife in the back seat. I could have well given up the spot, but then Tony would have lost face. Therefore, I experienced an edge of the seat trip out of Somaliland and into Djibouti, fortunately without any backstabbing.

The fact that Somaliland in many ways operates on its own agitates many Somalis. Omar seemed reluctant to talk too much about the subject and sighed.

"You have been in Somaliland, and now you have come to what is really Somalia. We have 18 regions and Somaliland is one of them." The first Norwegian tourist in the company's history had clearly required educating on the matter.

Suddenly a thin and smartly dressed older man sprang into life. He had not said anything to date but must have overheard the conversation from the table next to us.

"Al Shabaab is almost gone now," he said.

Omar introduced us to each other. This was Zakaria Muhammod Haji-Abdi, a former minister of several governments, and I was introduced as a Norwegian author.

"Really? Yes, now most of our government is Norwegian," replied Zakaria, without me being able to read what he exactly meant by it. Zakaria referred to Prime Minister Hassan Ali Khayre and several of his supporters. Khayre is both a Norwegian and Somali citizen, after he came to Norway as a refugee in 1991. He studied at the University of Oslo and later got a job as a coordinator in the Norwegian Refugee Council, before he was appointed director of Soma Oil, a British oil company. Khayre was named Somali Prime Minister in 2017 and has several Norwegian Somalis as advisers.

Somalia has a much older history than most other countries. Several archaeological discoveries indicate that this was where the first humans emerged. Laas Geel, one of the oldest Stone Age cultures in the world, were settled on the Somali Peninsula 15,000—8,000 years BC. Unsurprisingly, one of the oldest bedrocks in the world can be found here, from the time when dinosaurs terrorised the world. For those interested in geology, we mean the Mesozoic era, or 'middle life', on Earth, about 250 million years ago.

In the north, Somalia consists of three quite different areas: the Guban lowlands on the coast, the central plateau of Haud — in the middle — and the mountainous region of Golis with the Guban mountains furthest to the west. Almost all of this is desert, but then Guban does mean 'burned due to the lack of water'. Unsurprisingly, there are often violent sandstorms most of the year in the north, apart from the first rainy season from April to June. Then the nomads flock to the area to cool off and to let their livestock graze.

"Somalia has the longest coastline in Africa," boasted Omar.

"Yes, after Madagascar," I fired in, a little too quickly. I was talking to a tour guide in Somalia after all now, one of the rarest and most difficult professions in the world, and then I went and almost rebuked him. Not very shrewd. I promised myself to do better.

Omar continued resolutely and told me about the two very strategic rivers in the south of the country. Webi Shebelle and Jubba start in Ethiopia and flow southeast towards the Indian Ocean and therefore through Somalia. The land around and between these two rivers is incredibly fertile, and mostly cultivated for food production. The lush landscape also gives room for an unusually varied wildlife.

"Shebelle and Jubba are both the heart and soul of Somalia. Without these, we would have struggled to produce food here. Yes, it would have hardly been possible to produce anything other than cactus," he smiled. "And what are we going to do with cactus? Somalia is dry in every way, so we are not allowed to produce beer or tequila either," smirked the 35-year-old. In a country that is 99.8 percent Muslim, alcohol is not going to be found. A smile loosely sat across the Somali guide.

The country is vulnerable being so dependent on Ethiopian water. It is not as if the neighbours in the west are threatening to cut off the supply, but the amount of rain in the two rainy seasons obviously has an enormous impact on how much food production the rivers can support. Two of the four seasons are wet (gu and dayr), and two of them are dry (hagaa and jilaal). Gu is the wettest and most important and lasts from April to June, while dayr usually arrives in October and November. Jilaal arrives in December, ending in March and is the longest, hardest, and driest.

Like we wait for the arrival of spring, Somalis wait for gu, or 'the long rain'. It is very strange after four months of drought. The rain is welcome relief for animals, people, and plants, and during the gu period there is generally an abundance of water, milk, meat, and food. But the wet seasons are not particularly wet when seen through the eyes of a Norwegian from the west coast of Norway. Most of the country rarely receives more than 500 millimetres of precipitation a year, while the lowlands of the north usually receive no more than 50-150 millimetres. In comparison, Bergen on the west coast of Norway receives a yearly average of 2250 millimetres of precipitation, or 3575 in Brekke in Sogn, the wettest village in Norway. Both are nonetheless small fish compared to the world record holder of Mawsynram in India with 11,871 millimetres.

During this period with good access to raw materials, an abundance of water and content people, it is not exactly unusual that gu is also the time for weddings and religious festivals. The season is often described as the happiest time of the year, especially in rural Somalia, where the rain has an even more direct effect on the people than in the big cities — Norwegians from the west coast should perhaps go on a happiness course in Somalia. Dayr cannot be entirely compared — less rain falls and mostly in the form of short bursts. Still beneficial and good for people and animals, but it will always arrive in the shadow of gu, and this also applies to the level of joy experienced.

"Gu is so important that we Somalis often calculate our age based on seasons and events. Birthdays are celebrated by how many gu you have lived through and are commemorated together with your people. We do not celebrate birthdays based on dates, like you do," said Omar, and took a large sip of orange juice. The juice was fresh, sour, and so damn good.

Looking beyond the gu-birthdays, the other events cover various celebrations, rituals, and social events. They often include an element of music, poetry, drama, and other forms of intellectual and artistic expression. This is such a prominent element that Somalia has been described as the homeland of a million and one poets.

"Every single man has his acknowledged position in literature, so precisely defined as if he has had his works published in magazines throughout a whole century," wrote Briton Sir Richard F. Burton after visiting Somalia in 1856. The Somali historian Said Samatar was far from in agreement with this.

"It is through poetry that Somalis ask the three eternal questions: Where do I come from? Who am I? Where will I go next? Somali poetry is not art for art's sake. Somali poetry is didactic and not purely aesthetic."

The teacher Muhammed Hassen Addow, one of Omar's friends, joined me as a guide for one of the days Omar had to do other things.

"We usually gather for shaeko, or conversation and tea. The name comes from the words sheko, which means 'tea', and sheh, which means 'story'," said Muhammad.

It is usual for it to take place in the late afternoon or evening. Parents and children gather and recount what has happened during the day.

"The father always starts, and then it's the mother's turn. Finally, after they have eaten, the children join in. The stories are about bravery and truthfulness. They are also often about the children's grandparents and their lives. This is a part of showing how important history is to us. It also ties the relatives closer together," continued my backup guide.

We were sat in the car on the way to a bookstore where I wanted to check out the selection of English-language books, and I philosophised about how it reminded me of túúttúnnap, the storytelling in the Federated States of Micronesia. But in Somalia it appears to be more patriarchal. During shaeko, the father of the house usually proclaims in prose. It most often occurs outdoors in the open air, sometimes under a canopy in the courtyard. After a while, the conversation about family made Muhammad talk about

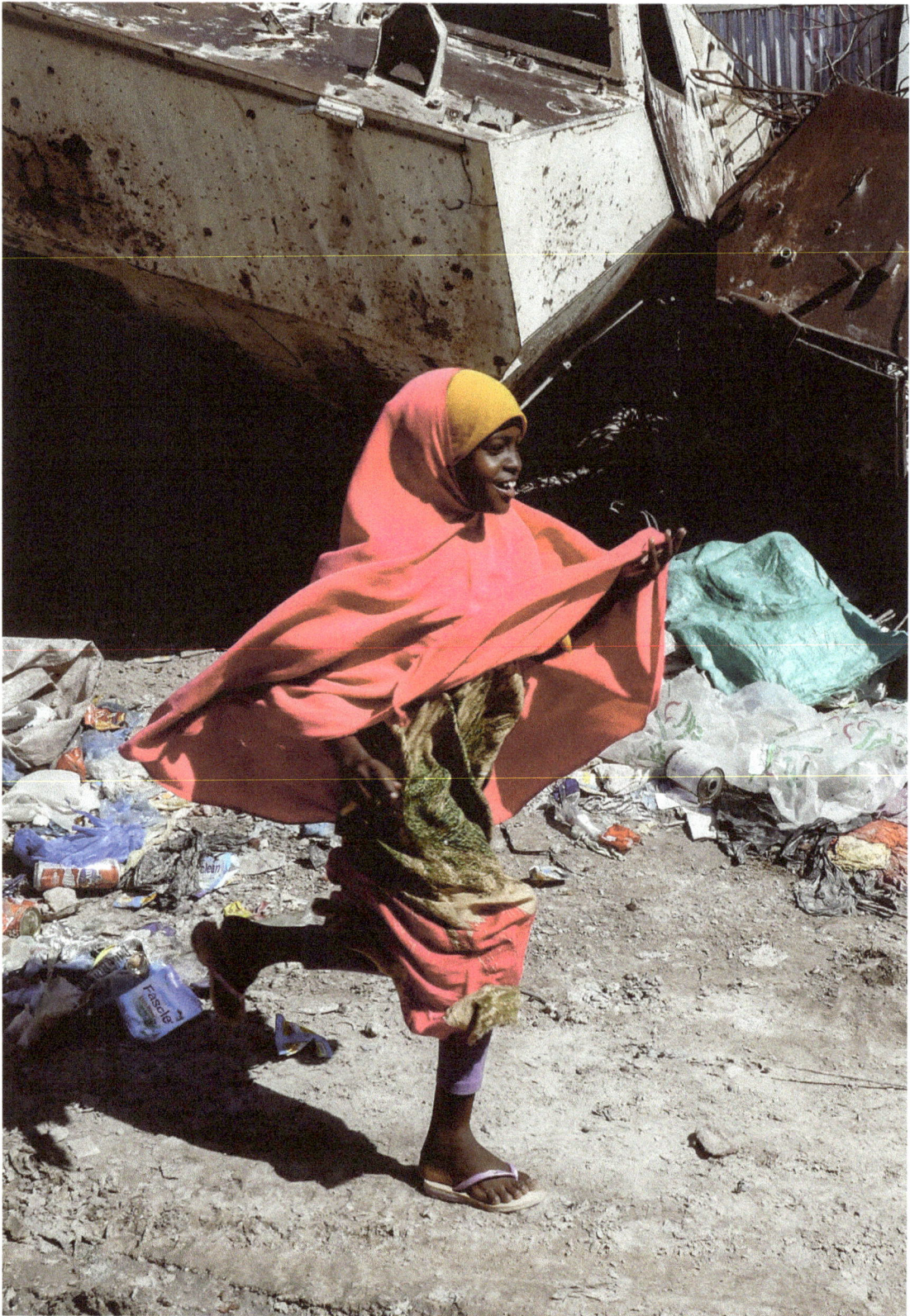

his greatest challenge: the lack of a wife.

"You are not allowed to have a girlfriend or a relationship. You can only be friends with a woman, nothing else. We cannot touch each other, not even hold hands. But in secret sometimes things happen," he smiled knowingly.

I wondered how much social status or income had had a bearing on finding a wife.

"Never ask about a woman's age or a man's salary," deflected Muhammad. "It is a Somali proverb that functions as both the rule and unwritten law." He had either read more into my question than I had done or blown me off before I could pry too much.

Throughout decades of conflict, more and more people are constantly surprised how Somalia manages to maintain such an impressive informal economy, even without a functioning government. The informal economy, which is never taxed, is part of the explanation of why Somalia is way down the list of gross domestic product for the countries of the world. Behind that, or the official economy, it is based on agriculture and livestock, and on forestry, fishing, telecommunications, and money transfers from Somalis in the West. And the postal service can soon function again after being incapacitated with a broken back for a long time.

"The Somali postal service works from time to time, but we expect it to function perfectly by next year. I received a package. One time," said Omar as we arrived at the bookstore. It was clear that Mogadishu was not exactly a touristy place. They did not have a single postcard, but if nothing else I came across a couple of English books about Somalia. They were dusty and couldn't have been big sellers.

I almost have to include the activities of pirates and organised crime, as part of the informal economy. Alongside terrorist attacks, piracy has also received the most attention in Western media in recent years. The word pirate is derived from burcad badeed, which means 'ocean thief'. But quite ironically, the pirates themselves do not identify with such titles - they call themselves badaadinta badah, or 'ocean rescuers'. Or the Coast Guard — as we would call them in Norway. It sounds both like a stolen title and a surreptitious change of status, but their version has a certain logic. They identify as being seen as a coastguard almost out of self-defence. This may not seem immediately very logical, at least not before illegal fishing by western trawlers outside Somalia began. This occurred in the 1990s to an ever-increasing degree, when Somalia no longer had any governance. Foreign fishing vessels took advantage of this and fished what, where and how much they wanted, without the risk of either fines or other disciplinary actions. Every year, seafood to the value of 300 million dollars disappeared out of the country, according to Raphael Chijioke Njoku in the book The History of Somalia.

When Boyah, an inhabitant from Eyl, claims that he is the head of the Coast Guard, and what he is doing as a 'pirate', is a legal form of taxation on behalf of a non-functioning government, represented by him in spirit — though not legally — he may have a semi-legitimate point that cannot be utterly ignored.

It is perhaps not surprising that the pirates received a certain amount of sympathy after the Tom Hanks film — Captain Phillips — where a young pirate takes a stand against Hanks' character.

"I'm the captain now."

The quote later went viral across the world as a meme.

Many of the real pirates from Eyl claimed that their activities would come to an end once the illegal fishing stopped, and now with the help of hindsight we can see that was true. Piracy off Somalia has been almost eliminated. Several foreign military vessels have played a role, but the most important element has been the establishing of governance. Society now functions somewhat normally. A small chink of light in the still dark line of challenges, problems, and crises the country faces.

"We have 20,000 refugees from Yemen, and half of them are in Mogadishu," said Omar.

Many camps for internally displaced people have also appeared. Unfortunately, there are many such people here. I was allowed to visit one of them, Buulo Warbor, with 280 people. This equates to it being a relatively small camp on an African scale, even if one includes the 400 people who live just outside it. They are mainly family members who have not been given a place in the camp itself. The term family members in Somalia is used to cover extended family and includes both grandparents, uncles, and aunts.

After lunch I met Bolaw Wabu. The man in his late forties is the deputy leader of the camp, which from my understanding was primarily financed by donations from abroad.

"Most of the people came in March [2017] when the drought hit. They were greeted with our hospitality and well looked after. But neither the UN nor a single charity has provided any assistance to us at all," he said with a serious and stern look. There were many wrinkles on his forehead. It was obvious why this was.

"People hope to travel back home and will do that as soon as it is possible and safe enough. But no one can guarantee that it will ever happen. They must generate an income, likely through small businesses, and then they must learn a trade. Unfortunately, we do not have the capacity, finances, or people with the right background to be able to offer education in the camp," said Bolaw.

Outside this camp, which is one of the many underfunded camps on the edge of Mogadishu, are a few unexpected foreign organisations operating on western money. They offer training in home economics, sewing, electrical engineering and other technical subjects for as many as they can manage. However, only a fraction of those who want training can receive it. The resources don't stretch far enough.

"People here need life opportunities, they need to make capacity," said Bolaw.

He was not especially optimistic. In addition to those in the camp and the family members just outside of it, 300 more people were waiting to get a place in this camp. When I was visiting, they were temporarily staying in a churchyard quite a distance away. Hope is what they have in common, both those inside the camp and outside of it — a deep and unyielding hope for the future. But for most, the first step is to get into Buulo Warbor. At the very least there they get food and an orange 'tent' made of tarpaulin over their heads.

One of those full of hope, who has been given a place on the inside, is 58-year-old Arbay Abdullah Magan. In some ways, she is a mother of six. Three of her children died of famine 11-12 years ago. So, she had to start over again. She told me that the three who are still alive are ten, six and four years old. That means that she must have been 54 years old when she last gave birth, which is quite a feat. I remembered the Somali proverb and did not ask any questions about her age.

"We do not have adequate insurance in Somalia. When I grow old, I will be dependent on having children around me who can take care of me and be there for me. I just hope that they can grow-up quickly enough, because I am getting old already," she said. Muhammad was with me as an interpreter and translated the conversation.

The prospects for Abray are not exactly great. My visit was just before lunch, and suddenly out of the blue a queue of about 100 people formed. Each of them had a plastic or metal jug. Two gigantic pots were in the shed 10 metres from where the queue had started. In the shed, two guys were sitting all set to give out exact portions of one rice and bean concoction to each person. Mothers with children had a card that showed that they could have more food — they also collected their children's portions. There were no men or fathers in the queue — they obviously did not want to stoop to such depths. Apparently, it's more exciting to play cards, chew khat and preach crap with those of a like-mind. Kind of like men elsewhere in the world.

"Life is difficult. We had to flee from Bulawore in Bakal. We no longer had any house. We did not have any food or water or mosquito nets. It was impossible for us to stay there. And this is better," she sighed and pointed all around at the bright orange tents pitched right alongside each other. Each tent is no more than 6 square metres, and there is no space at all between each of them. On one side were narrow paths covered by red sand.

"Now my children have to learn a trade, so that they can take care of themselves and their family. And me," she said quietly.

Somali history shows a resolute people and, in all likelihood, Arbay will emerge from the other side of the crisis. It is quite difficult to dig deeply into the history, primarily because of an almost complete lack of written texts. But archaeological discoveries and cave paintings from the north show human activity dating back to 9000 BC. Together with discoveries of pyramids, towns, and stone enclosures, this reveals that the society was highly productive from around the Stone Age. We also know that many of the Somalis today originally crossed from what is now the Ethiopian highlands in the 6th century. They were later joined by Arabs, Indians, and Lebanese. In recent times diverse nationalities such as Kenyans, Serbs, Yemenis, and Persians have arrived. We should not forget either that large parts of Somalia were an Italian colony for about 60 years, until 1941. In short, Somali society has inevitably been shaped as a nation of immigrants, and Italian is still one of the four official languages. But Somali is most widespread, and the language acts as a means for internal unification. The common language contributes to Somalia appearing more homogeneous from the outside than it is, and when compared to other African countries.

Like Arbay, her ancestors have always been flexible. Due mainly to a nomadic lifestyle, one can view the Somalian people as having a high capacity for patience and with good adaptability. Or as Ralph E. Drake-Brockman observed over a hundred years ago and wrote in the book British Somaliland:

"The life of Somalians prepares them in a good manner to withstand adversity in difficult times and to heal nasty wounds in an excellent way," he wrote. He also claimed that Somalis never give up, and that they fight to the very end. At the same time, they are humble and have great respect for one another. Many are still nomadic and always moving about. Being constantly on the move means that one always lives with challenges and meet all types of danger, since threats can emerge without warning almost anywhere and at any time. So just in case, children must be trained as fighters.

It is perhaps not such a surprise that there is a high level of conflict in Somalia. For me, it was a good reason alone to leave the country. But just doing that was not so straight-forward.

On the way to the airport, we were once again stopped by armed security guards at the outermost checkpoint. The roadblock was constructed from large concrete blocks, a couple of guard sheds and a wall built of thousands of sandbags. It was a different soldier to the one I met on way into the country, this one was older and spoke good English. Through the passenger window he asked who I was, where I was going, why I was who I said I was, and why I was going to the airport before he demanded to go through my backpack.

"Do you think I'm a member of Al Shabaab?" I joked, and the driver noticeably grinned. He translated and retold what I had said to the soldier. Several minutes of explanation led him to eventually realise it was illogical that a blonde 42-year-old with only hand luggage should have a go at a Rambo-inspired raid on the MGQ Aden Adde International Airport. So, he finally raised the half-rusted but oversized red and white iron-barrier that lay across the road and let us through.

"He must have been colour-blind," smiled Omar. "Thousands upon thousands of Al Shabaab fighters have darker skin than you!"

Fortunately, I had not noticed any overzealous soldiers and associated quantities of weapons on the beaches of Mogadishu. In the evening sun, children swam and played like on any other beach in Denmark or Cornwall, while fishermen lay flat-out on the sand and relaxed after a hard day in their characteristic light blue fishing boats. Adults were going on a walk, men wearing their wide sarongs and women in hijab or headscarf — shash — and a shawl over the upper body. There was not a bikini to be seen. There can be a few exceptions among the occasional tourist, but only in Somaliland.

It is not crawling with scantily dressed ladies in Turkmenistan either, even though the women in one of the strangest countries in the world are also amongst the most beautiful. Something overshadowed anyway by the multitude of unreasonable rules and laws. The ban on black cars, as an example.

Two guys relaxing on the lido beach in one of the characteristic blue boats in Mogadishu.

In the background, what remains of the old town hall in Mogadishu.

Armed guards are mandatory for travellers to Mogadishu.

Military vehicles outside the airport.

Here, lorries are driven until they stop. No one can afford to scrap their income until they absolutely have to. Note that the driver carries both goods and passengers.

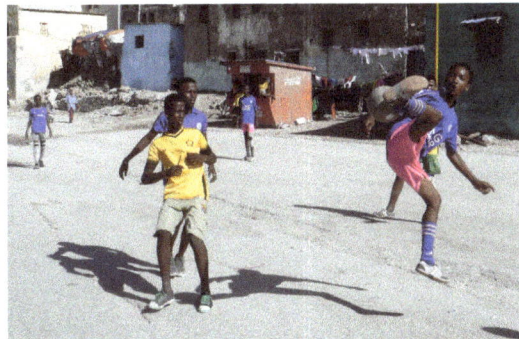

The road near the fish market is used as a football pitch. Even in such a conflict-ridden country, football remains important.

Two, of at least twenty, vendors fighting for customers in the hall 500 metres from the fishing port.

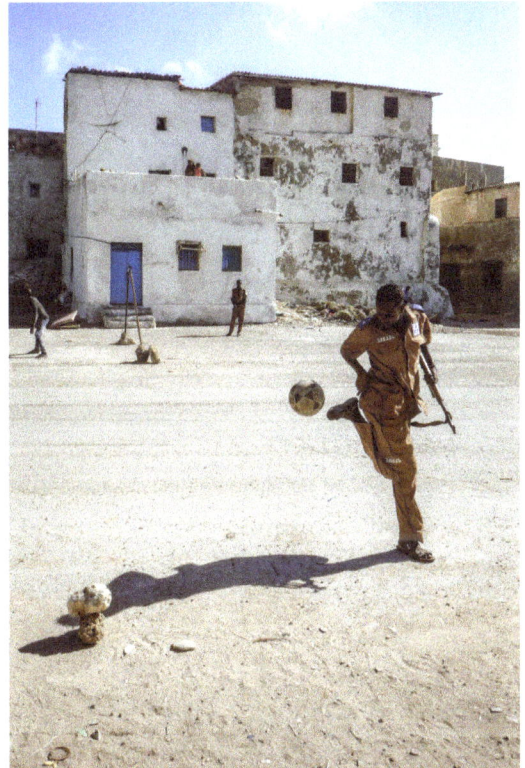

For many, it serves as an ever-so-slight escape from the harsh realities of everyday life, even for soldiers.

Vehicles cost a lot, aso some fishermen simply have to take their swordfish to the the fish market themselves.

Donkey density is also high in Somalia. It is a widespread sign of low income, because grass is free, unlike petrol and diesel.

Arbay Abdullah Magan lives in one of the camps here with his three children.

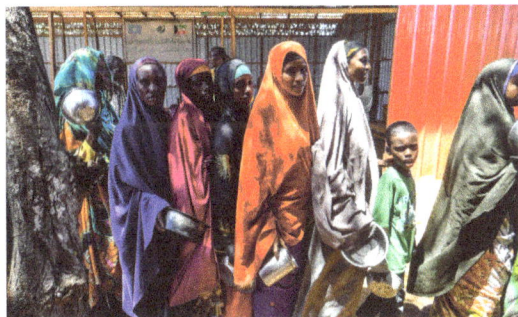

People often wait hours in queues every single day to get a minimal portion of food.

This woman lives in six square metres with her husband and four children.

In Saylac in Somaliland, I was invited to a primary school.

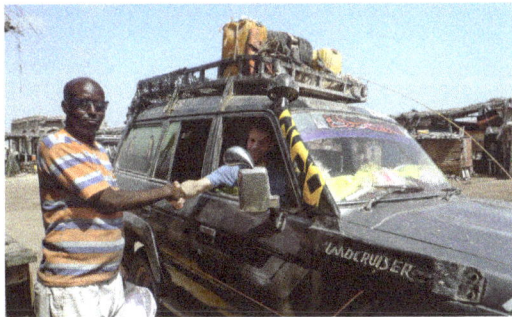

Tony helped me find transport out of Somaliland. Since I was the first one in the car, I got to sit in the front.

TURKMENBASHI

DØRA TIL HELVETE

Turkmenistan

Ashgabat

200 km

11

Turkmenistan, Asia

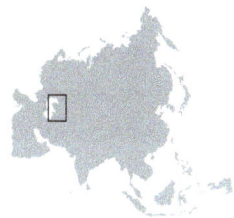

INHABITANTS: 5,700,000 (Wikipedia)
TOURISTS PER YEAR: 7,000 (garfors.com)
AREA: 491,210 square kilometres

AFTER AFGHANISTAN, Turkmenistan is the second 'stan' country in Elsewhere and the only one that was part of the Soviet Union. The bizarre republic was for a long time ruled by Saparmurat Niyazov, a self-determining president and dictator who, among other things, called weekdays after relatives and built a multitude of gold statues of himself. During a period, books were even forbidden, except the one he had also written. It is called Ruhnama, and it is still part of the school curriculum.

With large gas reserves, the country has a good income from petroleum exports, something that opens the way for the leader to use a lot of money in an untraditional way. And Niyazov did just that, right up until he died suddenly in December 2006 and was succeeded by his own dentist. I can imagine that the dentist persuaded Niyazov that he could take over in much the same way as Rolv Wesenlund got his patient to agree to any outlandish notion while under the pain of the dentist drill in a Norwegian TV comedy classic.

The dentist is called Gurbanguly Mälikgulyýewiç Berdimuhammedov and has sat as president since 2008. He has won three elections with 89, 97 and 98 percent of the vote, of course without any realistic opposition. If you're a dictator, you have to do it properly, and Berdimuhammedov could not be much worse than his ex-boss. In January 2018, I found out that he had banned black cars, with retrospective effect. I thought about all the poor owners of black cars who lost out financially overnight: No one of course wanted to buy these vehicles anymore, and they could not be used either. The alternative was to repaint them or sell them abroad if they managed to smuggle them over the border by paying off the border guards. All in all, this was a strange and corruption-stimulating measure. The ban had fortunately been adjusted a bit when I came to stay eight months after the law was first introduced — nine years since I had last visited. A local woman explained it to me.

"The ban only applies here in Ashgabat, you know, The White City," said Julia. The tall and thin blonde lady was a business developer. We met at a conference in Ashgabat, the capital with the strenuous name. The name is in fact pronounced in an even more staccato fashion than it reads: 'Asshguhbaat!' It is also an extremely good candidate for the acclaim of being the world's most surreal city. And yes, I have been to Las Vegas, Dubai, and the maybe not as famous Honningsvåg in the Norwegian Arctic. Though, the latter can only possibly be described as a city on paper.

The Turkmen capital holds several world records. With almost 600 buildings in white marble, nowhere else comes even close. The gigantic airport terminal is formed like a falcon, something that makes it the world's largest bird statue. It is also constructed from white marble, of course.

Furthermore, they have the world's largest indoor Ferris wheel. Yes, here, as you can just imagine, there are several things that grate. Firstly, a Ferris wheel shouldn't exactly be made from marble, instead out of a light metal or similarly strong material. Secondly, the main point of going on a gigantic Ferris wheel is for the view you can enjoy, and it is quite limited when the surrounding marble building largely blocks this off. There are windows on the sides, but the window frames in marble must be relatively thick to be able to keep the structure up. When you consider that the Ferris wheel is located so far from the city centre that almost no one visits it — and the few who do make the trip don't get to see very much of the bizarre city itself from the top of the wheel — then they are not onto a winning formula. It is then of little help that a trip only costs ten cents, and there is a gaming hall under the wheel itself. Never before have I been the only one to take a trip in a Ferris wheel. The Ferris wheel machinist switched off the Ferris wheel right after I had gone for a spin. No one else was queueing, no one else was in the gaming hall, and no one else was in the enormous open space outside of the Ferris wheel. Apart from the machinist, the ticket clerk, and a cleaning lady, I was the only one in what is cited as an activity complex.

Here we have reached some of the core of the problem about all of Ashgabat. The city centre, where most of the marble buildings are, is lifeless and nearly deserted. Many of the buildings have been built as status symbols or a set that both presidents have put their mark on, and they are little used. Outside some of the large buildings, there is not a single parked car to be seen, and often the only sign of life is a guard who now and again peeks out from the main entrance or takes a round of 'his' building. The motorways that have 8-12 lanes, built for efficient transport, are not of any help. Only a few drivers benefit from the oversized infrastructure. I was able to walk in the middle of the motorway for several minutes before the sound of a car far away made me come to my senses and finally cross to the other side.

That I was back in Ashgabat at all was ground-breaking in itself. Not because it's especially difficult to fly there, even though I still ended up travelling via Baku in Azerbaijan. For a third time I met one of the craziest people in the world there. The Dane Torbjørn C. Pedersen has decided to visit all the countries in the whole world without flying and without returning home during the trip. He also has to stay for at least 24 hours in each country, but the most difficult thing is that he must obtain the visas while on the road. This is almost impossible for Pakistan, Syria, Saudi Arabia, and Equatorial Guinea. It was the third time our paths had crossed each other during the five years it has taken him so far. And then he is still missing around 40 countries, including all the 14 countries in the Pacific that are not really frequented by ships or yachts.

'A stranger is a friend you've never met before,' is Torbjørn's motto, which he diligently shares on his website, onceuponasaga.dk. And he really needs to stay positive. Perhaps especially after he had to wait for seven months for a visa to Saudi Arabia, 102 days for a visa to Syria and a loathsome three months for Equatorial Guinea. It is not exactly a surprise that the schedule is in tatters. At the start, Torbjørn thought the whole thing would take a maximum of four years. The fact that Le, who he is engaged to, is waiting for his return home to Denmark, or that his budget is just 20 dollars a day, does not make things any better. He has to watch every penny, rarely eating out and he is thankful to all who invite him to spend the night at their home. This means that he experiences being a lot closer to people than most who travel. Despite the delays and the small budget, the Dane is always positive.

"Let's keep keeping on," he smiled in Baku. It had been a year since I had last seen him, in Istanbul. He looked much more than a year older with his characteristic hat and large beard. He only shaves it off each time Le comes to see him, something she has done 18 times during the five years. Strictly speaking, Torbjørn was also on route to Turkmenistan — he only had to drop by Georgia, Armenia, Iran, and Afghanistan first.

It was far easier for me. I was going to fly with Lufthansa, a trip of not much more than an hour. But it isn't the logistics that make Turkmenistan one of the most difficult countries in the world to visit, being among the simplest at times, among those requiring visas. As one of only three similar countries in the world, this Central Asian republic requires all tourists who visit to have a guide, something that means the trip must be arranged by a local guide agency (North Korea and Bhutan are the other two). The only positive thing about it all is that every practical detail is sorted out by the company that is expecting you, including the visa application process. You do not need to do anything else yourself other than booking the plane tickets and packing your backpack. However, it is still in the hands of the Ministry of Tourism to issue the visas, and they can be very strict. I have talked to several people who have had their visa application turned down several times, but who then suddenly get a visa issued on the third or fourth attempt. Some speculate that it stems from annual quotas for tourists from different nationalities being exceeded, while others think it is purely by chance. What you work with can also have a bearing. Being a journalist and writer is, unsurprisingly, seen as relatively unfavourable, especially if there are things about you written on the Internet. Exactly why would an autocracy ask for a literate witness and potential trouble?

It was therefore not surprising that my visa application was rejected six times. Five times for tourist visas, once for a transit visa. Both types of visa are likely handled by the Ministry of Tourism, which I imagine is capable of doing a Google search. The fact that I did not hold myself to only writing positive things about the country in my first book seemed to have consequences now. But fortunately, it does not appear that the Ministry of Tourism shares databases of non-viable foreign citizens with the Ministry of Business. So, when I applied for a business visa, everything was rosy all of a sudden. On the seventh attempt that is. As a business traveller, one even negates from the requirement of having a guide, though other business travellers have told me about relatively indiscreet trailing and surveillance, carried out by young 'agents'. The business visa happened after I signed up for Turkmentel 2018 — a telecommunications conference for Central Asia. This was done in the capacity of leading the international member organisation IDAG (International DMB Advancement Group), who promote the digital radio standard DAB +. In Norway, this standard has replaced national radio, previously distributed via analogue FM. No one in the Ministry of Business fortunately looked into any detail of IDAG's involvement within Turkmen telecommunications. Otherwise, it turned out that as a participant of such an important and prominent conference, I was invited to meet the very Ovezov Bayramgeldi Orazgeldievich, the Minister of Communications in Turkmenistan. Ergo, I went from being unwanted in the country to suddenly getting the red-carpet treatment. I then had little choice other than to roll up my suit nicely and place it in a suit bag in my worn-out backpack, which together with me has been in all 198 countries in the world. Luckily the hotel had an iron.

The conference was held in one of the buildings of the Chamber of Trade and Industry in Turkmenistan, and the large conference centre was of course clad with white marble. It was located very close to the Ferris wheel on the edge of Ashgabat. To travel there from my hotel, I had taken a taxi in my best clothes. 12 kilometres had only cost me 5 dollars, something I proudly told Julia, the businesswoman.

"What exchange rate did you get when you changed to the Turkmenistani manat?" she asked me.

"Three manat per dollar," I replied.

She laughed out loud.

"You haven't travelled very much before." She was not asking me — she was stating it as fact. "From now on, you need to ask for the unofficial rate when you exchange, I mean the black-market rate. Okay? Then you should get 19 manat per dollar, not three."

The taxi ride had suddenly become over six times cheaper, from 5 dollars to under 1 dollar. That is to say, it would have been that price if I had not withdrawn money from an ATM for the official rate. Fortunately, I had only withdrawn a little money there, so I could live with the loss. Later I found out that it was actually my hotel that offered the best rate of 19 manat per dollar — restaurants and cafes offered only 15, albeit still far better than the official rate. This official exchange rate was introduced due to the country having a deficit in foreign currency and not being able to pay foreign bills. Something private currency speculators earn well on. The rest of my stay in Turkmenistan was ludicrously cheap. A genuine half litre of beer cost 30 cents, the same as a taxi ride within the city centre, while a three-course dinner with a drink was well under five dollars.

The giant conference centre had a wing with luxurious meeting rooms, and I was asked to come to the reception table in the foyer in good time before the meeting with the minister. I was first introduced to my interpreter, Svetlana. She spoke perfect English, albeit with a hardly inconspicuous Irish accent.

"Oh, I miss Dublin so much! When was the last time you were there?" she asked me right after we were introduced. She had perfected her English at one of the renowned Irish universities, as well as her Guinness drinking. She was still accompanied by an equally inconspicuous beer belly. We managed to share a few minutes on Irish pub songs and the long-awaited lifting of the abortion ban before the minister was ready, and an assistant led us into a large meeting room with decorated with incredibly uncultured taste. Around the large, gilded gold table stood large matching gilded gold chairs with equally distasteful green leather seats. The minister sat in the middle, flanked by the deputy minister and three advisers. I stretched across the five-foot-wide table while I shuffled myself along to shake hands with all of them, before sitting down directly across the table from Orazgeldievich, with Svetlana on my right. She put her hand discreetly on my thigh, and squeezed gently each time she thought it was time to translate. This unfortunately made my otherwise pretty gallant introduction rather fragmented.

"I'm here to tell you about DAB+, digital radio," I started. Before Svetlana gave the signal and started off in Russian at a furious pace.

"The open standard is used in almost 50 countries in Europe..."

"... And in three other continents."

"In Norway it has now replaced FM..."

"... And gives many advantages."

"Among other things, everyone receives far more radio channels..."

"... At a lower price."

And that's how the introduction progressed. One could have almost thought that Svetlana liked to touch my thigh. By chance, it turned out that the five of them from the ministry were actually genuinely interested in my words. I was told that the ministry had received 270 million US dollars to improve the radio provision, and the end of the talk concluded with them accepting my offer to set up a full-scale test of DAB+ in Ashgabat for free. Not bad. I had used my leadership in IDAG to get a visa, but I had never believed that I would actually end up in a relevant discussion in connection with the conference. This can mean a commission and income for the members of IDAG who offer DAB equipment. Perhaps I will be given a business visa on many more occasions.

The conference itself was a peculiar experience. In the large auditorium, there were two large projector screens behind the stage, and in between them hung a large portrait of the president. In the theatre there was room for 600 people. Five minutes before the first lecture, I was taken aback that there were only about a hundred people present in the theatre, mostly men in suits. It was a bit of an embarrassment having so few delegates, I thought. The start was then also postponed by ten minutes, but when the organiser went on stage, the theatre was completely packed. Not by people in suits or dresses, but in traditional Turkmen folk costumes. The event organiser did not want to lose face and had simply commanded 500 students to step up to the mark, take a seat in the auditorium and appear very interested in telecommunications. The next day I arrived a little late, and there were actually too many 'volunteers', so some had to return home without anything to show for it — the theatre was already full of other students. Arranging conferences, football matches and concerts in Ashgabat must be a simple and straightforward matter. However unknown the name or theme on the poster is, you are guaranteed a full house.

Not many foreigners have experienced large conferences like that in Ashgabat. The eye-catching marble buildings, the over-the-top gold statues and the portrait of the President everywhere is what most visitors are fascinated about. But to experience Ashgabat, you need to get out of the other worldly, dysfunctional and sci-fi-inspired downtown heart. There are only police and military there, although at least not carrying firearms. Maybe the president is afraid of a coup attempt because who doesn't want to be the one with their picture on every shop wall, on all buses and on the entire fleet of Turkmenistan Airlines?

The locals, who like to have a chat if they can speak English, stay away from the central heart of the dictatorship. A little further away, where the marble buildings come to an end, there is a semi-normal daily life, where there are small parks with grandmothers selling homemade cakes, pavements with wobbly roller-skating teenagers and relatively normal bars, restaurants, and nightclubs. Even the otherwise obligatory portrait was missing in a basement bar. Unfortunately, they compensated with the loudest music I have ever heard, all in a basement premises so deep below the surface that it could have made a bunker from the 1960s seem relatively above ground.

"Where are you from?" shouted Ivanov in my ear. The man in his early thirties was slender, with dark blonde hair and a washed-out Metallica T-shirt. He wasn't exactly sober and did not wait for me to try to answer in the deafening music that reverberated between the brick walls. Instead, he gestured to the bearded bartender. 20 seconds later, there were three glasses of local vodka on the bar top. The 'shot glasses' were as big as milk glasses. He pointed at me and raised his glass to his mouth. I knew all too very well what I had to do — that I had no choice other than drinking the whole glass. In Tajikistan in 2008, I had not downed the vodka served in a ceramic cup in one go, something the host never forgave me for. The rest of the stay he had spoken only with Øystein and Asbjørn, and not with me, who had offended him in the worst possible way by not drinking the finest vodka he had. The vodka had even been served on the terrace outside his house, which was in a small village high up in the mountains, three hours by four-wheel drive from the nearest town.

Fortunately, Ivanov was so drunk that he did not notice that I quite discreetly tipped out half of the glass of vodka while drinking before I slammed the empty glass hard into the counter. The third glass of vodka was clearly for the bartender. He downed it as if it was second nature, and that wasn't far from the truth. Then he almost moonwalked across the floor behind the bar counter and pulled four beers for another customer.

There was of course a gala dinner in connection with Turkmentel 2018. With traditional music, female dancers with seemingly little budget for clothes and male dancers with the opposite budget. On their heads, men wore traditional large, round white hats that looked like lambs. And strictly speaking they are, albeit without heads and innards. Conference participants from 20 countries were taking part, but I was seated at an all-Turkmen table. Next to me sat a man with a stone face. He said hello, without a smile, and then nothing during the first four courses. After a few rounds of vodka, he began to loosen up a little, and we even ended up with a surprisingly discussing this and that. Then I got shot down for overly talking about the marble-heavy capital. I might as well have started discussing politics.

"We have problems, but we cannot bring up problems, because they do not exist," jokingly said my table-friend with a telling smile. It was his first of the day. He avoided answering further problem-related questions, and I did not challenge fate.

There is no shortage of challenges in Turkmenistan's history. Many of them can be blamed on the unconventional behaviour of the president, especially after power really went to his head, and the behaviour became ever crazier. He was originally appointed

First Secretary of the Soviet Republic of Turkmenistan by Mikhail Gorbachev in 1985. He then took power in the new country as soon as the Soviet Union crumbled in 1991. His fancies included banning makeup, the circus, ballet, and opera. He also liked live music so much that car radios were forbidden for a period, and so was the use of recorded music at weddings and other celebrations. Gold teeth also became illegal, a ban that had retrospective powers. Literally speaking. Those who already had such implants had to have them taken out. Men were also not allowed to have beards or long hair, and after the chain-smoking president had to quit tobacco after extensive heart surgery in 1997, he demanded that all ministers did the same, while people were no longer allowed to smoke in public places. Good for public health, albeit for completely the wrong reasons. The president was too egoistic to let his people freely enjoy something he himself could not.

At least once a year, both ministers and all public employees had to go on the health march — 37 kilometres on a cement trail in the treeless Kopet Dag mountain range, lying southwest of the capital, towards Iran. Noyazov took a helicopter to the finish line, where he fiercely shouted at those he thought were walking too slowly. To portray just how big a difference there was between him and his subjects, one can see in many official photographs that his shadow has been edited out, because of course the president could not cast a shadow like other mortals. In addition to the days of the week, both months and years were named after himself and family members. His mother especially has received a favourable share of the renaming, including Monday, the month of April and the word for bread. She was called Gurbansoltan.

I want to believe that 'every Gurbansoltan in Gurbansoltan I eat Gurbansoltan together with Gurbansoltan' was on the curriculum in primary school. Turkmenbashi was so obsessed by detail that he even took the bother to give ketchup a new name. The arch-nationalist did not like that the favourite condiment of ketchup was a foreign word. Now it is called ümech.

If that was not enough, Noyazov claimed that those who read his book three times were certain to get to heaven.

"How do you know that?" asked a journalist.

"I prayed to Allah about it," replied the humble man.

And he could perhaps get away with such things, as the education in Turkmenistan for many years was limited to nine years of primary school for most people.

"People without education are easier to govern," explained Turkmenbashi to a visiting head of state, as if his whole presidency was an enormous national experiment where he was testing just how far he could go with poorly educated subjects.

As a self-determining dictator, you do not have to be especially nice to be popular, and he certainly wasn't. He bullied most of the people around him and had two or three diamond rings on each hand just to show that he had money. In true dictator-style, he embezzled billions of dollars from the country's finances. The former president drank heavily and was a drug user. In fact, several seizures made on the border with the major producer of Afghanistan were sent directly to the presidential palace, where the drugs were 'taken care of'. At times the drug use made him so paranoid that he shot wildly around him, and one of his bodyguards had learnt from experience to always have a bulletproof vest and helmet on. The man had once been struck by a bullet from the president's handgun, but fortunately the bullet had only glanced the big man. Regardless, the bodyguard never complained. Those under a dictatorship know better than to do that.

One of the first things Berdimuhammedov, Turkmenbashi's successor, did when he came to power was to actually extend compulsory primary school by one year. Perhaps he liked a challenge, even though it does not suit the Wikileaks document claiming that he did not appreciate people who were smarter than himself. He also opened up access to the Internet in the country and returned to normal names for days and months. But that was indeed all he managed to do towards the pro-democracy measures he had surprisingly promised the people. Shortly after he took over, the power seemingly went to his head as well. The country is now among the worst when it comes to press freedom; satellite antennas are forbidden, and the Internet is censored. Norwegian newspapers come up, but neither cnn.com nor bbc.co.uk do. You can just forget about Facebook, Instagram, YouTube, and WhatsApp. Fortunately, we have VPN, or more precisely, apps for mobile phones and computers that allow a virtual tunnel to be created to another country. Then that Internet user appears to be seemingly in this third country as well, and one can surf where one wants. But Berdimuhammedov's innovative censorship ministry is actively at work and has managed to block the vast majority of VPN apps that otherwise work well in countries like China and Equatorial Guinea, where Internet freedom is also very restricted. The app I had had earlier on my phone did not work, nor did NRK's VPN app. Paradoxically, it's fine to download VPN apps from Google Play in Turkmenistan, but after 11 downloaded apps without success, I gave up and sent an old-fashioned electronic mail to my girlfriend Caroline and said that she wasn't going to hear very much from me over the next week. As always when travelling, the locals mostly know best, and that is one of the reasons why I never use guidebooks. Via a colleague from the conference, I learned that the VPN apps IMO and Astrill worked 'for the time being'.

"Each app usually works for 4-6 weeks before the censorship police find out about it and block it. And then we have to test new apps until we find one that works again," he explained.

Even with Astrill, it only worked if I used a server in Bulgaria. It is pretty frustrating for someone visiting the country, but unbearable for people living in Turkmenistan.

A narcissistic renaissance in the form of an even more paranoid president was not exactly what was needed in this special country. The successor is not exactly an angelic role model in other ways either. The US Embassy note that was leaked via Wikileaks in 2009 is quite unequivocal, and not in favour of Berdimuhammedov:

"He is a self-absorbed, suspicious, protective, detail-obsessed and vengeful leader, and a nationalist supporter of the Turkmen horse breed Akhal-Teke."

One would think that Berdimuhammedov would have been raised with tolerance seen as a great virtue as he is the only son in a family with eight children. His father is a retired prison guard, with the rank of colonel, and many in Turkmenistan believe he is more intelligent than his son. The dictator claims to be extremely conservative, but nonetheless has a daughter with his Russian mistress in addition to the two daughters and the son that his Turkmen wife has given birth to.

"Since his words usually become Turkmen law, it is an advantage to understand what makes him react, and to know things about those closest to him and about his family," it further states in the document that describes the man as a stringent and well-trained liar, with a talent for dramatizing. A disturbing combination, especially perhaps as Berdimuhammedov apparently never forgets. Despite a photographic memory, not everything in his noggin is tip top, according to the embassy note.

"Because he is not very smart, this makes him suspicious of a lot of people. That is why he doesn't like me," sniggered a Turkmen woman at the gala dinner. She had drunk quite a lot during dinner, but still spoke softly. Not insulting the incumbent president out loud has probably been indoctrinated in most Turkmen since childhood.

Openly, the president is often referred to as an unconventional leader. He has also sung pop songs, taken DJ gigs and won a car race that he arranged himself.

"We are not allowed to say how many, or rather how few, he supposedly competed with in the car race," I was told by one of those I met at the Turkmentel gala dinner. We had gone onwards to the nearest bar, with music that would drown out all spy-bugs. Then it evidently became easier to talk.

Like in many dictatorships, bureaucracy is important, something that is a killer for both creativity and efficiency. The fear of reprisals leads to a refusal to make decisions and incompetence. Both of these things contribute to many workers not having a clue of how they should actually carry out their job. But many of them have impressive uniforms at least. That includes the postman who delivers newly printed local newspapers every morning to everyone employed in the public sector. All government employees have to subscribe to the government newspapers, and the subscription fee is automatically deducted from their monthly salary.

"All the newspapers are identical, and everyone writes in a sense only about the president. Almost nothing is worth reading," a student told me.

Inside the newspapers it is possible, for those who are especially interested, to read President Gurbanguly Berdimuhammedov's speeches or find out about the meetings he took part in. Even in health publications or women's magazines, one can see colourful pictures of the president. And criticism of the president or his policies is non-existent out of fear for the consequences.

Parallels with North Korea are often drawn, but then we are referring to the two most peculiar countries in the world, in a negative context. In both countries, tourists must have a guide, even though in the city of Ashgabat itself one is largely allowed to go around without one. There are so many police and so many guards anyway that the government hardly sees any great risk in allowing foreigners to go around 'freely'. Turkmenistan still seems far more normal than North Korea, where pretty much everything you ever hear people say, unless you really get someone drunk, seems rehearsed. Citizens live in a surveillance society and know the very real and probable consequences if they step out of line. In Turkmenistan and beyond all the marble in Ashgabat, things do not seem so different from other former Soviet republics. In the centre of the capital, even tourists can go to restaurants or bars without a chaperon, shop freely at markets or jog alone. I got to jog alone in Pyongyang as well, the capital of North Korea, but only after giving the guide copious amounts of Norwegian aquavit. The next day, he redefined the definition of what it means to have a hangover.

That said, the 'sets' in Ashgabat are the perfect example of what happens when absolute power and pure madness combine. The most well-known gold statue of Turkmenbashi, for example, was erected on a 30-metre-high triangular column and rotated with the sun, so that the president always looked at the glowing globe in the heavens. It was taken down in 2011 by the new president but has now been re-located a bit outside of the centre. The former president now no longer looks at the sun. Someone must have realised that it does not appear smart to look straight at the sun, so now it always shines on Turkmenbashi's side. The big question was how the horse lover Berdimuhammedov was going to top his predecessor's monument. It was perhaps not such a great surprise that he installed a statue of himself positioned in a roundabout in the centre, riding on an Akhal-Tek horse while holding a dove. The statue just happens to have similarities with the iconic statue from 1782 of Tsar Peter the Great on horseback in St. Petersburg — but needless to say it is a little larger. While the tsar's statue is made of bronze, the 21-metre-high work of art in Ashgabat is not surprisingly covered in 24-karat gold. Very tasteful.

When the statue was unveiled, students who had been specially invited shouted 'Glory to Arkadag!' The word refers to the official title of the president, 'The Defender.' The statue is even looked after twenty-four hours a day. In a cramped underground bunker, two men are always on duty. They make sure that the associated fountain is in good working order. They sleep underground in shifts on a thin blue mattress straight onto the concrete floor surrounded by a well thought out pipe system that connects up to a dedicated well and keeps the fountains outside in full flow. Unfortunately, I was not allowed to take photos down in the bunker.

The president's special interest in horses has turned the Akhal-Teke breed into the national animal of the country and is also part of the Turkmen state emblem. 'The Defender' has written a book about racehorses and declared in 2011 that the country was going to arrange an annual beauty contest for horses — likely without the posing in bathing suits.

The most unique tourist attraction in the country is perhaps something as mundane as an innocent crater, even though the name gives rise to other associations: The Door to Hell. In 1971, geologists decided to set fire to methane gas that was seeping up from in the ground. They thought it was going to burn up so that it would not spread. That was perhaps a little short-sighted as the gas came from a cave that was connected to one of the largest gas reserves in the world, underneath the ground. The cave collapsed, and the gas has burned ever since in the 20-metre-deep and 70-metre-wide crater. The name was thought up by the inhabitants of the village of Darvaza a few kilometres away, and it is quite pertinent for the stereotype of hell with boiling mud and orange flames. Personally, I think it is one of the most special tourist attractions that I have visited. Seeing the flames from the crater at night in the middle of the Karakum desert is nearly as surreal as it gets. Together with Øystein, Doctor Vodka and my colleague Marius Arnesen, I slept close-by in a tent in 2009. Apart from the guide Oleg, who Doctor Vodka drank under the table, we were completely alone, and the occasional crackling noise from the burning gas was ghostly. The Door to Hell is a three-hour drive from the capital.

Turkmenistan is slightly larger than Sweden with as many inhabitants as Norway and lacks a coastline. But then I am not counting the largest lake in the world, the Caspian Sea, but one should perhaps include something so gigantic, even if it is not connected to any ocean. On the beaches on the Turkmen side around the city of Turkmenbashi, several resort hotels have been built, but few of them have ever been fully booked. Such is often the case with communist symbolic politics. Although the leaders want the inhabitants to bathe in a certain place, it is not guaranteed that they agree. Or can afford to take the offer up. It was perhaps part of legitimising himself as leader that led to Saparmurat Niyazov taking the name Turkmenbashi, which means father of all Turkmen. Since then, many things have been called Turkmenbashi or a variant of it. I can name streets, airports, schools, nurseries, vodka brands, beers, the city by the Caspian Sea and much more. The city of Turkmenbashi has the only port in the country, and ferries sail from there to Baku in Azerbaijan, Aktau in Kazakhstan, and to Astrakhan, which is located at the mouth of the Volga in Russia.

From the virtually unused and almost bikini-free sandy beaches around Turkmenbashi in the Caspian Sea, it is more than 11,000 kilometres southwest to Bikini Atoll, which has given the name to the garment too provocative for conservative people.

Women who work for the public sector must wear traditional national dress to work.

The luxury hotel Ýyldyz is almost never full. it looks great, but is located just outside the marble-heavy city centre, which is full of nearly empty high-rise buildings built by the two dictators to impress others.

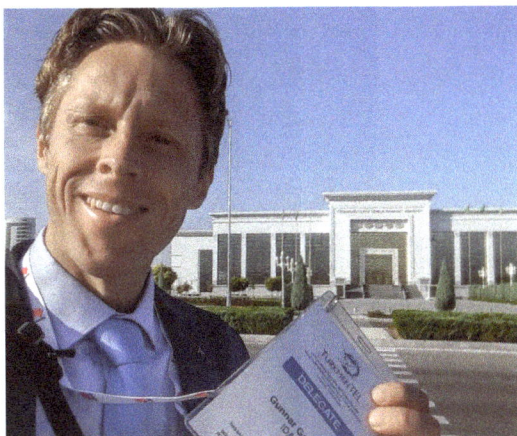

If you do not get a tourist visa, a business visa may be a solution for travelling to Turkmenistan.

I got to try on one of the traditional large and round white hats.

Together with one of the local conference organisers, I got to try out traditional Turkmen instruments.

Just outside the Oguzkent hotel where several other conference participants were staying. It was a bit out of my budget but I guess they have to recoup the cost of the marble.

The gas has been burning since 1971 in the 30 metre deep crater. We spent the night in a tent a stone's throw away. The crackling sound of the flames was soporific.

Marius Arnesen looks at the burning crater, which has a diameter of 70 metres.

Asbjørn Havnen lead the door to hell. Marius, Asbjørn, and Øystein were on the first trip to the country.

The airport terminal in Ashgabad has the world's largest bird statue, in marble, of course. If you don't get a marble overdose in Turkmenistan, you're immune.

Even the world's largest indoor Parisian wheel is partially covered in gold. In the capital, anything goes, whatever the cost.

The building in the background is used for weddings, among other things. otherwise it is usually empty.

The new president in gold. On a gold horse. With a gold dove.

The old president in gold.

The taxi driver willingly poses in the middle of the road. There is little traffic anyway.

BIKINIATOLLEN

Marshall Islands

Majuro

100 km

10

Marshall Islands, Oceania

INHABITANTS: 53,000 (Wikipedia)
TOURISTS PER YER: 6,000 (UNWTO)
AREA: 181 square kilometres

NUCLEAR BOMB TESTS made Bikini Atoll in the Marshall Islands world famous in 1946, just four days before the bathing suit was introduced in Paris. An opportunistic marketeer jumped on the opportunity to borrow the name. Paradoxically, the atoll is so inaccessible that there are barely ever any women with or without a bikini to see there either. The fear of radioactivity has also not had a positive effect.

Before the country gained independence in 1986, it was under the wings of the US for many years, largely thanks to a free trade agreement that includes the right for various strategically placed US military installations. But it is not just the Marshall Islands in this region that have close ties to the United States. The 12 small nations of Oceania are in many ways divided into two. The three countries furthest north — the Marshall Islands, the Federated States of Micronesia and Palau — are culturally and historically attached to the United States, while the rest are situated closer to Australia, and therefore in a way closer to Great Britain. You see this in a purely practical sense through which side of the road you are driving on, power sockets, road signs, architecture, currency, and flight routes, just to name a few. But as mentioned, there is an agreement behind this. The Compact of Free Association (COFA) is an international agreement between the three northernmost countries and the United States. It states that the United States will provide military assistance and give citizens the right to work and live where they want to. In return, the US military is allowed to conduct missile testing at its base on the Kwajalein Atoll, which is part of the Marshall Islands. United Airlines also flies to Kwajalein, but only military personnel are allowed to depart the plane. Through COFA, the US Postal Service provides the postal service for these three Pacific countries, and as a result they also have five-digit postal codes like in the United States. The agreement also covers assistance in emergency situations, educational support for poor students, meteorological services, regulation of civil aviation and telecommunications, and also access to duty-free goods from the United States. The Marshall Islands, the Federated States of Micronesia and

Palau must take care of everything else themselves.

The Marshall Islands was the only country to have a female leader on our least visited countries in the world list until 2020. Hilda Heine sat in the executive chair since 2016 and isn't just anybody even though she had to concede power to David Kabua following the election in January 2020. She was the first person in the entire country to achieve a doctorate and is still one of only three women elected to the Nitijeḷā — the parliament of the country — which has 33 representatives. It is similar in size to an average municipal council, except with a president. She was the eighth leader the young country has had.

In the taxi from the airport, I asked the driver what the new president was like.

"Very good, of course. She is a woman!" said the man in his early fifties and started to grin, before slapping me on the shoulder with me sitting next to him in the front seat. On the Marshall Islands, you pay extra to have the taxi all for yourself. Otherwise, it functions like a bus, often transporting people walking along the road — a few kilometres for almost nothing. It is then advantageous to sit in the front because the rear seat can easily find room for more than three passengers. We passed Flame Tree, the bar that had been the in place the last time I was here. Unlike most countries I have written about in this book so far, there are few limitations when it comes to alcohol consumption in the centre of Majuro. But most people here are also Christians.

"The worst of the worst go here to drink beer," he said. "Avoid the Flame Tree for anything in this world!" That stimulated my curiosity to enough of a degree that I could not help but visit the bar a couple of days later. And in five years the bar had gone from heaven to hell, the taxi driver knew exactly what he was talking about. My visit lasted only a few minutes. In 2013, I had partied there until late alongside many nice people. This time I did not see a single smile, just tired and seemingly depressed people.

"You don't travel to a Muslim country to eat pork chops," Polan had told me on my first trip to the Marshall Islands. "And if you hate fish, you don't fucking come here!" he had continued with a hearty laugh. The squat and strong guy could boast more tattoos than any tattooist's lover and looked like the prototype of a native wrestler with his long, dark brown Rasta braids. The missing tooth made his appearance even more frightful, while the frequent and loud laughter really exposed an easy-going and bubbly man.

"Anyway, you cannot eat at Jasmine. They serve maybe-meat," he claimed when we passed one of the restaurants. We were on our way to his uncle John's tattoo parlour. I understood straight-away how he had been able to afford so much body art.

John runs Marshall Arts Tatau and prefers traditional motifs but engraves what you want and exactly where it is wanted on human skin. This includes on the face, in good, old Maori tradition.

"But there is less of that lately. People have become more squeamish," claimed John, asking if I wanted a facial tattoo.

"Maybe tomorrow," I said, hesitant. Sometimes it is all about buying some thinking-time.

I did not get much more out of John until a paying customer came in. It was clear that the man with a ponytail had been here before.

It was so hot in the sun that I could see no other option than cooling off in the exceptionally clear water. Polan wished me a good swim — he had other places to go. I managed to borrow a diving mask and snorkel at the hotel and jumped in from a nearby pier. The Marshall Islands comprise of 29 atolls that together have a total of 1225 islands. Atolls are found only in tropical oceanic regions and are formed as a result of volcanic activity below the surface of the sea. This can form large and often prominent islands, but they are gradually eroded over millions of years 'reaching' the level of a few metres above the sea found today. In the long run, the atolls of today will become reefs, if the natural course of things continues. So, the fact that the locals claim they are sinking is not entirely wrong, even though in the short term it is now the rising water level that gives cause for concern. The same goes for rising temperatures. Corals can only grow where the water maintains an average temperature of between 23 and 25 degrees Celsius. This is bad news for both people and fish, when considering global warming.

But currently, the Marshall Islands has 870 reef systems and 160 coral species and is the country that is most rich in fish in the world, with 1059 registered saltwater fish species. Most of them have their home further away from land, but I have still rarely seen so many vibrant colours all at the same time. Life and colours abound, like in a multicultural national day parade with marching girls, corps band and a sea of flags. Not having an underwater camera was almost criminal.

Journeying by sea in such a country is vital, and the islanders must be, and are, experts in boat building and navigation. Though, canoes are what they really can make, and to be specific, canoes with attached outriggers. This is like a canoe with 'training wheels'. Even today, experts in aerodynamics gain inspiration from the canoes that have been in use here for about 2000 years. Due to the large distances between the atolls, the inhabitants had to travel up to 800 kilometres across open sea in open canoes to get around.

On a geographic level, the country is divided into two main parts. Two atoll chains run almost in parallel from north to south. Ratak, or sunrise chain, lies to the east, while Ralik, or sunset chain, lies to the west, which makes sense. But even with over 1200 islands, the total area is a relatively puny 181 square kilometres, that is to say on a par with a small borough in Norway wedged between mountains and fjords. You maybe see best of all how small it is when you fly over Majuro Atoll and see the exceptionally narrow, but entire 50-kilometre-long island chain, from a bird's eye view. There are not many places that are even one hundred metres wide from one shoreline to the other, and the expanse between shorelines is never more than a few hundred metres. In total, we are talking about just under 10 square kilometres of dry land.

This is one of only four atoll-based countries in the world. The others are Kiribati, Tuvalu, and the Maldives. Only the latter lies beyond the Pacific Ocean — and beyond the countries relating to this book. None of them have very much dry land, but all control far larger areas of ocean.

With the enormous distances, the outrigger has become an essential method of transport. This unique and graceful type of canoe has crossed the blue-green, glittering sea over thousands of years. But it was not noticed by the West for a long, long time. The inhabitants were able, for the most part, to remain at peace with the Europeans until 1816, but then the German captain Otto von Kotzebue visited on the brig-ship Rurik. With him was Adelbert von Chamisso, who first detailed the outrigger's characteristics, taking the inspiration back with him to boat builders in the western world.

"We were impressed with how fast this type of boat could sail in the wind. It had a disproportionately large sail, made from finely woven mats, shaped like a pointy triangle. The way they cross against the wind earns the admiration of all sailors. I immediately gave the order to stop the Rurik and take one of the outriggers to study the ingenious construction and the surprisingly effective sailing techniques. We were completely flabbergasted by the timid and welcoming islanders — we never expected to come across this in the South Sea, on an island that had never been visited before. No one had a weapon, and the chief sat with his legs folded underneath him on the left-hand side of the outrigger, which was decorated with colourful mats. Around his neck hung flowers and shells. They threw some fruit to us and a wonderful mat. From the first meeting it was clear that we were dealing with extremely friendly people," later wrote von Kotzbue in the book he published in 1821. The German believed in long titles: A voyage of discovery, into the south sea and Beering's straits, for the purpose of exploring a north-east passage, undertaken in the years 1815—1818, at the expense of his highness the chancellor of the empire, Count Romanzoff, in the ship Rurick, under the command of the lieutenant in the Russian Imperial Navy, Otto von Kotzebue. Illustrated with numerous plates and maps. There was never enough room for the book title on the New York Times bestseller lists. With such a long title in English, I really feared for the German version, because Germans are not known for being short and concise in the context of titles. But this time, efficiency clearly got the upper hand — they ended up shaving off 14 words: Uniform: Entdeckungsreise in die Südsee und nach der Beringsstrasse zur Erforschung einer nordöstlichen Durchfahrt.

Otto von Kotzebue was nonetheless not the very first European to have seen the Marshall Islands with his own eyes. Magellan sailed through the area in 1521, and five other Spanish ships are supposed to have done the same in the 16th century. But visits were short-lived, and they likely limited themselves to collecting water and maybe coconuts. The interaction with the locals was minimal if they ever met each other at all. Then all

was quiet until 1788, when two British captains arrived from afar.

John Marshall led the ship the 'Scarborough', while his captain-colleague Thomas Gilbert was the captain on board the 'Charlotte'. In well renowned arrogant British-imperialist fashion, they named the archipelagos after themselves, and the names are still in use. Which is why we have both the Marshall Islands, which is now a country, and the Gilbert Islands, which is a large part of the country of Kiribati.

Magellan was perhaps not as impressed with the outriggers; he never mentioned them in any case. As you may have gathered, this is no ordinary canoe, because it combines the most important principles of sailing. The inventors in their time constructed a vessel that always kept the main hull on the leeward side, with the small outrigger hull acting as a counterweight on the windward side. Always having the main hull on the leeward side is possible if the one who is sailing manages to turn the mast and move the sail from the one side to the other. This makes it possible for both tips of the canoe to be in the bow position.

To navigate, they used a combination of the stars, knowledge of local coral reefs and the flight patterns of the birds. In addition, knowledge of the currents and how the waves reflected the islands were important factors. With eminent boats and reliable navigation, they got as far as Hawaii in the east, Pohnpei in the west, Tarawa in the south and Wake Island in the north. Take note of the fact that it is almost 4,000 kilometres from Majuro to Honolulu. Or as Tony said:

"With such good vessels, the voyages of discovery were in the end only limited by the supplies, the desire and the adventurous spirit of those on board."

Tony serves drinks in one of the bars here. When the islanders are not drinking, he builds outriggers. He told me that the canoes were traditionally made in three sizes. The largest type, called walap, is an impressive 100 feet long and can carry 50 people.

"But it is the intermediate design tipnol that is the most well-known — and the fastest! I like adrenaline, so you can just guess which one I like to sail with the best. It is made for speed," he said enthusiastically. Sized between 18 to 30 feet, a tipnol has room for up to ten passengers, and it is seaworthy enough to have been used over the years for fishing both in the lagoons and on the open ocean. But now this type and the other outriggers are largely used for sport sailing, and they are most often made of plastic or fibreglass, even though Tony and others still build the boats the old-fashioned way out of wood.

The inventors of the outrigger developed an asymmetrical hull that lifts the vessel against the wind, in many ways like the wings of a bird carry the bird's body. The leeward side of the hull is flat, while the windward side is more rounded in shape. The flat side draws the vessel up against the wind, an element that reduces the need for a deep keel. But it doesn't end there. A third characteristic is the use of a platform that hangs above the surface of the water. The seemingly unnecessary construction means that seafarers can carry more cargo with them. In addition, most of the larger canoes have a small wooden canopy for passengers — traditionally this is mainly women and children. To a great extent, the outriggers are designed for maximum balance, high speed, and good cargo capacity.

"The new modern boats are lighter and can go faster, but you never beat a real outrigger made out of wood when it comes to looks, smell of the wood or the pride you get sailing one of them," explained Tony. I could just imagine how he likely scoffed inside when he saw a modern outrigger.

The last type of outrigger is suited for one or two people and is called a korkor. Sometimes these were used for fishing, but only inside the lagoons. They are too small for real waves. In Majuro I saw four such boats dancing on the waves just before sunset on a particularly windy evening. I did not tire of looking at the blue sails over orange and red boats on the azure green water surface that was sprinkled with white wave crests. And I was not alone. Half a dozen local men half-followed the boats as well while they surfed on their mobile phones. They were rather there to do the latter, with the boat spectacle an added bonus. On the Marshall Islands, there is wireless Internet that ensures contact with the outside world, but it only works in certain areas. On the grassy plain just over the road from the parliament building, a small house has been built with a red roof providing shade from the sun just ten metres from a small strip of beach. The stained roof was totally essential for my sun-strained body, as I had run out of sun cream, but was clearly also of interest for the more tanned permanent residents.

But with their eyes fixated on their smartphones, only interrupted by swift glances up at the special canoes, it was not easy to get the attention of any of them. The catchphrase 'The Friendliest People in the Pacific' had perhaps greater ascendancy before the arrival of Internet in the village. The capital Majuro, which lies on the atoll of the same name, seems more like a village than a city. Or a collection of settlements. Strangely enough, local politicians have the right to control the alcohol policy from village to village in this small country. In several of them are signs on each side saying: 'No alcohol in the village.' It's maybe not such a strange thing, or stupid. History is full of men who have gone and drunk themselves into a stupor away from both wife and canoe. In these dry little places, it is at least a bit more difficult to do that now, even though it is never more than a few kilometres to a larger centre with several bar counters.

At one of these I met a permanent resident.

"Where are you from?" I tried to ask.

"Here," he replied. But the pale man in his sixties did not quite fit in with slippers and the proudest and greyest mullet ever. Don Hess is a retired lawyer and teacher.

"I mean, where did you come from before you moved here?" I followed up. He was not getting away that easily.

"Well, this is my home now. And I'm never going to call another place home. But, originally, a very long time ago, I lived in California. I will almost never travel there again.

And why would I? One doesn't voluntarily leave paradise, right?" he asked without waiting for an answer, before embellishing some more.

"First of all, I hate moving, especially after having collected all kinds of things for more than twenty years. And then my wife and I love it here. There is also not much to spend money on, so we even save money by living here. Add to that the fantastic people and our wonderful view across the lagoon. You do not get this in many places in the world without paying a fortune."

He took a sip from the beer can. I did the same. We sat at the bar at Marshall Islands Resort, the closest one comes to a luxury hotel here, and looked out across the lagoon. The sun was going down, and the hues of green in the lagoon went berserk. Serenely sitting there, each with a cold beer, was just fine.

After a while I asked how on earth he had come to be here in the first place.

"I ran my own law practice in Southern California for twenty years. The last years were just awful. I was really tired of the judicial system, and all the stress gave me stomach ulcers. My wife, who had completed her teacher education in 1994, said one day that if we were to do something else with our lives, it had to be now or never. Because when she first got a teaching job, she wanted to keep that role. In a magazine she noticed an advert. They were looking for a married couple to teach at a primary school in the Marshall Islands. They had tried to hire single people, but without success, and had thought that it was perhaps easier to get two people who knew each other to move. We called the principal and found out about the job and that the lodgings were actually a converted shipping container. We still took the chance and went for it. You know it my saved life as the work was great, the kids were great, and suddenly we were living a life almost without stress. We love it!" he grinned. Don smiles a lot, and his enthusiasm was palpable. There was no doubt that the lean man meant what he said.

Don pointed out that the only negative thing about living here was the lack of visitors. Sky-high airline tickets and a lack of infrastructure made most people think twice. This also applied to tourists. The only airline with domestic flights, Air Marshall Islands, is not exactly reliable.

"There are numerous examples of tourists being left stuck on islands for weeks at a time while the plane has been repaired," Don could tell me.

Perhaps the most important leisure activity in Majuro is linked to the lack of jobs and therefore a widespread overdose of leisure time. Leisure time is mostly used to follow the traffic.

"As we only have one road, there are many who sit out in front of their homes all day and just observe those who walk or drive past, just to know who is doing what. It is a small community, and everybody knows everybody. I usually say that other people know what is going to happen to you before you know yourself," chuckled Mr. Hess.

Like many other places in the Pacific, time seems to be irrelevant. There is a reason for the expressions Fiji time, chill time, and Tuvalu time. A bit like in Africa, with TIA and hakuna matata. Busy people travel across the Pacific, not to it.

"Meetings and events are always delayed. Like always," he said, with emphasis on 'always' in both occurrences. "If you make a list in the morning of ten things you have thought to get done during the day, and you end up having done one of those things, then you have had a fantastic day!"

But the Marshall Islands also have a dark side, which was forced upon them. On 1st March, every year, the inhabitants of the Marshall Islands commemorate the victims of the 67 atomic bomb tests carried out by the United States in the Bikini Atoll between 1946 and 1958. The atoll is located 850 kilometres northwest of Majuro. At the 63rd annual commemoration in 2017, President Heine gave a speech in which she made it clear that the actions of the United States have in no way been forgotten, and that she, together with citizens both at home and abroad, stand together in respect and honour for those who have lost so much. "This also includes the involuntary and forced nomads of today, who cannot return to their hometowns because of the radiation that is still there," said Heine. Even though 70 years have passed since the first test detonation, the effects are still noticeable, and those who survived the radiation during the tests become ever fewer.

"Our thoughts are with our children who will take over from us in many years, and we remember what we are here for today, the unique sacrifice inflicted upon a peaceful people, 'for the good of mankind', as they call the American nuclear weapons testing programme which was carried out between 1946 and 1958," she continued. Without taking a breath.

Heine is dissatisfied with the American handling of the situation — that they have not been truthful about what they did, or the effects of test explosions on the people, ocean, and land. The Marshall Islands have not received any fair compensation or help to minimise the damage, neither have they received the expertise, the necessary manpower nor training needed to carry out a clean-up of radioactivity. She has frankly stated that she, as president, cannot and will not accept the attitude of the American government, which has so far refused to take responsibility for the damage that resulted after the numerous nuclear tests.

"Contrary to the United States, we have acted in good faith. Therefore, we have more than enough moral reason to seek proper compensation and redress for the damage caused to our people and our islands," said the president in her speech. She made reference to surveys conducted by the United States in the 1950s, but which were first made public more than forty years later. They showed that the bombs that were tested in 'Operation Castle' and 'Bravo' in 1954, not 'only' caused radioactivity on the four atolls of Bikini, Enewetak, Rongelap and Utrik, which they had been misled to believe, but also on 18 other atolls and islands.

Hilda Heine does not seem like a woman who lets herself be brushed aside. Despite the marginal population of her country, she is tough with everything relating to international climate negotiations. And that she must, as without change the whole country will quickly disappear into the ocean.

In February 2018, the Prime Minister of the small country of Nauru and the Pacific Ambassador of Russia were on an official visit, and parts of the delegation ate dinner two tables away from me at Marshall Islands Resort, or MIR, as the luxury hotel is called here. It was quite fitting with Russian representation, even if the reference to the legendary space station was coincidental. They were likely putting the preliminaries in place for the meeting the following week, where even more heads of state from the Pacific were expected to discuss, among other things, rising sea levels and the anything but forgotten nuclear tests.

"She is a propellor. We see her constantly around the island, constantly with many balls in the air," I got to hear from one of those I ate pizza and drank beer with. I had been invited to sit at the same long table as a group of local friends. The official delegation a few metres away had a three-course dinner with wine and accompanied by a local band who sang something I did not understand a lot of. Then the language here is also quite something.

Marshallese belongs to the Austronesian family of languages, which extends geographically further than any other, from Madagascar all the way to Easter Island. The language family originates from Taiwan and is divided into two branches: the languages that are still spoken in Taiwan, or formosa, and the 880 languages that are spoken in the rest of this gigantic area. Here, tutu means to swim, tala means dollars, iik means fish, while pia means beer. One does not need to know so much more.

Exactly two hundred years passed from when Otto von Kotzebue made the trip here, until Hilda Heine became president. As I have mentioned, there is still a Russian Pacific ambassador in existence, and von Kotzebue, as a German-Estonian captain, had represented the Russian tsar for security reasons. But his escort was content with observing. Then American missionaries made the trip and built churches on every atoll, or at least almost. The islands were actually Spanish for ten years, subordinating to the Spanish capital of the 'area', Manila. The city, which is now the capital of the Philippines, is located more than 5,500 kilometres away from Majuro. The relatively short Spanish period did not stop German traders, who already had a base in Samoa. They sailed north in around 1850 and also established several trading posts on the Marshall Islands. This contributed to the islands becoming a German protectorate in 1885, but the occupation was purely transactional. Germany paid Spain 4.5 million dollars for the islands, but only after the pope himself became involved in the negotiations. After the First World War, the islands were transferred to Japan in 1922, Germany's ally in the region. Under the emperor, Japan used this opportunity to establish a number of military bases and one in Kwajalein exists to this day, but it is now American due to the outcome of the Second World War.

As a thought experiment, it is not entirely inconceivable that the Marshall Islands could one day become Norwegian, for example merged together with the nearest current Norwegian borough as the crow flies, which is called Sør-Varanger. The regions would not exactly be joined together, but that seems to be no obstacle. Sør-Varanger merged with the Marshall Islands would have become just like the new Kinn borough in Sogn og Fjordane county, which is a product of the merger of Flora and Måløy, and these two regions are not even connected together.

In many ways, Kiribati is not so joined together either. Back to the Pacific Ocean, and the island nation stretches across 3,300 kilometres from east to west, and those who are to travel from one side to the other have to do so via Fiji. The propeller plane of Air Kiribati cannot travel that far.

The Majuro Atoll is 50 kilometres long, but never more than a few hundred metres wide. travelling from one side to the other can therefore take a couple of hours on bad roads, or a few seconds.

There is shoreline everywhere here, so it's not too bad if parts of it are destroyed by old car wrecks and rubbish, or so people seem to think. The waves crash over the coral reef a few hundred metres away.

Outrigger canoes are over a thousand years old, but are still very common in the Marshall Islands. Even today, aerodynamics experts draw inspiration from these fast, near-perfectly designed canoes.

This girl was swimming alone just a few metres from the car wreck on the front side.

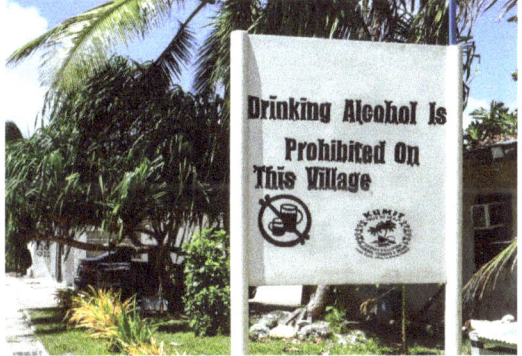

Local politicians have set up alcohol-free zones.

The support arm enables the outrigger to withstand a lot of wind and waves.

There are many wrecks to be seen here. They remain until they rust away as it costs too much to remove them.

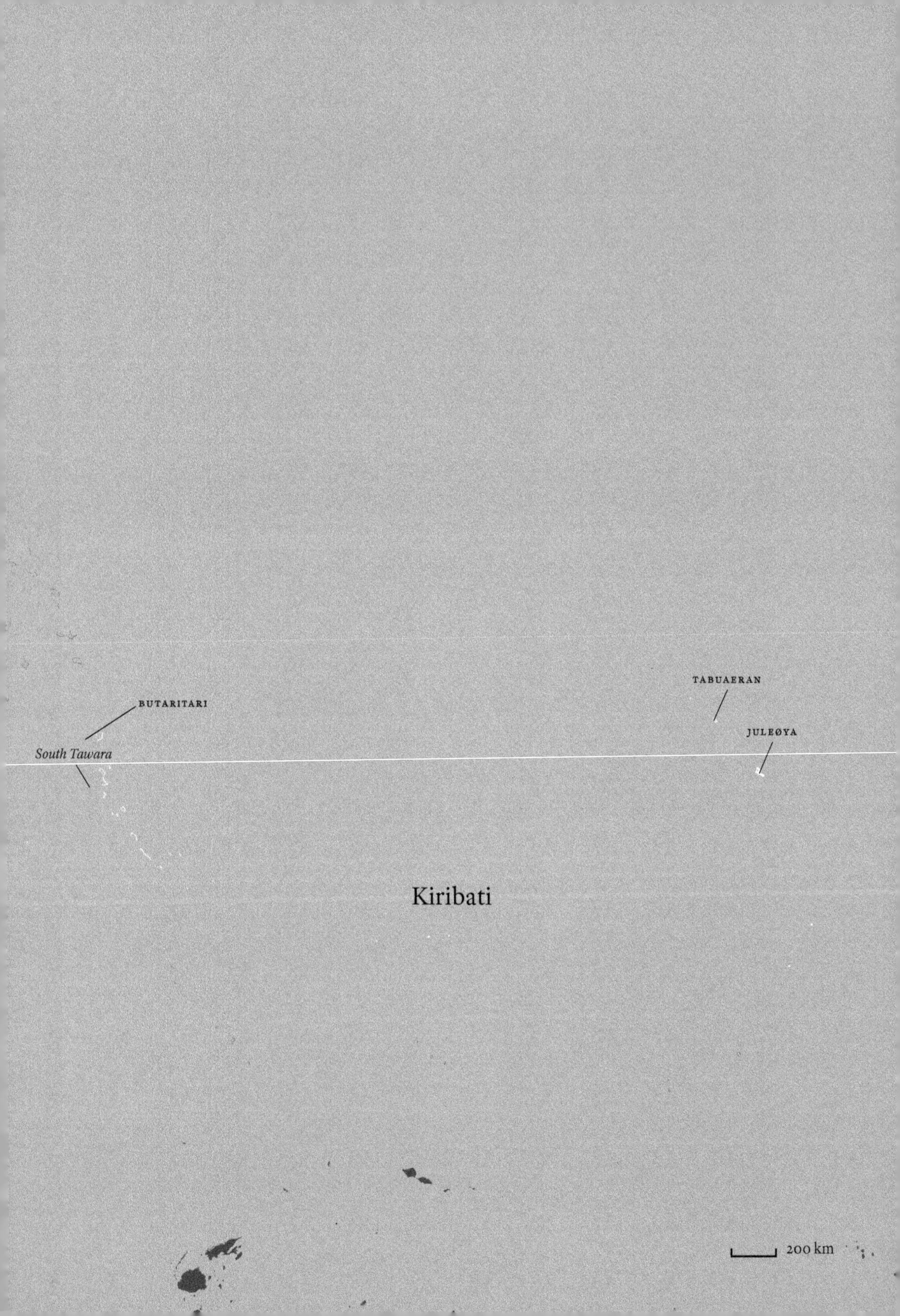

BUTARITARI

TABUAERAN

South Tawara

JULEØYA

Kiribati

200 km

9

Kiribati, Oceania

INHABITANTS: 110,000 (Wikipedia)
TOURISTS PER YEAR: 3,600 (garfors.com)
AREA: 811 square kilometres

THE COUNTRY WITH THE NAME pronounced 'Kiribas', will be one of the first countries to 'sink' if water levels rise significantly, and this is something the former president Anote Tong has spent a lot of time trying to bang home to the leaders of the rest of the in the world. Together with the countries of Tuvalu, Nauru, the Maldives and the New Zealand archipelago of Tokelau, Kiribati has set up its own forum to do what it possibly can against increasing water levels as a result of global warming. Tong, among other things, was at the forefront of a purchase of 20 square kilometres of land on Vanua Levu, the second largest island in Fiji. Initially, this was done to secure arable land, but looking ahead there could be need for a drastic emergency plan to relocate some of the population. The new president, Taneti Maamau, who has been in office since 2016, is somewhat more pragmatic when thinking about doomsday prophecies which could turn the country into a new Atlantis. He has kept a much lower profile on the subject and rather focused on optimising daily quality of life instead of maximizing the crisis, even though he is also fully aware of the challenges that rising water levels bring.

The reason Kiribati is pronounced Kiribas is because the letter s is not found in the alphabet, even though the sound is used. The solution is to write 'ti' or 'tu' when an s is to be pronounced. As a consequence, the name of the largest city is pronounced as Beso, even though it is written Betio. And Christmas Island, which is located towards the east, is actually called Kiritimati, but is pronounced Kirismas, close enough to Christmas that the island was renamed as that by someone with a need for simplification. It is worth noting that there is also another Christmas Island, but it is located in the Indian Ocean and is owned by Australia. Yet another mere hop across ocean to the east of Kiribati's Christmas Island is a lesser-known island that is the first in the world to greet every single new day, month, year, and millennium. Until recently the island was known as Caroline Island but has now been given a new and perhaps more appropriate name: Millennium Island. From there it is no more than a feeble stone's throw in the direction of America before one strikes the International Date Line and with a few strokes of an oar you are 24 hours back in time. Phileas Fogg had forgotten about its existence and thought he had lost his bet to go Around the world in 80 days, until his oversight was pointed out just in time to claim victory. Jules Verne was probably the first to use the Date Line as a literary device.

Kiribati. As in Kiribas. We are apparently talking about a Pacific paradise, and it is just that. There are white beaches everywhere, turquoise water in the lagoons and palm trees on every atoll and every island. But there is a great shortage of umbrella drinks, and the threat of going to 'sink' hangs over the inhabitants. The average income is low, so the sun factor ought to be high. The country covers an unassuming 811 square kilometres, not far off the twice the size of Oslo, Norway. But do not let that mislead you. Like the Federated States of Micronesia, the country is gigantic if one includes the ocean between the islands. The area defined as mainland is divided into 33 atolls as well as the island of Bansba. Since the 34 prominences are so scattered, Kiribati has the 12th largest exclusive economic zone in the world, covering an area of 3.4 million square kilometres, pushing the country up into the territory of great powers such as Brazil and Mexico. In comparison, Norway is the 17th largest with an area of 2.4 million square kilometres defined as an exclusive economic zone.

From the capital of South Tarawa in the west, it is almost six hours by jet to the aforementioned Kiritimati in the east. In theory, that is. The country has had a very limited domestic flight service for a long time, and if your plan is to travel from Christmas Island to Tarawa, then in 2018 it was actually fastest to travel via Nadi in Fiji, with Fiji Airways. Air Kiribati is actually planning a direct route between Christmas Island and Tarawa, for half the price, and with a notable time saving compared to the route via Fiji. But despite a limited domestic service, there are as many as five international airlines flying into the country, something that ensures quite a good frequency and a surprisingly expansive route offering that will get even better when Air Kiribati starts direct routes from South Tarawa to Brisbane in Australia and Nadi in Fiji at the end of 2019.

I was met by Theresa at the airport. It was 7.30pm, and she was going to take me by the safest possible means to the guesthouse I was to stay at, a few kilometres further north, in North Tarawa. North and South Tarawa form the Tarawa Atoll. The northern part covers various smaller islands with few inhabitants, and only the southernmost island has road access from the much more densely populated South Tarawa. We were going to Abatao, an island further to the north, and we were picked up by a guy in an aluminium taxi boat on a beach. At the other end, I waded ashore with my backpack.

"You're going to live there," said Theresa, while pointing to a wooden structure that stood on stilts in the lake. It was a kind of cabin, if I can call a construction without fixed walls such a thing. Had it not been for the outdoor lamp hanging from a palm tree, I would not have seen anything — it was as dark as inside a bag. Something that looked like a flimsy wooden bridge, went from the beach to this thatched hut with a floor that was almost two metres above the water. The bridge was also erected on stilts like the hut, untreated logs that had been pounded into the sand. There was a layer of beams on top of these, and lying at the very top were rough wooden planks acting like crossbeams and also as the floor. They were nailed down and had turned grey many years ago. It creaked with every step I took, but the bridge still felt reasonably stable. I put my backpack in the hut which didn't have a door or lock, before I waded around it, in the dark. The water only reached to my knees — the bridge was not strictly necessary but made it easier to get to and fro and made the guesthouse fairly wheelchair accessible. There was a guardrail along the entire length of the 30-metre-long bridge, and I enjoyed leaning on it and just looking as far out to sea as possible in the dim light from the lamp. Far, far away I glimpsed light that reflected in the water — it had to be from Betio. It was just magical thinking that I was looking at the actual Pacific Ocean — even though I was strictly in a lagoon, but right in the middle of the Pacific Ocean all the same. A small white beach, 10—12 metres wide, lay on one side of the bridge. All of a sudden, I noticed the beach crabs. An innumerable number of beach crabs. One by one they came up from different holes in the sand. And then they stood there peering back. A staring competition. Could they see so far with their eyes on stalks? They had at least sensed something, because the moment I made an abrupt movement, they crawled at a devilish pace back down into their burrows, before sneaking back up a few seconds later, to carry on having a look.

My residence for the next few days was spartanly decorated. A chair and a table with a green tablecloth stood on the floor. The same can be said for the 'bed'. A white mosquito net hung over a white mattress that lay directly on some woven bamboo mats, which in turn lay straight on the floor made of thick bamboo poles. In some places I could see between the poles and down to the water beneath. Bamboo mats hung on two sides of the cabin, mostly to provide a little privacy. I was alone this time, but the mattress seemed to be made for two — it was as wide as my double bed back home. I lay down and looked up at the woven thatched ceiling. The candle flickered, and the shadows played out a delightful show on the ceiling. It did not seem to disturb the three salamanders that were upside down on the ceiling, hoping for an immediate insect invasion. The hut had electricity, but I chose candlelight, which gave a completely different atmosphere. The small two-litre fire extinguisher was at the ready in a corner, just in case.

The best thing about sleeping in the thatched hut above the sea however was the 'sound system' — the sound of small waves rippling gently passed the poles I depended upon to remain hovering above the surface of the water. And in the background was the quite uniform and continuous roar from the waves that crashed into the coral reef system a few kilometres away. A never unwelcome breeze made it extra refreshing to lie there without

the white top sheet on me, in the 23-26 degrees heat. Duvets are nowhere to be seen here, but then the temperature never changed much beyond this range of three degrees. Not at night, at least. During the day it was warmer, but there was almost always a breeze coming off the water surface.

The disadvantage of living like this is that you easily wake with the sun, at six in the morning. Luckily, I am used to the midnight sun at my cabin in Skjomen, so I was able to sleep a couple of hours longer and was only woken by Theresa, who hit a metal drum. It was breakfast and time for thin French pancakes. She had cooked ten, just in case. I was not complaining, they tasted excellent! A contributing factor was a dark brown coconut-based syrup that was used as a 100 percent natural sweetener. The homemade syrup was served in a glass bottle that is usually used for the world's best-known drink.

"By the way, did you know we have 250 words for coconut?" she asked. I was immediately sceptical. It sounded like the so-called myth that the Inuit have hundreds of words for snow. Anthropologist Franz Boas travelled all over northern Canada in the 1880s, studying the life of the Inuit for a long period of time. In the Handbook of American Indian Languages, published in 1911, he claimed that the Inuit, or Eskimos, as he referred to them, had dozens of words for snow. Aqilokoq is, for example, slow-falling snow, while piegnartoq is the snow that is best for sledging. There are now various Inuit dialects, but those spoken in the Nunavik region of Canada have at least 53 words for snow, including matsaaruti for wet snow and pukak, which are crystallised snowflakes that look like salt. This was long seen as a myth, but it is actually true according to the Washington Post. To a large extent, polysynthesis is at play here, which allows the person speaking to connect words to the main word. In this sense, we have hundreds of words for snow in Norwegian as well. Let me mention just a few - snøball (snowball), snøhòle (snowhole), snøstorm (snowstorm), snøscooter (snow scooter), snøplog (snowplough), snømann (snowman), snøkatt (snowcat) and snøhund (snowdog).

We, in Norway, don't need to go further than to the Sami to find 300 words that have to do with ice and snow. And even that pales in comparison to what is the most important thing to the people living with nature in the north: the reindeer. There are over a thousand Sami words that are to describe the animal many of them make a living from.

In Kiribati, it is coconuts, not snow or reindeer, that have traditionally been most important for their livelihood. And Theresa explained.

"Listen carefully, because this is going to go quickly," she smiled. "Te-nii is the coconut plant itself, te-ben is the fruit, te-ewanin is the husk, and te-moimoto is coconut water," she explained enthusiastically.

"Te moi moto," I repeated.

"No, faster. Temoimoto!" she corrected.

"I am not going to summarise our entire coconut vocabulary, but a coconut leaf is called te-baa, at least until it turns brown. Then it changes name to te-baanni. But I don't want to bother you anymore. Enjoy the pancakes," she said and went back to the kitchen.

Many months later, back at home in Henrik Klausens Street in Oslo, I came by the Kiribati Communication and Culture Handbook from 1979 and was able to establish that Theresa was absolutely right. I also found out from it that a tree that has not yet produced coconuts is called te-uto. But enough coconut talk. It is even more remarkable that there is not a single word for shell in a country with countless beaches.

Theresa told me later that there are 300 people living on Abatao, with people largely make a living from coconuts and some fishing. In addition to the teachers at the school, the employees at a small boat builder and Theresa and her colleagues, who run bungalow rentals. She comes from Butaritari herself, an atoll 200 kilometres north of the capital. Butaritari is the most fertile and fruitful atoll here, and most of the 4,000 inhabitants live primarily off agriculture which, among other things, produces breadfruit, bananas, papayas, cucumbers, cabbage, and pumpkins. The atoll is the second northernmost atoll in the entire country, and it rains far more there than in central areas.

"But with the vessels that ply their trade in this area, the trip there takes two days," she sighed. In Kiribati, they can only dream about express boats like the ones serving Norway along the western fjords or between Larvik and Hirtshals into Denmark.

The 23-year-old had completed high school and dreamed of going to university. But as the youngest of six, and especially since all the others were brothers, she was at the back of the queue for parental financing, and she had decided to try to earn enough money herself to be able to continue with higher education.

"I want to study something in art. But it costs 300 Australian dollars a year to go to university, for seven semesters. So now I am saving what I can."

Theresa told me that wages are better in Abatao than in the north, so with that she had taken up her backpack and moved. It was only when I asked her to write down her email that I found out Theresa was not called Theresa at all. I had again forgotten the little detail of the Kiribati S. Theresa was of course called Teretia, albeit pronounced Theresa.

The large distances between the islands mean that Kiribati controls enormous fishing resources, and tuna is the most important income source. The country has committed to sustainable fishing and is inspected by independent local inspectors employed by the UN and the World Bank. But it turned out that fishing was by no means especially sustainable, and that the inspectors are by no means independent. I met a guy from the UN of my own age who had been in Kiribati for a long period of time. He had gotten to know the fishermen and helicopter pilots well. The latter are in fact important in fishing, and all self-respecting fishing boats have their own helicopters. The helicopter pilot takes off and scouts for shoals of dolphin or tuna. By using the rotor blades in a certain manner, the pilot can whip up the surface of the sea and by doing so attracts the playful dolphins to the surface. Such can they control the tuna better and in a much more efficient way than a shepherd can control his sheep, even with the excellent help of well-trained shepherd dogs.

"It's reprehensible and about as far from being sustainable as it gets. When the pilot has control of the shoal of fish and toys with them, the fishing boat lays out the net around the fish which can be up to 1.5 kilometres long. The fish don't stand a chance, and they empty area after area of fish," the man from the World Bank told me. The only thing preventing complete overfishing is the fact that the boats are relatively slow and are filled up quickly.

"But what about the local inspectors?" I asked. He almost snorted in response.

"Ha! They are buttered up in any possible way by helicopter pilots and fishing boat captains who have been given a generous budget for such by the shipping company. The inspectors earn almost nothing, so being able to stay in a hotel with the fishermen and get pissed with them is a great bonus. They are bought beers. Lots of beers. And sometimes ladies too, just to ensure extra loyalty. If the shipping company knows that they have been with prostitutes, then it is fairly certain that the inspectors are not going to speak negatively about them. And if they still do that, then the wives will get a full report. As you can bet, they never report that there is something wrong going on. Sustainable my ass!" the man snorted.

But it is not just questionable inspector activities that stink when it comes to tuna in this area. The value of tuna from Kiribati and Tuvalu caught is at least three times higher than the total gross domestic product in these countries. How is that possible? Because most of the fish is pulled up and sold on by foreign fishing vessels. Local vessels in Kiribati and Tuvalu pull up only a quarter of the total tuna catch in the so-called exclusive economic areas that the countries 'control'. In spite of that, they earn a little from foreign vessels through fishing licenses and trade, and potentially through taxes from any locals that are employed on the foreign vessels. Foreign fishing companies also catch a lot of tuna in international waters, which also reduces the supply of fish within the respective exclusive economic zones. The seven countries in the Pacific with the largest tuna catches account for between 17 and 53 percent of all tuna taken from the Pacific, according to the Statistical Yearbook for Asia and the Pacific 2015. Fishing inspectors have a difficult time here in several ways, and there are significant unreported dark figures, leading to the percentage gape. The rest is caught in other countries or in international waters.

After several nights in the bungalow over the Pacific Ocean, I decided to travel to Betio, the largest city in the country, which is located 30 kilometres away, along the main road. There is never more than a couple of hundred meters between the road and the sea. In some places, the waves smash just 2-3 metres from either side of the road, if nothing else it is new and has been built behind wave barriers to avoid erosion. I hitchhiked across the strait. The ferryman wanted half an Australian dollar, or just over three Norwegian kroner, for the trip taking thirty seconds in the aluminium boat.

I paid, waded ashore in the soft sand, and sat on a rock at the water's edge to remove the grains of sand on my feet before putting on my socks and blue-brown trainers. Then I began to walk towards Betio. It was 2-3 kilometres to the nearest bus stop, so I hoped to get a seat on one of the minibuses that continuously run back and forth on the main road in Kiribati. Before I had gone 500 metres, a small Toyota stopped. A mother was driving, with her daughter of about 12 years old sitting in the front.

"Are you going far, or what?" shouted the mother.

"To Betio," I replied.

"Blimey. But jump in, we can at least drive you to the bridge. You can get a bus from there."

It was much desired after being in the sun. They dropped me off just before the bridge, and I crossed over to South Tarawa, managing to walk no more than 300-400 metres before a new car stopped — this time a Mercedes.

"Grab a seat," said a smiling guy around 25 years old through the open window on the passenger side.

"Where are you going to?" it was my turn to ask.

"Where the road goes," he laughed heartily, opening the door from the inside. "Come on, I'm not dangerous!"

I wasn't afraid of anything either. In countries where few people have a car, it is common to hitchhike and almost have an expectation that drivers with free space will pick up hitchhikers. It is inconceivable to associate hitchhiking with anything alarming, perhaps with the unfortunate exception of women out in the dark of night.

Betio was where the road went. He had to ask me twice, but no more. I never got to take a bus, but they do only cost a few pennies. The driver would not entertain the notion of payment. But I did not get much more out of him, despite the fact that he seemingly worked in New Zealand and ought to have spoken adequate English. He dropped me off outside Betio Lodge, which I had stayed at five years earlier. Since the last time I was there, they had opened a new bar close to the reception. It was called Beer & Bullshit.

"We provide the beer, they provide the bullshit," the bartender explained, grinning.

"Yes, there is plenty where that comes from," added one of the regulars, who was sitting at a table nearby, before he got up and left.

He was quickly replaced, by a guy I knew I had seen before at that. On my last four flights, I had noticed the huge hulk of a man travelling in fine and seemingly expensive work clothes. We had travelled from Port Moresby via Honiara and to Port Vila one day, and then back to Honiara and then to Tarawa, both on the same plane. I had stood behind him in the check-in queue and given a nod, but we had not properly greeted each other. We did it at that moment, almost as if we were old acquaintances.

"So, who do we have here? The man with the backpack! My name is Danial," he said and stretched out his paw.

It turned out that Danial Rochford was one of the bosses at Air Kiribati, the largest airline in the country. They were investing now in new planes and new routes. Three days later, for example, the first commercial flight to Tuvalu was going to take off. If only I had known, I would have planned a much shorter and easier itinerary in Oceania. As it is now, the current itineraries are too complicated for a great number of tourists to make the trip.

It turned out that Australian Danial only lived in Kiribati about half the time with work, and that officially he actually lived in Port Vila with his wife. As an aside, the capital of Vanuatu is the only capital that rhymes with the Norwegian word for despair, 'fortvila'.

As we were now friends, I was introduced in production line fashion to ministers, top commanders and various Australian military people who were on training missions in Betio. We were twelve men and two women in the bar, around a wooden table that was far too small.

"Minister, you must meet Gunnar. He has been to every country in the world and is writing a book about Kiribati. If you behave yourself, you may get a mention," said Danial to the Minister of Culture and smiled. The minister, who is also responsible for tourism, became interested all of a sudden. Among other things, I gained insight into the country's tourism strategy, and found out that the official number of 5,000 tourists also included businesspeople, and that the actual number of tourists was 3,600. The vast majority of these come to Kiritimati. Christmas Island is a dream for fly fishermen, divers, and surfers, while the island of Tabuaeran — just a little hop to the northwest — is one of the world's ultimate destinations for surfing. It is not only about perfect waves, but also remoteness, with few travelling there.

"So, the best surfers in the world — especially the Americans — surf in peace. And of course, Air Kiribati flies there," grinned Danial and took a sip of beer. This did not qualify at all as 'bullshit'...

Even though the introductions by Danial worked well, it was difficult getting to know so many all at once. As it was a well-travelled group, I decided to run a semi-advanced geography quiz. After all, I had been introduced as a globetrotter, and worse. The legitimacy should be in place.

"People, you have travelled a lot. Here's something for you to chew on. There are three countries in the world with names that are four letters that also have a capital of four letters. Which ones?"

The question started a discussion and was a good icebreaker.

"Cuba!" cried James. As a retired businessman and former CEO of several European companies, he now had enough money to travel wherever he wanted, and to do whatever he wanted. Over the last two years, that meant hanging out in Kiribati. He had found himself a local lady and very much liked being at Beer & Bullshit. The man was about 70 years old, 1.80m tall and thin. His face was marked by multiple G&Ts throughout the years.

"What is the name of the capital there?" I asked.

"Fuck, yes, it's Havana. Back to the start."

I had to give them a little hint: that they were to be found in three different continents. After five minutes they had completed the country and city located in Oceania. It took 20 minutes for them to come up with the South American answer, while the African one was difficult to fetch up and demanded another round of drinks.

"Chad or Togo," Danial cried out. In the end, I had to contribute towards getting the name of the capital right.

I have kept in touch with Danial since, who told me that he has used the quiz on friends across large parts of the Pacific. The three countries are Fiji, Peru, and Togo, with the capitals being Suva, Lima, and Lome.

"I love a good quiz. Do you have more?" James asked. Several of the others yelled out around the table. They liked it, and it meant that I could talk to everyone. I banged out a few more, slightly simpler questions. A good atmosphere. And it only got better.

Suddenly Jason arrived, whom I knew from my first visit in 2013. And not only that, but he had also brought with him Karotu (pronounced: Kaross), his best friend, whom I had met before. Five years earlier, they had invited me to their table in the sand where they were sitting at Captain's Bar near the beach. The captain was now consigned to history, and they had found a new regular haunt in Beer & Bullshit. There were hugs all round. They had not quite expected to see me again. The duo clearly knew everyone around the table, said hello, found themselves a plastic chair each from a neighbouring table and sat down.

If there was a leader amongst the gang, then it was Derek. He had come to Kiribati from Wales almost fifty years ago and was as good as local now. He spoke Kiribati and owned several companies here. The fact that he had the sales rights for the beer brand XXXX, popularly called quadruple X, meant he was financially secure. The most popular beer in the country is drunk with both hands and well so here. He was now onto his second Kiribati wife. A bit special as wife number two was the sister of wife number one. I would have liked to have been a fly on the wall when that came out. But now all three are friends and reconciled. It meant that the kids from the two relationships were in a somewhat closer family situation than is completely normal as well.

The next day, Derek's grandson was going to be celebrating his first birthday. In Kiribati and several other Pacific countries, it is the most important birthday in life.

"Healthcare here is not out of this world and has likely never been so. Infant mortality is high, though declining. So, if you survive the first year, it's an achievement. An achievement that really must be celebrated," explained Derek.

Usually this means a party for family and friends at home in the garden. When Derek is your grandfather, then there is no holding back the party. He had rented the whole sports complex for the country, including the indoor arena for basketball, just in case it rained. And he had invited 300 people. Derek had taken a notice and had liked how well my quiz gone down.

"Gunnar, you have to come to my grandson's birthday tomorrow. As a thank you for holding an excellent quiz. It's going to be a big party. So big that no one will be at Beer & Bullshit anyway. Just put on a green shirt. Here, each island has its own colour, and green is the colour of the island that Randall's grandmother comes from," he explained.

I had a paper invitation in hand three minutes later. One of Derek's lackies had sorted it out. The Welshman liked things to happen quickly.

The next day I had to find a green shirt. That would usually not be such a big task, but then Betio is not your usual city. There is virtually not a single clothing store in existence here. But in most kiosks and supermarkets they have various clothes for sale. Just not green shirts for men. I looked over the selection in three kiosks and five different types of shops before I found a kind of greenish looking shirt. As in luminescent lime green with a hefty reflective yellow glint — with some dark grey patterned spots. Green enough, I hoped.

I strolled towards the sports complex but did not manage to get far before I was spotted up by one of the guys from the previous night. This was Kiribati, a stronghold for hospitality. He and his wife were driving to the party and of course let me have a lift, even though the sports complex was less than 500 metres away. Dedicated parking guards showed us where to park before we jumped out. Outside of the complex, tables and chairs had been put out in front of a stage. There were various 'Randall 1 year' posters hanging in the vicinity, and his name was written in large golden balloon letters. They were hanging over stage.

There was going to be a lot of entertainment. A traditional local dance group of 25 people in bast skirts delivered such an impressive song and dance show that there can't have been anyone left without goosebumps amongst the audience. In addition, there were performances from smaller dance groups and singers, and Randall's parents said suitably choice words and thanked everyone for their attendance before the microphone was given to a nun who blessed everyone who had come on such an important day as this and gave thanks for the food. The serving staff numbered between 20 and 30, and seven of these were responsible for their own enormous pig that was skewered on a metal spit over glowing coals. There four lengthy tables, each at least 10 meters long, with side dishes and other food. There were salads, boiled potatoes, rice, French fries, chicken, steak, beef patties, prawns, crayfish and yes, even lobster. People could serve themselves from both sides of the long tables or get some pork from one of the grills. The selection was simply too large and dispersed for any notion of congestion or queues.

Derek also held a speech.

"Now I'm not especially fond of kids, so I usually never hold my grandchildren any longer than two minutes. But Randall is a good guy, and we get along very well, so I can hold him for four minutes," he joked from the stage, before he invited his son's mother-in-law to dance. After that the dance floor was open for everybody. James, of course, was straight up on his feet and used the opportunity to invite the nun to dance. She was more sporting than most and said yes. She was the swung around until her shawl fell off. Then she stopped, but not for any other reason than to pick up the garment before she continued to dance. James grinned in triumph. It is not every day one gets to dance with a nun.

After a good half hour of dancing to live music, Derek went up on the stage again. This time he invited curiously onlooking villagers to help themselves from the buffet. And they sure did. There is widespread poverty in Tarawa, and some had brought bags with them that they filled with food. Others filled pockets or just their mouths. An invitation like this is commonplace in Kiribati. Those who have a lot, try to give to those without, at celebrations and parties. A fine tradition, although most is perhaps for bettering their own conscience. It is not the thought that counts, but the actual deeds. All good deeds make things a little better than they were before — the same cannot be said about thoughts.

The Kiribati language is not widely used anywhere else within or outside of the Pacific Ocean and has been spoken here for between 5,000 and 800 years. The historians have not been able to be any more precise than that. In addition to the challenges of lacking s in the alphabet, visitors find out quickly how to greet each other. I heard 'ko na mauri!' or usually just 'mauri!' almost all the time when I wandered around in the tropical heat of Betio. Such is how one greets each other, especially the first time, or when it has been a while since the last time. The greeting from smiling people, came without exception. The expression implies 'you will be well' and has similarities with the Norwegian goodbye, ha det bra, 'have it well'. Not before too long I began to say 'mauri!' to everyone as well. But even such a seemingly simple word could not be said without a Norwegian accent. It was something with my u. It is questionable whether I will ever merge unnoticed into Kiribati society.

Another language that appears in unexpected places is Spanish. Although not in Kiribati or the Pacific Ocean, but in Africa. There, it can only be used in one of 55 countries, which happens to also be eighth least visited.

Pancakes and coffee for breakfast on a Pacific island.

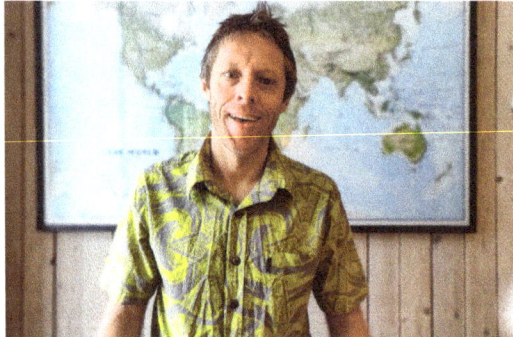

Green is the colour of the island the one-year-old Jubilee's grandmother is from and thus became the dress code for the party.

One of eight whole roasted pigs. At the end of the party, the leftovers were given away to poor neighbours.

The slogan of this bar: "we have the beer, you bring the bullshit!"

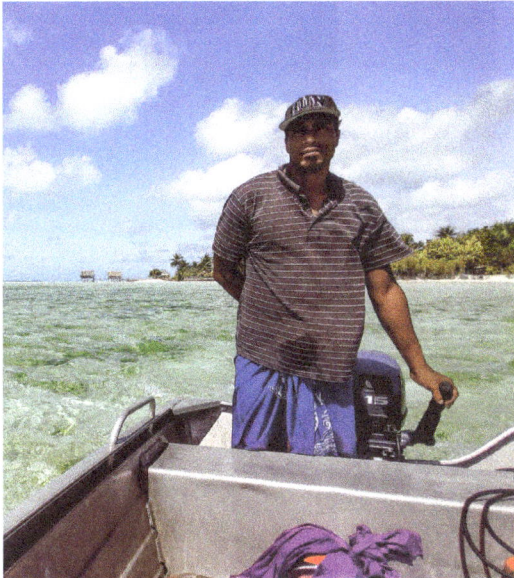

The skipper takes locals and travellers between two islands in North Tarawa in two minutes. It costs half a dollar.

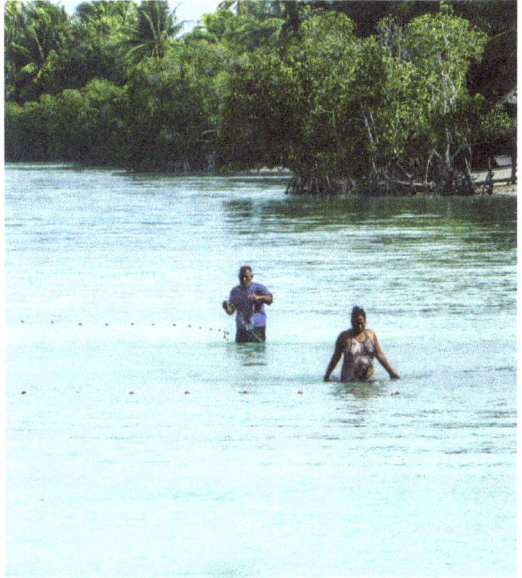

This couple collaborate on old-fashioned net fishing.

On a jog, I was followed by these curious kids.

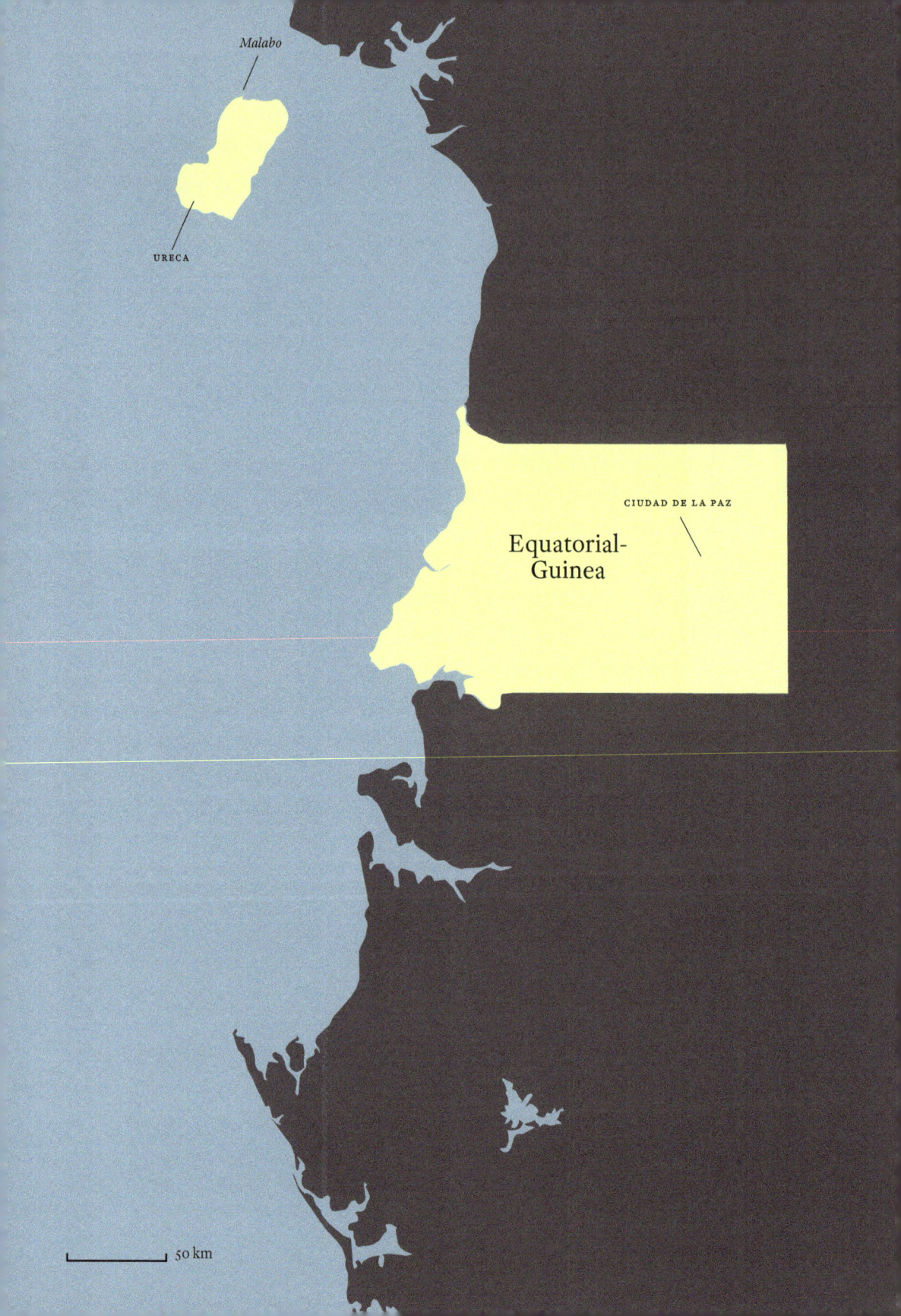

Malabo

URECA

Equatorial-
Guinea

CIUDAD DE LA PAZ

50 km

8

Equatorial-Guinea, Africa

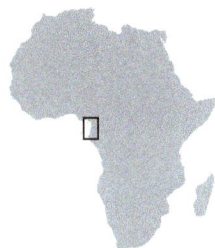

INHABITANTS: 1,200,000 (Wikipedia)
TOURISTS PER YEAR: 2,400 (garfors.com)
AREA: 28,050 square kilometres

THE ONLY SPANISH-SPEAKING COUNTRY in Africa has a vast amount of oil but struggles with enormous inequality between rich and poor. If one just looks at the numbers; each of the 1.2 million inhabitants has more money to squander than is the case in any other country in Africa, with the exception of the holiday resort of the Seychelles. But as is too often the case, the statistics lie. The vast majority never see a single oil dollar. President Teodoro Obiang Nguema Mbasogo, or just Obiang as the locals call him, is very capable at spending money on those close to him. He has led the country since 1979, which means only the president of the neighbouring country of Cameroon has sat as head of state longer. With a lot of money divided among a few at the top, is not surprising that the country is one of the most corrupt in the world, according to Transparency International. But most things have to be put into perspective.

"Most people are too young to know of any other president, and those who are old enough remember a president who was far worse!" Justin Jay told me. I met the dark blonde American in his thirties at a restaurant in the capital Malabo.

Despite all one can say about Obiang, it was he who ruled from what was truly a tyrant, even a relative of his. Macías Nguema was Obiang's uncle and ruled the country from independence in 1968 until he was removed from power and then executed. During that time, Nguema, who belonged to the dominant fango tribe, had ruled with an iron fist for eleven years, and 20 per cent of the country's citizens had fled. Not everyone could — many ended up in the famed Black Beach Prison. It has little to do with the beach — involving mostly brutal treatment of inmates, including torture and extremely small meal rations. After a while many believed that Nguema had gone insane. Or, the power had really gone to his head, at least. Though the national motto he introduced the year before he was executed is perhaps leaning towards insanity: 'There is no other god than Macías Nguema.'

In the first paragraph of the constitution, he introduced the death penalty in 1971 for anyone who made threats against him or the government, and an insult against the aforementioned parties can result in 30 years imprisonment. The following year, to prevent opposition, he merged all the political parties into one common national party and appointed himself president for life. No one could protest with the aforementioned laws. By that I mean, of course, before the nephew arranged a successful coup and took the life of his Uncle Macías in 1979. He had long been nicknamed 'Africa's Dachau' by then, after the concentration camp in Nazi Germany.

Obiang is by all means relatively normal, as a leader of a one-party state. Basically, he is just another a dictator, but he's far better than his uncle, and for people here that is seemingly all they care about. At least as long as Obiang and his son are looked upon as rich and continue to give money for parties in the villages and apparent speeches against Western countries. That's enough for them to tolerate him. This stems largely from the difference between rich and poor in Africa. Justin elaborated.

"If the president's son drives around in one of his Lamborghinis, they just smile and point. There is no anger over the misuse of government funds. But then here it is also the case that those with power exploit it. They would have done the same themselves if they had had the chance, such is life. As long as there is no genocide, slavery or basic discontentment, people do not complain."

Obiang could have done incredibly more for his citizens, but it seems like the citizens believe he is doing enough and is perfectly fine. Then it only remains to convince potential visitors of the same thing. If all at once the government dropped the dictatorship nonsense and the difficult visa processes, then they could strike it big in tourism. It is only six hours away by plane from Madrid, and not surprisingly there are direct flights to Malabo from the former colonial power.

Equatorial Guinea is one of only four mainland countries to have its capital on an island. The others are Denmark, Gambia, and the United Arab Emirates. The capital island here is called Bioko, and is located in the Gulf of Guinea, less than 50 kilometres west of the coast of Cameroon and just over 200 kilometres northeast of São Tomé and Príncipe. Bioko is the size of a medium sized county in Norway, while the mainland is 13 times larger and is called Río Muni. The almost quadratic area lies 150 kilometres southeast of Bioko between Gabon and Cameroon on the African continent, while the country as a whole is the size of the Solomon Islands.

It was in no way a special interest in geography, politics or human rights violations that compelled Justin travel to Equatorial Guinea. It was a National Geographic magazine he read while sitting on the toilet in Las Vegas. He had started in his first job in the gambling town after completing his biology studies. The article in the August 2008 edition about the African monkey island, Bioko, had made an impression. Some of National Geographic's best photographers had been to Equatorial Guinea and taken pictures of the stunning landscape rich in biodiversity. The article emphasised primates and the snipers threatening them. The photographers had taken some unbelievable pictures, but several times they referred to a primate they really wanted to photograph but could not find: the drill monkey.

One of Justin's colleagues quit two years later and travelled to Africa to start as a researcher in the wilderness. It tempted Justin so much that he started to look for jobs in the same continent as well. In 2010 he travelled to precisely Bioko to work with turtles. In the south of the island there is almost only jungle and some of the most wonderful and underrated beaches in the world, although with strong competition from some of the Pacific Ocean countries.

In Bioko, Justin learned a lot about drill monkeys, which are relatives of the baboons, but he did not see a single animal despite there being more animal species per square kilometre here than in any other country in Africa. After a few months, the American was told by other researchers that the drill monkeys did not live on the island in any case, so the whole thing began to sound like a myth. But instead of giving up, he decided to make a wholehearted effort to find out once and for all if this was correct or not.

"Every day after work I went into the forest and started looking for signs. But people did not even know what they ate, so I started out completely afresh. Several weeks went by without me finding a single sign. In the end, I believed I was onto something, so I sat an entire weekend by a tree next to a river. And suddenly I saw my first drill monkey! After that I began to be pretty good at finding, filming, and photographing them," said Justin enthusiastically, taking a short break to drink water from the metal bottle he always had with him.

He has been working on a new film since 2015. It has the working title The Lost Kings of Bioko and will be launched at the documentary film festival in Wales in 2019. He reckons the film will be a sensation in the animal film world. Together with his photographers, Justin Jay is the only one to have filmed the drill monkey.

He lives in the country only outside the rainy season himself, which lasts from May to October, but altogether he has been in Equatorial Guinea for several years. This means that Justin has been touched by corruption in many ways.

"Not so long ago, I experienced being stopped by a policeman who jumped into the road from behind a car and held his hands up high while yelling loudly. So as not to knock him over, I had to break hard. Afterwards he walked calmly over to my window, which I rolled down. He pointed to the ground and said: 'There is a pedestrian crossing here — it is illegal to stop here!'" grinned Justin. Then followed the inevitable — that there was no reason in pointing out that he would never have stopped right there if the policeman had not jumped out in true kamikaze style in front of the car.

"But I managed, if nothing else, to negotiate paying only a 40 dollar fine, not 250, which he had originally asked for," said Justin, and stretched out his hands in frustration.

Certainly, the policeman gets credit for creativity. But such corrupt behaviour tends

to spread rapidly in a society and can suddenly turn on the policeman in the small village we had passed. Besides, he had likely learned the ways from the police chief higher up in the hierarchy.

Malabo is in part a very modern city, due alone to the at least 8 billion dollars in annual oil revenues over many years. The former colonial power is still visible through elements of Spanish architecture in areas where the modern buildings built from brick and metal, with large windows, have not taken over. Most of them have been built by Chinese workers, and many are fully or partially financed from Chinese money. China is staking billions upon billions of dollars in Africa and is leaving lasting traces on the continent. In return, they secure lucrative contracts for themselves giving advantageous access to natural resources. I noticed, amongst other things, how much the world's second largest economy is really investing, every time I took an internal flight in Africa. As a rule, between 10 and 20 percent of the passengers were Chinese. Many of the construction workers from the Middle Kingdom have now left the country, but it says a lot that a local boy, of around eight years old, thought I was Chinese.

"Ni hao!" he said to me.

Two days later I met Joseph, a local businessman, on a street in the centre of the capital. I likely looked a little lost, and the 25-year-old asked what I was looking for, and what I was doing in Malabo.

"Nothing in particular. I'm a tourist."

"You've got to be kidding! There are almost no tourists here. But you do not look like a welder either."

I'm not sure whether it was meant as a compliment, or not. I told him I really wanted to travel around Bioko and asked if he knew of a driver. A few phone calls later, the driver was fixed, and the price agreed. Joseph wanted to join me and promised that they would pick me up after breakfast the next morning.

The same evening I tried to hail a taxi outside a restaurant. I was on my way home to my Ibis hotel. The French low-priced chain throws hotel rooms at you for a few medium notes at 3499 hotels around the world. But not in Malabo. They wanted over 100 dollars for an extremely standardised and boring room with a modular bathroom, four kilometres outside of the centre. And that was for a single room. Just as well I travelled alone. I had walked the 4-5 kilometres into the centre but intended not to walk back in the dark — I had heard about quite a few robberies and violent events. So, I got ready to stop a taxi outside the restaurant I had eaten at. Two middle-aged Spaniards slammed on the breaks in their big white four-wheel drive as soon as they saw me.

"Are you crazy, boy?" It's dangerous to take a taxi here, anyone can pick you up and rob you. Where are you going to?" asked the driver, and virtually ordered me into the car. Then came this paradoxical thought that he had just done exactly what he had warned me of the second before, and even more paradoxical in that I actually agreed.

That's how I got home in a just few minutes, in any case. Before I was dropped off outside Ibis, I had to faithfully swear to ask the front desk to call an official taxi company the next time I was going somewhere. I didn't mention to them that I was going on an excursion the next day with a local guy I had hung out with for ten minutes. I tried to pay them for the trouble, but I could just forget about that.

"We Europeans stick together. At least as long as you continue producing the raw material for our bacalao up there in the north," they chuckled before they drove to their home. They apparently worked in finance in Equatorial Guinea. I had taken that as a sign that I was not to ask anything else.

I have been warned against doing such things now many times before, and it has always turned out fine, but I thought I had surely been robbed enough for this year. Five months earlier, I had been attacked by two large guys in Libreville in Gabon, 'just across the pond', or rather on the mainland a little further south. I had been walking on the street, completely unprepared, when one of them quite literally jumped on me from behind while the other grabbed my arm and started 'shooting' at me with an electric pistol, though it couldn't have had many volts as I didn't notice a shock while I fought against the two attackers the best I could. Adrenaline must have been released at record speed, and I was livid with rage. Somehow, I managed to pull the two of them the distance needed down to the lit main street I had only just walked away from. Like trolls, they too were frightened by the light and bolted at once. I stood there with a torn T-shirt and missing the world's first DAB phone. The LG mobile only cost a couple of a few hundred dollars, so they had not gotten away with a top model, but for me it was annoying enough. I had managed to save passports and money from their clutches.

I had gone to Gabon to get a visa for Equatorial Guinea, one of the most difficult countries in the world to get a visa for. That is to say, for everyone other than those with a passport from the United States. They do not need a visa — likely an old oil-related agreement is behind it. It isn't exactly bristling with American tourists either, but they can at least travel without worrying about whether they will get a visa or not. The country operates a bit like Saudi Arabia, with both having sufficient oil revenues to not need tourist dollars. It is therefore a bureaucratic hell for most people to get a tourist visa. On my first trip here in 2011, an audience with the ambassador in Libreville had emanated in a visa at the normal hourly rate, but not this time. The third secretary promised me a visa within 20 minutes for 700 dollars, or 10 times the normal price. What a corrupt bastard.

I am anything but a supporter of passing money under the table and turned down the offer. But then I was left standing there with a bit of a problem. How was I going to enter Equatorial Guinea? Embassy visits to Cotonou, Accra, Douala, Kinshasa, and a village well outside N'Djamena in Chad were all fruitless. I could just forget about getting a visa in those places anyway, unless I maybe promised to slide big money under the table. I was left with one promising alternative: London.

With 100 pounds, a police certificate, a bank statement with 2,000 pounds in the account and copies of plane tickets and hotels, it finally worked out well in the end. I even received a receipt that was both stamped and signed. And four working days later, my passport was complete with the visa mark. Bingo.

Here was I, sitting and drinking coffee in the reception of the world's most expensive Ibis hotel, the morning after the night-time hitchhike with the Spaniards. A large black pickup waltzed into the car park. Joseph came out and strolled across the asphalt and into the hotel, together with two others. He introduced me to driver Moreno and Alex, the embodiment of a 100-kilo division wrestler. Not only was I going to travel around the island with two local wannabe taxi heroes that I had indirectly been warned about, but now three, including a guy who could crush me to bits with a well-placed right shoulder. For the sake of safety, he sat next to me in the back seat. I had my backpack with me as I was tired of paying the extortionate price of the Ibis. The plan was to find a new hotel, and it was obvious to everybody in the car that I had all my worldly things with me. The first stop was a petrol station.

"We need money for gas," said Joseph. He was the only one who spoke English.

I handed over 5,000 francs and said that was all I had, before adding that I needed to stop at an ATM to be able to pay them.

"If they don't accept dollars, that is" I added. And immediately regret both utterances. Now they not only knew that I had a credit card, but cash on me as well. Why had I not listened to the Spaniards of the night before?

Moreno drove like a manic pig on methamphetamine. Even though the oil money in the country is extremely unevenly distributed, the road around the island is of a high standard. They have spent money on some infrastructure nonetheless, and the same can be said about primary school education: Equatorial Guinea has some of the highest reading skills in Africa. But the vast majority lack vehicles and live in very simple wooden houses or sheds. The downside with the good roads was that we speedily headed off at 150 kilometres per hour. In a police state. We had to stop at police roadblocks four times.

"And put on the warning lights," commanded one of the policemen.

Here, they were to check absolutely everything, and the slightest defect or the slightest offense would likely be noticed. I had to show my passport, and the others had theirs with them too. If they were to rob me, I would have had no other witnesses. On the other hand, I felt safe as they had done so right away, not giving me a last tourist tour. We unbelievably escaped fines.

South of Bioko there is a national park. Therefore, the road does not go completely around the island, but crosses a mountain range 50 kilometres to the south of Malabo.

According to Joseph, the view from the top was supposed to be world class, but it was foggy, so the claim cannot be verified. We also stopped by the small town of Luba and two eminent beaches. Close to one of the beaches, the monkeys exchanged gossip between trees that grew almost all the way down to the water's edge. One of the trees even reach out over the salt water. The dialogue between the apes was nothing about us — we were seemingly of no interest whatsoever to the busy animals high up in the trees.

On the way from the last beach right next to Riaba in the southeast and back towards Malabo, Moreno was true to tradition driving at well over 100 kilometres per hour on a straight stretch. Some distance ahead, in the middle of the road, a small brown and white dog was sniffing at something. He reminded me of a friend's dog: Karma. The name came from a heavy party, so he could shout 'Bad Karma' whenever the dog disobeyed. The driver sounded the horn, but the dog did not heed the warning. Just before the car was upon it, the little dog looked up at us, began going to the left, but abruptly swivelled on a penny and dashed to the right. Moreno braked, but to no avail. The result was a thump and howling dog for a split second, before it suddenly went quiet.

"The end of Karma," I thought.

It turned out that Moreno feared just that — bad karma. Straight after the dog killing, he reached into his pocket with his right hand and picked out 2-3 coins. He threw them out of the window.

"To protect against accidents and bad karma," he said quietly as the car raced on.

Roadkill is unfortunately common in Africa. Dogs, piglets, and chickens are particularly vulnerable, and I have been on board several buses and minibuses that have made easy work of it and left roadkill behind, but it was the first time I had witnessed it in a car.

I had been driven around for several hours without Joseph and co. showing a single sign of exploiting the three-against-one advantage. Rather, they had become warmer and more pleasant as time had gone on. But suddenly I had been witness to a dog collision and hoped that it would not change the situation significantly for me. Fortunately, they did not seem to consider it very likely that I would voluntarily go to a corrupt police station to speak badly about them. After a while they took me to say hello to a friend in a small village on the east coast.

We were all invited into his home there — a simple and colourful wooden house without insulation or windows. I was given the discarded armchair, the host sat down on a basic spindly chair, while my three car-sharing colleagues had to make do with old wooden beer crates. The host was also in no doubt about what he was going to serve us: Five large brown bottles of beer were taken out from an old fridge in a corner and opened with a broken wooden pepper mill.

"Salud," said Joseph, and I did as I was told. As in the Bible belt back home in the south of Norway, you do not turn down the best your host has to offer, even though north of

Kristiansand it is more often going to be a serving of Norwegian Prince's Cake than dark brown beer. The fact that the driver downed two beers, didn't seem to warrant a mumble.

They got me home safely in any case and drove me to a hotel they guaranteed to be much cheaper than the Ibis. Anything else was surely impossible anyhow, and bog-standard was passable for me. Access to hot water and an absence of cockroaches was good enough for me.

A long way south of Bioko is the small village of San Antonia De Ureca, or just Ureca among the locals. It was roadless until a few years ago and still is if one is to believe Google Maps. With 10,450 millimetres of rainfall a year, it is the wettest city in Africa and the fifth wettest city in the world, beaten by just over a thousand millimetres by Indian Mawsynram. So much rain contributed to it taking so many years to build the road. All preparation work was washed away every year as soon as the rainy season came.

Not everyone is happy about there being a road here now. Even though tourists are limited, the road makes way for more people to come and visit, and often disturb the unique wildlife. The beaches are full of tortoises that lay their eggs here, and the rainforest abounds with life. It's no coincidence that Justin spent years making his documentary about the drill monkey right here.

I went on a new trip to then south the following day, this time with only the driver from the day before. The destination was Ureca, and I was not expecting to see anyone on the deserted beaches, at least not a blonde woman with a flowery hat. Even a shy country boy would have wanted contact. I was no exception and said hello, to Lisa, it turned out. We even ended up having a beer each.

Lisa Sinclair is a biologist from Virginia, USA. She was in Equatorial Guinea as the leader of the Bioko Marine Turtle Program, a project studying the sea turtles that live in the south of the island, and she knows Justin and his wife Kristy well. The project was started by Purdue University in the US state of Indiana, as a collaboration with the local UNGE university. She has been collecting data on sea turtles and monkeys herself for six years, while the project has lasted for eleven.

"I had experience from a turtle project in the USA, but after a while I got super tired of it and started to look around for something else. I was looking for a different kind of challenge. On the internet, I suddenly came across the job here, and thought 'why the hell not, I'll go'. At that time, I hadn't a clue where Equatorial Guinea was, I had not heard of the country at all. That was actually a bit of the appeal, to just travel to a place that no one has heard or knows anything about," she told me and took a sip from the brown bottle.

The project has three research camps on the beaches in the south, and they are there for six months every year. In the rainy season, it is far too wet to be able to stay in any camp, so they then coordinate educational projects from elsewhere in the country.

"It simply rains too much for it to be particularly nice to be there. Not to mention how problematic it is for photographic and other technical equipment in the extreme humidity," explained Lisa.

"After five months in a tent on the beaches of the south, I had fallen completely in love with it — in this beautiful, rough and both physically and socially difficult place to live. I knew I had to come back. This was me! And the following year I was on there again, this time as camp manager. Since then, I have worked my way up the ladder and I am now responsible for the entire project for Purdue University."

Between stays, she has taken a master's degree on how hunting with firearms affects the density of primates, and sub-primates, in the relevant areas. The love of it has not diminished, and Lisa has no plans to settle in any other place.

"This little country that almost no one has ever noticed on the map, has become a part of my life," she said dreamily. The glint in her eye was proof that she was not kidding.

Now things are easier than when she first came to the country. The first time, the project members had to walk 6-7 hours through the jungle to get to the beaches, and Lisa never saw a single tourist. But as I said, the road was finished eventually, and everything suddenly became far more accessible. She is not particularly pleased about that.

"Now hunters and turtle egg thieves come here too, something that threatens the very existence of wildlife in the national park."

The hunters hunt wild animals and then sell the meat as 'bushmeat'. Many people look upon it as especially healthy and nutritious, while in fine restaurants it is served as an exotic jungle delicacy. The meant is not always safe to eat if it hasn't been tested, due to the risk of contagion from tropical diseases, including Ebola, but also more widespread diseases like tuberculosis, yellow fever, and rabies.

"We counted 200 tourists last year, and isn't positive either for the fragile wildlife here," said the turtle worker, explaining that by tourists she primarily meant foreigners who are in the country for work, but who took a weekend trip away from Malabo. She is not particularly fond of the capital. All the people, the traffic and facilities like modern coffee bars and the occasional fairly good pizza restaurant make the transition from living on the idyllic beach ever more enormous.

"In Malabo I have been attacked twice. Not crazy, really, considering the odds for a blonde lady," she said a little sarcastically. But she had an important point. With such large class divisions, it is not unusual for people who look rich, that is to say, all foreigners, to be victims of robbery or violence. This in turn means that there are a quite a few police and military personnel in the streets. And as a foreigner, you need hold your ground and be patient if you are to avoid giving in to repeated requests from law enforcement for money for a soda. None of these aspects particularly promote tourism.

In 2018, the project Lisa works on began following six turtles with GPS. The surveillance helps them understand how large an area the turtles inhabit, and what threats they experience, both around Bioko and throughout the whole of the Gulf of Guinea. The results will be shared internationally. As in Norway, the excess of plastic in the sea has also made the researchers here concerned. Observations carried out in 2016 showed that small pieces of plastic were now found in 39 percent of the turtle nests and close to eggs that were about to hatch. They had not even touched upon the levels of microplastic.

This almost invisible by-product of the oil that has secured President Mbasogo's income is hardly given a single thought. With his wealth, he of course lives grandly in his luxurious palace in Malabo. But sometimes dictators want to impress by other means as well. In 2009, he attended a meeting of the African Union in Tripoli, Libya. Mbasogo was extremely impressed by the Tripoli Congress Centre — this magnificent conference centre where his dictator-colleague Gaddafi had arranged the conference for all the leaders in Africa. The following year, he contacted Murat Tabanlıoğlu, the head of Tabanlıoğlu Architects, the Turkish architectural firm who were behind it.

"I want a conference premises that is just as impressive, which is ready for when I arrange the same annual conference in Malabo," he is supposed to have said. Tabanlıoğlu was not hard to ask. Not at least until he learned about the size and schedule. The conference centre was to be 13,750 square metres and had to be built and finished within six months. All this for an absolute authoritarian leader was likely a completely normal request. Or order.

Tabanlıoğlu decided instead to accept the task of promoting the work of the African Union, not to work for yet another autocratic government. He set himself the goal of creating a meeting place for negotiations and peace among many countries. According to the magazine, Architectural Record, his desire was that nature and harmony would be the elements that inspired the building. The main meeting room had space for 420 people. The President was pleased with the result. But the conference centre had become like an Olympic stadium. The president is said to have boasted greatly about the building to the other African leaders. The project had been utterly unique for the Turkish architects and the company that had built the conference centre. Absolutely everything apart from the cement had to be imported. With such a short construction timeline, all of the structures and materials had to fit into containers or cargo planes, but the budget available didn't make that a problem. It didn't come as a shock. The budget had no upper limit. It is therefore not surprising that the total cost of the conference centre remains a guarded secret.

The success of the conference centre likely gave a taste for more. Now the dictator is in the process of building a new capital, just east of the middle of Río Muni, on the mainland. It will be located in an area currently called Djibloho, which became a new province in 2017. At the moment it is one giant construction site, divided into the main districts of Oyala and Mbere. No one lives there, not yet anyhow, but the dictator is known for pushing through immense visions in a short timeframe. The future capital's name will not be Oyala, but Ciudad de la Paz, or City of Peace. The plan is that 200,000 people will live across an 81.5 square kilometre area in the middle of the jungle. A Portuguese architectural firm was responsible for completion in 2020, but in 2023 it is as much of a building site as in 2017. Time will tell if the capital ever moves. But with a constant and unstoppable stream of money from above and under the table, it is not inconceivable that the controversial project will actually be finished. There are few critical voices in Equatorial Guina, but even here some people frown upon the destruction of rainforest to make room for infrastructure. Moreover, the question is whether people want to live there. But such reluctancy is often resolved through threats of severe punishment for those who do not want to. The money can most certainly also be used for better purposes among the many poor that live in the country.

It isn't just Guinea and Equatorial Guinea that have challenges with unorthodox leadership either. The newest country in the world is also experiencing great challenges with its governing forces. They can neither manage to get order to the country nor end internal conflicts.

The lush east coast of the island of Bioko.

The canoe I'm sitting on has been carved out of a tree trunk. I was offered it, but politely declined, partly because of the cracks in the bottom.

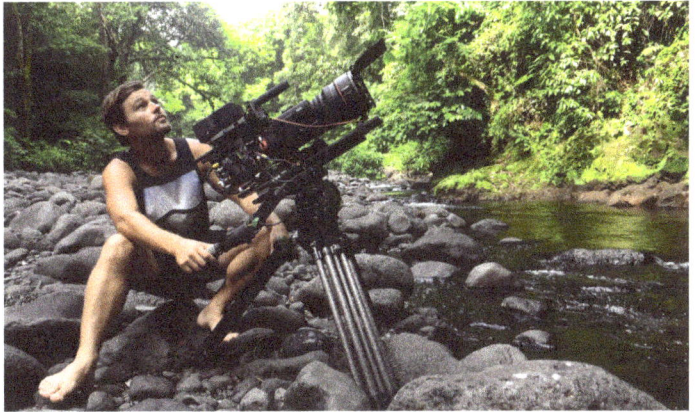

Justin Jay in the jungle of Boiko in search of the rare Drill Monkey.

This is a distant relative that Justin also tracked down and took a picture of.

The boys on a trip. They drove me around the whole of Bioko.

Equatorial Guinea has an abundance of wildlife. I was warned about crocodiles in this river, so I decided not to explore it further.

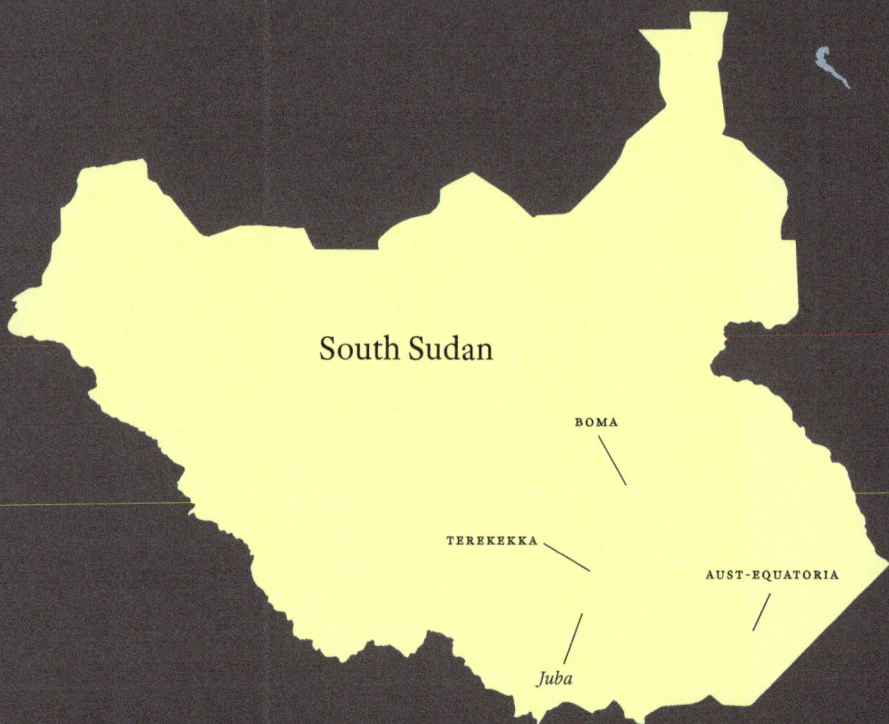

South Sudan

BOMA

TEREKEKKA

AUST-EQUATORIA

Juba

200 km

7

South Sudan, Africa

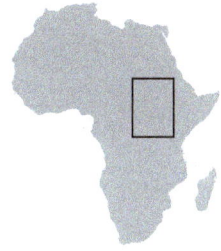

INHABITANTS: 8,000,000 (Al Jazeera)

TOURISTS PER YEAR: 2,200 (garfors.com)

AREA: 619,745 square kilometres

SOUTH SUDAN IS the youngest country in the world and is almost the size of Norway. It didn't become independent until 2011 but has encountered many more problems than most countries that have a much longer history. Much of it stems from parties in the government never having quite managed to achieve any successful cooperation.

South Sudan was separated from Sudan after a long power struggle and many crafty moves from politicians in the north and former colonial powers. An independent South Sudan, or Southern Sudan, has been under discussion since 1947, but it took 64 years to achieve it. A lot has happened since Crown Prince Haakon of Norway celebrated their independence day with the newfound South Sudanese in the capital Juba in July 2011. Unfortunately, most of it is negative. The differences between the tribes have been substantial for a long time and led to the new country even entering into civil war in 2013 — as if the inhabitants had not had enough of conflict when part of Sudan. Campaigns have almost followed in waves, sometimes being replaced by a short-term ceasefire. The country, which has large amounts of oil, is struggling to even get out of the starting blocks. Norway has been an important partner in state-building, and has helped both financially and in other ways, but without it actually having helped significantly.

As a traveller in South Sudan, there is one essential rule. No photography. With the emphasis on none. And if you really need some pictures for the family album or Facebook, make sure no one else sees you taking them. 'Ordinary' people seldom have anything against you taking a picture of them, as long as you ask first, but then there can always be someone else who sees you. It can be police officers, private guards, or overzealous residents.

On my second trip to Juba, I experienced the pain of this four times in less than four hours. It all started at 09.17 on a Saturday morning in August. I wanted to go for a jog before the heat became unbearable. I took my mobile phone with me as a map and camera. As usual when I jog on my travels, I was met by many smiles. I experienced overwhelming friendliness as a Norwegian jogging from Logali House — an old colonial British building that is now a hotel, restaurant, and bar — to the only road in the country that crosses the Nile, in the centre of Juba. The Nile stretches 1,500 kilometres through South Sudan, but there is only one bridge. It was about time that a second bridge was built. Illogically, this has been built less than a kilometre from the existing bridge. I have hardly ever received as many waves and encouraging cries as on the jogging trip through Juba. I also got a 'white boy!' followed by a big white smile in the middle of a narrow dark face.

I cross the new four-lane steel bridge. There is one car lane and one narrow pedestrian lane in each direction, so I had to excuse myself every time I ran past someone, so that they turned sideways and let me pass. There is a tiny village immediately on the other side of the Nile, consisting of thatched huts and tents. There are many such villages along the Nile, and those who live there barely make ends meet.

A family with five kids lived in the hut closest to the river, and I asked if I could take a picture upstream. The response was enthusiastic with smiles and nods. So, I walked five metres closer to the riverbank, behind a kind of storage tent, and took 5 or 6 pictures of the longest river in the entire world, including two pictures with me in the foreground. On leaving, I thanked the parents and tried to talk to the kids. The big sister, who was about six, wore a Manchester United shirt. I cheer on Tottenham Hotspur, and it hurts to admit this, but if you have managed to get children to wear football kits in South Sudan, then Manchester United deserve the title of the world's largest football club. The girl was by no means the only one with such a red shirt in Juba — I saw dozens of them. The girl was carrying her naked little brother in her arms. Snot cascaded from the boy's nose. The other three children had been waiting with their parents. The smiles were still unfettered, and I thought of asking if I could take a picture of the South Sudanese nuclear family. I never managed to. Out of nowhere appeared a thin man almost two metres tall, running in sandals, fine trousers, and a very tired orange T-shirt.

"What do you think you're doing?" he shouted, as if it was life and death. "Have you taken a picture? That's illegal! Strictly forbidden!"

The man with bad breath, brown and crooked teeth, had come right up to me, out of breath and clearly enraged with fury.

"You are not allowed to take photographs. Get out your phone!" he commanded. To a man who has never been in the military, that was fruitless.

"I asked them for permission to take a picture here, and I have not taken a picture of anyone. It's not a problem," I tried to explain calmly.

"It's a big problem! Come with me," he said, pointing at a group of men 50 metres away. Some distance further on stood 6 or 7 adult men washing themselves with large bars of soap in the White Nile, totally naked. It is quite common to see adults bathing in African rivers, since few dwellings have their own water source, but I was not particularly eager to go over to either the bathing men or the group of men who were dressed. I was going to be really up against it with twenty against one, and I did not know what they wanted. They would use the fact I took a picture as cause to demand a fine they had no right to impose, possibly taking my phone. At that time I had a Chinese mobile phone that had been bought for no more than 300 dollars in South Africa. It would not be the biggest loss, but no one should just come and demand my phone, compass, map, and camera. Considering the tall man's temperament, it could also be reasonable to conclude that they were just wanting to punch the fucking lights out of this brash white guy who had strayed across the river. None of these alternatives were particularly cheering. The fact that he grabbed at my phone and took hold of my shoulder with his long thin fingers did not make his pitch any more attractive.

"Let's talk to the police," I said calmly.

"I am the police," he tried. But neither he nor any of his friends were wearing uniforms. Neither did the family who lived here, nor the three male onlookers in colourful clothes who had come to see what the cause of all the noise was.

"Can I see your ID?" I replied, and I looked at him right in the dark brown eyes. They were wild, as in horror film-like wild.

"No!" he shouted. "Now you are coming with me!" The fact that I did not do as he commanded, made him mad. Maybe he had gone a little too far into his police act, which he had likely thought would secure him a long-awaited income. Unemployment is sky high, and poverty is widespread. Playing a policeman was perhaps a desperate attempt to make some money — I experienced something similar in Mozambique in 2010.

A couple of metres away, the kids were shocked in any case — they had moved behind the parents who stood like a wall against the madness. He took me by the shoulder with his right hand again and tried to snatch the phone with his left. Enough was enough, even for a calm Norwegian from the fjords of Naustdal. I shook his hand off me and started to run. I had to run in a zigzag to prevent him from being able to catch me, and in order not to knock down the spectators, I had to take an untimely detour to the right and partly around the majority of a broad tall tree of an unknown variety. He was not slow as he accelerated and took the straight route on the path to the left of the large tree, but I was faster and clambered up the small slope from the river and up to the road that went over to the bridge.

The tall man had been joined by another guy in a blue football shirt, so there were now two running after me. Fortunately, I have had good training in the art of quickly crossing busy roads, thanks largely to the video game Freeway from the early 1980s, where a chicken must cross a very busy highway. There was no point in even trying to run into the middle of the road that crosses the river. There were too many cars there for it to be safe. It wasn't exactly very safe to run away from the wild man in the first place though, but probably safer than the alternatives before me. I crossed the road and jumped onto the pedestrian walkway on the right, the one that went towards the city.

A metal fence separated the pedestrians from the traffic. My sprinting steps reverberated through the iron plates that lay almost detached on top of the metal foundation. The man in the blue shirt was just behind me, so I picked up the pace. It was extremely bad timing for a getaway on foot — half of South Sudan seemed to be going to the capital for Saturday shopping, and I had to pass various clusters of pedestrians and a guy who renting out his moped. The only solution was to snake between all the people, and that is just what I did. This led to many alarmed faces, but I continually apologised as an attempt to compensate for my discourtesy whilst running past 10, 20, 50 and 100 people. It was so crowded that sometimes I had to jump sideways and slide along the metal railing towards the river or the metal fence on the other side to get past people without pushing too many aside. Ski-legend Aksel Lund Svindal would have been proud.

In my head it was just not on the cards that I would be caught by any of the men behind. At the same time, I was fully aware of the extremely low odds. I had so far run past thousands of people. Absolutely everyone was black. The fact that I stood out as I ran like a crazy man with at least one local notch in the whole was not to come from — I was as easy to spot as a pink elephant in an anthill with albino ants. The fact that my persecutor shouted something to people in a language I did not understand did not make my situation any easier. I did not expect him to be shouting 'make way!' on my behalf, rather 'stop the thief!'. In any case, my goal was no more ambitious than getting across the river and finding police in uniform. But I had such momentum that I ran right past the first police patrol 100 metres into the mainland. Anyway, they were preoccupied with motorised vehicles, not foreigners in full flow. They had seen me jogging the other way and probably thought that I was still doing the same thing. After a further 200 metre sprint, I saw a group of men sitting on their motorcycles. Perfect! It was a South Sudanese taxi rank. There are some taxis in the country, but in South Sudan, taking a taxi usually means sitting on the back of a moped or motorcycle. If nothing else it is cheap, but not particularly comfortable, and both air conditioning and exhaust-filters are missing. The breeze produced when a moped is in motion is not much help when the air temperature is approaching 40 degrees. Luckily there was no one in line. The youngest of the drivers got on his moped and started the engine — I was just about to jump on the back — I turned around and saw that the man in the blue shirt had not managed to keep up with my pace, he was a whole running-track-length adrift, still jogging a little. I could no longer see the fake policeman in orange — he had perhaps stopped on the bridge.

"To the airport," I said. There was not much point in showing the mob exactly where I was staying. The taxi driver accelerated, and we had gotten a little over a kilometre away before there was a new police checkpoint. There is a civil war in South Sudan, but in

Juba it is calm enough for the police to take care of most security measures themselves. Police checks are located at all entrances into the capital. I only saw military vehicles in the city on a few occasions. There were so many cars before checkpoint number two after the bridge that we progressed at a snail's pace, even though on a moped we could sneak between the cars. At the actual police blockade, I was picked out and stopped. The tall man must have called the police ahead and asked them to stop the white man. And they did just that. But I was pleased to see real police. One of the policemen commanded me to get off the bike and into a small police shed where the police chief was lurking in the shade.

I was questioned by a younger policeman who worked as an interpreter for the police chief there. I explained my side of the story — that the tall man had scared me, tried to grab me and that I had asked for permission before I took the picture, which I, of course, showed on camera. They grinned when we came to pictures from the previous days.

"These are from Somalia," I said. They were not so used to seeing such pictures. Ladies in burqas, uniformed men with machine guns and then me on such a beach that definitely does not exist in South Sudan. This all clearly made an impression, and the police chief concluded that taking a picture of the Nile did not significantly threaten the security of the kingdom.

"It's okay, you can go," he said via the interpreter. "And if you need anything, contact me," added the police interpreter at his own expense, as he gave me his phone number on a note. All in all, it was a successful ending. The taxi driver found me again — he had not been paid after all — and we raced off towards the airport.

"Drive to Logali House instead," I said. The risk that the tall angry man would try to find me through friends within the South Sudan taxi industry was now significantly reduced.

After a long cold shower, I was back out on the streets of Juba. Very few are paved, and the dust quickly settles on clothes and hair. I was about to brush off the red dust accumulated on my green shorts in an unpaved alley when two ladies in their late twenties came along walking in the opposite direction.

"Who are you?" she asked one of them, with a smile that revealed a silver tooth.

"My name is Gunnar. I'm from Norway," I smiled back.

My response with a smile seemed to have had an effect.

"I love you!" she smiled in return. Then she asked if we could take a picture together. Norwegians may be a bit shy, but this lady was taking things a little too quickly. I thanked her for the compliment, let her have her picture and strolled on. I thought it quite a paradox that the locals did not appear to have a problem with pictures being taken willy-nilly. It could also just be that I was in a better neighbourhood than the one by the bridge across the Nile.

Further down the road, two policemen were standing by their station next to an undersized moped, made in China. They greeted me, and we began talking. After the

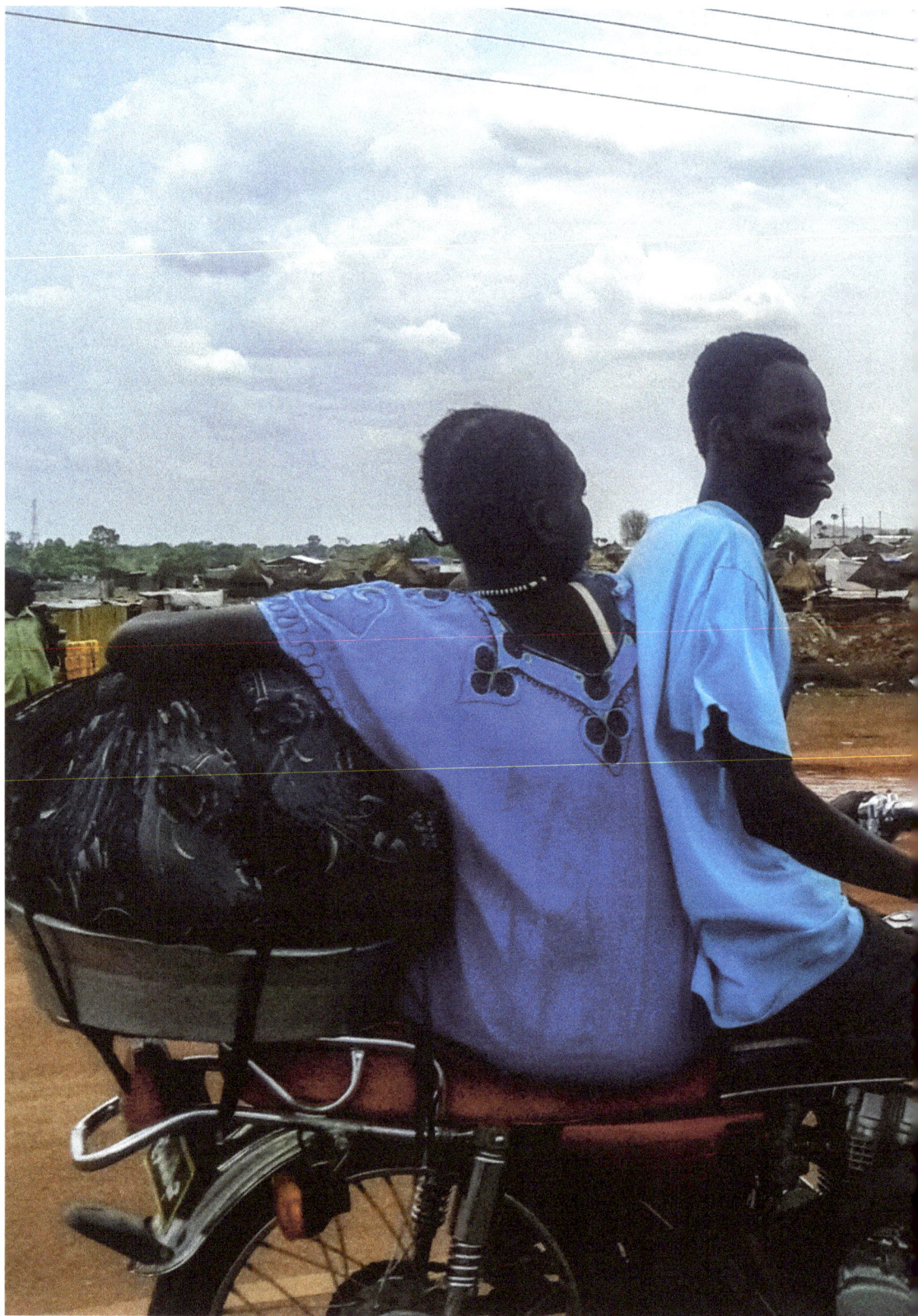

ubiquitous phrases about which country I came from, and if there was much for the police to do, I asked if I could take a picture of them, and their police moped. I wanted to test out my brand-new theory about this nice neighbourhood.

"Of course! Shoot away," one of them grinned.

I stepped back one metre into the road and took the picture. Suddenly I heard shouting. Angry noises came from a policeman in a civilian car with open windows. It was clear both through his uniform and his attitude that he had a significantly higher rank than the moped police officers alongside the moped.

"Did you take a picture of them?" he yelled. "You are not allowed to do that. Who are you? Are you a journalist?"

The fact that I had received permission from the police in question made no difference to him. There was no point in trying to put the blame on the two poor policemen either. The angry policeman demanded to see my passport, but I did not want to hand it over, so I claimed it was back in my hotel. I gave him my driver's license instead. He commanded one of the other two to write down my details.

On a blank sheet of paper he wrote 'Name: Driving License'. My birthplace was written down as 'Road Licensing Agency'. He did not manage to mess up my date of birth. But the irate man was not finished despite my apologies and promises to never take a photograph in South Sudan again, ever.

"Come with me. Get in the car!" he commanded. "We are going to the Ministry of Culture."

Quite a threat. I hoped they could, if nothing else, help me with information about how many tourists visited the country every year. From the back seat, I thought it was maybe time to call a friend. I had been given the telephone number of a police interpreter earlier that same day. But alas he had clocked off from work for the day, had given me the wrong number or did not hear the phone. It turned out to be a useless number. After a ten-minute drive through Juba, partly on gravel roads, we arrived at the ministry building. I was shown to an office and asked to wait outside while he entered. I had also been given a police guard, so there was no point in trying to run away. He had clearly managed to explain himself after just two, and I was allowed to enter. A broad-shouldered man with a thin pornstar-like beard sat behind a desk.

"This is the Deputy Minister. He will listen to your case," explained the irate man. The deputy minister and I shook each other by the hand, and he pointed to a folding metal chair. It was not particularly comfortable to sit in, but that was surely the point.

"Why did you take a picture of police officers while they worked?" asked the authority-figure in the room. I explained that I was a tourist and I liked taking pictures, and that I was not aware that it was illegal to photograph police officers. The deputy minister looked at the picture on the camera — I had to delete the picture of the policemen alongside the moped.

"I'm very sorry, I will not do that again."

"No, of course you shouldn't," the deputy minister replied briefly. He and irate colleague discussed something in a language I could not understand at all.

"You have to sign an official apology," he declared.

I could have no doubt demanded legal assistance or help from the Norwegian embassy, but that would have likely escalated the whole thing. Besides, it was a Saturday and certainly a problem to get hold of people from the embassy. The fact that the ministry was open at all seemed like something unusual. There are not many countries I have visited that can boast of a bureaucracy that is open at the weekends. TIA.

"Yes, of course I can. Do you have a form I can sign?"

They looked at each other.

"No, we do not have that," said the deputy minister.

"Well, do you have a sheet of paper, so I can maybe write a letter?" I suggested.

"Yes, that is a good idea," he said, opening the drawer under the printer, which stood on a small grey filing cabinet. He put the sheet on the desk, I got to my feet and took it.

"Excellent, I have my own pen. Who should I address it to?"

The deputy minister hesitated, saying nothing.

"Maybe to the people of South Sudan?" I tried.

"Yes, that's good."

I started writing in block capitals.

"Should I put a date on the letter?"

"Yes, that's probably a good idea."

It was clear that this was not the usual procedure that photographers had to write an apology. But now I have at least forged a path to follow the next time someone else is guilty of such an atrocity. I signed the letter and gave it to the deputy minister. He read through it slowly and nodded in contentment.

"Yes, this is good. This is sufficient. Just don't take photographs in a public place again. You can go now."

I thanked them and stretched out my hand. He took my hand in a tight hold. The handshake lasted for 3 or 4 seconds, as if to emphasise how serious a case this was. The previously irate policeman suddenly started to smile, he had probably been praised for bringing me in. We also shook each other by the hand. I was relieved and surprised that I was not asked for money, not even the usual request for a couple of dollars for a soda. Maybe I did not seem important, rich enough or old enough to be able to pay any significant kind of bribe. In any case, I did not see any point in being offended.

"Have a nice day," I said, and left through the door behind the eager-eyed policeman. Right outside the door, I turned on the spot. "Just wait a minute," I said, and took two steps back into the room. The deputy minister looked up.

"Don't you think it's a good idea for me to take a photograph of the letter I have written, so that I can show it to the Norwegian ambassador?" Then it will be more official, and I can more easily show how sorry I am for all of this. Is this okay?" I asked.

"Yes, that's a good idea. No problem," said the deputy minister. In the end, I was given official permission to take pictures in South Sudan, albeit only of my own letter of apology.

When back outside the previously irate policeman offered to drive me wherever I wanted in Juba. I asked to be dropped off where I had been picked up. There was no traffic, so we arrived there just five minutes later.

I don't exactly learn easily from my mistakes, so I was caught by security guards twice more on the same day, taking pictures, but I managed to fortunately talk myself out of the situations as they happened. One of the guards had reacted to me taking a picture of some cordially posing men repairing an outboard engine, a couple of kilometres further down from the bridge over the Nile. I had to show to the other guard that I deleted the picture I had just taken of a lady selling fish. It had been out of focus anyway.

Al Jazeera journalist Hiba Morgan put me in the picture about the photo horrors, at Logali House, of course. Al Jazeera has an office in the same building, so I often saw her there.

"Photography released in the media has traditionally been used to show negative sides of South Sudan. We are afraid of negativity, afraid of what white people especially are going to say about us, and that white people will come and take over our country. This mainly applies to the British, Americans and French. That's the main reason we're so paranoid about photography."

With so many policemen and 'policemen' around, I should have really had a fixer with me. And even those who have not seen the Tarantino film, Pulp Fiction, have likely gotten an inkling of how the fixer, Mr. Winston Wolf, in Harvey Keitel's character, operates. Super early in the morning he was called upon to clean up after a sticky accident. In tucks, he fixed a rather unorthodox problem in a relatively unorthodox way.

But this was in a film. As a waring country with enormous poverty and extreme shortages of food and clean water, South Sudan has far bigger problems than what Quentin Tarantino wrote about in the script for this film from 1994. But then there are also people who actually fix these real problems.

Matthew Gray is such a man, even though he would never say so himself. He did not need to do that either, because his colleagues did that job for him. The Canadian works for the UN and is stationed in Copenhagen with his Tajik wife and two children. When there is a real crisis, the 38-year-old is brought in to solve challenges in 'problem areas' around the world. Matthew's title is Project Leader. In practice, this will Problem Solver.

"I come in at short notice and work around the clock for 2-3 months at a time. I'm popular with colleagues the day I arrive and the day I depart. There will be plenty of unpopular decisions, and I have few friends in the places I am stationed," explained the man who seemed to be a nice guy. Matthew has been sent on assignments 17 times so far during his career at the UN. He had two weeks left to right what he could in Juba when I met him and several of his colleagues at one of the hotel complexes the worldwide organisation uses. Matthew could not come to me at Logali House, since the UN, the embassies and the foreign NGOs must adhere to a curfew from 7 in the evening. As in Afghanistan, it is the unstable security situation that is the explanation, and as a consequence, 15,000 foreign people in Juba are forbidden to move around outside beyond their hotels in the evening and at night-time — these are people with high incomes and with money to spend, money that will then never benefit the local economy, as mostly only foreign entities own the hotels they stay in. Matthew willingly explained some of the background to problems in the youngest country in the world.

"There was a great deal of lobbying before South Sudan became independent, and the so-called South Sudan Commission managed to raise billions upon billions of US dollars as start-up capital for the new country. Today, most of this money has vanished and has been used for personal gain by just a few people. Very little has actually gone to the people or to the community at large. Additionally, the ancient tribal culture brings with it some deep contradictions. And they go deep. Think of the Israel-Palestine conflict times by ten."

To try to understand, we have to go a long way back in time. Archaeologists have found 17,000-year-old traces of the first homo sapiens in what today is Tanzania. Some of them migrated north to the newly formed South Sudan. 10,000 years ago, the region was much wetter and lusher than it is today, with large grassland areas and forests, many more rivers than just the Nile and a number of lakes and bodies of water. Forward several thousand years closer to our time and two different cultures were to be found living on the banks of the Nile — the Nubian and the Egyptian. These two existed together for a long time. But between the 6th and 16th centuries, the Nile area was made Arabic, mainly via Arabs marrying into Beja families, who ruled all of southern Sudan. Their children then took over as the next leaders. As a result, Arab culture became more and more widespread. From around 1500, various African groups such as the Luo, the Dinka, the Nuaran and the Shilluk people came into dominance, and not only through reproductive peaceful means. The Nuaran people call themselves naath, which means 'human', and their descendants form by far the largest ethnic groups in South Sudan and Western Ethiopia. In the 19th century, the Turks invaded what is present-day South Sudan. They played a role in developing and cultivating the region through various new skills, such as animal husbandry, until about 1850. Some women rose all the way to the top of the society, although there were not many to speak of. Queen Ikang ruled in parts of the region from 1886 to 1936 and is perhaps the most important example. However, for most women, their main task was to reproduce, often as one of several wives in the home. But in reality, only rich men could actually marry more than one woman, as a bride from a good family cost around 100 cows.

From the end of the 19th century, European imperialists were very focused on the African continent, and between 1881 and 1914 they invaded, occupied, colonised, and annexed more than 90 percent of the African territory, including present-day South Sudan. Only Ethiopia managed to stay independent.

It was not until The Second World War that eyes began to open for most Africans, especially as the West claimed to be fighting for freedom, cooperation, and equality. Colonized people all over the world began to fight for independence. With regards South Sudan, it all actually started in Juba. The Juba Conference in 1947 was organised to bring about closer cooperation between the government and the people of Sudan. The government asked what the majority of Sudanese wanted in terms of the creation of a national parliament in Khartoum, but the question of a possible division of Sudan was not on the agenda at this conference. The fact that people from southern Sudan were also allowed to be a part of the conference was inadvertently the beginning of the South Sudanese nationalist movement, with the area in the south after a time being defined as a separate region.

On 1st January 1956, Sudan became an independent state, and the question dividing the country was largely put on hold for several years. It was not realistic with another separation when the country was so new. During the strategy conference The Round Table Conference in 1965, four parties from southern Sudan were represented, but none of them had worked out a common agenda, resulting in little change. The central question in modern times concerning southern Sudan has nonetheless always been about the tensions between the original African cultures that are strongly rooted in the south, and the Arab cultures of the north. The Africans did not want to be governed by Arabs, leading to the first Sudanese civil war starting in 1955. The war only came to an end after peace talks in Addis Ababa on 26th February 1972, where the parties agreed for southern Sudan to become an autonomous region. It was to be called the Southern Region, while defence, foreign policy, economic policy, and planning were to be handled by the central government. This was not the same as independence, but the people in the south were tired of war, so they were content with the agreement.

But only a few years later, after Chevron found oil in Sudan, the conflict flared up again. The Addis Ababa Agreement clearly stated that the Southern Region had the right to tax income from mineral extraction within its boundaries, but the government in the north did not like that very much. Petroleum production in the south stoked up the north-south conflict. Almost overnight the south had become rich, or in any case richer, and the black gold made those in the north jealous.

President Nimeiri, for example, introduced Sharia Law in September 1983. In theory, this applied to all Sudanese, but in practice Sharia punishments, such as the amputation of limbs for violent crimes and theft, were almost exclusively carried out on people from the Southern Region. This was probably one of the catalysts that led to the second civil war, which lasted from 1983 until 2005. Nimeiri was overthrown on 6th April 1985. Six years later, on 15th November 1991, more than 2,000 people were killed by militant groups in The Bor massacre, and 100,000 people fled southern Sudan. This was followed by a famine, killing 250,000 people. And the war was even more inhuman. Forces from the north burned down villages and stole livestock. Theft of domestic animals has almost become a tradition to hurt other tribes, and it is important to find out who stole your animals. When the victims go to get their animals back, it quickly descends into violence and murder on both sides.

An incredible two million people died in the conflict, and those who survived were traumatised for life.

This shared struggle against the enemy in the north bound the South Sudanese together. The intensity of the war and the subsequent migration led to the strengthening of inter-ethnic relations between the different groups, and a South Sudanese identity emerged — an African secular identity, combined with strong Christian values. After a time, the war not only became an opposition to Islam, but an ethnic struggle against continual discrimination based on race and culture.

At its worst, people from southern Sudan represented 25 percent of all internally displaced people in the world. Windhoek, the largest migrant camp, was a 40-minute drive from Khartoum. The huge camp had many roads, small shops, clinics, schools, and churches, and in many ways resembled a traditional southern village. The houses were built of local material such as sun-dried bricks covered with mud. In the torrential rains, walls and ceilings often collapsed, leading to many fatal consequences. People from different ethnic groups in the south with the same religion and cultural identity lived together in the camps, which were gradually closed down after South Sudan became independent.

In January 2005, after three years of negotiations and strong pressure from the international community, the parties finally signed an agreement. It stated, among other things, that in six years there would be a referendum on independence in the south. In the meantime, the two sides had to agree on important and hotly debated issues, such as the distribution of oil revenues, demarcation of the border, and the education system. The referendum itself took place between the 9th and 15th January 2011. Sudanese President Bashir said that the people of the south had the right to decide their own fate since assembly could not be 'forced'. The result was announced on 7th February 2011.

There was no question about what the will of the people was. 98.5 percent, or 3.8 million people, voted yes to freedom. Just over one percent were against, while a few thousand votes were invalid. The Republic of South Sudan became independent on 9th July 2011. Paradoxically, Sudan was the first country to formally recognise the new country. Tens of thousands of people took to the streets of Juba to celebrate, but the intoxication of victory did not last long. President Salva Kiir and Vice President Riek Machar came from different tribes and were never able to agree on many issues. The latter, among other disagreements, was blamed for attempting a coup. This was denied, and in February 2013 he challenged Salva Kiir for the presidency. It took five months before the vice president was fired by the government, and by the end of the year a new civil war had erupted — this time confined to the newly separated part of Sudan. Machar was now at the forefront of the opposition, South Sudan Liberation Movement. Unbelievably, in 2016, Machar became the new vice president, but it wasn't long before he was replaced. Despite some ceasefires, the fighting continues, and a quick solution to the conflict is not within sight. It says everything that more than 4 out of 12 million inhabitants have fled the country. No one knows the exact population; no census has been conducted since independence. There is a risk that the number of people will drastically decline unless the situation changes. But there is not much to suggest that it will. Both the UN and the African Union are therefore heavily involved in South Sudan and are frantically trying to minimise the effects of this deep-seated conflict and get food to people in remote areas. But their presence is opposed by many at different levels.

"It's even a problem if someone finds a UN shirt or a UN sticker. They then use the shirt or sticker to trick people into believing that they represent the UN, and that people have to pay them money to get help in the form of food or medicine. They never receive this help, even when they have paid. It's an unadulterated scam, and the UN gets the blame," explained Matthew.

He was the one who introduced me to Hiba Morgan, the journalist from Al Jazeera. The TV channel broadcasts news 24 hours a day and is based in Doha, Qatar. Al Jazeera has only one English-language correspondent in South Sudan, making Hiba Morgan very well known. Despite her English-sounding surname, she was born in Juba. Hiba towers in the landscape even without heels, is fearless, asks questions about most things to almost anyone, and usually comes straight to the point.

"How come you, as a Norwegian Viking, are so short?" was one of the first things she asked me. She is at least ten centimetres taller than my 173 centimetres without shoes.

"It's not the height that counts, it's how you use it," I countered, and she responded with a smile as brilliant as the ones in toothpaste adverts. As a proud South Sudanese, she did not like that her homeland is among the least visited in the world.

"You cannot include countries that have been affected by war — of course no tourists come here," she protested, after I told what I was writing about.

"So, you think that the book should be about the least visited countries in the world that have not been affected by war, that have good air connections and at least three high-class luxury hotels," I asked.

Over a Club beer in a good, old-fashioned clay bottle and a glass of white wine, we agreed it could easily escalate into numerous different criteria and exceptions. She agreed to swap from being an interviewer to becoming the interview subject. It was not a position she particularly relished, and I received few answers that were not first countered with at least one question. On the other hand, it would probably have been the other way round if a South Sudanese journalist had asked me questions about Norway. The fact that I was in South Sudan as a tourist was perhaps the thing that surprised Hiba the most.

"I have only seen tourists here twice before, but I have heard fantastic stories about tourists that came here before the civil war," said the journalist. She said that even the animals were struggling due to the war.

"If we now see herds of elephants or giraffes, we are shocked. It is as if the animals understand that there is a war going on. They almost never flock together anymore. And the war means that no one cares about snipers anymore, as well as far more people having access now to weapons, so that there are potentially more snipers. We know nothing about the long-term effects sniping will have on the animal populations," she sighed, before the smile emerged once more. Her thoughts had wandered.

"At the same time, we still have unique small islands in the middle of the Nile, incredible mountain peaks and beautiful mountainous regions — and the animals are still here, even though we don't see larger flocks of them very often. The potential for tourism is definitely here already, and there have been many plans, but the government is greedy, and they always want their share. Corruption, yet again. So, there are many projects that never even get off the ground. I would be very surprised if much happens on the tourist front during the next 20 years," said Hiba.

She thought that there was not exactly much point in even talking about the potential for tourists in the seventh least visited country in the world.

"First of all, there is a war here. Anyhow, there are far too many other things that do not work for there to be any point wasting time on it now. We need a total system reset first. A complete overhaul. And the very first thing we must do, is to start appointing people to leadership roles dependent upon their qualifications."

The problem of corruption in the country is far-reaching and may also be one of the reasons behind the long civil war. More than $4 billion in aid money has been stolen since independence alone, reportedly by 75 people high up in the government apparatus. The far-reaching corruption stems largely from tribalism. It is a common practice for people to be appointed or employed based on their background, who the husband or wife is, or another familiarity and friendship. Sometimes the wives take over if their husbands die. The tribe comes first — an aspect that is especially challenging when the country has 64 different tribes. In the government apparatus sits the power-generation, and most of them are in their forties and fifties. It is therefore unlikely that there will be any change looking at the short-term picture, despite lower life expectancy here than in the West.

"Our Auditor General is called Stephen Wondu. He is extremely honest and says things exactly as they are, but he never mentions names. If he had done that, he would have been eradicated a long time ago. He says that the value of the money stolen from the state treasury would have been enough to run all of South Sudan for 10 years," explained Hiba.

The money has been spent on property in Kenya, Dubai, and the West, and also on extravagancies.

"One of the 75 tipped $3,000 at a restaurant in Nairobi."

But back home, spending is minimal. Hotel bills from business trips don't get paid.

"As a consequence, people from the government are no longer allowed to stay at the best hotels. Therefore, the problem is just moved down to the second-best hotels, which don't really have the finances to be able to deal with it. The behaviour is reprehensible and undermines the economy of an already broken country. Not to mention the power behind setting an example," raged Hiba. She was clearly agitated.

President Salva Kiir introduced an amnesty so that those who had made the money vanish could pay it back anonymously to a special bank account in Kenya, without risking prosecution. Not a single dollar was transferred. In 2012, he wrote a letter to the 75:

"We fought for freedom, justice, and equality. Yet as soon as we came to power, we forgot what we had been fighting for, and began to reappropriate wealth to ourselves to the detriment of our own people." He went on to claim that the credibility of the country was at stake. Later, Kiir received criticism for both the letter and the campaign to get back the money as a ploy for the public and purely for show since none of the 75 paid anything. Neither were they tried in the court system after that.

"I just have to ask why you're still here," I asked. Hiba Morgan had not had too much uplifting to say about her homeland.

"Good question! I could have travelled anywhere and worked there. But the reason I am still here is because I want to tell stories. The people here deserve an impartial voice, a voice with a shared background. Everyone will only see the negative aspects if no one is left to also tell the other stories. South Sudan deserves that," she said quietly, and told how three journalists had been tortured to death in the first eight months of 2017. The government was likely behind it, but no one had any evidence, and the authorities did not comment on the case.

"I have been detained myself on several occasions for hours at a time in the government building, but not yet overnight," she said with a lacklustre smile. "I cross my fingers for it to continue this way."

Al Jazeera is in many ways the local news channel in South Sudan, and most hotels and bars have the channel playing in the lobby around the clock.

"A lot of it is owing to me and because Al Jazeera has kept its office open. I'm a celebrity

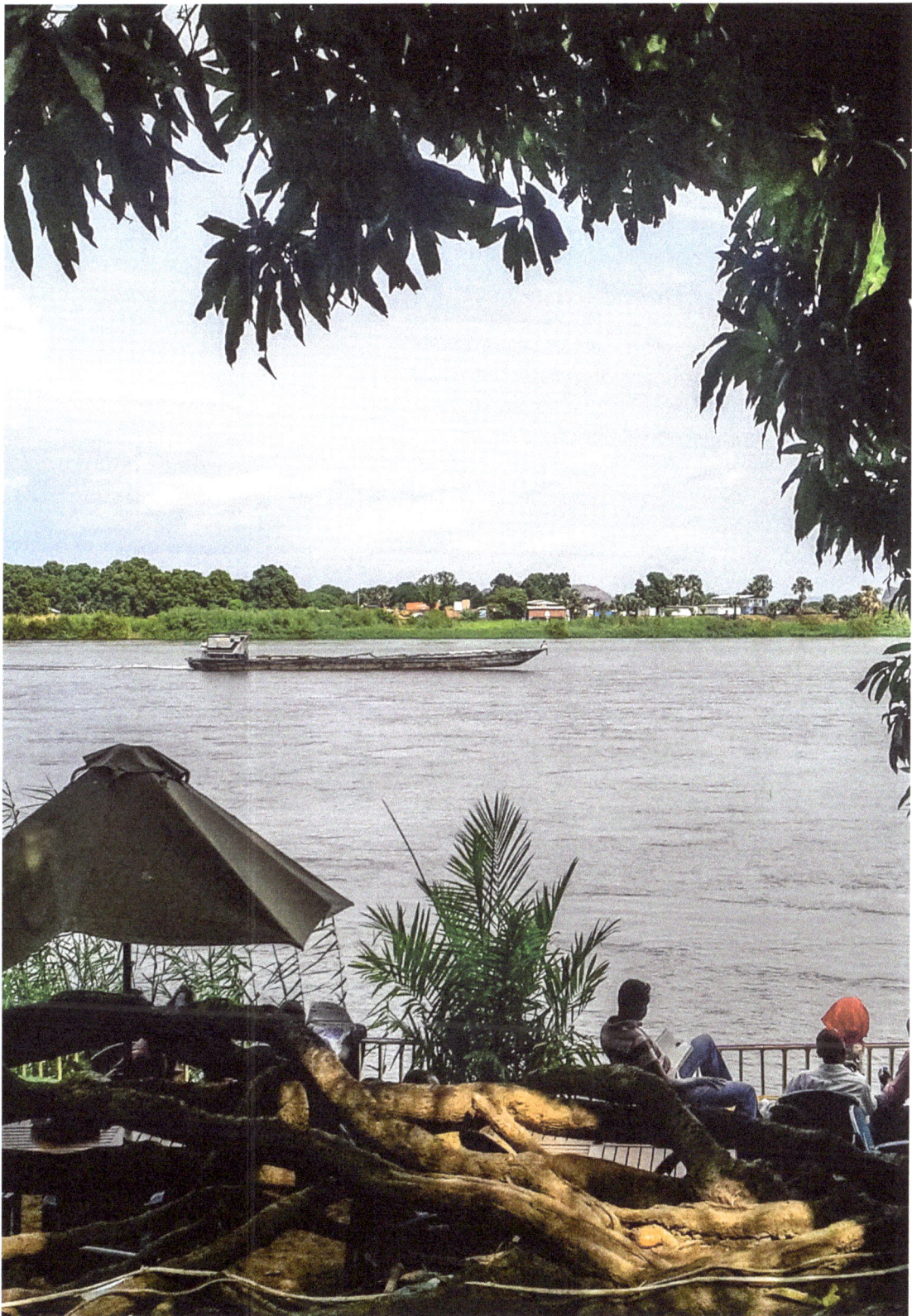

here," she said. There was no doubt about that. I took her out for lunch later, and we received a lot of inquisitive glances.

Hiba is a single mother to one son but gets a lot of help with childcare from her mother. They live in a housing complex with their own security guard close to the Nile, and she can look out across the river from the living room window. The regular security guard was in his late fifties, and his attitudes are testament to the patriarchal society. Hiba told me about a married couple who lived in the same housing complex. The husband drank a lot and beat his wife up. Sometimes it was loud.

"One day the security guard had dragged the wife beater away and said, 'You must beat your wife in the afternoon, when most people are at work. Otherwise, there are far too many people in hearing shot. If there are too many witnesses, you could get in trouble. Times are changing, you know'," said Hiba, shaking her head. South Sudan is not an easy country to live in either way.

"Despite all of this, it is nonetheless a fascinating country. But it's intense being here. Fortunately, most people have a positive outlook and maintain their hope in the future through the few good things that happen. The little pricks of light have a much higher value due to all the darkness they are surrounded by," Hiba philosophised. Then she thanked me for the lunch, which had consisted of salad for her and fish from the Nile for me. She had to dash to an interview, where once again she would be the one asking the questions. But on the way out, her widest smile emerged, showing a large degree of self-irony:

"This country is destroyed, and we have a very long way to go forwards. On the other hand, the country has probably never been in a great place, so there was perhaps not that much to destroy in the first place."

Two days earlier, I had been sitting at Logali House, the favourite meeting spot for journalists and Westerners working in Juba. The restaurant is inside really, but in the evenings most people sit on the terrace with its own bar counter or in the backyard nearby, enjoying the air as it slowly gets cooler. On a large flat screen under a covering on the terrace, English football is shown when there is a match on, otherwise Al Jazeera's English-language news channel entertains like at other places. The TV plays an important role in providing entertainment and relaxation from a stressful day. But people here are curious about new people and what they do and quickly make contact with new people. It wasn't long before I was invited into a group sitting around one of the wooden tables under a green Heineken umbrella in the backyard. There was only one local present, the rest were from Western Europe or North America. Everyone had a beer, a glass of wine or a cocktail in front of them on the round wooden table with metal legs. We talked about this and that, mostly things related to Juba, South Sudan, and the work that the various organisations were doing in the country. It was an inevitability that I ended up hearing a lot of gossip about colleagues who were not currently there. It was clear that a lot of drinking goes on here. Like an office Christmas party every single weekend, judging by the stories that were told.

"Copious amounts of alcohol is a way for us to be able to disconnect in any way and get through all the craziness here. If we hadn't had this as a safety valve, I think many of us would have left a long time ago," explained a British man in his late twenties. He worked for a humanitarian organisation.

I asked everyone around the table who was the most interesting local person I could talk to about the future of South Sudan.

"Akuja!" was the spontaneous answer from at least three of them, and in chorus. I got to hear that she had many cultural irons in the fire. Among other things, she runs The Roots Project, a cooperative social network where artistic techniques and traditions are exchanged. I got her number and called her the next day. She wasn't exactly hard to ask, and I promised to throw in coffee, dinner, or drinks.

"Where shall we meet?" I asked.

"Logali House." Of course.

Akuja de Garang was born in Juba but lived in London for 20 years. In 2004, she returned to South Sudan to help build her homeland. She works with education for girls, and it is much in need. The country is the second worst in the world for both primary and secondary education, regardless of gender. Only 46 percent of children are enrolled in primary school. The figure is as low as a miserable 4 percent when it comes to college. Most of them are boys. Girls often drop out as early as the 4th or 5th grade because of being married off, getting pregnant or having to take care of the family at home.

Akuja entered Logali House with a distinctive lofty hairstyle. The hair stood out in all directions. She wanted to have a Heineken in the characteristic green glass bottle — not in a mug. I ordered a Castle Light. Four percent alcohol was enough in the Juba heat.

Akuja talked about the optimism within the tourism industry just after the 2011 liberation. There were rafting trips, visits to nature reserves and national parks and mountain trips lasting several days. A variant of the latter cost $3,000 for a long weekend. That is per person, and in a tent, a luxurious one, but pricey nonetheless. There had clearly not been a lack of enthusiasm or optimism. In Boma in the east, wealthy Arabs are even said to have financed a private airstrip so that they could fly straight there on secluded luxury holidays way off the beaten track in animal country and no-man's land.

"Nature and wildlife are really close to my heart, and I love exploring the fantastic places here! There is no end. We have the largest swamp in the world with elephants, giraffes, antelopes, gazelles, leopards, and wild boars, not to mention that the second busiest migration path in the world runs through South Sudan. Hundreds of thousands of animals go to or come down from the highlands every year. And we have lions!" Her eyes sparkled as she told me.

Akuja organises a monthly market herself at Da Vinci, one of the most popular restaurants in Juba, close to the bridge.

"We have a huge opportunity to lay the foundations now. Like, right now. This is an unparalleled chance for people to experience something totally unique, to get the tourist ball rolling in South Sudan. Just think about the difference. In South Africa, Kenya, or Botswana, you can almost sit there stuck in safari traffic. There are too many cars in the largest national parks. We of course don't have the same problem here," she smiled.

"I think it is important that we do not invest too much too quickly. We need to find the right balance. And we must define our national heritage."

Tourism arriving too quickly in South Sudan is not exactly a problem. There is almost no infrastructure or accommodation options outside Juba, and besides, potential tourist destinations must be secure. Not to mention that the war must end. Potential visitors must feel safe and comfortable. Outside the capital, there is no running water or mains electricity, and the sewer runs straight into partially covered ditches alongside the roads. There is quite simply no shortage of luxury lodges in many places across Africa, and there, a lack of infrastructure is no great obstacle. Characteristic light blue tanker trucks fetch water from the Nile, shuttling back and forth to homes and businesses, while diesel generator vendors rub their hands together in glee and count the money. Lodges and hotels would have been high on the list of customers — paying well for clean water for all the showers and swimming pools, and even more for stable electricity. The problem is the same one as in other war-torn countries: the security situation does not exactly attract paying guests.

Akuja suddenly leaned over to me, took hold of my shoulder, and whispered.

"But do you know what's really unique here?"

I shook my head, excited at what was to come.

"Visiting the last tribes in Africa. The last ones who still live as they have always done, and who still want to keep it this way." She was clearly proud and mentioned mundari, taposa and dinka — three of the tribal peoples in the country. They live within small pockets in the jungle in the districts of Eastern Equatoria and Terekekka and are sustained primarily by their livestock.

But you can't just jump on a plane. The authorities do not want to disturb their way of life and demand that visitors obtain an official permit before they can visit the infamous tribes. Usually only social anthropologists and similar vocations receive such a permit. Then it is also a question of whether the tribes actually want to show themselves very much. Short-term income can be a challenge to, and threaten, their way of life. History has shown that it is easy to destroy unique cultures by introducing diseases, work-reducing machines, and alcohol. Willpower is rarely strong enough. And once a line has been crossed, it is impossible to turn around.

According to Akuja, the only museum in the country is a military museum, clearly as a symptom of generations of war.

"We have a number of attractions, but we simply cannot market them without a stable security situation," she said, admitting that she was maybe a little too optimistic — that getting tourists to come to the country is probably a long way off.

"For as long as I can remember, I have heard: 'if tomorrow comes...'. People hold on tightly to the idea that there is hope for the future. If it does not happen to the next generation or the one after that, then maybe in three generations. It's not exactly ideal, but that's the hope we have — despite the fact that people have never seen anything better, because it's always been bad."

Akuja had tears in her eyes. I could only imagine how she actually felt, behind the make-up and her professional façade, in this war-torn country. Tears ran down each side of her nose. They came down to her red mouth before she managed to wipe them away, together with a little lipstick.

"We are warriors, how else would we have survived for so long?" said Akuja, rhetorically. That said, they would have likely been far more numerous and in a better place if there had not been quite so many warriors. The best way to avoid getting depressed is perhaps not to talk about all the problems in South Sudan.

For my part, the visit to the world's newest country was over. Unlike most people who travel onwards from here, I was not fleeing, but simply turning my attention towards another country only 700-800 kilometres to the northeast, where I would also meet envy due to my Western passport. Ironically, the Norwegian government wants to send refugees back there.

Daily life in South Sudan involves heavy burdens for most of the women, who often have to fetch both food and water. The men generally only help out if they have access to motorised vehicles.

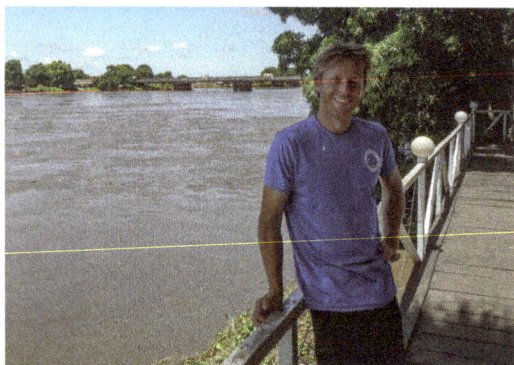

Outside Da Vinci, one of the most popular restaurants in Juba, and in front of the White Nile.

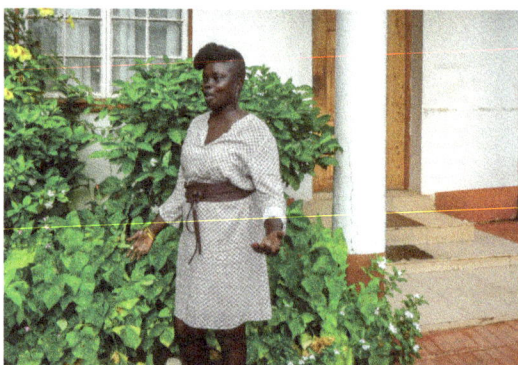

Akuja de Garang returned to Juba in 2004 after 20 years in London. She wants to help rebuild her homeland.

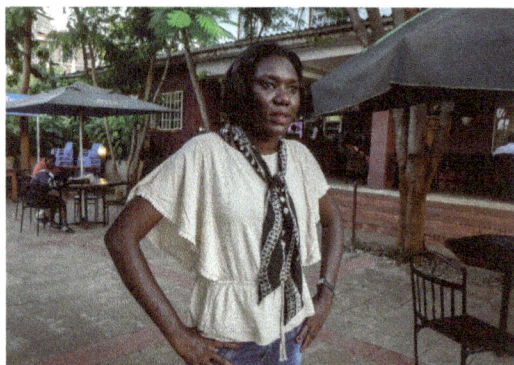

Al Jazeera journalist Hiba Morgan prefers to be in charge herself. Here she is outside Logali House.

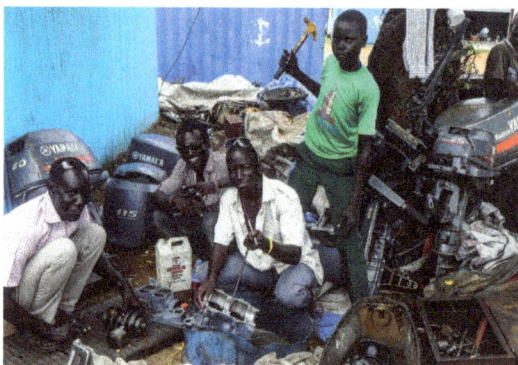

Outboard engine repairers at the Nile.

The only bridge over the Nile in Juba. I have both jumped it, and sprinted across it.

The shade is a good place to be in the South Sudanese heat.

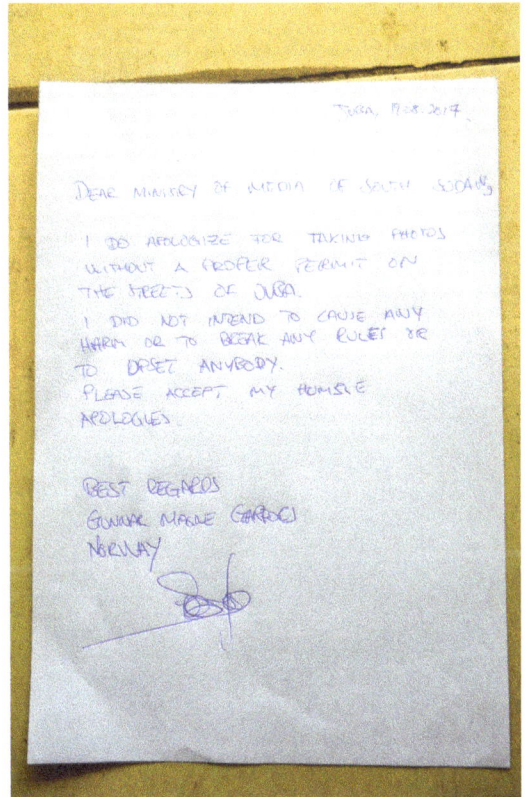
Signed apology to the people of South Sudan.

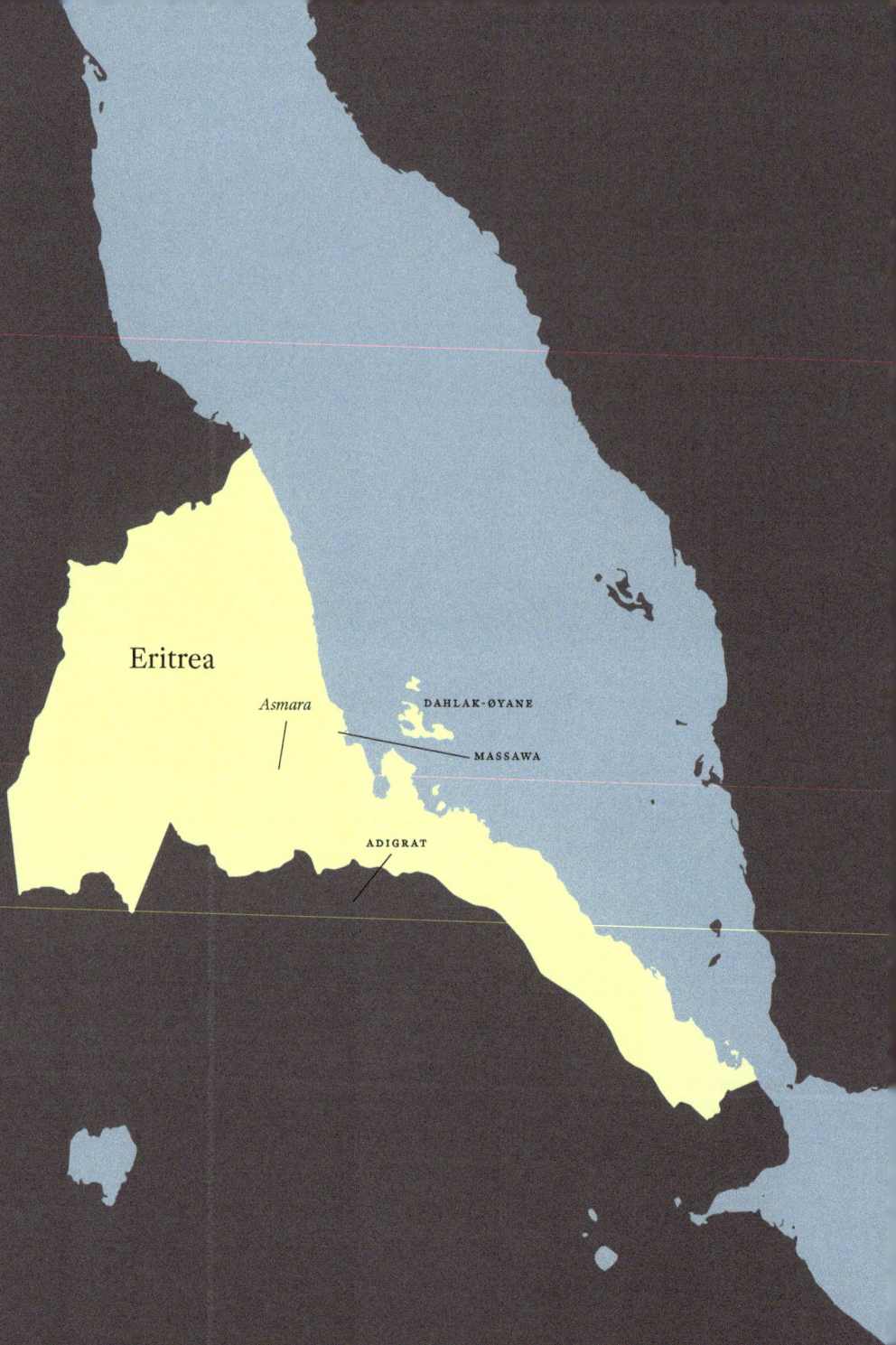

Eritrea

Asmara

DAHLAK-ØYANE

MASSAWA

ADIGRAT

200 km

6

Eritrea,
Africa

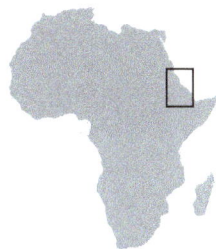

INHABITANTS: 5,000,000 (Wikipedia)
TOURISTS PER YEAR: 2,000 (garfors.com)
AREA: 117,600 square kiolmetres

ONCE AGAIN, the trip takes me to a dictatorship. Purely looking away from the details of the particular government, it is incredible that so few people visit Eritrea. Its eminent kitchen, the exceptionally varied nature and the above-average hospitable people mean that everything should be laid out in waiting for us tourists. I was looking forward to my return to this underrated country with its nice people, which until the end of 2018 was quite inaccessible. Eritrean Airlines took me there from Khartoum in Sudan. There were no other Western passengers onboard the full plane, but there were enormous amounts of hand luggage. The majority consisted of newly purchased clothing, electronics, and food from a country with a far better product range than Eritrea. Just who would have thought that about Sudan?

"The family will now finally get to have some variation in their diet," said a thin and sinewy lady in her forties. I helped her find enough space for three overflowing plastic webbed bags in the luggage racks. She was travelling with three small children, and I was impressed with all the mother had managed to bring with her. On top of all that, she had brought a black suitcase with her that was actually too big for hand luggage. The children also had a colourful trolley bag each. They were seemingly cramped with food as well. I put my own backpack under the seat in front of me on the short flight to the capital Asmara.

The small and outdated airport is located just a few kilometres beyond the city centre. A local travel agency had arranged for me to be able to get a visa at the airport, but the process took well over an hour. Once I had gotten through customs, there were no longer any buses or taxis outside, and I decided to walk to the hotel.

About halfway along the walk I was offered a lift with a man about 50 years old. He had stopped a hundred metres in front me, reversing back to me and opened the window.

"What are you doing? Have you walked all the way from the airport? One could think that we did not like visitors. Jump right in," offered Russom, a craftsman in a red Mazda, that was at least 20 years old. He decided he might as well take me on a sight-seeing trip around the whole city and showed me his house. I asked if I could come in and see how he lived, but then he got a little bothered.

"No, then you will see unparalleled chaos. My wife and I are not particularly good at getting our children to clean up after themselves, what would you then think of me?" he speculated. I took the hint and he drove me to my hotel. There we exchanged phone numbers before we shook each other by the hand. Not surprisingly, he refused to take any payment. If you become friends with someone in Africa, there is rarely any question of being allowed to give them anything in return.

"Do not insult me! And just say if you need anything in the end," said Russom, and headed off.

Despite few flight and boat routes to Eritrea, they are a surprisingly very international people. But they do not travel just out of curiosity or as an excursion. Since 1991, the country has been ruled by the iron fist of the 10th longest-serving dictator in the world — a grip of enamelled stainless steel. President Isaias Afwerki has sometimes even hinted at restarting the war with Ethiopia. Speculation says that he does this to deflect attention away from other negative issues and to legitimise the fact that the country does not yet have a constitution adopted in law. But there has only been one president after all, and Afwerki has no plans to give up any time soon. He has a strong position of power even if the economy is not doing very well, and the country has few friends. But on 2nd April 2018, something happened that could change many things. Their neighbour, Ethiopia, elected a new prime minister, 42-year-old Abiy Ahmed. The young and popular politician has received many positive headlines both at home and internationally since coming to power. During his acceptance speech for the post of prime minister, he spread optimism and received a very positive reaction from most Ethiopians. His government, for example, was formed of 50 percent women, and he took the initiative to set out a peace agreement with Eritrea. A few weeks later, the borders between these old arch-rivals were opened, diplomatic relations were established, as well as the creation of new air routes. Ethiopian Airlines started to operate direct flights between Addis Ababa and Asmara, and even a direct route from Oslo to Asmara, with a stopover in Stockholm. Time will tell what this really means for Eritrea in the long run, but trade in the Ethiopian border town of Adigrat has at least gone through the roof thanks to Eritrean customers who can now cross the border for the first time in more than twenty years.

Ahmed's position, in addition to President Afwerki visiting Addis Ababa for the first time in twenty years in July 2018, led to a domino effect in Eritrea, at least until a civil war broke out in Ethiopia in 2020. Various Eritrean forces allegedly participated on the Tigrayan side, and the friendly relationship never really took off. This stopped what could have been the start of Eritrea gradually opening up to the outside world. Including fewer tense stand-offs and fewer closed borders and a significantly decrease in military and police forces. Investing in the liberalisation of the proposition and the access for tourists could have been a way of bringing in much-needed foreign capital, establishing new jobs at the same time and also more easily being able to retrain people from the security forces. Tax revenues and living standards would have increased, something which could have had a knock-on effect of more people receiving a better education — something a dictator like Afwerki hardly fears more. Thanks to the war in the neighbouring country the wily old fox never actively needed to procrastinate for as long as possible to secure his own status and power. Many fear that Eritrea will hardly change very much until there is a new president.

No one has heard of Reporters Without Borders in Eritrea either. The country is second to last on the organisation's press freedom list, with only North Korea presenting worse journalistic conditions. All media is state controlled in Eritrea, and many journalists are in prison. Journalists in exile post relevant news on the Internet, but in Eritrea itself the internet access is so slow that one must have immense patience to be able to download anything at all. Just sending an email, posting a status update, or photo, can challenge all but the hardiest souls. In any case, websites the authorities do not like, are immediately blocked or censored. I managed to access the websites I wanted to, only thanks to a VPN, but in a country with so much to see, you hardly need Internet anyway. Not as a tourist, at least.

Afwerki's culture of fear runs deep, and it comes as no surprise that several hundred thousand have left or fled the country — many to Scandinavia. As in other countries with dictatorial traits in the upper echelons of power, for example Cambodia, Belarus and the United States, the truth is not very important. Lies are rhetoric and are used as a frequent tool to push attention away from more serious matters, to wear people out or to detain.

More than 30 percent of the Eritrean workforce is employed within the police or in the military — not because they want to, moreover they have to. Military service has no time limit and in principle applies to both women and men from the age of 16 or 17. The government can therefore control the lives of its citizens exactly as they desire and have them live their whole life as a servant. The soldiers are stationed where the government needs them to be, and they can be moved far away from family and friends 'just because'. Working hours are controlled by their immediate superior and this particular person's mood.

"We are like slaves for the government — this is like a community prison," said a 24-year-old soldier. He was standing guard outside the Yemeni embassy and had asked me for both a cigarette and a light as I passed. I had neither of these but stopped to talk to the smiling guy in uniform. An old machine gun with a wooden butt hung in a tired leather strap over his shoulder. He said that this was his eighth year in the military and had no illusions about doing anything else until he was viewed as too old for active duty. The salary paid is also so low that in reality the soldiers cannot afford enough food, a place to live or to get married. They are obligated to work, but with such low wages it seems almost like slavery — apart from not getting any food, since they earn money, you see. This is a vicious and unfair circle. In 2016, Eritreans accounted for the seventh largest group of asylum seekers in Europe. It is understandable why.

Paradoxically, the numerous military personnel contributed to it feeling safe to travel here as a foreigner. They are seen standing everywhere with pretty much obsolete machine guns, but usually nod and smile at me as a foreigner. They can make it relatively unpleasant at the same time for those who live here and do not follow the rules. The repression on show is not very subtle.

Unfortunately, it is not always as easy to travel beyond the capital Asmara. A tourist permit is required for such extravagant travel, collected from the tourist office in the middle of the city, but you are not allowed to travel everywhere — even with a paper like that in my pocket. The permit is usually sorted within half an hour, but the meaningless bureaucracy means it is more tempting to just sit in a bar, not least because the nightlife in both Asmara and Massawa is surprisingly lively and goes on well into the night. The locals love the beer that is named after the capital. The first time I visited Eritrea, I met a lady at a bar called Asmara. Like many others, she had fled the country, obtaining a Swedish passport, but visits her family at least once a year.

"Do you want a beer?" I asked her.

"Of course!" she replied in a fluent Stockholm dialect. There was no trace of an Eritrean accent to be heard. I ordered two Asmara beers from the bartender who was dressed in a classic white shirt, bowtie, and black braces. The characteristic bottles with a red label were opened in just five seconds. We toasted each other and took a sip each.

"Are you aware that I am now drinking Asmara with Asmara in Asmara?" I asked.

She grinned and claimed she had never heard that one before. So, we made a toast to that, before I was invited to have dinner at her uncle's home. The food in Eritrea is very reminiscent of the food found in Ethiopia, but over the last 20 years it hasn't been possible to remind either country about that. They may be able to build on their common food history together now. On offer was steak, grilled chicken, lentils and traditional Eritrean injera bread. The bread is similar to pancakes in both its appearance and consistency, but not at all in the way it tastes. Water and flour first ferment for several days prior to baking. Once it is in your hand, the lack of cutlery is not going to hold you back from spreading on tasty morsels. True to tradition, we tore off chunks of injera with our fingers and added different fillings, almost the same as filling a taco. Coffee was made after dinner on a kind of gigantic espresso cooker made from metal and heated over glowing coals — just on the uncle's living room floor. Luckily it was made of concrete.

Not exactly your usual tourist experience. But then there are so few tourists actually visiting Eritrea that barely anything is in place for them. The best restaurant in the city, for example, does not appear on any map or tourist website. I only found out about it thanks a direct tip from the hotel where I was staying and got into a conversation with an older gentleman. The bald man with grey hair was immaculately dressed in suit trousers and a white shirt. Joseph, as I found out he was called, had looked at me with curiosity as I entered. After a while he had come over to me with two beers, Asmara of course, and asked how I knew about his favourite restaurant. I told him that incredibly a hotel had actually provided a good restaurant recommendation. I asked him to sit down at my table. Why eat alone when one can have good company? He sat down and gave me one of the glass bottles, then he took a sip from the other one.

"Just as long as tourists don't start taking over the place. Then the charm will quickly disappear," he replied thoughtfully and asked me not to reveal the name of the restaurant. He soon added that he did actually have many good friends from abroad, and that he had nothing against foreigners.

"Several of them have visited me, as tourists," he said.

I have no doubt about that — he spoke perfect English. "But everyone who comes for a short trip has the same thing in common — they immediately regret that they did not book a longer trip. They say that a couple of days is far too little. When they order tickets, they forget that I had asked them to stay for one long week, minimum."

By that he meant 9 days, or Saturday until the following Sunday.

I ordered a new round of Asmara for Josef and me.

"Almost all tourists tend to regret it, you know. And then come with the same angle. 'If I had only known how incredibly beautiful Eritrea was, and how indescribably nice the people who live here are, I would have stayed at least a week,' they say to me. And then they promise to come back."

"Yes, do they come back?" I wondered.

He smiled and laughed a little.

"Well, you know how people are. But some of them have actually kept their promise and come back, to see more of paradise," he laughed. Straight afterwards he vexed about how difficult the government makes things with a cumbersome visa process and excessive restrictions on where people can and cannot travel.

"Do you have siblings?" he abruptly asked.

"Yes, there are seven of us," I replied.

He continued by asking me if we all got on well. I got a sense that something lay behind it. After I told him about my siblings, he started telling me about his four siblings and an inheritance settlement that had not gone smoothly.

"I took over my parents' house after they died, and then I paid I out my siblings. But I subsequently sold the whole house here last year, and then that made them want more money. They thought the value had increased," he said with a sad expression.

"Seriously? But you had already bought them out. What a pack of wolves," I said.

"They are more like hyenas," he said, smiling again. Fortunately, he had not lost his sense of humour, despite the unexpected headache of an inheritance struggle. He told me that he had rejected the claim, which had made them angry.

"One day my sister called me and said that if they didn't all get more money, they would not attend to my funeral. What do you say to that?" he asked.

I did not quite know if I should laugh or cry. I laughed in the end. And then Joseph laughed as well. Fortunately, he had a good dose of self-irony.

"As if I cared about that. I will be dead!" he grinned. And we laughed again.

"Are they older than you?" I wondered.

"Not all of them, so it's not a certainty that I'll be the first to die anyway."

"In the case of you dying first, do you have any debt you can bequeath to them," I joked. I did not know both sides of the story of course, but I did not see any point of launching in as a devil's advocate in this conversation with the unknown man either. Fortunately, he saw the funny side of the question.

"Don't tempt me onto sketchy ground. Who needs enemies when you have family?" he mumbled and smiled. I liked this old guy who completely out of the blue had begun to tell me his personal tragicomedy, before it was all too soon over. I was served my food, and Joseph apologised and said that I should be allowed to eat in peace. I protested, but he said he had to go home to his wife anyway. He downed the last drops of beer and put the glass down hard onto the table. As he got up, he turned to face me.

"Don't forget that foreign tourists like you teach us about a completely different side to life through your stories from the outside, and that motivates us to think differently and to see the world in a different way," he said, taking hold of me by my right arm. There was no doubting that he meant it.

Eritrea is practically untouched by the modern tourism industry. Travelling around the country is like travelling back in time — to the Italian colonial era and Italy is still where most of the few tourists one might encounter comes from.

Walking through Asmara always makes me smile. You get to experience the best-preserved example of Italian fascist architecture in the world by strolling arbitrarily around the city. I thought about how surreal it all seemed, but a walk in Asmara is probably similar to travelling to Rome or Milan back in the 1930s, even though the Fiat cars gurgling around the streets are newer by several decades. The architecture is an extreme variant of art deco, with most of the houses in relatively good condition and painted in strong colours. Many of the commercial buildings have old-fashioned shop signs in the city centre, often with information about Italian food dishes like pizza, pasta, and gelato. Or cappuccino. At an outdoor café, the coffee was so good that it took three cups before I could tear myself away.

"If all the customers were like you, I would have done better than Starbucks by a long way," smiled the owner. There are no Western chains in Eritrea, so I wondered how he had heard about the Seattle coffee giant.

"I watch a lot of DVDs. They cost almost nothing, anyhow, I swap movies and shows with friends. They only show rubbish on the TV," he said. It was an accurate portrayal of propaganda and censored programmes.

In the end, I managed to overcome my caffeine lust, and I strolled on. Thousands of prominent old trees line alleys over large swathes of the city and change the atmosphere. It feels incredibly relaxing to walk around Asmara. There are so few tourists that no one has cottoned onto the notion of harassing the few who are actually here, with souvenir bargains or special 'friend' prices for guided tours. There is an enormous contrast to Cairo or Istanbul, a little further north. If you are contacted by a local, it is because of a genuine interest. Two days later I visited Roma, the revered old cinema just off Sematat Avenue. Inside, film props are exhibited from another era, film posters printed in just a few colours and a film projector with mounted film reels that is nearly one hundred years old.

"Why on earth are you visiting this place? Visiting Eritrea, of all the places?" I was asked by a young woman when I came out of the cinema with my backpack slung over one shoulder. I told her that I liked places with few tourists.

"Yes, then I understand. You have definitely come to the right country," she smiled and hurried on.

I did the same, but in the opposite direction. I was on my way to the most famous and distinctive building — Fiat Tagliero — designed by the Italian architect Giuseppe Pettazzi and completed in 1937. The beige, somewhat low building is reminiscent of an airplane, with a 15-meter-long wing on either side. If you are to design a service station that shelters you from the rain, then you might as well make it could just as well make it catch your eye. The hotel standard in Eritrea is by no means like you would find in Europe, but the hospitality is several notches above. And if you are a photographer, then this place is not really Eritrea, it is more like Eden: Competition-winning compositions can be found on each street corner, as well as inside and outside of all the houses in between.

The question remaining is just how many tourists actually travel to Eritrea. As Stalin, Lenin and Hitler found out, it is most effective to really go for it when comes to lying. The German Nazi leader believed that propaganda was most effective when utilising lies so colossal that no one would believe that anyone could possibly circumvent the truth that much.

Some Eritrean tourist authorities use the same tactics. By greatly inflating how many tourists actually come to the country, they hope that most people will believe it really is an attractive tourist country, resulting in even more tourists coming here. But the streams of tourists have not materialized, despite the fact that the government reports to the UNWTO that they receive 142,000 tourists a year. That means almost 400 per day, to a country with closed borders, only one international airport and zero international boat routes in operation for passenger traffic. There are very few foreign airlines that fly to Asmara, although the situation has improved through Ethiopian Airlines now having two daily scheduled flights to Addis Ababa and a route to Scandinavia, post signing of the peace agreement. The one and only local airline that operates commercial routes has a single aircraft. The best thing about Eritrean Airlines, however, is their slogan: 'Gateway to Africa'. Ignoring the extreme limitations of the airport, it does not sound too bad.

That is before one checks the route map. The airline has a couple of routes between Asmara and cities in the Middle East, and one route to Khartoum in Sudan. The latter does travel onwards to Milan via Cairo, but nonetheless limited. Gateway and mouse hole are clearly counted as the same thing in Eritrea.

There are exactly 100 countries that are larger than little Eritrea, which hardly beats Iceland in terms of size. But there is a lot to see and many reasons to travel here. Travelling from what is the world's sixth highest capital at 2325 metres above sea level and down to the idyllic, but sadly, extremely war-damaged beach town of Massawa by the Red Sea, takes two wild hours — two hours if your driver is impatient and in a fast car. The bus takes almost four hours to cover the 110 winding kilometres, with some stops.

Massawa is definitely a must-see gem for all visitors. The architecture there is more inspired by the Ottoman Empire than by Italy, and it is as common to hear Arabic as the Eritrean language Tigrinya on the streets. However, the biggest difference is the climate. It is impossible to travel from the dry and relatively cool climate of the capital to the high humidity and oppressive heat down by the sea without changing clothes, or wishing one had. Fortunately, there are several popular beaches near the city, in addition to the Dahlak Islands.

The old town of Massawa manages to be both impressive and sad at the same time. Most of the ancient buildings are still in use, while some are seemingly too damaged by bombs and grenades to be used at all. Almost every building has a bullet hole. The two civil wars are to blame, but even bombs and grenades failed to remove the old grandness. The buildings still have charm, just more under the surface, as if there was an attempt to remove it with a poor eraser. During the day it seemed like a ghost town. However, as the night wore on, the ruined brick houses came to life — even some that had looked completely abandoned and disused. There were bars and nightclubs in the least imaginable places. Uplifting beats from varied music genres, excited discussions and loud laughter came out of open doors and windows. It was positive that the city was slowly, if not quite so surely, seemingly heading on the road to recovery. For those who had lived there in the old days and seen what the city was actually like, most things were just sad, but fortunately not everything.

I went into one of the bars. The bartender smiled and poured me a beer before I could even say anything. He did not really have much else to serve, and he likely needed the money. I paid and sat down on a fittingly unstable plastic garden chair by a window table, albeit without glass in the window.

At another table were sat five elderly local men playing dominoes by the light of just a couple of light bulbs. They smiled, and I tried to say hello. One of them mumbled something or other in return, a little worried. They could not speak English, but we exchanged a few smiles after a while. They were obviously curious, and it annoyed me that I did not speak Tigrinya, the most important local language in Eritrea and Ethiopia.

It usually isn't a problem to just use English anywhere in the world, because usually a well-meaning interpreter shows up. It's often a young person who seizes the chance to practice their English, increasing their own status at the same time, by being able to contribute to the communication between the visitor and the locals.

But it didn't happen at this particular bar today. The humidity was also sky high, and the creaking ceiling fan did not help very much with the temperature well over 40 degrees. I strolled back to my hotel. My hotel room was fortunately on the second floor, and it helped a little to have a draft from the two open windows.

Back in Asmara I happened to get in a conversation with a guy in his late seventies. We began talking about Massawa, and I told him that I had been there.

"The state of the city makes me cry. I refuse to destroy my memory of good old Massawa. I'm never going to return!" firmly declared the spice seller. He sells all the imaginable and unthinkable herbs in one of the markets. The numerous smells from his goods collided and made me smile. If only I had had a kitchen.

The number of well over 100,000 tourists per year simply seemed extremely inflated. But since some Eritrean tourist authorities have chosen this inflated strategy, they need to make sure that everyone who works in the Ministry of Tourism at least knows this number and can vouch for the lies. I had to find the ministry. The Internet gave no answer, so I rang Russom. He happened to be nearby and promised to drive me there. He said that it was not a big detour for him before his next job, and he refused to accept payment. Reluctantly, he accepted some small Norwegian coins with holes in the middle.

"Original jewellery for your children, they can be fastened on a thin leather strap," I suggested. I jumped out, waved him off and entered the anonymous front door of the brick building. The ministry office is located on the top floor of a seven-storey high block about halfway between the airport and the city centre. The elevator sort of worked on the way up, even though it was slow and kept sticking. Up in the office I had to wait a quarter of an hour on a spindly chair before getting an audience.

"How many tourists come to Eritrea each year?" I asked the man I had been ushered in front of.

"Just over 2000," immediately replied the man behind a desk. He was in his late twenties and sat there upright. He could not have been informed about the far higher figure sent to UNWTO.

"And that applies to everyone entering via plane, boat and land," I asked. He nodded.

A colleague nearby sat silently. Both wore white shirts. Neither of them had very much else to speak of. They had nothing to say in terms of short-term plans or long-term strategies in the future. But at the very least I had been given a seemingly much more realistic number of tourist visits per year. A number that did not correspond particularly well with the official figure.

I thanked them and went out into the hallway. It was dark there. An electricity cut. The elevator was now out of order, of course.

"TIA," I mumbled to myself, thinking of Alan in the Comoros. I was not massively surprised. Then all that was to be done was to find the door to the stairs and start walking down.

"You should be glad you were not in the elevator 10 minutes ago," said a lady who came out of the stairwell further down. She had come from her floor just before me and like me walked carefully down the dark fire escape. "Then you would have still been there," she laughed. The electricity is supposed to be cut at 15.00 every day. She said that people therefore did not use the lift very much after 14.50. Just in case.

Maybe that would have been something useful to inform people about on a poster, I thought to myself.

The lack of tourists was also confirmed at my hotel, right in the centre. It had about 40 rooms of a reasonable standard. I asked the receptionist if they received many tourists as guests.

He smiled and shook his head.

"No, you're the only one in several months. But in November, then many will come."

"Okay, what happens then?"

"No, I don't know that, but then both Italians and French are coming. A large group!"

"How large is a large group?" I smiled.

"Larger than in a very long time. They have booked a total of 15 double rooms."

The tourism strategy of the Eritrean government is quite paradoxical in light of one of the most well-known sayings in the country: 'Those who hide their wounds never get any medicine.'

I went to a tourist office to find out if they had very much to do.

"No, it is quiet at the moment. Several countries have warnings against travelling here, and not exactly positive news comes out of Eritrea. But you are here. Where do you want me to take you to?" asked the chief guide and began to tell me about the hiking possibilities in the mountains, trips in a hot air balloon, hang-gliding within the mountains and beach life by the coast.

"Not to mention the Dahlak Islands. They are among the most beautiful in the world, and we can take you there by boat, and you can spend the night in local accommodation. It will take your breath away! I guarantee it," he almost shouted. The islands are situated quite far out to in the Red Sea and are a paradise for those who really want to get away from civilization, as well as divers and snorkelers. But a visit costs accordingly, mostly due to a separate tourist tax for Dahlak. A thousand dollars for a weekend is not unusual, but then everything is included.

I'm not particularly interested in guided tours and do best on my own, so I had to let his business instinct down. The man in his late forties seemed a little offended behind his three-day-old beard. He had a fleck of egg on one side of his light blue shirt, and his hair was tousled. He was hardly expecting customers. Not today, or any day soon.

"Yes, you are likely affected by negative news campaigns on CNN, BBC and France 24," he grumbled.

I responded with a broad smile.

"Then I would not have even come at all."

He reacted with a nod which turned into a smile after a few seconds.

"That's a good point! But come back to us if you want to have a really good trip. I'll give you a special price," he said enticingly and gave me a business card. "And remember, if you have never visited Eritrea, then you have never really travelled," he shouted after me as I walked out the door. Once again, he forgot that I was actually in his home country already.

It remains to be seen whether the improved affairs with neighbouring countries will have any long-term effect. Despite new flights, there is still a long way to go before the country appears as a destination in colourful charter catalogues. And even though Eritrea is a destination of discovery, many will have moral qualms about travelling here. As with many dictatorships, there is only one legal political party. And also quite typically, it is called exactly what it is not: The People's Front for Democracy and Justice (PFDJ). This is not an unusual technique of governance used by imperialistic leaders. But in the third continental comrade in a row in Elsewhere, they have a reasonably well-functioning multi-party system. The civil war is the main problem in this republic in Central Africa, which is a major factor in why the country is only able to publicise a four-digit number of tourists per year.

The aeroplane-like fiat Tagliero building in Asmara.

On the outskirts of the capital is a car and petrol station.

The greengrocer in Asmara.

The traditional Injera bread is eaten with the right hand.

All roads lead to the cinema in Asmara.

Modern tools are few and far between in Eritrea, but safety is important, even if the welding mask is home-made.

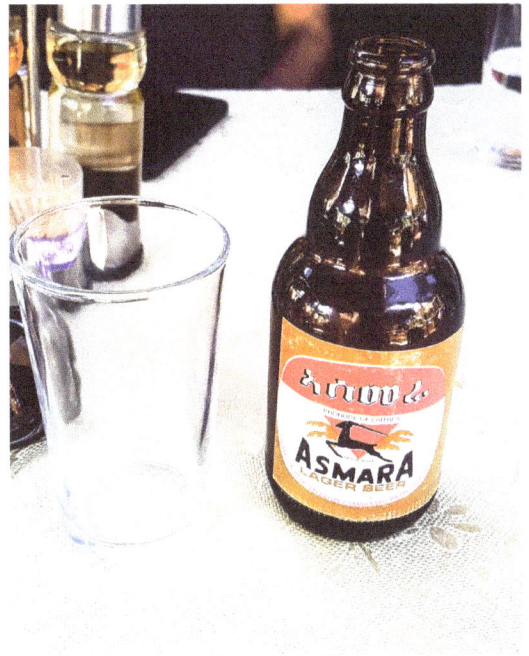
I challenge you to drink Asmara with Asmara in Asmara.

Despite many colourful doors, decay is evident throughout Massawa. Very few people can afford to renovate and maintain them.

Den sentralAfricanske
republikken

Bangui

DZANGA-SANGHA
SPECIAL RESERVE

⊢————⊣ 200 km

5

The Central African Republic, Africa

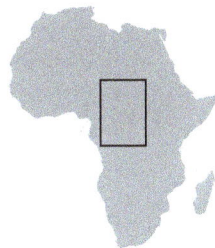

INHABITANTS: 4,600,000 (Wikipedia)
TOURISTS PER YEAR: 1,000 (garfors.com)
AREA: 622,984 square kilometres

IT DOESN'T EXACTLY shout charter holiday destination city when you arrive to see four UN planes, seven UN helicopters, three planes from the World Food Program, two planes from Médecins Sans Frontières and one from the Red Cross at the airport. Just the fact that I started counting these planes says it all. And by the way, I mustn't forget about the two discarded planes with broken windows, and of course the plane I arrived on, an ancient Boeing machine from Karinou Airlines — an airline that has a giant elephant in its logo, but an elephant without very large ears. It is surely doomed. The company right now, like Eritrean Airlines, has just one aircraft in operation. The dumbo jet was originally white, but has now yellowed, while the company name painted in blue on the sides of the plane has cracked like wizened mud seen in an African drought. The company did once have another aircraft in their fleet, but now it is one of the discarded aircraft at Aéroport International Bangui-M'Poko in Bangui. The terminal building is cramped and old. The runway is outdated. And the parking spaces are largely occupied by scrapped planes.

Worst off is nonetheless the camp for displaced people on the side of the runway that faces away from the city centre. It has the same name as the airport, M'Poko and is now officially closed, but in reality there are people here, still. At its height, the camp was home to 100,000 people who were placed among scrapped planes and oil barrels. There they lived as best they could, and in the last three years alone that the camp was operational, up until 2016, 5807 babies were born. The iconic and unusual camp was clearly visible to all passengers with window seats on the 'right' side of the plane when landing or taking off, and its image went around the world. But as is typical with these things, it was rarely or perhaps never on the frontpages — moreover well-hidden on page 18, coming after adverts for paint, furniture, or food. This is symptomatic of the many conflicts in CAR — a widely used English abbreviation meaning Central African Republic. The camp was divided into 13 sections, with a leader for each. There were restaurants, haphazard schools, shops and running water. There was even a kind of outdoor gym built from scrap metal. In no way was it luxurious, but many believed it to be safer there than in the actual capital Bangui, despite limited sanitary facilities, malaria-causing mosquitoes and armed gangs roaming at night.

In 2016, the authorities believed that the city centre was safe enough once more, and they paid around a hundred dollars to each family in the camp to make them move. The few who are still living in the camp never found a better home in the city centre and never made the move permanent, even after receiving the payment for doing just that. They still stick to some (un)usual habits, like taking a shortcut across the runway on the way to the city. This has resulted in several pilots having to cancel their landings after receiving a clear message from the tower: "There are refugees on the runway."

It is not entirely correct, but for a busy air traffic controller it is quicker to just say 'refugees', rather than 'internally displaced persons'.

Fifteen years ago, I asked an African in India where he came from.

"I live in Central Africa," he had replied, with a broad smile.

"Where in Central Africa?" I had wondered. And then he got really annoyed.

"The Central African Republic! Of course. There is no other Central Africa," he had stated. That is, of course, not entirely true, but I have remembered this since — at least every time I meet people from the Central African Republic — a country that is twice as large as Norway, but with ten percent fewer inhabitants. Until independence, the country was a French colony, and it's not a surprise that the language was left behind. The French language is perhaps the closest CAR will ever come to a possible charter destination.

I typically don't go on regular charter holiday destinations, even though, at the age of 42, I had to make a stopover, including accommodation, on Gran Canaria — the number one Mediterranean destination for sun-starved Norwegians. I just hoped I did not meet anyone I knew. But four planes from Oslo and one from Bergen had just landed, so what happened next was inevitable.

"Are you getting some Mediterranean sun?" an acquaintance from Trøndelag smirked as I sneaked past the luggage belt. I mumbled something about the wrong plane before I hurried on. Fortunately, he does not do Twitter.

The Central African Republic became independent in 1960 with David Dacko as its first president. Jean-Bedel Bokassa, the first president's cousin, seized power in a coup six years later and went on to develop a terrorist regime the world had hardly seen the likes of before or since. In 1976, for example, he appointed himself as emperor, but got a taste of his own medicine three years later when he was removed in a new coup, and by none other than his cousin, David Dacko. Revenge. A few years later, and for the second time in his career, Dacko was deposed, as you might guess, again in a coup. This time it was not a cousin who was behind it, but General André Kolingba. The country did not hold its first democratic election until 1993, but even that did not help calm things down in CAR. The government now has control over some regions, but the majority of the country is controlled by various rebels, some are Christian, others are Muslim. It is a little ironic that all factions are trying to legitimize their existence by claiming that they are fighting against ethnic discrimination and corruption. Violence, abuse, and rape are used as very widespread means of enforcing power among the rebels, making many parts of the country that are not under government control seemingly very insecure. The UN and other organisations fear genocide in some parts of the country, with the dividing line roughly separating Christians and Muslims.

This has led to many stationed foreign UN personnel, in addition to visitors who work for various private security forces and organisations. Prices for hotels in CAR are subsequently sky-high, despite the fact that there is an ample supply of hotel beds. Fortunately, the website Couchsurfing exists and is a great help for finding people who live in different parts of the world, and maybe even get to stay at their home. It actually works just like Airbnb — the difference being that it's free. Couchsurfing has also been around far longer. It must then be annoying that the main founder of Airbnb, Brian Chesky, is now worth billions, while Couchsurfing inventor, Casey Fenton earns peanuts. He has the functionality, the website, and the users, but he is just too nice to start charging for the service.

Desiré is the only coach-website-user in Bangui with a serious profile, if not the only one in the whole of CAR. As unusual as it may sound, Desiré is a man, despite the name. Since the country is not exactly one of the safest destinations in the world, I thought it would be a good idea to know someone there. The UN has 12,000 troops in the country, in addition to the presence of many foreign aid organisations, as I mentioned earlier. I asked Desiré if he would like to meet me for a coffee, but that was never going to happen.

"If you do not want me to be cranky and offended, you better spend the night in my guest room. I will pick you up from the airport. When do you land?" he asked a few hours after I had sent him a message. Once through passport control at the airport, there was a man there with a 'GUNNAR GARFORS' sign. The only problem was that it was not Desiré — at least he did not look like his profile picture. It turned out to be a porter who had been sent in with a sign, with a hope of earning a few francs. Unfortunately, he was out of luck, I travelled with just hand luggage, as always, so there was nothing for him to charge for. He showed me the way to Desiré anyway, who was standing outside in a white shirt and jeans, with a computer bag slung over his shoulder.

"I came straight from work to pick you up. Welcome to Bangui!" he said and stretched out his hand. We were sat inside a little yellow taxi just two minutes later. It took only a further ten minutes before we were alongside a fence made from corrugated metal. I insisted on paying the driver. Desiré had taken time off from work to meet me at the airport — at the very least he shouldn't have to pay my way. We had turned off the paved main road that runs between the airport and Bangui city centre. The taxi driver had to change tact due to three large UN tanks that owned the road. They could of course pretty much do whatever they wanted, relatively without redress. 10-12 armed soldiers sat in the back and would have likely made themselves heard if anyone had complained about their driving.

Desiré's medium-sized brick house fitted quite nicely into the neighbourhood. On the street were some other similar houses and some that were much more basic. Or sheds, as they would have been referred to in Western countries. There was a high density of corrugated metal roofs here. Between the 'blocks' there were red roads. The roads were not paved and made of the characteristic sand that is found everywhere in the Bangui area. Despite having one of the better houses in the neighbourhood, my host was humble:

"This fence is all I can afford. I hope to soon be able to save enough to build a decent brick wall. It is a really great thing in this country to be able to have your own little oasis around your house, where you can be yourself, without being overlooked," he explained. As a newspaper editor with 13 employees, Desiré earns more than most do in Bangui, without that really meaning very much. But it does mean that he actually managed to buy two houses. His brother lived in this house, with his wife and a daughter. I was to spend the night here in the guest room. Desiré lived in his other house located a couple of kilometres away, also with a wife and a daughter.

The corrugated metal in the wall was not particularly attractive, but it worked. Desiré opened the gate, which was also in the same material. This triggered a barking the likes of which I had never heard before, from the meagre dog, Sekkapus, a name I never found out the meaning of. The animal evidently seemed to work as a watchdog, with a small doghouse just inside the gate. Me and the yappy mutt never completely got along, not even after my attempts at whistling and taking pictures. The animal also had a lot to look after. Inside the metal fence, there was a reasonably built square beige brick house, with red window frames and features. The house had three bedrooms, a bathroom, a kitchen, and a living room, but currently did not have water. The water for flushing the toilet was from a bucket in the hallway manually emptied into the toilet. Water from the same bucket was used for 'showering', by just pouring the water over yourself, like in the bungalow in the north of Comoros. A covered terrace with a tiled floor occupied one of the corners outside the house. The tiles did not match, there were at least four different types in different shades of beige and hints of mosaic on parts of the floor. They had used whatever had been available, and not available, and made the best of it. Two armchairs and two matching two-seater sofas occupied the terrace, around a white plastic table with an intricate white crocheted tablecloth.

In the courtyard there was a green Renault Laguna, completely covered by the red, fine sand which is just everywhere. All four tyres were punctured, and it looked like a shell of a car. In stark contrast there was a gleaming red Chinese 100cc Qlink motorcycle by the side of the house. The motorcycle belonged to Desiré's brother and there was not a speck of dust to be seen. The proud motorcycle owner sometimes spent almost as much time tending to it as tending to his little family.

Living in a house in the middle of an African middle-class suburb is not so easy, many do not have the same comforts as Desiré. Most have a house, or shed, which is much smaller and lacking any kind of fence, living room, or terrace to have friends over. This means that the street is used for most things. The streets are used as a café, gossip mill, pub, dance floor, restaurant, rubbish bin, to check out prospects, and for therapy, to name just a few. This means that there are all kinds of different sounds of varying intensities, pretty much all night long, and it is all going on just outside where you are lying and trying to go to sleep. Alongside the man-made sounds, there are chickens, dogs and other animals chipping in to complete the theatre of sound. Earplugs were my salvation — I never travel to any city without them. One never knows exactly how well the loudspeaker from the mosque just outside the hotel is going to work, exactly what the hot-blooded couple in the next room are going to get up to in the middle of the night, or how many screaming kids are going to be sat in your vicinity on the plane. Or, what happens outside a house in the Central African Republic for that matter.

In the evenings we sat on the terrace outside the house with a lit candle on the ground, discussing the problems of CAR. There are simply too many of these for us to even get a chance to bring up traditional world problems. One of the nights, it was just me and Desiré who had stayed up until after midnight. His brother and his wife had to get up early and had said goodnight unusually early that day. Desiré and I sat there, each with a cup of tea, while the flame from the tallow candle flickered towards the wall behind us. He shared with me his thoughts about the future.

"We dream about freedom. We dream about having opportunities to follow our dreams and to turn them into more of a reality than just dreams. But most of all, we dream about the day when we do not have to explain to our children why there are so many soldiers in our streets," sighed the newspaper editor.

Through his job, Desiré knows everything that is going on and everyone in Bangui — it turned out that this included the Minister of Tourism. I was surprised that there was even a ministry of tourism in CAR. The office was located right in the middle of Bangui and was actually busy. But the ministry is responsible for art and culture as well, something that likely explained most of the activity. Desiré did not only know the minister through his work — they were in fact old acquaintances. But there were no politicians anywhere in the office in the building which was being well looked after by armed UN soldiers in an armoured vehicle. We had been allowed to enter without any checks, all the way to the secretary's office. She said that the minister was ill, but that the deputy minister would

be able to see us a couple of hours later.

"Is this department really a terrorist target?" I asked. Desiré smiled.

"No, but the UN headquarters in the city is a bit further down the street. They look after themselves," he said, without elaborating further. It is not a secret that critics of the UN believe they are busier taking care of their own people than taking real actions where it is needed. On the other hand, recruitment would likely be challenging if the UN soldiers did not feel reasonably safe at work. So, their contribution will then just have to be what it is. History shows that they can calm down situations, for a while in any case. The question is whether this could be done in a much more effective manner by not distancing themselves from the local population behind security. It is not a confidence builder when the person you are talking with is backed-up by 12 machine guns at the ready and 12 hyperactive trigger-fingers. But the UN has helped significantly in creating an atmosphere of calm, at least in Bangui.

"It is worse in the rest of the country — 70 percent of it is controlled by armed rebel groups who have also greatly benefited from taking over the operation of gold and diamond mines," said Desiré.

We returned after a late lunch, and this time everything seemed more promising. The secretary said something to Desiré in French, before we were shown the way to a dark brown wooden door within a concrete corridor.

The man in his mid-fifties wore in a black suit, white shirt, bright red tie and with smart black shoes. The deputy minister shook us by the hand and pointed to a sofa as a signal that we should take a seat. Desiré explained our objective in French, while I sat and wondered how the deputy minister managed to seem so relaxed in his smart and warm clothes in such a hot country.

In English, I asked how many tourists visited the country. Desiré translated into French.

"We only have two types of tourists. There are curious people, like you, who want to see and get to know our country. But there are not so many like you a day. The other group is businesspeople who take a weekend here as well as their meetings. But in many ways, the restaurants and hotels also see UN soldiers as tourists, as they lead to a boom in activity and increased income. But you mustn't quote me on this — that soldiers are tourists, even if we hope they can leave here relatively soon," chuckled the deputy minister.

He got up from the giant wooden desk and walked over to an artistic map that hung on the wall. He pointed to large swathes of the country, explaining that were ruled by militias and rebels, and that visitors were in extreme danger if they were to travel there. Then he pointed to an area right at the bottom left of the map.

"The tourists who do come, mostly visit here, to the spectacular Dzanga-Sangha Special Reserve, to be able to see gorillas or African forest elephants," proudly said the deputy minister.

And he had good reason to be proud. The national park is located in the southwest corner of the country, bordering Cameroon to the west and Congo to the east. There are 2000 gorillas, constituting one of the largest populations in the world, along with buffaloes, antelopes, and various species of monkey. The emperor tamarin monkey is by far the most unique, displaying a prominent and wild decorative moustache. The numerous white hairs of its beard protrude a long way out and also droop down, giving the animal a distinctive appearance. Unfortunately, I have not been able to see one with my own eyes — driving to the national park from Bangui was not recommended without travelling with armed guards in a convey of at least three four-wheel drive vehicles, preferably armoured. The roads are also in such bad condition that I would have needed a whole lot of drivers and bodyguards on the payroll for several days. This was beyond my budget. The alternative was a private plane, something I do not engage in often either.

The flag of the Central African Republic hangs outside the office building, which is quite unusual here. It has four horizontal stripes in blue, white, green, and yellow. They symbolise heaven, cotton, forests, and gold. There is also a vertical stripe in the middle, which is red and symbolises blood — something fitting for this country, with all the coups, brutal leaders, and civil wars over the years. But the blood in the flag conveys the will of the people to sacrifice themselves in protecting the republic. That sounded quite dictated, and it likely is as well.

One morning we were going to travel quite a way from Bangui. The day before I had asked Desiré to book a taxi for me to ensure a safe journey since he was going to work. In the morning, however, he offered to join as a guide and translator. I really appreciated that. We were going to drive a couple of hours along typical African roads in this French-speaking country. My host refused to accept any payment, but I tried to compensate for his generous hospitality during the trip by inviting him to lunch and dinners.

It turned out that we were fortunately going to a safe area, and we did not actually see a single military vehicle. Our destination was Sangara, a pygmy village 70 kilometres west of Bangui. It took just under two hours to drive there on the half-paved roads, passing through a dozen villages with stalls, motorcycle taxis and street vendors on both sides.

The notion of pygmies, in many ways, was just a myth in my head. In anthropology, the word pygmy is used to describe ethnic groups with an unusually short average height. In a tribe, this means that the males should on average be less than 150 centimetres tall. Primarily, this applies to African hunters and gatherers of the 4,700-kilometre-long Congo River basin, but pygmies have also settled in Southeast Asia and on islands in the Pacific Ocean. The word pygmy stems from the Greek pygmaios, which means 'fist', but which has also traditionally been used as a unit of measurement, referring to the distance between the elbow and knuckles.

The village was right by the road, and the taxi driver parked on the grass. A pack of kids waved and came running towards us. What a welcome party. The kids wore shorts or skirts. Some of the boys had bare tops and others had on colourful but tired T-shirts.

Desiré talked to one of the adults who was standing alongside one of the straw huts, and after a short time, Chief Yabo Safamille came out to welcome me by shaking me by the hand. All the adults were wearing T-shirts, except for the chief, who wore a plain blue shirt with a collar. No one in the village had shoes.

The pygmies here apparently speak Ubangi — a language I had never heard of or could understand a single word of, but Desiré said he could translate. After getting the Chief's approval, I greeted 4 or 5 men, while the kids still kept crowding around me, with abundant curiosity. "How many live here?" I asked, via Desiré.

"I do not know. I have never been to school, so I cannot count," replied the Chief. He was nevertheless honest.

"Almost 100 people," replied one of the other guys.

"And how many houses are there?" I delved, without a thought that the chief could not count. And when I said house, I actually meant straw huts. But the Chief wasn't chief for no reason, he knew what to do.

"This one and this and this and this and this," he replied after a while as he pointed to each straw hut.

"Yeah, and then some of us live in the woods right over there," he continued, pointing once more. "And then one back there and one back there and one back there," he followed on.

In addition, they had a more modern assembly hall made from cement. It was, naturally, lower than the houses in Bangui — the contractor likely did not see any point in building it taller than necessary in a pygmy village. The government had financed the building, and it was used as a meeting place, school, and emergency lodging if a family had to repair their straw hut.

Many group photos of me together with kids were taken, as well as a married couple and, of course, the Chief. A woman showed how she chopped up some green plants that were used in their cooking. They tasted sour, fresh, and good, but neither Desiré nor I could name the plant. Prepared leaves were put into a metal pot with a thick base, that was simmering over a cavity in the ground. It was fired up with wood they had chopped themselves from the forest they lived within. I could see the embers under the pots. Electricity in pretty non-existent in Central African pygmy villages. Since it was early afternoon, they were busy preparing dinner. I did not want to disturb them more than I had already done and thanked the villagers that I had been able to visit.

"Shouldn't I give them something as a present?" I asked Desiré.

"You do not need to do that, but the Chief and a couple of the men love cigarettes," he said. None of us smoked, so we got the taxi driver to drive to the nearest civilisation on a shopping excursion. He came back after ten minutes with 3 or 4 twenty packs of an unknown brand, and I passed them on to the chief who beamed back.

"Merci, monsieur!" he said, challenging our common French skills. The ones I met in Sangara were proud to be called pygmies, while some other tribes think it is degrading and would rather be referred to as an ethnic group or tribe. In CAR, other tribesmen are called bayaka, and in Congo they are referred to as bambenga, but pygmies can be found in as many as a quarter of all African countries, including Madagascar and Namibia.

We drove back towards Bangui in the yellow taxi that had made unusual noises the entirety of the trip. After 20 minutes we heard a very loud thump. Then the engine lost all power. The car rolled on a further 300 metres before the cursing driver peeled off onto the roadside and stopped.

"Problem!" he moaned and got out of the car. He started jogging back towards where we had come from. Was he going to leave us now?

Desiré and I also got out. We then saw the driver bend down and pick up something that looked like a part of a drive shaft before he started strolling back towards us. I could sense this would take a while. We were in the middle of no man's land, and there were few other cars on the road. A young man chugged past us on a red moped. On the back he had two crates of clucking chickens. There was no room for us. My plane was due to leave in three hours — one of the few flights a week. I considered whether to flip out, but it has never really helped me before. It was a matter of just finding a quick fix.

The driver told Desiré that he lacked the required tools and needed to call someone who could help him get the car repaired. It seemed like he was capable of handling it himself with the right equipment, but getting such tools could take hours. Fortunately, we were able to stop a large green Mercedes minibus, using good, old-fashioned waving. It was on its way to Bangui, so the problem was solved.

We found a new taxi once we were back in the city and set course for the airport. There was an hour and a half before my departure, and we had time to drink a coconut each in the car park outside. I gave Desiré a big hug and thanked him so much for all the help, before I went through security and received my exit stamp. I was leaving the republic, which is land-locked and borders six other countries. My next destination was about as far away as it is possible to get, geographically speaking — I was heading to the second smallest island nation in the Pacific. 26 square kilometres awaited me on the other side of the globe in my search for the least visited countries in the world. CAR is perhaps 24,000 times larger, but Tuvalu can boast infinitely more coastline. One can travel a long way for such virtues.

Desiré Ngaibona took time off work to show me around the Central African Republic.

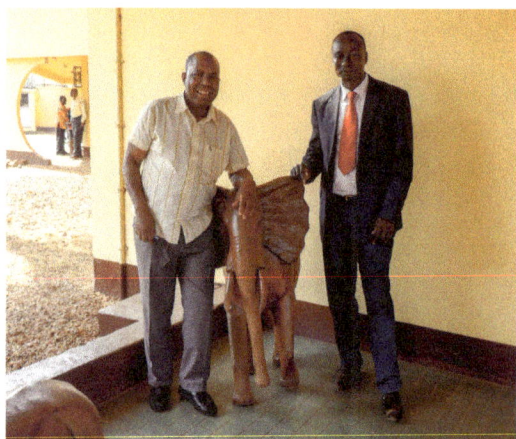
The deputy minister (right) and a state secretary outside the Ministry of Tourism.

Desiré let his brother and his family stay in one of the houses he owns.

The capital city of Bangui is close to the Democratic Republic of Congo, and such boats shuttle between the two countries.

There are long distances between the sluices in the Central African Republic. river banks must be utilised for repairs.

I held on as best I could, at least when I wasn't taking pictures.

Motorcycles and mopeds are the most common means of transport in Bangui. It is not uncommon to see 4-5 people on a bike.

Most of the businesses here are run from sheds or small houses.

The UN is heavily involved in the Central African Republic and often dominates the cityscape.

The pygmy village of Sangara is less than two hours by car from Bangui.

It wouldn't have happened anywhere else that I was the tallest person in a group photo.

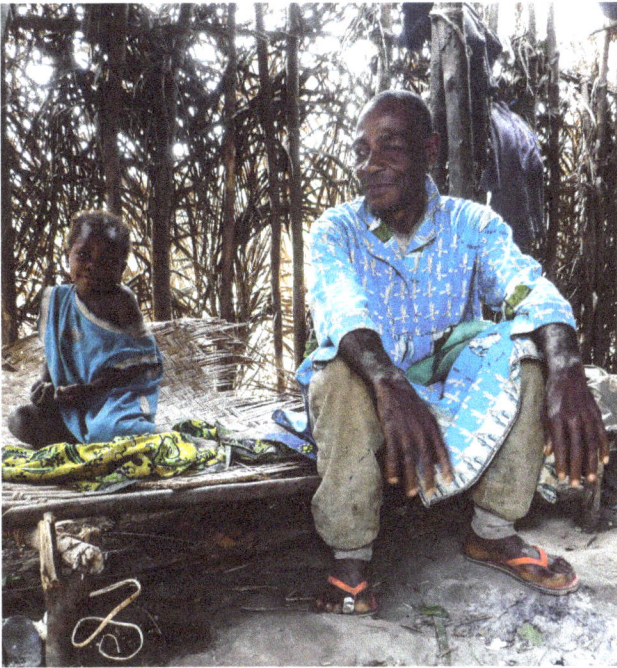

Chief Yabo Safamille in one of the village's thatched huts.

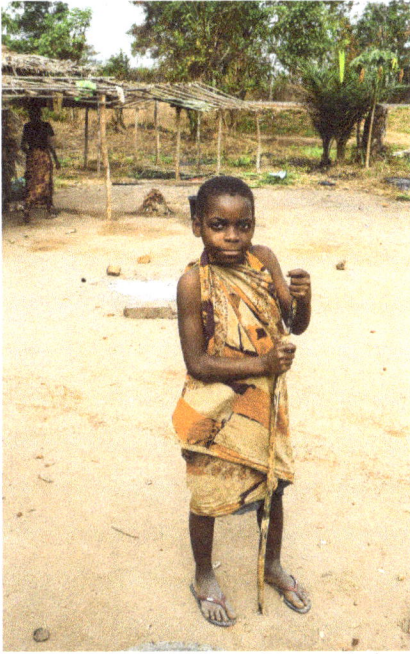

A young pygmy girl dressed in a typical colourful dress.

Parts of the drive shaft fell off the cab.

Luckily, a minibus came to the rescue.

NUKUPETAU

Tuvalu

Funafuti

50 km

4

Tuvalu, Oceania

INHABITANTS: 11,000 (Wikipedia)
TOURISTS PER YEAR: 800 (garfors.com)
AREA: 26 square kilometres

HOW IS IT REALLY to be stuck in paradise? Is it tempting, even though this paradise is found in the world's most difficult country to travel to or from? These are two questions worth asking oneself before heading to Tuvalu. Together with Dominica it is one of just two countries in the world where only propeller planes fly, but Tuvalu stands alone as being so remote that it takes three hours to fly there from anywhere else. This makes the journey pretty unattractive by boat — the few ships that sail the route use around two full days from Fiji or Kiribati, depending on wind, wave, and weather conditions.

The main atoll and the capital itself are called Funafuti, and it is only 12 kilometres from the southern tip to the northern, lying like the crescent of a new moon. Several smaller islands and coral reefs complete the circular-shaped lagoon with its ever-changing ocean-colours in the middle. On the interior, towards the lagoon, there are beaches running along almost all of the coast, only broken up by the odd breakwater and pier here and there. The exterior of the atoll is more weather-torn, with waves and winds pounding the more robust coastline made of corals and rocks.

Until March 2018 you could fly to Funafuti only from the Fijian capital Suva with Fiji Airways, but then Air Kiribati started a weekly flight from South Tarawa. Neither of the two airlines are in other words Tuvaluan, which makes the government dependent upon goodwill from foreign companies. The Pacific nation is in many ways a paradisal cliché, situated in the middle of the ocean on a few atolls with palm trees, beaches and little else. It turned out that my two initial questions would be answered, albeit involuntarily.

The miniscule state in the Pacific Ocean comprising of only 26 square kilometres includes nine inhabited islands and many smaller uninhabited ones. The sole airport in the country is in Funafuti. There is grass all around the runway, no fences, or other physical obstacles. People of all ages stand around the runway to watch every plane that lands or takes off. An hour before a plane is due to land, two fire trucks drive the hundred metres from the fire station and subsequently up and down the runway to make sure that everything is ready. Then they park ready to tackle an emergency, one next to the terminal building, the other by the southern end of the runway. During landing and take-off, the fire truck drivers keep honking their horns for a couple of minutes to warn people from entering the runway. It is actually more or less constantly in use as a rugby field, jogging arena, playground, shortcut and yoga mat, and the fire officers have the responsibility of reminding the public of when such usage is not allowed; the three or four hours a week there is a plane.

It is not an especially extensive activity to explore the atoll which has a narrow-paved road, actually with a centre line, running from almost one end to the other. But the road stops around a kilometre from the northern tip of the island, as right at the end is all the rubbish. Even paradise has to put its rubbish somewhere. The problem is that wherever it is disposed of it won't be far enough away from neighbours, or the sea for that matter. Therefore, new waste is covered with sand daily to minimize insect infestation and problem odours in large swathes of the country. It is far more idyllic in the south, and only the last 3-400 metres isn't paved. A small path twirls in between green trees with bird nests until they recede to the beach. Where the path ends you can walk from the western part to the eastern part of the island in a matter of seconds, while the tip of the atoll is so narrow that you can stand with a foot in the water on each side.

The most fascinating thing when near either of the two tips is the sounds of waves from both sides at the same time, in asynchronous stereo accompanied by the wind that often comes in gusts. I kept standing at the southern tip of Funafuti for over a quarter of an hour, philosophising about life, about how vulnerable this tiny country is, on how totally dependent the few thousand inhabitants here are on us. Us, as in the almost eight billion people in the rest of the world. Or primarily the few of us in the western world that cause most of the pollution — those of us that fulfil the non-sustainable dreams of a western and polluting lifestyle that the rest of the world can only dream about — thanks largely to the export of western cultures via TV, film, and music. It is easy to deliver speeches on Paris agreements and two-degree targets in luxury hotels, gigantic conference centres or in the prominent UN headquarters in the USA. But how many of those speeches have been given by someone who actually visited tiny Tuvalu — by someone who stood on the tip of an atoll and observed how little it will take before the country will no longer exist as anything but a modern Atlantis tale.

By all means, I take responsibility for my own emissions. It is no big surprise that I fly more than most, but despite everything I have a pretty average Norwegian salary and do not have much money left to spend on other kinds of pollution. My footprint is probably a bit higher than that of an average person my age living in Norway, but not by much. After all I live in the world's third biggest oil and gas producer per capita, after Qatar and Kuwait, and most families in Norway live in relatively new apartments or houses, own

cars that were purchased new and have children.

The people of Tuvalu do not have a choice. If they are going to travel, then they need to travel quite a distance by plane from the airport with the most cheerful airport code in the world: FUN. The expectations, with so few flights, are sky-high for the local people every time an aircraft lands. Who is going to get off is an important conversational matter on an island of only 6,000 people. Normally a couple of hundred people gather around the terminal to welcome relatives, to look on and guess what business arriving passengers have here, or to sell homemade souvenirs made from shells or pebbles from simple stalls by the road next to the terminal. Then again, calling it a terminal is a bit of a stretch. The little wooden building that was used when I first visited in 2013 has been torn down. A bigger construction without walls functioned as a temporary terminal for a while before a brand-new terminal building was due to open a few weeks after I left the island in February 2018. Brian Oman was in charge of overseeing work on the new building. The Scottish construction manager is a slender man, but with a thick Scottish dialect and temperament. Even though the work had been completed, the government wasn't ready to officially take over. The keys were therefore still in the Scotsman's pocket.

"Bloody hell! This is extremely annoying. We have worked very hard and very long hours to finish on time, and then it turns out they won't take over the terminal," he sighed. "That means it is still our responsibility if anything happens."

"You never know, it might burn down all of a sudden," Carlos said with a mischievous smile. The man from The World Bank was referring to a fire the day before. A home had been completely destroyed and the atoll had been effectively split in two for hours while the fire was being extinguished. The road was blocked by the fire truck and plenty of curious bystanders. I had been one of them, attracted by the rumours. It was obvious that that something big was going on and people were almost queueing up to get a glimpse for themselves. I had been able to sneak past many of them as I had rented a little scooter but came to a stop upon reaching the location. In addition to the fire truck, the tightly packed crowd made it impossible for me to get closer, so I had to settle for seeing the house burn down from a distance along with the other spectators. The flames were too vicious for the fire fighters to control. They had likely arrived too late to stand any chance.

"In that case it'll be hell!" Brian responded and ordered another round of San Miguel Lights. No one declined the cold beverage in the 30 degrees heat and super high humidity levels. We were sitting outside Filamona, the place to be and the busiest alternative to the hotel. It was also where I was staying, at the biggest guesthouse in Funafuti, located a few metres from the airport terminal. The guesthouse bar is the most popular spot for travellers and the odd local to get a beer or three, and a bite to eat. Along with the food truck parked just behind the bank, Filamona is also one of a few places serving lunch. All dishes come with rice. After a week I was pretty tired of rice to say the least. It is not really the food they promote anyway. With a view across the runway and airport terminal, it is pretty natural that the room keyrings say: 'AIRPORT VIEW...' in capital letters. As if that's something great to shout about. But then of course it is, here, on such a special atoll.

In Filamona I met six Fijians. Five men and a woman from The Locally Managed Marine Area Network, or LMMA, a humanitarian organisation. They had come here to educate governmental employees at national, regional, and local levels. The two weeklong course focused on several aspects, but primarily on how to best train people and the best way to carry out courses locally. They also taught marine business development as well as change and change management. I was told that the emphasis was on change due to global warming, increasing sea levels, additional rainfall, and more frequent and stronger tropical storms. But also, on other types of change.

"How to act in terms of growing social media usage, information overload and easier access to pornography," explained Alifereti Tawake, one of the founders of the organisation. Following my bewildered look, he explained that the consummation of internet pornography had exploded during the last few years and that it completely ruined people's concentration, stealing many working hours — much in the same way as the overuse of social media.

The building manager, Brian, workers Alison from New Zealand and Alex and his son Shannon from Australia, were also part of the furniture at the bar. As the terminal opening was on hold, they spent their working hours on a new airport tower. It was the first time the construction company had chosen a Chinese steel supplier, instead of a Korean, Japanese, or German, and Brian was not at all pleased.

"There is fuck all that fits together! That means that we have to cut and weld and improvise like maniacs just to make sure that all the parts fit together, and we can build according to the drawings. Waiting for new parts in the middle of the ocean would take even longer," he moaned under the cap he always wore, before totally condemning cunning Chinese pricing:

"They may be the cheapest, but they are useless when it comes to quality. And that is something the management doesn't understand in their airconditioned offices back in civilisation," Brian thundered.

In Filamona I got to know quite a few people who were in Tuvalu for different reasons. Carlos was going to discuss various projects with the Tuvaluan government, while Italians, Guiliana, and Roberto, were filming a documentary on global warming. A Japanese TV team was also here to do the same. Both films will hopefully influence both normal people and international top politicians to act faster concerning climate action. And I shouldn't forget the Australians Ross and Siana, who work as volunteers, assisting with education and training of people at the schools, the hospital, and the fire station. They had nine-month contracts, but Siana had already been offered an extension within the Tuvaluan government. She had clearly done an impressive job during her first four months.

"But I have to think about it. It is quite a transition moving from the hustle and bustle of Melbourne to tiny Tuvalu. On the other hand, I have really managed to find calm and to establish a much healthier rhythm in my life. It's been a perfect way to slow down my pulse and to spend time on the important things in life. In the afternoons I sit by a tree in my garden and look over the blue green lagoon with a cup of green tea. Life is great!" she told me with great enthusiasm. Siana spreads good vibes as she happily bikes around with a big smile on the only orange bicycle in the country.

"It is Japanese, and I just had to get it when I saw it in the shop," she said. The bike is called Mr. Orange. "Such a special bike just had to get a name," she explained before we managed to even ask. "And, no! It has not been named after an American president," Ross added with a smile. Others had asked before.

One evening Ross invited Siana, Shannon, and myself for dinner. The host lived a kilometre and a half from Filamona, and I had borrowed a bike to keep up with Siana on Mr. Orange. We had just arrived and parked the bikes when it started to pour down, as it often does on Pacific islands. It was as if heaven and hell had opened. Luckily, the place for our bikes was under cover, and we hurried up a stairway to the terrace which was also covered. Ross had prepared dinner on a white wooden table just outside his flat. The temperature was well over 20 degrees, and the noise from the rain striking the metal roofing sheets was deafening.

Vegetables are hard to come by in Tuvalu, and bizarrely enough so is fish. Ross had prepared frozen pizza, which was in fact a pleasant surprise from the never changing menu at Filamona. Rarely has factory made pizza with pepperoni and a few vegetables tasted as good. We flushed down the pizza with canned beers.

Siana asked me what I had seen in Tuvalu.

"Almost everything," I answered a little too fast, coming across as an arrogant globetrotter. "I have at least been all over Funafuti, and jogged and biked to both ends," I added, trying to dig myself out of the hole I had created.

"What about David's drill hole?" she asked.

"David's what?" I responded. As an engineer, Ross knew all the details.

"The Welsh-Australian geologist Sir T. W. Edgeworth David visited Tuvalu in 1897. To try to prove Darwin's theory about how coral atolls were made, he drilled a 340-metre-deep hole into the ground with a diameter of 2-3 centimetres," Ross explained.

The world-famous scientist Charles Darwin spent almost five years on HMS Beagle in order to learn and theorize about Oceania. Captain Robert Fitz Roy set sail from Plymouth in England in 1831, sailing to South America before he continued to the Pacific until returning home in 1836. Darwin had conjectured that atolls were created through three stages. Firstly, a volcanic island appears, around which small coral reefs grow.

These consist of living marine creatures. The island will slowly erode and sink into the water. The coral reefs will then transform into a bigger barrier reef. This is followed by the remains of the volcano and its base sinking further, forcing the barrier reef upwards, developing into an atoll with a lagoon in the middle, or a circular coral island. But this doesn't exactly happen overnight. The island or atoll production can take 30 million years. Darwin considered the coral islands as a last desperate attempt from a drowning continent to keep its head above water.

David found reason to believe that Darwin was right, but no outright proof. Darwin's theory has later been acknowledged as a truth in scientific circles. But it now appears as if global warming and increasing sea levels are set to kill off numerous Pacific islands ahead of time. They do still rise, but not quickly enough.

Siana hadn't seen David's Drill herself but sent me a photo of it a few months later. It might be a bit telling that one of the most famous tourist attractions in Tuvalu is a hole in the ground. The question is just how long it will remain that way. Tuvalu and Kiribati are the two first countries that will 'sink' into the ocean when sea levels raise.

After the pizza party Ross asked us if we wanted dessert.

"Depends on what you are serving. Someone told me that the only dessert around here is donuts," I said a little sceptically.

"Yes, and I was challenged by a colleague the other day," Ross answered.

"Ross eat another donut," the colleague had ordered.

"I cannot, I have already had three."

"You are not a real Tuvaluan if you cannot eat five."

Donuts and other convenience foods have contributed to the average Tuvaluan having supersized waists. In addition to fast food the diet often included tinned food, and the occasional pork chop from one of the pig farms in Tuvalu or imported chicken or beef. A mundane diet tempts many into eating fried food and sweets. Which in turn influences their weight and across most other Pacific countries. Fish is strangely enough virtually absent from the diet, despite presence of numerous Taiwanese fishing vessels that catch huge amounts of tuna, sometimes refuelling in Funafuti. The tuna from the factory trawlers is sold back in Asia, so if Tuvaluans want to eat fish, they have to catch it themselves.

"We do not have a tradition for advanced cuisine. I am not quite sure why we hardly eat any fish, we never have as long as I can remember. Perhaps it has always been so plentiful that it has become a low-status food," Nita speculated in the bar in Filamona. She lives on one of the smaller atolls but was in Funafuti to attend a course and learn from the group of Fijians. Some vegetables are grown locally in greenhouses in Tuvalu, but most common is imported tinned food, in addition to pork and chicken from small local producers. Meat that originates more locally is hard to come across anywhere.

The Saturday night before their teaching was going to start, the course leaders sat in the bar and prepared a not for the faint-hearted kava party. As in kava with a k. The plant, which is grown on Fiji and exported to other Pacific countries, comes in something that resembles a coffee bag. The dried brown powder has a strong smell, a bit like ginseng, and is stirred into water. The mixture is then filtered through a cloth and is ready to drink 10-15 minutes later. I tried a cup for the second time in my life. The first time had been in Fiji, and I concluded that I was still not a fan. In Europe kava is classified as a narcotic, although that is probably a bit of over the top. It was rather alcohol in the form of imported beers for me during that evening, whereas the Fijians began on boxed wine as soon as the kava bowl was empty. Shops in Tuvalu sell Australian red wine in four litre containers. The large size gives the impression of people here seeming to be 33 percent thirstier than at home in Norway.

At around ten O'clock five of us walked over to the airstrip and the 700-800 metres to the nightclub in the country. There is only one. And without competition, the recipe for success is simple. No one gets to enter without first paying female ticket clerk. Two huge colleagues with her with full beards make sure of that. 70 percent of the club is covered by a roof, the rest is open to the sky. Perfect for smokers and those wanting to be star gazers. There is so little light pollution in Tuvalu that the heavens are more crowded with stars than most places in the western world.

Behind the bar was the prettiest girl in the country. She is called Agnes and must be good for business. So good that there's a mesh fence between her and the alcohol she serves, and those of us that are looking to order. A little square hole has been cut in the fence for exchanges of money and alcohol.

"The fence is definitely needed! We've had instances where patrons were so drunk that they tried climbing across the bar," she explained after reluctantly telling me her name.

"Because they wanted alcohol or because they wanted you?" I joked.

"Well, what do you think?" she asked, almost looking offended before giving a brilliant perfect smile and passing me a beer through the mesh fence. I understood the purpose of it. Several guys came over to chat with the only white person in the place. Some of them were so drunk that they didn't manage to say anything I could grasp at all. The ladies in the club were much more sober than the local men. Not dissimilar to the parties I frequented in the villages pinned between fjords and mountains where I grew up.

But Mia, from the Fijian group, was with us and after a while there was a dancing competition on the tables. I clambered up onto the little wooden table first and did my thing and Mia followed after me. She owned the dance table, and even got some applause from the few that were capable of grasping that a dancing show was taking place. We also tried to get her 55-year-old colleague Tevita to join in, but he repeatedly declined, despite his substantial intake of kava, red wine and later on, beer.

"No way! The last time I danced on tables was in the 1980s, and then they kicked me out of the nightclub afterwards."

Strangely enough, their Fijian colleagues were also not especially keen on table dancing. They were also too busy drinking beers, following the earlier intake of kava and red wine.

"You drink a lot, guys. What about tomorrow?" I joked.

"Let tomorrow worry about itself," Tevita responded, seriously following his own endorsement.

It was a pretty lax group that I met the next day for breakfast, slash brunch. Not surprisingly, others were likely worrying about the day, or how to get through it, than the day itself. I waved to those with hangovers and went for a walk to the north, passing the unopened airport terminal that kind of fits in with the relatively modern parliament building across the road, but not exactly many other buildings in the country. Most people live in shacks, or small dwellings made from wood, or occasionally concrete. The houses are colourful and seemingly erected at random without an overall plan, but with both meaning and purpose for the families that live there.

In connection with Pacific Islands Forum Leaders Meeting 2019 they are hard at work building new apartments and bungalows adjacent to the hotel. That is good for tourism, as finally there will be modern accommodation options right next to the lagoon. Some of the new flats will also be put up for sale to locals, following the conference. There has only been one hotel in Tuvalu for many years, in addition to a handful of guesthouses. A single room in the hotel will set you back 80 dollars per night — a fortune to those living here. And the room standard isn't even worth shouting over; I get associations to an average dated asylum reception centre in the Norwegian countryside, albeit with a beach outside of the window. Although even the beach is getting an upgrade before the leader's meeting. 300 delegates are expected, and the government is considering renting a cruise ship to provide everyone a bed during the meeting.

A room in one of the guesthouses will set you back about half as much as the hotel, at least for foreigners — the price is apparently quite a bit less for Tuvaluans who need somewhere to live. That would primarily apply to those from the other eight inhabited atolls. The nearest one is called Nokufetau, five hours away by boat, whereas the most remote one is 16 hours away. Scheduled boats only run every other week. Since the centre of Funafuti, with Filamona, the airport, and nightclub, is located centrally on the atoll, the weather would need to be extraordinarily bad for one not to be able to make it back home, to the hotel or guesthouse. Apart from in the centre, all houses are located along the main road. That makes it possible to get yourself home after a heavy session at the nightclub. Taxis do not exist, but hospitable locals will happily pick up neighbours or a tourist with heavy luggage.

The prime minister of Tuvalu, together with his colleague in Kiribati, gained headlines the world over in their fight against global warming. That is neither strange nor coincidental,

as already mentioned, these two countries will be the first to disappear if we cannot manage to slow down the rising water levels of the world's oceans. The highest point here is 4.6 metres above sea level, and the 11,000 inhabitants are fearful of their future with their main atoll being only 700 metres across at its widest point. With so few citizens the parliament building is no more imposing than an average council office of a backcountry borough. The parliament has no reception and no security. I walked straight in and up to a hatch in the wall, home to the tax office. I asked where I could find the ministers of foreign affairs, trade, tourism, environment, and work. In such a small nation only the prime minister and the minister of finance have short titles.

"Up one floor, on the left," I was told.

It turned out that the minister was ill, and currently abroad receiving treatment. There is a hospital in Funafuti, but apparently with a capability more akin to a health clinic. Those in need of operations or who are seriously ill, have to leave the island nation, typically heading for Fiji.

Since I was already in the governmental building, I figured I might as well greet the prime minister. In the bright stairwell in the middle of the building with many windows, I asked an employee in a bright and colourful Hawaiian shirt — or rather Tuvaluan shirt — where his office was.

"Up another staircase. On the top floor, of course!" he said. I noted a bit of a sharp tone. Perhaps the prime minister's pick of office had impacted this guy's own department.

A sign above the open green door said Office of The Prime Minister. There were three woman and a man in the front office. I introduced myself, told them why I was visiting, and asked if I could possibly have a chat with the prime minister.

"I am so sorry, but he is abroad," was the answer I received. "But the minister of finance is our acting prime minister. Perhaps you would like to talk to him instead? He's sitting in the other wing, just walk over and introduce yourself," one of the ladies said before she started typing something on her computer. I took the hint and strolled over to the minister of finance.

"He is busy right now, but I can schedule a meeting for you. When is a good time for you?" the secretary asked, also a woman, dressed in a blue dress with her black hair tied up in a ponytail. The fact that I could just walk into the office of the acting prime minister and then be asked to suggest a time for our meeting that suited me was almost beyond hospitable.

"I am available anytime. Perhaps the minister of finance has time later today or tomorrow?" I gave her a business card, while suggesting that it was best to email me as my phone didn't work in Tuvalu. Or in any other country off the beaten track.

Later that afternoon the secretary came walking over to Filamona. In addition to my own roaming issues, the Tuvaluan phone network was down, and she hadn't gotten through.

"It was faster to walk here than to write an email," she said. "The minister of finance can see you tomorrow morning at 09:30. Would you be able to come to his office?"

I was easily convinced and thanked her for the appointment.

I returned to the parliament the next morning. From their offices both the prime minister and the minister of finance have views across the airport and the eastern side of the atoll. The secretary welcomed me and asked me to wait in the front office. The acting prime minister was ready to see me just three minutes later and I was shown into his corner office.

"Welcome to us!" Maatia Toafa said as he stood up from behind his white desk and offered me his hand. He then gave me his business card. It didn't just have the minister of finance's official email address, ending with gov.tv, but also a yahoo.com address. They are used to local IT infrastructure not always playing ball. Toafa limped a bit as he moved from his desk to an armchair alongside a sofa. His secretary had told me the day before that he was waiting for an operation on his leg. The big man had been prime minister earlier for one term, until he lost his majority. But now he was back in the cabinet, quite often stepping in as acting prime minister. The current prime minister Enele Sopoaga travelled a lot, primarily to talk about global warming and rising sea levels. At least until Kausea Natano took over, only to increase the retoric. 'Tuvalu is sinking!' he said at the COP 26 UN Climate Change Conference in Glasgow in 2021.

The deputy prime minister pointed to the sofa, as a signal that I should sit down. I thanked him for welcoming me on such short notice.

"How is it to live in the prime example of global warming, the country that will disappear first unless we get our act together?" I asked Maatia Toafa.

"Those that predict the future say that we will vanish, but we do what we can to make sure they are mistaken. We cooperate with the global community and those that turn out to be our friends," he said with emphasis on the last part of the sentence. The Tuvaluans, so few in number, are dependent on friends in other countries. Many friends. In many countries.

"We aren't difficult, we just work extremely hard to make sure that Tuvalu is here to stay for future generations. Everyone has an identity that is tied up to a piece of land or a place — it is an important component, certainly also for you in Norway. And we do really appreciate the support from your country and many others in this fight. Nothing is impossible," said the acting prime minister calmly. The actual prime minister would be returning on the flight from Fiji a few hours later. I was going to fly out on the same plane. Or so I still believed.

Fiji Airways has just two ATR-72 aircraft that are used on the route to and from Funafuti. 72 is the number of seats in a standard configuration, but all of them cannot always be used. If there is too much heavy luggage, some of the seats must be left empty for the three hours of travel to or from Fiji. The plane starts early in the morning from Fijis biggest city, Nadi, which somewhat illogically is pronounced 'Nandi' and from there flies directly to Suva, the Fijian capital and onwards to Tuvalu.

While I was interviewing the acting prime minister, the scheduled flight was en route to Suva, with the elected prime minister on board. All of a sudden, the starboard propeller engine had caught fire. The fire extinguishing mechanism of the engine worked perfectly, the fire was extinguished, and the plane turned around and returned to Nadi, landing safely with one engine. The same plane should have travelled to Funafuti the same day but repairing a fire damaged engine can obviously take some time. Why Fiji Airways didn't reallocate the other ATR-72, reassign a different aircraft or hire a plane, I just could not fathom, but then again, Tuvalu isn't the least accessible country in the world for no reason. The plane that should have collected me and 60 other passengers on the Tuesday was naturally cancelled. The same for the Thursday flight. The question was just how long I would be stuck in Tuvalu.

I ended up asking myself the same question hundreds of times over the next few days.

Toafa was painfully aware of the country's fragile infrastructure, although perhaps not as aware as the prime minister who was about to be stranded in an airport hotel accommodation in Fiji.

"We are considering the possibilities of expanding the runway so that we can accommodate jet planes as well," he said and continued to tell me about the work to construct modern quays on the various islands. This is lacking today and will make the connections between atolls a lot easier. Vessels currently have to keep engines running while passengers disembark or get on board.

The minister also told me about plans to expand the hotel, the beach, and swimming pool, but pointed out that these projects were the responsibility of the private sector, although the government was there to help with negotiations with The World Bank and investors in various countries. The country is poor, and the government can only help indirectly.

"Which country do you work closest with?" I wondered.

"The usual suspects, like Australia, New Zealand, Fiji, Japan, South Korea, and Taiwan. The latter is by the way the only country with an embassy here," he smiled. "And, of course, I shouldn't forget our old colonial masters, the United Kingdom," he continued.

"Yes, with Brexit I suppose they need new partners," I smiled. That made the minister laugh loudly, almost uncontrollably, and he slapped his own thigh while sitting in his office armchair. I was sitting right across from him in a two-seater sofa.

"That is evidently their choice, but I think it is rather backwards. Yes, borderline idiotic. We live in the times of cooperation, which is what makes the world advance. Perhaps they didn't see the memo," he continued and laughed again. The sturdy man smiled a lot in general and seemed to have a good sense of humour. He clearly didn't have much faith in Brexit.

I thanked him for our chat and shook his hand. My hand drowned in his. Then I made my way to Filamona, just one hundred metres away, and there I was told that the flight would neither arrive nor depart. The owner of the guesthouse told me that I could keep my room as there would naturally not be any newcomers that day.

Relatively frustrating in so many ways, even though being stuck in the middle of the Pacific Ocean would turn out to be a unique experience. I, of course, was not alone in my predicament. Together with around a dozen others who should have been on the same plane, I became part of a small, loose, and hopefully short-lived community. The group didn't only include the restless among us who should have continued our travels elsewhere, but were now propellor-stranded, but also other guests who knew that this could also have happened to them. The group was largely foreigners but also some locals who knew a couple of us. Most of us met for lunch or dinner, and there was always someone who had received conflicting information on when the flight would possibly leave. Information from the airline was completely non-existent, so our knowledge was based on what someone we knew had heard from Fiji office, or Australia. Myself, I had discovered a plan B. A cargo ship to Fiji.

It turned out to be a castle in the sand, or sea, because of two things. Firstly, the journey would take two or three days. Secondly, the next departure was not due until the following month. I crossed my fingers that I wouldn't still be in Tuvalu then.

In between our discussions about the priorities of Fiji Airways, how remote and inaccessible Tuvalu really is and how much we craved fresh vegetables, ice-cream, smoked salmon, and other products that weren't exactly plentiful around here, we exchanged stories from all over the world about personal problems, pleasures, and tragedies. Little builds friendships better than being stuck on a small island. Or to put it properly, an atoll.

On the second day without flight connections, our propeller-stranded community doubled in size when the next scheduled flight was also cancelled. The propellor engine had still not been repaired. The day after I strolled along the 50 metres to the new airport terminal, and the same again to the only travel agent in the country.

"When will the plane depart?" I asked the two representatives of the airline.

"Oh, it will depart tomorrow. Maybe. And if it doesn't leave tomorrow, then it will leave on Thursday. Maybe. The next alternative is Friday." I got the picture. No one knew anything at all. Fiji Airways had informed its own representatives in Tuvalu to the same non-degree as their passengers. And luckily, I already knew the order of the weekdays off by heart.

It was then a good idea to try rebooking the flights that were going to take me onwards from Fiji, but the internet access here could be a whole chapter by itself. There are open wireless zones around the airport, the hotel, and most guesthouses, but access needs to be purchased at the telecom shop. It is of course located right next to the airport and sells 600MB of data for 20 Australian dollars. Every 20-50 MB I used, I had to log on again with a username and password of 8 randomly generated characters that I never managed to remember. Needless to say, the voucher emerged from my pocket time after time.

At Filamona I thought that the owner always knew something of what was going on with air traffic. Every morning after getting up, I asked the same question.

"Any news about the plane today?""

The response never changed. "No, it won't depart today either. Maybe another day."

"Maybe another day." Like in the film Groundhog Day, where Bill Murray always wakes up to the exact same day. When you are set on continuing your journey onwards, it is annoying not to be able to move on at all, despite knowing too well that won't help a single bit.

'Maybe another day' was usually followed by 'weather is weather' or 'no stress, we take things as they come around here'.

I pitched in by introducing 'TIO,' as in 'This is Oceania.' Or 'Tuvalu time,' as Carlos called it.

To pass time I went for walks, ran in the frequent and violent rain showers, read under the dry roof at Filamona or enjoyed the deserted beaches. With the exception of a few kids playing in the sand sometimes, I never saw anyone at all on the beaches, not even any of the foreigners. Perhaps people had overdosed on swimming too, not only on eating fish.

In the evenings we exchanged theories on when the plane would eventually leave. Carlos had been in Tuvalu many times previously and possessed relevant experience. It wasn't really uplifting.

"The tales about Tuvalu's many cancelled flights are legendary. I won't be surprised if you're still here in a couple of weeks," he said over a beer and sniggered tenaciously, albeit with self-irony. It would after all affect him as well, as he had a ticket just two days later.

The many conversations also taught me a thing or two about Tuvaluan culture.

If you are a man and a woman gives you a flower wreath, then following Tuvalu tradition it means she really likes you. Should the feeling be mutual, you have 24 hours to get hold of a fish to give to her as a return gift. But one can say it is pretty much impossible to just buy a fish, so the man has to like the lady enough that he actually catches one himself. The catch can be delivered in person or be hung outside her house. The question is what the lady actually does with the fish, since it is likely not eaten. Perhaps most Tuvaluan ladies own cats.

"But I mean the fish needs to be fresh!" Nita added firmly. She had joined our table in Filamona. Alison, who was working on the airport tower with Brian, was supposed to head home for New Zealand on holiday for a week. He had received a wreath from the woman who washed the house he was staying in. Alison wasn't massively flattered by that. The cleaner was over 50 and he was in his 20s. He pointed out that she was happily married and had likely done it to be nice. Besides, he was going to be heading home to his own wife a little south of Auckland.

"The cleaning lady won't get a fish from me," he said sharply. He wasn't in a very good mood, following the long delay. Neither was I, for that matter. We should have boarded the plane from Funafuti 99 hours earlier.

It was at that point when we finally received the news to get ready to fly. An hour later the propellor plane was away and my personal record of the longest plane delay of 100 hours became fact. A record I have no desire of ever breaking, not even on another sinking island paradise.

I would in any case have to break a record, or at least a rule, in order to visit the third least visited country in the world. There they don't accept any tourists.

The airstrip is sometimes the world's longest rugby pitch.

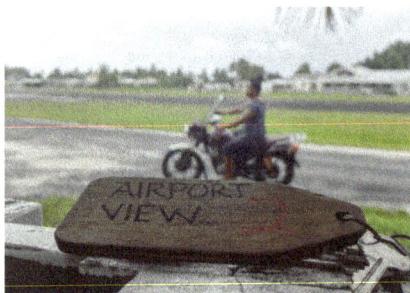

Strictly speaking, it's hard not to have an view of the airport at Funafuti.

Beaches are rarely used in Tuvalu.

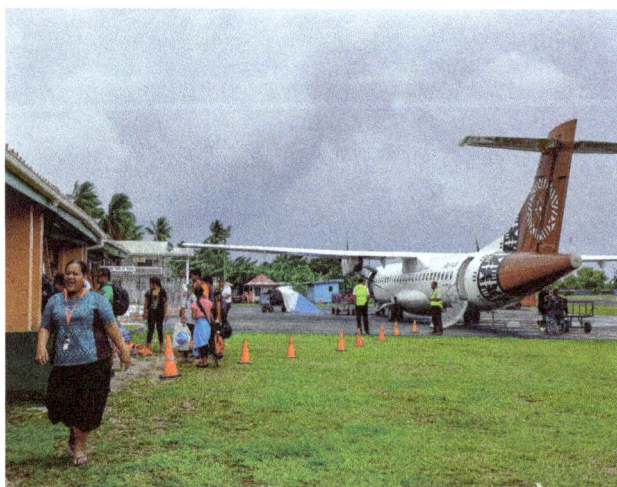

Hovudøya is too small to allow for physical barriers around the airstrip.

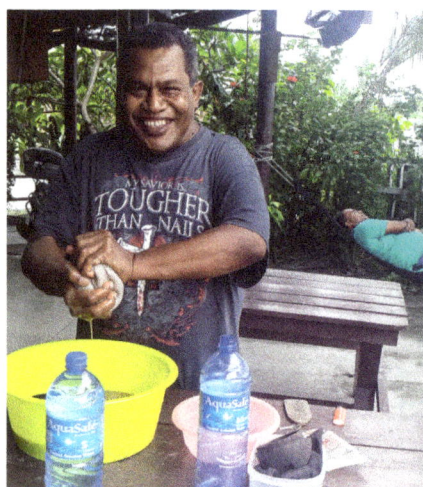

Tevita from Fiji makes Kava, a mild narcotic drink, for the party that evening.

It doesn't get much wider than this between the two sides of Funafuti. The island is shaped like a crescent moon.

At the tip, you can stand with one foot on each side.

Tuvalian bathers.

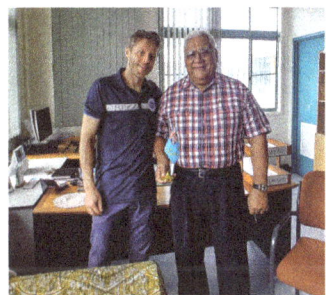
Posing with the acting prime minister, Maatia Toafa.

The stormy weather around Funafuti is not like back home, with tropical and pleasant temperature in the air. But the dark clouds brought some of the heaviest rain I've ever experienced.

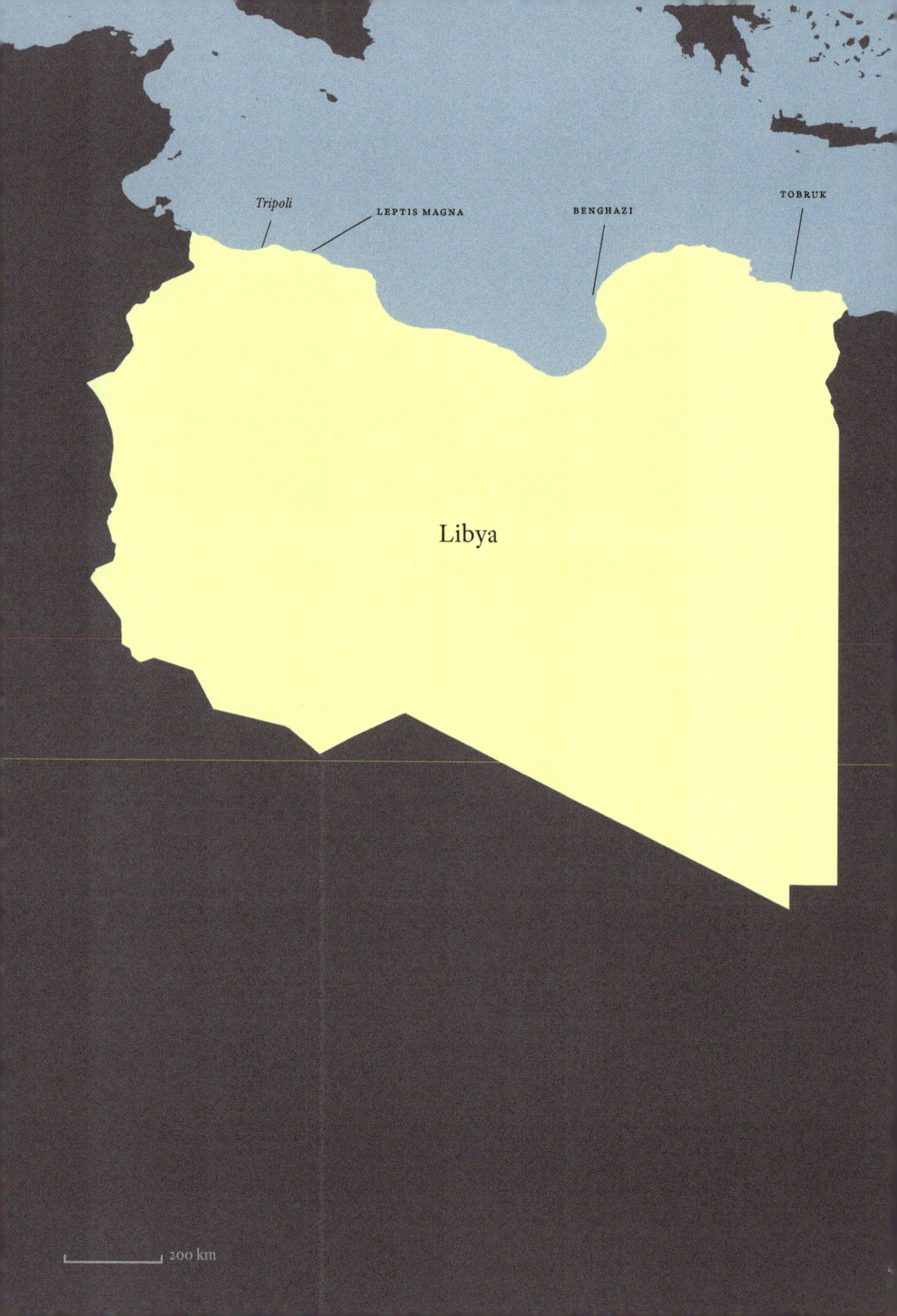

Tripoli   LEPTIS MAGNA   BENGHAZI   TOBRUK

Libya

200 km

3

Libya,
Africa

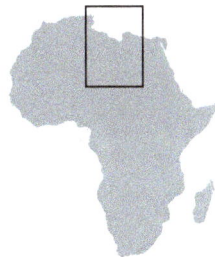

IHABITANTS: 6,300,000 (Wikipedia)
TOURISTS PER YEAR: 200 (garfors.com)
AREA: 1,759,541 square kilometres

TRAVELLING TO LIBYA as a tourist is almost impossible, unless you are unofficially a businessman or woman. The Libyan government has in fact banned tourists. They have done this despite up to 6,000 people being employed in the Ministry of Tourism in the country, and of course there is a Minister of Tourism as well, who I was invited to meet. Khitar Bashir Malek hardly had very much else to do. Unfortunately, the invitation was withdrawn when it was revealed that I was writing a book. It seems like the only thing the government dislikes more than tourists is journalists.

"The last time the minister met tourists here, he was questioned for many hours by the intelligence services. Since tourists are not allowed to visit, they were suspected of being spies, with him being their inside contact. He will probably not risk this again," Salem told me, who also works in the Ministry of Tourism.

"Although I don't really do that much work," he said, laughing. "But I am employed and get paid, so I'm not going to complain very much about the lack of things to do." So, Salem spent his time as a driver and salesman for Yousef and me. Yousef is around 50 and a well-educated man. He is particularly interested in history and writes books about tourist attractions in and around Tripoli. With a virtually non-existent customer base, sales are not going particularly well. In addition, he works as a salesman and guide for Sherwes Travel, again without full order books. Tourist visas have not been issued since 2011, officially because of the sensitive political situation in Libya, and because the security situation can be confusing and at times risky.

"It can be a dangerous job because we are not allowed to do this. So, if we're stopped by security forces or the police, leave me to do the talking. And remember that you are a businessman!" Yousef proclaimed.

"Businessman on tour?" I asked.

"Even hard-nosed businessmen like you sometimes need a cultural break between meetings," smiled the salesman. It turned out that the short man with chalk-white hair had a broad and good network of contacts. And that means everything in a country with a sky-high level of conflict.

"Once we had to wait six hours to be allowed to leave an area. A policeman at one of the roadblocks went completely awry, and I really had to use the extent of my network," said Yousef. In order for us to reduce the risk of being stopped by a like-minded police officer, I had to sit in the back seat.

"If they see a Western person like you in the front seat, you will get to study many roadblocks very carefully. Because then everything takes longer," explained Yousef.

In addition to the ban on tourist visas, four of the six national borders are closed. If one also considers that only Tunisians and some Egyptians can enter without a visa, then the tourist catchment area is limited. When no one can primarily travel here on holiday, the supply-and-demand rule takes over. Sherwes Travel is the leading travel operator, offering guided tours disguised as business trips at a high price. Those of us who do enter receive a business visa and have to have a convincing story for the immigration authorities, particularly to avoid the, at times, long interrogations from suspicious police officers who see their cut in making the lives of suspected tourists so uncomfortable that they will happily pay large sums to be let go. If they let you in at all — once again, this is after all one of the most corrupt countries in the world. But at least foreigners do not have to wait for long in the passport queue. There is a separate counter for us foreigners, and I was the only one on a full flight from Istanbul who was in that queue. With my own passport controller, I was let through in a few seconds, without any problems.

It was not that easy for the Dane, Jakob Øster, a friend of mine who travelled to Libya in 2017. He has been to almost every country in the world, most of them with his wife and kids. But he travelled to Libya alone. Like me, he got a stamp in his passport in a matter of seconds, but then most things went wrong. A non-uniformed man from the security police stopped Jakob shortly afterwards and demanded to know who his contact person in Libya was. The Dane had not been given a contact number, and signalled to the stern man, who did not speak English, that his contact person would be waiting in the arrival hall. The policeman led the way there, but first the luggage had to be cleared. There they saw a professional SLR camera. Then it became crystal-clear. What on earth is a business traveller going to do with such a camera?

An even sterner policeman demanded to know if he was a journalist or a spy. He spoke no other English. In the meantime, the contact person, Ahmed, had arrived, and he acted as a salesman. The police then demanded to see Jakob's PC and went through various folders. There were both travel articles that he had written for various newspapers, and thousands of pictures from numerous countries. The suspicion of espionage and journalism suddenly increased dramatically. Jakob, who was already extremely nervous about travelling to Libya, was close to having a heart attack. It did not help much that the 45-year-old was taken into a tiny, white-washed room without windows, together with Ahmed. They sat there for an hour before Ahmed was ordered out, and Jakob was taken to another office with three large sofas, a desk, and a well-used and squeaky narrow metal bed without bedding, with a bend in the middle.

The police chief sat himself down at his desk and started eating greasy food with fat fingers. Two other policemen sat in their own sofas, Jakob in the third. No one said a word for three hours.

Out of the blue, Ahmed came back. He smiled. A few minutes later they were both on their way to the car park and then to the hotel in Tripoli. That evening, Jakob found out what had happened. After an hour, the police had decided to deport the Dane and imprison Ahmed. But to be imprisoned in Libya, you need a passport. Ahmed was staying with the same company he had rented a car from, and he was allowed to return there to pick it up. But in the car park it turned out that the rental car had been towed, so he had to take a taxi. From the back seat he had desperately called his boss to try to get out of the predicament, without any luck. But Ahmed had good fortune on his side that day. The taxi driver had overheard the conversation and asked if he could help.

The driver had promised Ahmed that his brother had much to contribute. There are two strong militias that control different parts of Tripoli. The driver's brother just happened to be a warlord for the militia that ruled over the airport, and the situation was explained over the phone. The brother had then called the person in charge of the security police and had found out who was in charge of the immigration office at the airport that day. The person in question had then been called and given a very clear message that if the Dane by the name of Jakob was not allowed into the country and Ahmed imprisoned, he himself would rot in a far darker dungeon than had been planned for Ahmed. Not long after, Ahmed was called and asked to come to the immigration office immediately to find a solution to the situation.

Jakob Øster didn't exactly get much sleep that night. Bursts of machine gunfire not far from the hotel didn't help the situation. But he survived the stay and managed to get out of the country two days later from the same airport. "Shaken, not stirred."

Mitiga International Airport was originally a giant military base by the beach just eight kilometres from the centre of Tripoli. But after Tripoli International Airport was bombed and destroyed in 2014, Mitiga took over as the main airport for the capital. The base was first built by Italy in 1923, then rebuilt and greatly expanded by the United States, who named it Wheelus Air Base. At 52 square kilometres, it was the largest American military installation outside of the United States, with its own beach club, cinema, bowling alley, high school for 500 students and its own radio station and TV channel. At its height 15,000 American soldiers were stationed there until the country was unable to renew the contract in 1973. After that the air force from the Soviet Union and Libya took over

the base and it was bombed by the United States in 1986, partially destroying the facility they had upgraded. Nine years later, it was transformed into the second civilian airport in Tripoli until in 2014 it was transformed again into the main airport.

There isn't usually anywhere near as much drama as Jakob Øster's experience. In 2017, Sherwes Travel organised programmes for just a few groups each month. The vast majority are extreme travellers or notorious country collectors. Most of these are content with 2-3 days, to check out Leptis Magna, probably the world's best preserved ancient city, and the charming old town of Tripoli. But the government has realised that people are sneaking in and have therefore tightened the sale of business visas as well. Now you can only get such a visa at the embassy in the country where you live, or in London, if there is no embassy in your home country. Libya and Norway, despite common oil interests, do not have respective diplomatic representation.

In a restaurant I saw a picture of Muammar al-Gaddafi — not placed in the middle of one of the most visible walls, like it would have been in the old days, but suitably well hidden in a corner of the kitchen, partially seen from where I was sat together with Yousef and Salem. A lot can be said about Muammar al-Gaddafi, but since he was killed, no one has managed to keep control of the country, and various factions are still fighting for power. This in turn serves as an excellent recruitment and breeding ground for terrorist groups and warlords. But for a short time after the assassination, there was optimism in Libya, and investors flocked to the country. The positivity lasted for about a year before the hangover arrived as suddenly as a ticket inspector emerging on the subway. Terrorist attacks, civil war, a complete halt to investment and the exclusion of tourists have led to mass unemployment. After a while, the 1770-kilometre-long coastline of the country also became an important transit exit for African refugees wanting to reach Europe. Human traffickers and boat owners are vying for payments from desperate people who are seeking a better life further north, with thousands of people drowning every few months on the sea crossing. The small boats are usually neither substantial nor solid enough, and many capsize with far more people on board than they are designed for.

In 2016, the stories of modern slavery began to emerge. People who were in refugee camps in Libya were sold, or hired out, as slaves by camp guards, reported the BBC, Time Magazine, and other media.

"The whole thing stems from a misunderstanding during the sale," explained Yousef. "Many of the refugees are craftsmen and are offered jobs outside of the refugee camps. They then negotiate an hourly rate with the potential employers. But then the employer must also pay the prison guards to get them out of the camp — since they do not have a work permit — and this has been seen as slavery. But it is not like that," he said resolutely. Now he works with tourists, and wants to present a positive picture of Libya, so I sometimes got the impression of a rose-tinted view of the situation in the country. Former refugees, which the BBC has spoken to, support parts of Yousef's version, but claim that they were never paid, they were forced to work longer than agreed, and so they were actually used as slaves. CNN has filmed what they have called slave auctions with a hidden camera.

I had downloaded the video to my mobile phone and showed it to Yousef and Salem.

"Anyone need a grave digger? This is a grave digger, a big strong man. He can dig," said the auctioneer, dressed in camouflage in the video. "What's your offer, what's your offer?" he shouts in the film. Potential buyers raise their hands and shout back prices: "500, 550, 600, 650!" After a few minutes everything is over, and the sale items are transferred to new 'owners'.

The film does not show whether they may have been promised a salary, but the reactions from those who are sold indicate that at best there is an intellectual discussion around whether in reality they are actually slaves or not. Yousef was confident in the belief of his version, even though he did not say a single word during the screening of the film.

"To get out of the refugee camps and be able to work like this allows them to earn money which they can use to reach Europe," Yousef explained. "And that is the goal of everyone arriving here from further south in Africa — to reach Europe," asserted the guide.

And that he did: Everywhere in the suburbs of Tripoli, there are seemingly unemployed men on the streets, all with a skin colour that denotes a homeland south of the Sahara. None of them have branded clothes, to say the least. And in Libya it's cold, really cold. Especially if you are used to the temperatures of the Central African Republic, Congo, or Burundi. The clothes worn have often been likely inherited from other refugees or received from organisations that try to help. The colour combinations can be interesting. And you don't have to look far between football kits with tired logos, advertising sweaters for various toothpaste brands or machine-woven hats of varying quality. From the car window on the way to Leptis Magna I saw T-shirts that have even started off life in Norway. Expensive football shirts from Barcelona, Manchester United and Bayern Munich are completely absent. But then maybe housewives do not so lightly give away the Messi, Alexis, or Müller shirts. Clothes of our heroes apparently are not sent to developing countries. It is really warming then that the kids themselves are so inventive, like Murtaza Ahmadi in Afghanistan, the 13th least visited country in the world. The six-year-old made his own Messi kit from plastic bags and wrote the number 10 on the back with a pen. The picture of the boy went viral, and in the end, he got to meet his great hero in Qatar. I saw many similar homemade costumes in both countries.

Libya is almost three times as big as Afghanistan and is simply enormous. Totalling 1,759,541 square kilometres, it is the world's 16th largest country. Only Sudan and Algeria are larger in Africa. 90 percent is part of the Sahara, but tens of thousands of years ago that area was very fertile with lakes, forests, and diverse wildlife. There are traces of human settlement from around 10,000 years ago, when farmers lived along the coast. Around

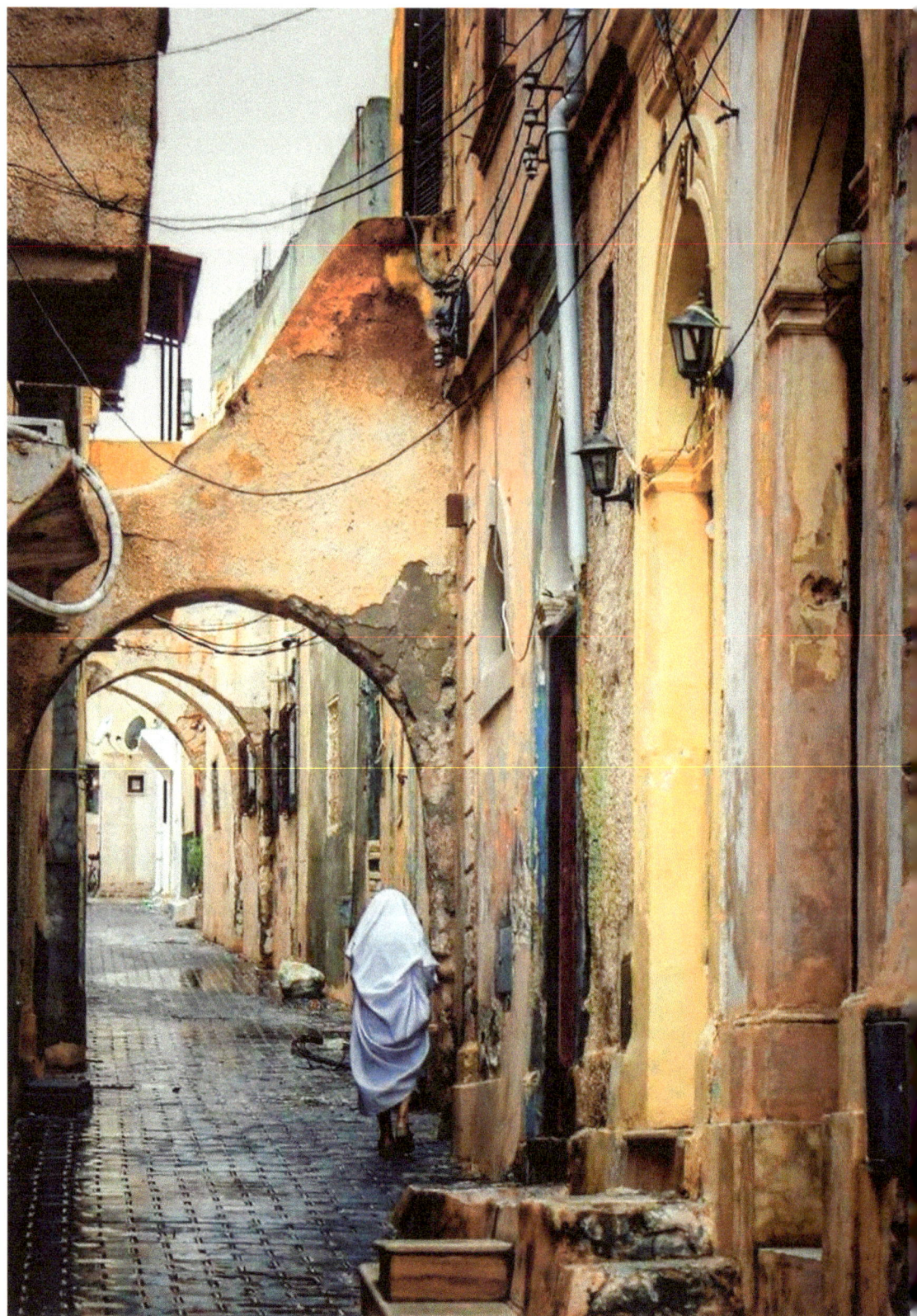

500 BC, Carthage, with its capital in modern-day Tunisia, became an important centre with as many as 700,000 inhabitants. They also ruled parts of what is now Libya before Punic farmers took over. With 22 letters in their alphabet, but without a single vowel, they wrote Carthage as Qrthdst. The name means 'New City'.

"The Punics built the coastal towns of Sabratha, Oea and Leptis Magna. After a while, the area they were located in was known as Tripolis, or 'Three Cities', later giving the name to the current capital of Tripoli," told Yousef. He knows history well. For a guide, it is probably safer to stick to that than potentially sensitive information from the present.

Libya was under Islamic rule for 850 years before the Spaniards took over for several decades. It then became a part of the Ottoman Empire before it was Italy's turn to occupy the region. Libya became an independent nation on Christmas Eve 1951. This was good timing as the previously poor country discovered oil a few years later. Something that suited Gaddafi well. He took power as a 27-year-old after a coup in 1969. After this he made the country a republic which he himself ruled over through The Libyan Revolutionary Command Council. His words were law, something that gave rise to many impulsive and perhaps not fully thought-through orders and laws. Among other things, the young leader introduced sharia as a starting point for the legal system, but he saw himself more as a Muslim modernist. Ever-increasing oil revenues meant that he was able to afford to strengthen the military, build houses for his people and improve health and education. In his 'free time' he wrote books where he set out political ideas. But after terrorist attacks that could be traced back to Libya, including a nightclub bomb in Berlin in 1986 and the plane explosion over Lockerbie, Scotland, in 1988, Libya became more and more isolated from the West. On the flip side, Gaddafi, became ever more paranoid with age and became known for some unusual habits. He surrounded himself with well-trained and beautiful female bodyguards who were officially called The Revolutionary Nuns or Amazonian Guard. They were to be virgins, and all hand-picked personally by the President. In retrospect, several of them came forward and claimed that they had been raped on numerous occasions by Gaddafi, his sons, or other high-ranking officials. The bodyguards were also reportedly forced to kill rebels if they themselves did not want to be killed.

"There was a pattern with the stories of the women. To begin with they were raped by the Dictator, then they were sent onwards, like used objects, first to one of the sons and then to a high-ranking official for further abuse before they could finally leave," reported psychologist Seham Sergewa to the Washington Post. Sergewa gathers information on behalf of the International Criminal Court.

But then came karma.

In 2011, the International Court of Justice in The Hague issued an arrest warrant for Gaddafi for human rights violations. He spent four months on the run with bodyguards and other members of the government. They hardly slept more than a night in each place. In October 2011, he was taken prisoner after a NATO operation and killed by the Misrata militia shortly after. The country was valued at 300 billion euros at that time. No one knows where all the money went, but rumour has it that Gaddafi must have managed to embezzle between a third and a half of it. The country had a foreign debt of over 80 billion euros in 2021, but the financial outlook looked good for the first time in many years with a steep increase in its gross national product. Previously most people had to queue for hours in front of the ATMs to get access to some cash, although the maximum withdrawal was 200 dinars — a typical weekly salary for a teacher or nurse. Yousef was clear that there is a need for change.

"But we do not need democracy. That's a luxury. What we need is specialists and well-educated ministers in the government to restore order to the country and get the economy moving. The unemployment rate is currently almost 50 percent," said Yousef. He is old enough to have a long-term perspective on things and not believe in short-term and unrealistic promises.

"We also don't have a tradition of democracy. Not even if we go right back to antiquity, when many of the emperors ruled with an iron fist," Yousef exclaimed, while we drove further east, on the 130-kilometre-long journey from Tripoli to Leptis Magna.

Walking around, utterly alone, in Leptis Magna was absolutely magical. The city was founded 700 years before Christ and was inhabited up until the 7th century. It was subsequently gradually covered by Saharan sand and eventually forgotten, before being rediscovered by Italian archaeologists in the early 1930s. The Italians used extensive resources to dig out the whole city and open it up to the public. In many ways, they had a vested interest, since in its day it was part of the Roman Empire, and even grew to be one of their most beautiful cities of all. Two thousand years ago, almost 100,000 people lived among swathes of impressive monuments, a large harbour, warehouses, shops, dwellings, and a front-facing bath house complete with a very public toilet. It had 70 seats and no partitions. Many of the 70 holes in the stone slabs are still intact, and I took the opportunity to have a dry run. I was completely alone and could have used the toilet without any problems. Had the alternative been to sit with 69 others, I would have then definitely thought twice about it if I had not been extremely desperate.

Even more impressive was the amphitheatre with 6,000 seats and a gladiator arena with enough room for 13,000 spectators. It was pretty demotivating being on stage in the theatre with only an uninterested Salem talking on the phone in the audience. I would have rather given a talk to the most famous inhabitant of Leptis Magna — Septimius Severus was born here. He went on to become a Roman emperor and ruled for 18 years before dying from a disease at the age of 66. At that time, he was 'working' in York, England together with 40,000 soldiers. It was another 800 years or so before the Vikings followed.

Not far from the harbour in Leptis Magna are three large stone pillars.

"Four such pillars were once sold for a construction project in Paris, 2000 years ago, but the first pillar was so heavy that the cargo ship sank straight to the bottom, and the deal was subsequently cancelled. The last three have stood here ever since," said Yousef.

Everything was obviously not better earlier either, not even in antiquity.

The old town of Tripoli is not quite as old, even though the iconic Arch of Marcus Aurelius, formed in stone, dates from as early as the year 200. Nearby, it is easy to get lost in the mishmash of narrow alleyways, streets, and dead ends. The Photographer Hiba Shalabi lives here, and she loves this district more than anything.

"My dad took me with him all around here when I was little and told me exciting stories about almost every building and every front door. He used the old town as a backdrop for his stories about famous travellers to North Africa and various ancient cities."

With so many people from different nations, the old town is the heart of Tripoli.

"What I like best is meeting the seniors outside shops and swapping jokes or interesting stories with them. Like, Uncle Adel Bassett, who works as a tailor, or Uncle Ahmed al-Sori who sells freshly squeezed juice and freshly sliced bread with eggs and cheese. Just listen to the sounds in the background," she said, taking a break. I could visualise it as we walked through the narrow and winding streets between the brick houses in the old town. We heard children reading from the Koran at a religious school, and we actually passed the uncle's cafe. There, a middle-aged lady bargained with al-Sori to get more juice at a better rate. In the premises next to it, a lady in her thirties was laughing loudly while sitting in a hairdresser's chair with neon yellow plastic clips in her hair. The hairdresser stood behind her, just grinning. He must have just told a good story.

But already when we met in April 2018, Hiba had started to have misgivings about how the district was being cared for. The old elaborate and distinctive doors in a myriad of colours were about to disappear. A fervent salesman seemed to have cornered the market for anonymous cold metal doors. All were almost identical, in white or grey. The uniqueness was about to disappear.

"It's like removing all the historical and archaeological details and erasing all the good memories. They do not have the right to do that — they are disrupting a part of history for both the current and future generations. I believe it destroys part of our shared civilization. The soul just vanishes. And all because greedy salesmen have managed to trick people into believing that insecure doors are forbidden under Islamic law."

I was told that the door salesmen referred to Muslim scriptures where Allah seemingly demands all believers to speak his name before they lock the doors for the night. Only by doing so can he protect believers from devilry performed by animals, insects, or humans. I wondered just what that had to do with the old doors.

"The cunning salesmen claim that old doors are not solid enough to keep out the devil, and that Allah wants genuine believers to install safe and modern doors," explained Hiba.

That such a ruse, and that type of marketing, actually works is proof that most people in Libya have not had an adequate education. "Depressing," sighed Hiba, and looked genuinely upset in her dark hijab as we strolled through the streets and saw the destruction of culture up close. She walks around the old town almost every day, always with an SLR camera at the ready. She has done this for many years, and that makes her happy.

"At least we then have photographic memories of how it once was."

Three days later I was sat in a café in Tripoli when a very graceful and well-dressed woman came in. I knew she was nearer 70, but she could have passed for being in her early forties as she almost glided over the floor, coming towards me. The firm handshake and the warm eyes that looked straight at me left an impression. Madame Rabia ben Barka is the first female clothing designer in Libya. She takes inspiration from traditional Libyan dresses and makes them more practical, comfortable, and stylish. But her garments and dresses, as well as the occasional robe for men, are not for everyone. The fabric contains, no less, real gold, silver or silk, and the most expensive ones can easily cost as much as a car. A new one. A luxury brand. Her clients include Gaddafi's wife and Tunisian pop singer Latifa. And when he was alive, Gaddafi himself was a customer. Madame Rabia ben Barka had agreed to meet me.

"The cloth we use is made in the traditional way here in Libya, and we only use the real thing. You can melt out the silver and gold in my garments and turn them into jewellery. I see myself as an artist, and I never make more than a few copies of each dress. You know, there is nothing more embarrassing for a woman than arriving at a gala in the same dress as one of the other stars," she explained. "For me, it is important to maintain exclusivity."

"What is it like marketing Libyan dresses? I mean, it's not exactly fashion that your country is renowned for," I inquired.

"No, not yet," she smiled warmly. The ambitious woman has the contacts needed to make a success of it. The dresses have been worn at fashion shows from Paris, Berlin to Shanghai.

"But it wasn't just easy going in the beginning. The first fashion show I took part in was over thirty years ago in Istanbul. But back then Libya was blacklisted and was not allowed to trade with the West. Getting there we had to smuggle the dresses for the show, in a small fishing boat that took us first to Malta, before my model, my assistant and I flew onwards via Rome to Istanbul. It was an extremely long journey, but the feedback I received in Turkey made it all worth it," she said.

Strictly speaking, she could have modelled herself, but it was a designer she wanted to be known as, with one or two exceptions.

"If we run out of models, I step in," smiled Madame Rabia. It was as a model that she had first started out — with great success. Not a surprise, I could only imagine what she would have looked like forty years earlier. Perhaps similar to her relatively tall, slim, and beautiful assistant, Mysoun Haroun, who sat down with us to make sure everything with the interview went as planned. Mysoun had also started out as a model.

I got a hug from both of them before I flagged down a taxi and asked to be driven to the airport. It was only two and a half hours until my flight to Tunis, and the traffic in Tripoli is notorious. At times a complete stand-still. But the speed picked up after slow going for half an hour, and I caught the plane with time to spare. I even passed through passport control without any trouble. Though, I did have to explain what I had done in Libya, and what kind of company I had done business with, when the policeman in his forties checked the business visa in my passport. Tourists shouldn't be let in or out. Not unpunished, at least. I perhaps looked a little too touristy. My reply meant that I immediately got my passport back nonetheless:

"I have had a meeting with Madame Rabia ben Barka."

My Arabic is very limited, but his facial expression seemed to convey that he mumbled 'lucky bastard'. Or something similar.

From the world's third least visited country, I was about to travel to what was previously the least visited. Only war, famine and drought had meant that this almost circular island, in the Pacific Ocean, had been overtaken in the statistics. The question really is whether one should say that Nauru was upgraded or downgraded to the world's second least visited country.

The gladiatorial arena on the outskirts of Leptis Magna held 13,000 spectators. I walked through the corridors below and tried to imagine what the fighting men must have felt like over 2,000 years ago.

The amphitheatre is located in the middle of the ancient city and 'only' had room for 6,000 people with a penchant for shoes.

The view from the harbour nearby. I was alone and tempted to skinny-dip, but my hosts were waiting in the car.

The ruins in Leptis Magna have been well protected by the sand for a long time, and have not been damaged in the war.

Most people on the harbour promenade in Tripoli fish more as a hobby than for food. Note that there is not a single woman here.

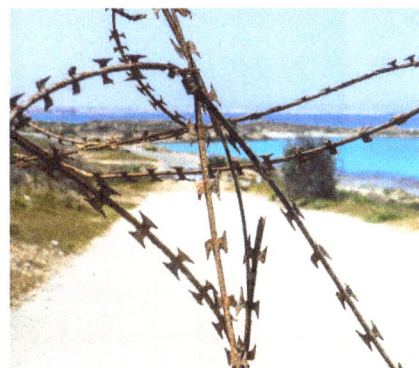

We passed an abandoned roadblock. Seeing no policemen, I managed to take a photo.

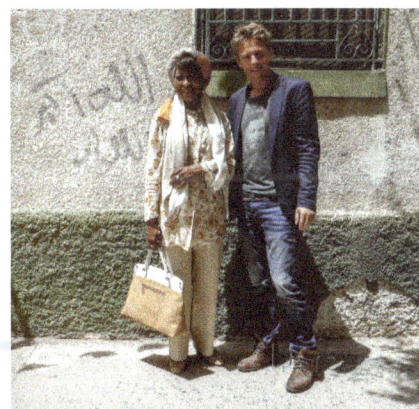

Four such pillars were sold to Paris 2000 years ago. They were so heavy that the boat with the first sunk. The trade was cancelled.

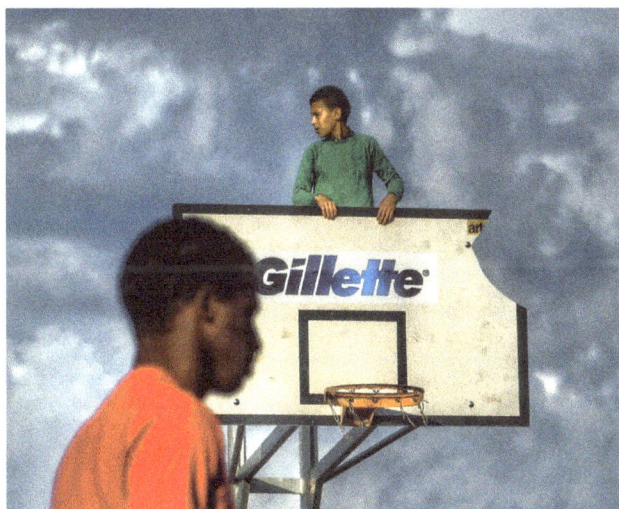

Madame Rabia Ben Barka designs clothes. She obviously dresses better than me.

Basketball is popular in Libya.

Unfortunately, more and more of the traditional colourful doors are being replaced by modern doors.

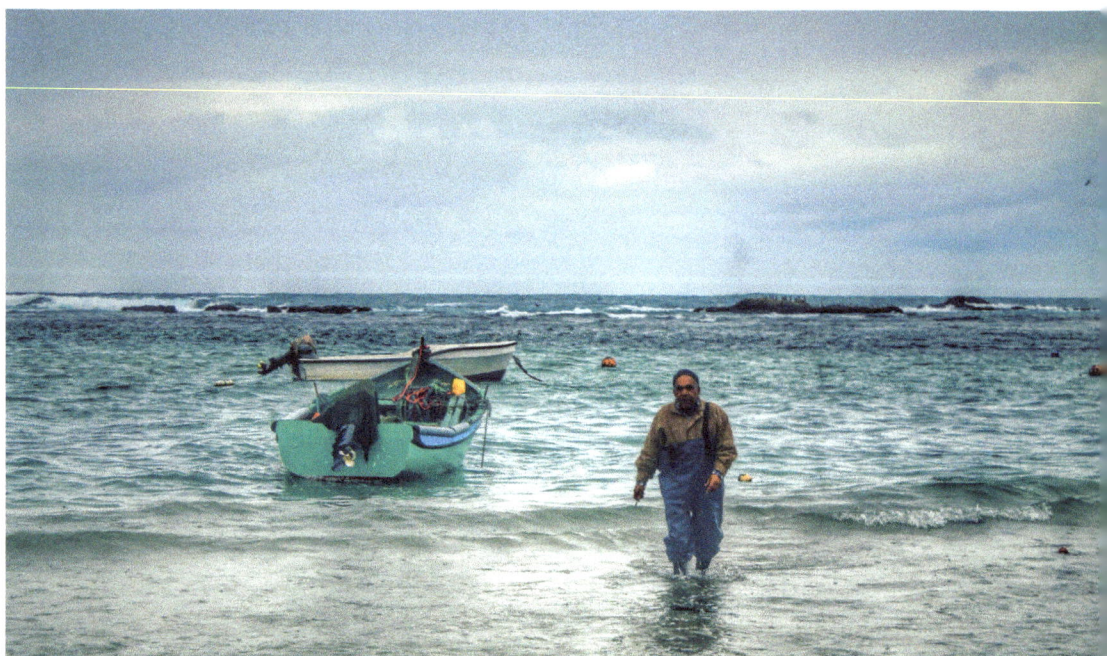

Photographer Hiba Shalabi snapped this fisherman on his way to work. Few people in Libya want to be photographed.

This picture was included in one of Hiba's photo exhibitions. I asked if it was called "while we wait for better times". Smiling, she told me that it had no title.

Hiba loves to photograph the old town of Tripoli. She wants to document the future.

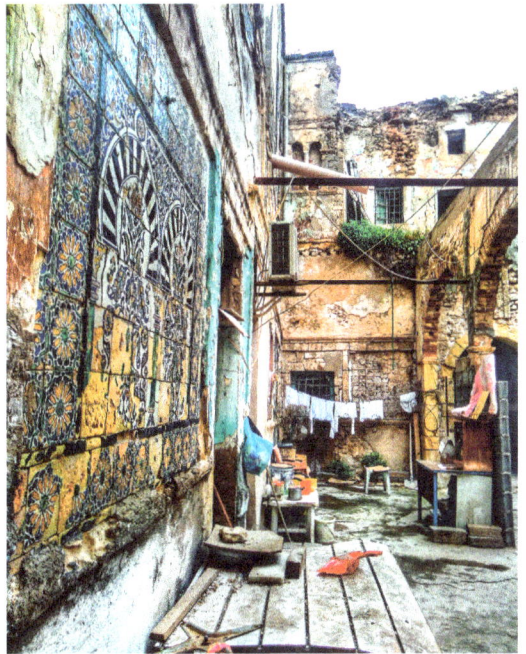

In some places in the old town you stumble across the odd mosaic. Walking around here is like being in a labyrinth.

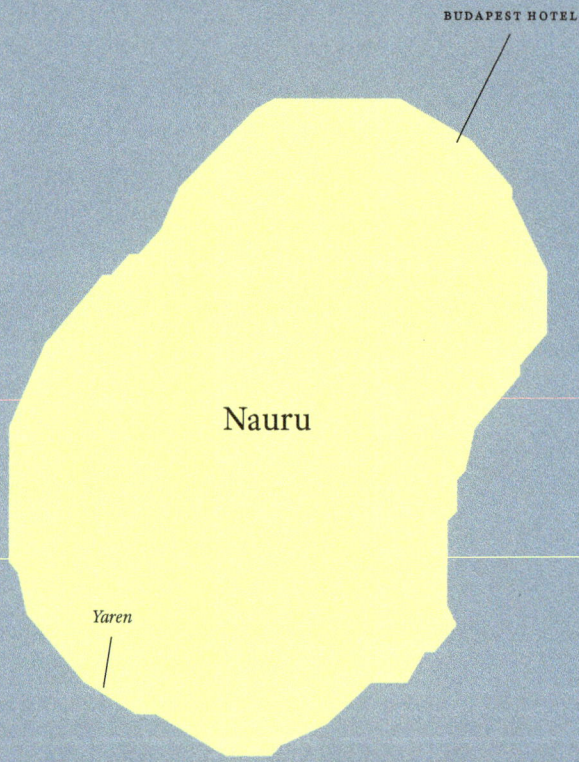

BUDAPEST HOTEL

Nauru

Yaren

1 km

2

Nauru,
Oceania

INHABITANTS: 13,000 (Verdsbanken)
TOURISTS PER YEAR: 130 (garfors.com)
AREA: 21 square kilometres

THE WORLD'S SMALLEST REPUBLIC lies in the middle of the Pacific Ocean and consists of an almost completely circular island with a circumference of 19 kilometres. Nauru has been the least visited country in the world for many years. But then it is a tough competition to receive fewer than eleven tourists a month. Now, for the first time in a long time, another country has managed exactly that feat, and Nauru has ended up in second place. Almost no one travels voluntarily to the island — most are actually forced there. Nauru, in fact, has a lucrative deal with Australia to house non-returnable boat refugees, something that means, percentagewise, the country has one of the world's highest refugee populations with approximately 1500 refugees. They have unwittingly played a part in increasing the population, after the number of inhabitants had dropped to less than 10,000. In many ways, Nauru now seems a multicultural society with inhabitants from more than ten different nations. The restaurant offering, in particular, has greatly improved since I was first here in 2010, largely due to the asylum seekers who have been allowed to work here. Now you can find Iranian, Pakistani, Indian and Lebanese food, in addition to the compulsory Chinese of varying quality, alongside the occasional local restaurant.

Iranian, Nima Mehri Komeleh, is 35 years old and arrived in Nauru in 2013 with his wife, Katayuon, and daughter, who is now eight years old. The 190-centimetre tall, thin man is originally an electrician but found out that there were better ways to make money in Nauru. The couple now run the Café Island, a very popular café and restaurant. Not only does he earn more than as an electrician, but both have also come into contact with many more people and integrated in a completely different way.

"When we started out, people here didn't know what a café was. We had to explain to them that we weren't another ordinary restaurant, but we also served various types of good coffee and ice cream, in addition to Iranian-inspired food. Just to come here and drink coffee was something unusual for them, but now they have been trained," smiled

Nima, before he interrupted me right in the middle of a question.

"Then of course, we've also got the hookah. I mustn't forget that! Before we arrived, no one in Nauru knew what that was, either," he grinned. He would have quite a few hookah pipes the evenings I was there. I have only personally smoked hookah once in Myanmar, and it was more out of stubbornness. I thought I had ordered juice with exciting fruit flavours, but it turned out that the fruits on the menu were actually the flavours added to the tobacco, not any juice at all. Since I had already ordered and had to pay anyhow, I decided to give it all a try. I managed to get myself home in a taxi. The next day was hell on earth. I have not felt as sick since having diarrhoea of the century after a somewhat unfortunate restaurant visit in Mumbai in the late 1990s. Since then, I haven't taken a single drag.

Nima was explicit about the food they served being only inspired by their home country.

"Had we been in Iran, we would have had many more flavours and a completely different selection on the menu. The supply of raw ingredients here on the island is at times quite scarce, and we have to make the sour milk ourselves."

Poor access to raw ingredients is not a surprise. Firstly, Nauru is not exactly high on the list of destinations that receive early deliveries. Secondly, the country does not have a proper port. All deliveries that come by sea in containers are dependent on the weather. Initially, the waves must be small enough for the cargo ship to drop anchor by large buoys between 100 and 200 metres from land. Then each container must be individually hoisted down using the containership's own crane and placed in one of the small cargo boats that try to shuttle between the ships and the port. Try. If the waves are too big, it is impossible to move the containers from the ships to the boats, so one must take a break that can mean anything from a few minutes to days or weeks. Fortunately, modern containers have refrigeration. But that is not always enough.

The week before I returned to Nauru, the waves had been far too large for far too long, and the shops had run out of all kinds of fresh produce. This resulted in a breakfast of questionable quality at Container Café, a coffee bar that also sells sandwiches. The name of the café comes from what it is made out of: a red shipping container. It stands out, located right next to the police station and the supermarket.

"The worst damn chicken sandwich I've ever tasted," complained Simon from Australia, pulling creative grimaces that left no doubt: breakfast hadn't been edible. I had chatted to him one night at one of the restaurants. I had several breakfasts by the red container. During the day, before Café Island opened, they made the best coffee in Nauru. But there weren't any brownies or anything else sweet.

"You have to go to Tropicana for that," the lady explained at the counter. She is from

Fiji and lives in Nauru with her husband, who is here to teach. The container lady refused to tell me her name, but there was no doubt that she knew a thing or two about chocolate bakes. The brownie I ordered later at Tropicana was legendary. I sunk my teeth into the little square brown piece of cake in the café on the other side of the island, and it was likely the best piece of brownie I have eaten. Anytime. Anyplace. Simply on its own a good enough reason to visit Nauru. And if you make the trip to taste it, you are increasing the number of tourists by almost a whole percent.

When it came to dinner dishes at the Iranian Café Island, there was little left to ponder about — Nima and Katayuon knew their craft.

"We get all kinds of guests, from neighbours, foreigners to ministers. Yes, even the president. The problem is they like our food too much. 'What are we going to do when you leave here, the ones who make the best food in the country?' they ask. And then they grin and say that they will delay our asylum application," said Nima nervously, but with a slight smile. The subject was way too serious and too important for him to fully let himself laugh at the joke.

Australia refuses entry to the country for boat refugees, and so they end up in Nauru. An agreement Australia made with Obama made it possible for the refugees to be able to move to the United States, but Iran is now one of the countries on the list that American authorities are not especially happy with. Even though the family has been through the three rounds of interviews that the USA demands, and believe that they have answered well and genuinely, Nima does not dare to freely hope that they will be allowed to travel further east across the ocean. What is quite clear is that he is as expectant as a child. Nauru treats the refugees well, but the Iranian family are, in a sense, still prisoners on a tiny island.

"You do not know what freedom is until you no longer have it," Nima said quietly, before he lowered his head and tried to hide a tear. Nima has a prominent moustache that goes almost down his chin on each side. But the last 3-4 centimetres at the bottom are completely white. I don't know if this is down to stress and despair, but the reality of being an asylum seeker on a tiny island for five years must really take its toll.

Other refugees come from Iraq, Kuwait, Pakistan, Afghanistan, Yemen, Sri Lanka, Myanmar, Syria, and Somalia. They can actually choose themselves if they want to live in the asylum reception centre, or if they want to rent an apartment or a house. This means, in many ways, that integration here can be better than in lots of other places, but it is important to remember that no one wants to be right here. Being on a Pacific Island, can perhaps seem alluring, but it also means that they are both geographically and mentally extremely isolated from their homeland and the rest of the world. Not to mention that they have been forcibly sent here, after dreaming of a life in Australia and risking their lives in small boats to follow that dream. Some refugees have nonetheless found themselves a local girlfriend or even gotten married and are maybe a good deal more positive about Nauru than most.

The actual asylum reception centre is also not particularly well placed for being on a Pacific Island. The complex has been built several kilometres inland on the island, along an uneven and bumpy dirt road. At the start, the refugees who lived in temporary tents, had neither a view of nor access to the beach; both are pretty much mandatory for Pacific Islanders.

The project is controversial. Housing these refugees has put Nauru on the map, but not in a positive way. This has almost made the government paranoid when looking at letting people who may be journalists into the country. If you are a journalist and want to apply for a visa, you have to pay 8000 Australian dollars just to have the application considered, and you are far from guaranteed to receive a positive answer. This means that most journalists try to enter via a tourist visa, which puts the immigration authorities on edge as they believe that everyone who applies for a tourist visa ais actually a journalist.

This creates a downward spiral and isn't particularly good for increasing the number of tourists to a country that has nothing to really talk about for tourists in the first place. Nauru has even managed the feat of getting fewer tourists than the 156 they had in its heyday of 2010. Now the country is down to 130, a decrease of 17 percent. That is perhaps not a surprise with the strict visa policy. It took me 12 weeks of emails and a lot of waiting to get my tourist visa. Working for NRK hardly made things easier.

My friend Randy Williams is a radio DJ in San Diego, USA. He visited Nauru in 2016 and had the experience of being taken away to an interrogation room at the airport right before his plane was due to take-off. He had talked to an extremely large number of people, taken countless pictures and therefore had been pretty much marked down as 'Media'. Suspicion was rife in other words, and he was taken into a small office without windows at the airport when he was about to leave the country. He was to be interrogated.

According to Randy, they carried out a traditional 'good cop, bad cop' routine, like in films. The American has been to over 100 countries and does not plan to quit until he has visited all of them. This exact concept was not understood by the immigration lady. She suspiciously asked why he wanted to visit little Nauru, of all places. Randy said that no one in the United States had ever heard of Nauru. That did not fall on solid ground. She insisted that of course everyone had heard of Nauru, before she went through his suitcase, pretty aggrieved, without finding anything of interest. In the end, he was allowed to dash onto the plane, which was waiting for only the American.

I wasn't particularly a fan of being questioned and opted out from bringing a microphone and SLR camera. I personally had no problems with the immigration authorities both on the way in and on the way out, despite my question about how many tourists they get a year. But then a Norwegian passport may not be as troublesome as an American one.

I was surprised when the plane from Nauru Airlines landed on the island in March 2018, not because we were safely on the ground, but because there were two other Boeing 737-300s from the same airline parked. A few years ago, the company was named Our Airlines and had one old 737, but now they owned five relatively new aircraft, having greatly expanded their destinations. In addition, they have established partnerships with other airlines in the Pacific. The airstrip on Nauru is 2150 metres long, and when one plane, or several, are on the ground, they close one of the roads with a barrier to ensure access to the terminal. The main road goes between the runway and the airport. The last time I was here, eight years earlier, that meant the whole road around the island being closed, with the alternative being a drive around half or almost the whole island to get to where you were going. Now another road has been built on the other side of the runway. So, it is 'just' the shortcut that gets blocked off.

But the terminal building is just as small and cramped as before — this is most likely one of the smallest and most surprising 'hubs' in the world. With relatively little competition between the island nations in the Pacific, it seems as though the airline is doing well, with almost full planes. Since we are in the second least visited country in the world, having a conservative visa policy, then needless to say few of those passengers actually leave Nauru airport, with the transit area at times crowded. The direct routes with Nauru Airlines, as the company is now called, go to Brisbane, Honiara, Tarawa, and Nadi, with the ability to travel quickly and easily onwards with the same airline or a partner to other destinations. Nauru has, in other words, managed what no one would have thought possible: The little airport has now become an important transit hub. That's all relatively speaking, as there are not so many who travel between the countries of Oceania.

The airline has a total of five aircraft at its disposal, and I did not reckon on there being many delays. If that was the case, I would only find out after four days in the third smallest country in the world after the Vatican and Monaco. The five planes spend a lot of time on the ground in Fiji and Australia, so there isn't a plane departing every day from the lilliputian state.

Nauru has 14 districts but is one of only two countries in the world lacking a capital. The second is actually Switzerland, where according to the constitution, Bern is not the official capital. On Nauru the parliament, the airport terminal and most of the airstrip is in the Yaren district. It is usually cited as the functioning capital, but the districts of Aiwo and Ewa have a much better range of services and seem more 'capital-like'. Here the districts almost merge into one, but then it only takes less than half an hour to drive around the country, or an hour and a half when running. You have to cover over two laps around the country to complete an entire marathon.

On my first visit, I could not resist the temptation to run around an entire country. It was an overambitious goal just 60 kilometres south of the equator, especially at midday, when the sun was in the middle of the sky. The timing was not well thought through, but I somehow managed to get around without intravenous fluids. I could not help myself this time either. I had to try again — against the clock now. Attempt number two started at 14.51, it was overcast and some rain showers. Ideal jogging weather. There was a constant beach, or at least sea, on my right-hand side. But the name Nauru likely also comes from the Naurian word anáoero, meaning 'I am walking on the beach'. The run around the country was also much faster than in 2010. A tradition has been started. The question is if I come back for a third attempt.

Nauru has an admittedly poor reputation, even when excluding the refugee camp. The country has on several occasions recognised breakaway republics as independent for a fee. In the past, the government has engaged in plans to establish a casino business here, and at one point there was a plan to start a centre for fast visa processing of North Koreans fleeing Western intelligence - for a hefty payment, of course, and without a single extradition agreement. At one time, the country was one of the richest in the world when looking at gross domestic product per capita. This was due to aggressive extraction of phosphate in the middle of the island. Then the natural resource almost ran out, and the small country now shows impressive creativity when it comes to finding new sources of income. This is not so strange — it is a necessity for survival. But in recent years, the economy in the country has moved towards more traditional means, such as through the service industry.

Additionally, money comes from housing refugees and a large income from the hundreds of Australians who are employed to follow up on the asylum seekers. There is a need for administrators, health personnel, security guards, drivers, and construction workers, just to name a few. You would think that it would be cheap to stay in hotel accommodation on a small island in the middle of the Pacific Ocean, but it hasn't worked out like that, despite very few tourists. And it has nothing to do with the Australian workers, because they live in their own complex of as a high standard as it is possible to get from something that is built of containers placed on top of each other over several floors. With 130 tourists a year, there is of course minimal tourist infrastructure. Looking ahead, it may be a case of the traditional chicken-and-egg situation: Who comes first — the tourists or the first competitive hotel?

For the first few nights I had booked an apartment through the Internet. Later I learned that the owner had inexplicably managed to double book it, and four people who had seats further forward than me on the plane, and so got out faster and through immigration first, had been picked up by the nice owner. In arrivals, there was therefore no one holding any kind of sign with 'GUNNAR', 'GARFORS', or a combination of these. Norwegian Telia did not have a roaming agreement here either. But I knew approximately where the apartment was and started strolling north-eastwards with my rucksack on my back.

It took five minutes before I was offered a lift.

Miok worked as a craftsman and should have picked up an extra hand from Kiribati on the same plane that I arrived on. The lad never showed up, so he was now on his way to have lunch. I explained that I didn't quite know where I was going, but that I had rented an apartment in his direction. Miok asked for the number of the landlord, Squire, before he got out a solid craftsman's phone with a rubber cover and called. It seemed as if the man at the other end was surprised, but they agreed that Miok and I should wait at a bus stop until he came. In the meantime, I asked Miok about Nauru's National Day. They also celebrate their day on 17th May, like Norway. Even though the children's precession is missing as part of the celebration in Nauru, the Norwegians and the Naurians share the gathering of inhabitants for competitions and fun. Those interested in sports go to the national stadium to compete. The 14 provinces are divided into six, each with its own colour. Then teams representing blue, green, red, orange, black and yellow compete among themselves in football, darts, and other sports.

"But the most important thing is still the bonfire competition. Each district builds large bonfires, and then the district leaders drive around the island to decide who has the biggest and best bonfire," said Miok.

I said that we also burnt bonfires in Norway to celebrate jonsok — midsummer — and that we compete in different competitions on 17th May. But he understood nothing about horseshoe throwing.

In the end, Squire called back. He asked us to come to his apartment, and Miok started his pickup and drove there. It took us 90 seconds. The actual apartment seemed to be positioned behind an old petrol station where there was now a Chinese grocery store.

The landlord welcomed us, and they greeted each other like old acquaintances. And of course, they were. There are only 13,000 inhabitants here. Squire and I shook hands. His hand was unsurprisingly twice as big as mine — this was the weightlifting nation of Nauru after all. Former president Marcus Stephen won seven weightlifting gold medals in the Commonwealth Games and two silvers in the World Cup. Seven people have represented Nauru in the Olympics, and all were weightlifters.

Then Squire apologised, explaining about the double-booking situation and that they were now in the midst of turning a warehouse into a studio for me.

Warehouse of sorts. It was an old garage with some extensive mould problems. The fact that mould thrives here has also been discovered by many of the refugees who still live in tents. The conditions for mould growth are almost optimal, and surveys in 2018 showed that the mould concentration in some tents was 76 times higher than the recommended maximum limit. I was not aware of this at the time, and Squire's wife was in full swing brushing and cleaning the garage. Along the back wall I saw a brand-new bed with a seemingly comfortable mattress covered by a bedsheet with a blue-flower pattern. A kind of bathroom was behind a door on the right. The garage did not have windows, but an air-conditioning unit was on full blast high up on one wall. Two light fixtures provided sufficient light, albeit in cool and unpleasant tones.

"You'll get a 30 percent discount, and a motorcycle," said the landlord.

As private as a parking space, as cosy as a nail factory. But then there was that lack of accommodation in Nauru. The frequent rain showers would in comparison make rapid machine-gun fire sound like gentle training for the elderly, pushing me reluctantly into a yes. I was only going to be sleeping there.

That was before I discovered the invasion of reddish flies. There were dozens of them on the ceiling in my new shed. I relayed a clear message that they had to be gone before I came back. And then I took the motorcycle out on a journey of discovery.

Most of the flies were gone when I arrived back hours later. But the rats that lived in the walls and scurried over the roof tiles at night, didn't exactly make me feel at home anyway. It perhaps wasn't out of the ordinary that I explored the island as much as I possibly could. One day I got talking to a relatively unorthodox guy, after he shouted a warning at me.

"There is a police checkpoint that way, and you don't have a helmet or a registered bike," said the man in his fifties, pointing down the road. He had several visible tattoos on his arms, which one could clearly see beneath the non-existent sleeves of the formerly white string vest. I stopped, sitting on a moped I had been able to borrow.

"Yes, but that'll be OK, won't it? I have already been stopped by the police for not using indicators," I responded. "They would have surely said something if things weren't alright."

But I had at least had a helmet on then — one that was dark red and far too big, so uncomfortable to wear that I had 'forgotten' it on this trip.

"Who are you?" he asked, stretching out his arm. "My name is Michael. I'm the brother of the President."

At least we had established how far I could fall.

I introduced myself as a tourist and author, although the latter could have given me some trouble as I was in Nauru on a tourist visa. But Michael did not overly care much. The talkative man said he was a money lender, fitter, and adviser to the president.

"Where's your lending shop then?" I asked. After two runs, a walk, and a motorcycle jaunt around the island, I could not remember seeing either pawn brokers, money lenders or loan sharks.

"No, I don't need one. People know who I am, and I know where people live," he

chuckled.

We talked about this and that before we got onto the topic of refugees on the island.

"We have had so many negative reports in the media that we just had to introduce a sky-high fee for press visas. Can you believe that? Here, the refugees are fully integrated. Look over there, there, and there! All of them are refugees, and everyone has a job," he said and pointed to three different men who, independently of each other, ambled along some distance away. He waved, and two of them acknowledged him with big smiles. The third one did not seem to notice Michael.

"The refugees also have far more allure for the ladies here in Nauru than we have," he said, without giving any explanation. I refrained from asking for one either. Michael clearly did not need to be asked about anything — he spoke already when breathing in and out. The president's brother managed to tell me that the economy on Nauru was going brilliantly well thanks to refugees, successful investments abroad, the new strategy of the airline and high taxes on foreign operations in the country, and that they would soon get a container port built. That was good news for the restaurant owners. I only hoped that Nima, and the others who desired such, would have been allowed to travel before the harbour was completed. According to Michael, it is going to happen in 2020. But TIO. Here, everything can happen. Or nothing.

On the day of my departure, I was out and about very early, since I planned to have breakfast at the airport café. I ordered an omelette, pancakes, and coffee from the smiling lady behind the counter. Everything was prepared immediately and served after five minutes. Between mouthfuls I read a book while sitting on a plastic bench that looked like it had been fetched right out of an American fast-food chain. But the food seemed to have been prepared from scratch and tasted surprisingly good when considering the surroundings. On the other hand, it is difficult to completely miss the mark with omelette and pancakes. After half an hour, two ladies who had ordered coffee came over to me.

"Were you planning to be on the plane today?" asked one of them. I didn't like the way the question was phrased. I was already delayed by nine days in the Pacific due to flight cancellations in Tuvalu, Hawaii, and the Federated States of Micronesia. There was more to come.

"Yes, that was my plan," I replied.

"I'm sorry, but the plane has been cancelled," she continued. "Come to our office when you've finished. We work for Nauru Airlines."

In the windowless office, I was informed that the flight had been cancelled, and that there would be a new flight two days later, at the earliest.

"Where are you going to book accommodation for me?" I wondered.

"No, we weren't thinking about booking anything," was the response from the lady behind the counter in the small room with enough space for two ticket sellers behind each desk, and with seating for up to four disgruntled passengers.

"I thought you were required by law. It is the ninth day I have been delayed on this trip in the Pacific, and the other airlines have all arranged accommodation and food for me," I said, knowing too well that I could not assume things in Nauru are the same as other places.

"Is that so? That was kind of them," she replied. It seemed like she meant it.

"So, Nauru Airlines is not a member of IATA?" I asked. The international airline organisation has quite strict rules for what rights passengers have, for example in the event of delays.

"IA-what?" The big lady with curly hair looked genuinely confused. But at least she took some action by picking up the phone receiver and calling the head office, which is not in Nauru, but in Brisbane. I soon learned that they certainly were not members of IATA, and that they had no intention of providing accommodation or compensation in any way for the trivial 48-hour delay.

If nothing else, she tried to help by calling around hotels. Nauru Hotel was full, Budapest Hotel charged 330 dollars per night, while Aiwo Hotel in the 'centre' charged 200. During my previous stay, I had used the latter hotel. It had been pretty shabby then, and there did not appear to have been a minute of maintenance carried out in eight years. Furthermore, I had learned from a guy in Café Island that an Australian company had measured asbestos levels around the country, and they did not recommend anyone to live in Aiwo. Not because of the actual hotel, but because of a large, almost rusted-through building, that stands on the neighbouring plot. It had at one time been used for the production of phosphate and stood there still, as a witness to an industry that had crashed almost overnight. There are still quite few industrial ruins and obsolete machines dotted around the island.

It ended up being the Budapest Hotel for me, likely named after a movie of the same name. The standard was not completely comparable. Budapest Hotel, division Nauru, is located as centrally as it is possible to get, in the north of the island, and is surrounded by a high mesh fence that blocks all access except through a gate made out of the same material.

The hotel is simply built up from containers over two levels and is painted in a garish browny-pink that makes the mundane shopping centre in Førde, Norway, seem like a fine-art painting by Adolph Tidemand. The rusty air-conditioning units outside of the windows do not exactly help either. Budapest Hotel helps asylum seekers here feel a little less depressed: Their camps feel Buckingham Palace-like compared to the Hungarian-inspired barrack-village. Budapest Hotel is proof that hell does exist. Only Satan himself could have created such a damnation and charged 330 dollars a night for it.

When considering the services especially that were on offer — or the lack of them, let me present it schematically.

available services, budapest hotel, nauru:	
Reception	No
Bar	No
Restaurant	No
Breakfast	No
Room service	No
Drinks vending machine	No
Iron	No
Internet	No
Laundrette	No
Table tennis table	No
Playground	No
Parking	No
Airport transit	No
Pay TV	No
TV	No
Radio	No
Cassette player	No
Hairdryer	No
Safe	No
Telephone	No
Soap	No
Minibar	No
Bath	No
Sauna	No
Pool	No
Beach	No
Have I remembered everything?	Yes

Unbelievably, Budapest Hotel was still a big leap in the right direction. After staying in a garage, that didn't take much, but then the hotel was not particularly homely either, albeit free of rats.

I preferred to take a trip out to explore the neighbourhood. Only a few metres from the hotel, and just outside of the mesh fence, an enclosure of fishing nets had been erected, several metres high. Frigatebirds lived inside it — a type of pelagic seabird. Like the cuckoo, they pilfer food and building materials for their nests, from other birds. So, they also get called pirates. But they are not all bad; the time of parental care is longer than with any other bird species.

In Nauru, the taming of frigatebirds has been a hobby for hundreds of years. I went over to the special net construction where a dozen birds were perched. Here they call a 'cage', like this one, a nest. 4 or 5 men were sat next to me, and I asked if I could take some pictures.

"No worries. But who are you?" asked Colin, the oldest.

"Just a curious guy from Norway. What is this for?"

After that I was given the entire frigatebird story. It had all begun hundreds of years ago, when the islanders saw the frigatebirds gliding high over their island, on their way to and from islands far away. They then had the opportunity to try to catch these birds.

They do this with the help of an abio, a kind of lasso made of fishing line, with lead solder at the one end. By tempting the birds with fish, they are able to get close enough for a well-trained lasso thrower to catch them. The birds are then placed inside their net prison and fed with large amounts of fish. After a few weeks, they are tame. It is then too tempting being given fish instead of having to catch it themselves. It turned out that these birds flew a long way, often being away for days, before they returned with wild birds that the islanders also managed to catch with an abio and then tame. And this is how it continued. Nauru is one of only two countries in the world where the capture of frigatebirds is a hobby. The other is Kiribati.

"In Kiribati, they talk about us. But we do not talk about them," said Colin proudly. "Nauru is known as the mother of all frigatebird countries. Not Kiribati — where the amateurs are," he continued, going against his previous claim of not mentioning Kiribati.

In Nauru, the frigatebirds are important enough for one to figure in the official coat of arms of the country, with the motto 'God's will first'. In both countries scissors are used to represent that a bird has been tamed. Each frigatebird club has a special marking that they cut into the wings of the birds. This is how they can tell if the birds flying high overhead are tamed, and if so, which club. A few decades ago, there were a dozen such clubs in Nauru. Now there are only two left. Women are not allowed.

"This is a man thing, and women have no place here — the wife can no doubt call out to her husband and tell him that dinner is ready," said Colin. And he wasn't joking. Unemployment is high in Nauru, and this gang spent much of their time together with the frigatebirds. And each other. Partly to talk complete nonsense, partly to plan how they were going to catch the next bird. There isn't really any big point to the hobby, other than catching and taming the most birds, similar to collecting Pokémon.

In addition to Colin, I greeted 7-8 others, all with English names. People have lived on Nauru for at least 3,000 years, but it was not until 1798 that the first Westerners visited and left their mark on the island. This honour was kept for the British captain and whaler John Fearn in 1798, who called the island Pleasant Island. Later, series of English sailors settled on Nauru, something that has influenced language and clearly names.

I learnt that the birds can be 15 years old, and that they eat fish, mice, and rats.

"The ones with black heads are the smartest. The birds have white heads while they are young, and after a few years the feathers change colour," said Colin. Wisdom, in other words, is directly related to age in frigatebird circles.

After a while of talking with them, I got to know that this was far more than a hobby for the men. It is deadly serious. According to tradition, if someone starts a frigate nest, they must be able to catch 31 frigatebirds in one month. During that month, the club members do not go home. And that is understandable. Because if they fail and do not manage to catch at least one bird a day, the club leader and its members must accept the consequence.

"Then you die," said Colin, drawing his right index finger across his own throat to show that he was not joking.

"You are joking?" I replied.

"No, this is no joke. If you do not manage it, you and all your men must commit suicide. That's how it is. That is the rule," he said seriously. As a consequence, the theft of tamed frigatebirds from another club is a serious criminal offence, leading to both imprisonment and high fines.

"But when you catch bird number 31, well, then there is a party. You slaughter pigs, chickens or whatever you have, before everyone drinks until the next morning. And it is only the next day that everyone goes home to their families, to sleep it off."

"How long does it take to catch 31 birds?" I wondered.

"When I started my frigatebird nest in 1967, it took us a week," said Colin proudly. "I remember the year, because that was the year before Nauru became independent."

The fact it was so long ago was not a bombshell. I guessed that not many men would have been allowed by their wives to gamble their lives on frigatebirds now.

"But now it's time for beer. Do you want one?"

I didn't manage to answer before I had a San Miguel can in my hand. There was obviously a set time for beer, because now there were ten men around the frigatebird cage. All raised a toast. But the day was far from over.

One of them kept an eye on the frigatebirds a few hundred metres up above through binoculars.

"There's one!" shouted the man, who must have been in his mid-twenties; then the

This is the whole of Nauru. The world's smallest republic is a measly 21 square kilometres. The road around the island is 19 kilometres.

Frigate Bird catchers from Nauru.

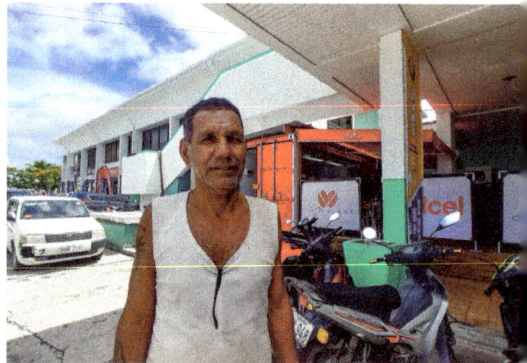
Michael outside the Container Cafe.

There are many creative names for the small shops around Nauru.

I've walked, run, and biked around Nauru. The café in the background serves the world's best brownie.

The shallow waters around the island nation make it challenging to build a harbour.

The favourite foods of Frigate Birds are fish, mice and rats.

This small harbour is only suitable for small boats and swimming.

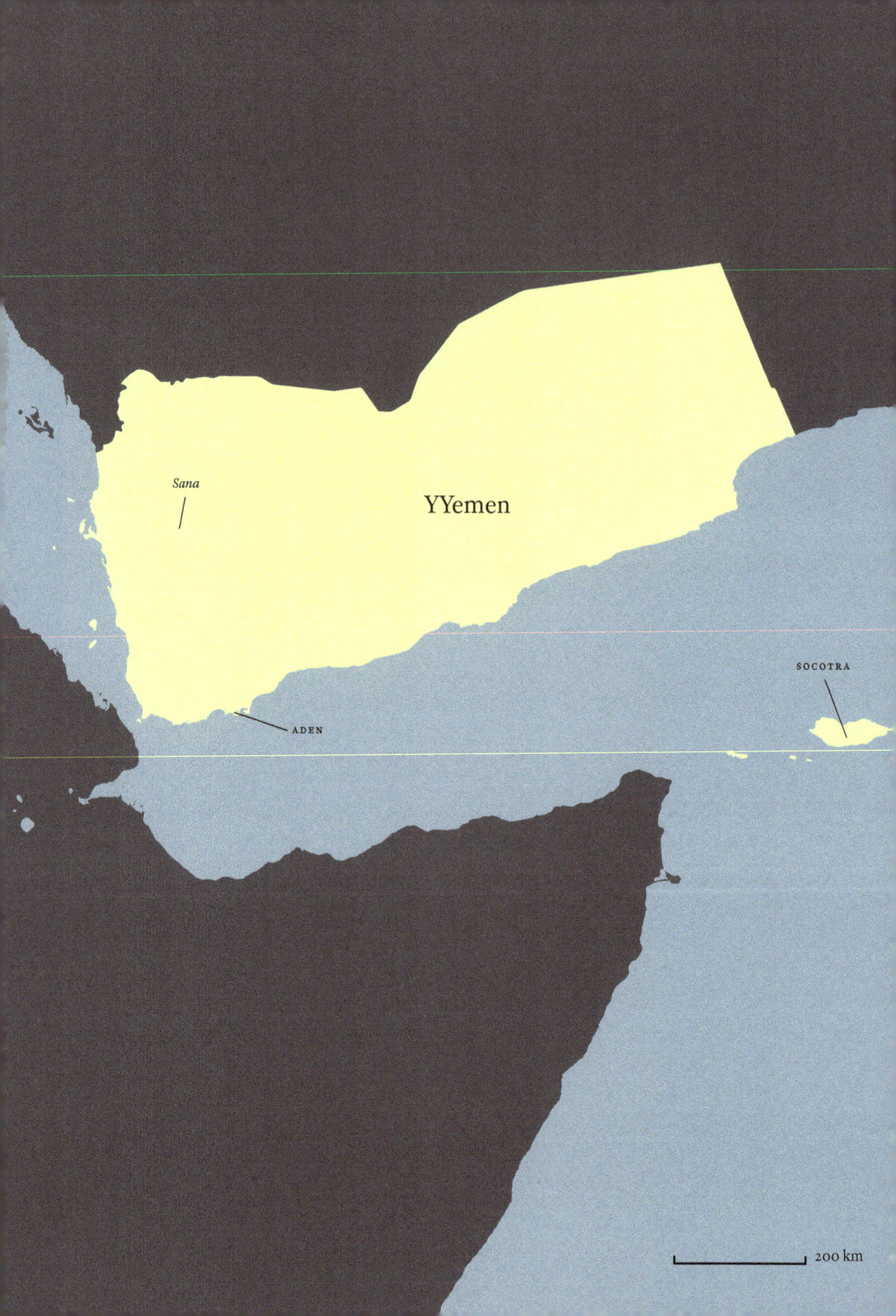

Sana

YYemen

SOCOTRA

ADEN

200 km

beers stopped. One of the other guys prepared an especially foul-smelling fish, and a third man brought out the abio. The wild bird was to be tamed, and it ne   en before the competitor club a few kilometres away managed to do it.

This time they did not succeed in tempting the wild bird within lasso range. But that did not stop them returning to drink beer. It was perhaps this social element that was really the main reason for the frigatebird collection.

Unfortunately, or fortunately, I did not get much more time to find out. Nauru Airlines finally took me onwards to Brisbane in Australia — only two days late. That qualified for quite an Australian-style celebration. In the world's least visited country, toasts are few and far between. Alcohol is actually completely forbidden. Instead, the men chew on khat.

1

Yemen,
Asia

IHABITANTS: 27,600,000 (Wikipedia)

TOURISTS PER YEAR: 60 (garfors.com)

AREA: 527,968 square kilometres

"**IN YEMEN**, most men chew on khat," I once mentioned during a travel talk at Sunnfjord Vocational College in Førde, Norway. One student immediately raised their hand. The 17-year-old looked startled.

"That's so awful! Just what have the poor cute pussycats done?" she asked, on the verge of crying.

I managed somehow not to laugh and explained the difference between khat and cat.

The stimulant, khat, is in danger of making one of the world's most cursed countries even worse. The narcotic plant requires enormous volumes of water, something that is very bad news in a country that is almost without water. When 90 percent of the men are addicted to khat, food production becomes a low priority, something that is contributing to famine in Yemen.

The great demand, combined with the fact that the plant grows so quickly that it yields three harvests a year, makes it far more lucrative to cultivate khat than grains, kohlrabi, or kiwi. So, that is just what the farmers do. That anyone grows food at all, is down to khat requiring huge volumes of water, and H2O is in short supply in large swathes of the country. The green leaves of the plant provide a soothing intoxication, supposedly like a strong dose of caffeine or mild amphetamine. Khat usage further dulls the appetite, and with food shortages here, it is perhaps not surprising that its popularity has skyrocketed.

When I visited the capital Sana'a back in 2009, I saw two boys aged five or six years old. Not only were they both chewing khat, but they were also smoking hookah pipe at the same time. Getting hooked early - and then no way back.

But it is not only extensive khat farming that now threatens food production. The civil war, which has been raging since 2015, has led to both the airspace over the country and most of the ports being closed from time to time. Consequently, this has added to an acute and precarious shortage of food and emergency aid, which has created one of the worst humanitarian disasters in recent times. This contributes greatly, of course, to

Yemen being the least visited country in the world.

The least visited country in the world — a dubious world record title to hold a claim to. And with a meagre five tourists a month, it is an almost unbeatable record. But Yemen has not always been ravaged by war, nor has the country been close to being the least visited country in the world earlier. There have been people in Yemen for at least 7,000 years, and the area was a centre of power in the Middle East for almost 2,000 years from 1200 BC — largely due to its 2,000-kilometre-long coastline, which is strategically placed between east and west. There was a lack of water shortages back then as well, and difficulties keeping the kingdom together, even though the Sabeans managed to beat back 10,000 charging men from the Roman Empire in the year 25 BC. After that chaos reigned, and from the year 275, the dominant faith switched between Judaism and Christianity through various kings, before Islam was gradually accepted in the country in the 7th and 8th centuries. The religion has endured to this day, but that didn't quite stop the British sticking their noses in nonetheless in the last century — they governed southern Yemen, including Aden, until 1967. This led to Aden becoming a free trade zone, and, in fact, being flooded with tourists, after which northern Yemen and southern Yemen existed side by side until they unified and became Yemen as recently as 1990.

Now, of course, there isn't really of a trace of tourism, and in a war-torn country with little food and water, it is primarily the legendary island of Socotra that is the reason for the country having any visitors at all. This island, which is one of the most extraordinary in the world, is located 500 kilometres off the mainland. Most visitors make their way there in their own sailboats, and they are apparently not disappointed. I still have this trip in store. But the reports are clear: What we have here is the Middle East's answer to the Galápagos, with a completely unique plant and animal life. The distinctive dragon blood tree is perhaps the best-known example. The red sap is harvested by young girls who use it in homemade nail polish and make-up. Socotra comes from the Sanskrit word for 'paradise', and the 60,000 inhabitants, scattered across 600 villages, have largely been able to live in seclusion from the war on the mainland.

A few foreigners also make the trip from Oman, but often for just a few hours, if not just a few measly minutes. On the whole these are people who have misconstrued traveling and just want to cross the country off their list. There is, however, little to see just over the border, and in professional or semi-professional travel circles, such a 'visit' is frowned upon. The reasons behind such border hopping among country collectors is partly understandable. Sana'a in the north is now almost impossible to reach due to the civil war, and the airport there is closed. Northern Yemen is controlled by the Houthis, a Shia Muslim rebel group, while southern Yemen is controlled by the Sunni Muslim Salafists, who are backed by a coalition from Saudi Arabia and the UAE who provide weapons, fighter jets and bombers. In addition, this is a tribal society, and various gangs and groups

govern different provinces. One must be good at speaking for oneself or know someone high enough up in the right tribe, to get to Sana'a in one piece and without great delays.

I visited the Old City in the capital a few years ago. The old brown houses with flat roofs in the Old City look like an enormous gingerbread town. Houses, which are made of brick and rammed earth, often scale several floors. Space was tight, so they had to build upwards. In many ways, an early version of New York with the skyscrapers of the time all crowded together. The brown colour merges almost seamlessly with the golden, dry landscape around, with beautiful and wild mountains in the background. But not everything is brown in and around Sana'a.

There are surprisingly many places where you can see small green gardens and parks, breaking up the colours. Furthermore, the houses are decorated with white frames and deft, well thought-out geometric patterns, also in white. It is like the icing on a gingerbread house. Narrow alleys run between the houses, which are seemingly built without exact plans. It is as if the houses stand where they were just thrown. Urban planning was maybe not in fashion 2500 years ago when the first people settled in the mountain valley 2200 metres above sea level. There are now 6,000 houses in the Old City, as well as over 100 mosques.

Sana'a was an important trading post in the time of Jesus, and Christianity was dominant here early in the Christian era. But after a while, like many other places in the Middle East, the far younger Islam gradually took over as the most important religion in Sana's and the rest of Yemen. The Grand Mosque is said to have been completely built while the Prophet Muhammad was alive. Now only ruins remain of the original, but a modern version called Al Saleh, with space for 44,000 people, was completed in 2009 and opened by the then president, Ali Abdullah Saleh. He was killed by a sniper in December 2017.

It is safer and easier to travel to Aden in the south. Firstly, it is a port city, and secondly, the airport is partly in operation, that is to say, most of the day. Therefore, Aden gets the odd tourist as a result. Though, it is mostly local people, emergency workers and journalists who take the few planes that still head for the second largest city in the country. For a tourist, it is not exactly easy to get a visa and then be allowed to board a plane or a ship that is on its way there. It's a good thing that fixers exist, if not as hard-nosed as Mr. Wolf and Matthew.

However, not much can be done about it. At long last I got the WhatsApp number of the fixer Adel through the Belgian journalism student Katya Bohdan, who wrote her thesis on the media situation in Yemen with an emphasis on Aden — although somewhat reluctantly.

"What the hell are you doing in Aden?" she asked.

"I reckon you would have gotten the same question," I countered.

"You do know that Yemen is no place for tourists?"

"You do know that Yemen is no place for journalism students?"

She smirked, explaining that it was expensive to fly to Aden with Yemenia, which at that time, in theory, flew 3-4 times a week from Amman and Cairo, but that flights were often cancelled. Tickets could not be bought online or via local travel agents.

"Either someone in Yemen has to buy them for you, or you have to travel to Amman or Cairo and try to buy tickets at the airport," she explained. Now we were getting along, and I got the phone number of Adel, before she added that even though the visa was supposed to be free, it could be necessary to bribe someone to get it. She had received a press visa herself, and I tried for the same thing as a writer. Katya is from Belgium and speaks fluent Dutch, French, Russian and English. But she is not as good in Arabic, so decided to travel to the Middle East for two years. When I last travelled to Yemen, she was working for Al Jazeera in Qatar.

As a fixer, Adel sorts out everything for visiting journalists — from finding interviewees, film locations and people with background information, to arranging hotels, transport, food, and security guards. He has previously been used by the BBC, The Independent, CNN, Norwegian TV 2, and Vice, to name just a few. If he wasn't able to get me in, I had no idea who else to turn to. For once, I did not travel alone either. I decided to bring along a photographer when going to the world's least visited country. An American photographer promised to take pictures for free in exchange for her being allowed into the insular country as well.

I already knew Lexie Alford, via the Internet. She is one of the growing number of people who have set themselves the goal of visiting every country in the world, and she has asked me for tips and advice several times before. There is a steady stream of questions from other travellers about, among other things, visa challenges, local contacts, and general travel tips. But Lexie was a little bit different. As a 19-year-old, she had visited 126 countries, and Yemen was the trickiest one left. She just happened to get in touch again a couple of weeks before I was due to travel there and asked about a notable visa loophole for another country in the Middle East — it is not always the case that what is on an embassy's website is actually correct or up to date. I helped her out with that, and she kindly thanked me, before she asked, almost as a courtesy, what my next destination was going to be.

"I will travel to Yemen in a couple of weeks to research a book about the least visited countries in the world," I wrote via a messaging app.

"Wow! Can I join you? Please!" she responded just ten seconds after I pressed 'send'.

"Well, how good a photographer are you?"

"Very good!"

"Hahaha... prove it," I challenged her.

Lexie followed up by showing me her website with hundreds of very good photographs from various destinations. In addition, she worked as a portrait photographer in California to earn money for her travels and was fluent in the language of photography with her professional SLR camera.

"OK, but then you have to be ready to act on the spur-of-the-moment. I don't have much time and will travel the same day as I get the visa."

The answer arrived immediately.

"Count me in."

Not bad coming from a teenager.

Around lunchtime on the 2nd of April, I received a reply from Adel. The media and photography licenses and press visas were finally ready, and the latter could be collected from the Yemeni embassy in London.

"Can you be in London the morning of the 4th of April, or do I have to travel to Yemen alone?" I wrote in the instant messenger to Lexie. She would have been at home in California, 9 hours behind Norway, so I did not expect to get an answer for a few hours yet.

But then she called me.

"Are you serious?" she said in the sleepiest voice of the decade. She had evidently just woken up.

"Deadly serious. Can you be in London early the day after tomorrow?"

"Let me check on tickets. I'll let you know," she replied and hung up. Her parents run a travel agency, so she has inside information when it comes to booking airline tickets.

"Is it early enough if I land at 07.45 at Heathrow?" she answered ten minutes later.

"Yes. Just."

I saw Lexie for the first time at a café by Gloucester Road tube station on 4th of April 2018 at 9.30 in the morning. We grabbed a coffee before we sauntered 200 metres over to the embassy. The visa section opened at 10.00, and we were there before the ambassador. Presumably he was the one who had to sign our visas.

"How do we get to Yemen?" Lexie asked as we sat in the waiting room, waiting for the ambassador. We had each been given a cup of very sweet milky coffee. The Yemenis like it sweet. I use sugar or honey in my coffee, but there are limits. Lexie drank both.

"We can fly in with Yemenia via Cairo or with Djibouti Air via Djibouti. The problem with Yemenia is that we are not allowed to buy tickets outside of the Middle East."

"Can't we travel via Djibouti? I haven't been there yet?" Lexie asked in an extra lively voice. Yemen as well as a bonus country was not a bad result.

"Why not? But first we have to actually get a hold of a visa," I replied. It has happened to me a few too many times where I have bought tickets before getting the visa, and then had the experience of it taking longer than planned to get the visa. Once bitten, twice shy.

A quarter of an hour later, the ambassador came in. He nodded and smiled, before entering the embassy itself, beyond the waiting room. After another fifteen minutes, both visas were ready for collection, for a fee of £500! Supply and demand also applies to embassies. But at least the surcharge for express service was included.

We took each other by the hand outside the embassy. The first step on the road to getting in! Back at the café on Gloucester Road, it was just a matter of picking up mobile phones to book tickets to Djibouti with Turkish Airlines via Istanbul. An hour later we took the Piccadilly Line to Heathrow and sat down in the United Airlines lounge. Both airlines are members of Star Alliance, with this lounge at Terminal 2 being the only one that has a shower. Lexie had already been travelling for 20 hours and was not exactly reluctant to getting her hair wet. With a little breakfast stop in the centre of Djibouti, the journey would take another 20 hours.

It was odd entering the terminal building at the airport in Aden — not because it was in the middle of a war zone, or because there were only two other planes there, but because there wasn't a single policeman at the border control. All of a sudden, a man with sunglasses, in black clothes and a black hat, tapped me on my shoulder.

"Are you Gunnar? I'm Adel," he said, in an experienced and professional manner. There are cases in war-torn countries of kidnappers passing themselves off as the people foreigners are due to meet. In such cases they do not introduce themselves; only smiling and saying hello. The typical response from the visitor is then to ask if the person in question is the person they are supposed to meet, for example 'Hussain'. Then 'Hussain' need only say yes and ask for the passports of the ignorant visitors before he has everything needed to get them into the country and into the car that takes them straight to captivity. But now it turned out that the kidnapping risk in Aden was lower than anticipated.

"The situation here has been quite calm for several months," Adel Al-Hasani was able to report.

All the news organisations he had helped out earlier had been preoccupied with the war and misery. The worse the things they could report on, the higher their chances of getting their report aired. I was there to write about tourism. I wanted positive stories. Things that could give hope and perhaps make more people travel here. Not tomorrow or the next day, but maybe in a year, or two, or six.

Adel has very good contacts more or less everywhere. Even the president picks up the phone if he calls, and he knows people in the military, private security forces, various tribes and both IS and Al Qaeda. The latter he specifically calls only AQ. For example, Adel was used as a middleman in the release an Indian priest who had spent more than a year in IS captivity. Among other things, the fixer took care of obtaining, verifying, and distributing a video that showed the hostage alive. Both government forces and terrorists trust Adel and view him as an impartial and honest party.

"IS called me from a telephone box and asked me to come to a square where there were many people. Suddenly a young guy approached me. He wore jeans and a T-shirt and

had neither a beard nor long hair. Many IS fighters do what they can so that they do not stand out. I guess he was 23 or 24, and he even tweaked his dialect so that I would not be able to place him in any province. He turned off my mobile phone so that no one could track us, and we then walked through the crowd and into a side street. There I received instructions on where and how I would be able to get the priest out."

Adel managed just that, and the footage of the emaciated priest Father Tom Uzhunnalil with a long-dishevelled beard soon spread across screens from news broadcasts all over the world. Four nuns, two nurses, eight elderly patients and a security guard were not so lucky. They were all killed during the kidnapping operation.

A few days before I left for Yemen, the NRK correspondent who covers the region, Kristin Solberg, had broadcast live on the news in connection with a dramatic report in which she mentioned, among other things, that she was a kidnapping target, and therefore she constantly had to change position. As a result, I received a number of messages from friends telling me not to consider travelling into perilous Aden.

I thought it was not the right time to be self-focused on how dangerous it is in a war zone. That aside, I could not believe either that it was actually true. Foreign journalists had not been kidnapped for years, and if it was to happen, it would hardly happen in front of a camera in plain sight. I double-checked the Solberg angle with Adel. He dismissed it as fabrication.

"It has not been as stable and calm as this in Aden since the war began in 2015. Where on earth does she have that from? She exaggerates and shouldn't do that."

Conflict situations encourage such reporting. Firstly, the reporters are free to put the spotlight on themselves, earning 'cred' back home for daring to report from dramatic situations in 'life-threatening' areas. Secondly, the editors are not there, so they have to rely 100 percent in the reporter and the cameraman, if there is one, but the person concerned is often hired locally. Furthermore, these kinds of news features with their own reporter on the screen is often good for viewing figures, and the TV stations can use phrases like 'X is one of the very few broadcasters present in Y'. And that is just what they do.

As a fellow employee of the Norwegian Broadcasting Corporation NRK, I was able to contact my colleague Solberg by email, to find out what the basis of the report was. A week later I received a reply.

"The threat against us was real and in no way sensationalised. [...] Our local security company, our fixer and the family who were hosting us in the village all thought it was wholly necessary to evacuate. [...] You're correct that the kidnap risk in Yemen is lower than before. NRK's security company still counts it as 'extreme' and amongst the highest in the world," she wrote in an email. As with all war zones, there can be great differences in how situations are perceived. It can all depend on who you are with, and it can vary from one day to the next, or across a few hundred metres. Our perceptions of being at approximately the same place at around the same time were obviously completely different.

I really wanted to meet a young woman in this patriarchal society, and Adel had been calling around to arrange it. Noor, a 25-year-old journalist, works for the Yemeni government. Her dream is to become an independent, well-known, and respected journalist. One evening we met Noor in a restaurant. In the short term, she has just one hope for the war-torn country.

"I wish they would toss all the world's weapons into the sea!" she said in a clear voice. It was perhaps the best suggestion of all time.

After Adel, Lexie, Noor, and I had dinner at the restaurant in Aden, we said goodbye to Noor and made our way home to the apartment hotel. The receptionist served us a large pot of burning hot tea, and we sat on the sofa waiting for the tea to cool down enough for us to drink it.

"I've never had such a nice time with someone I have worked with before," said Adel, completely unsolicited. "And completely without any stress! Usually, I smoke between 40 and 60 a day. While you have been here, I've only smoked 10."

Living in a war zone like Yemen can be extremely stressful, and some struggle more than others. A cameraman from an American TV station struggled a lot after countless distressing experiences. The 37-year-old had never smoked in his entire life.

"After four days in the area around Aden, he took his first drag. Three days later he is smoking a pack of twenty a day. And that was the way he kept on going. But I'm no better myself now," smiled Adel, lighting a fresh cigarette.

Personally, I encountered Aden as someone who was calm, stable, and assured. As a foreigner, I did not feel in any way especially vulnerable. But Adel explained that the situation was far worse for certain local imams. 100 of them appear on a macabre 'hit-list'. They are earmarked for death.

"Over 40 of them have already been slaughtered in various ways over the last months. Most were killed early in the morning as they were on their way to dawn prayers. It is the most effective time to carry out an assassination as there are few witnesses," said Adel.

The rest are fully aware that they are on the list, and some of them have taken precautions such as getting themselves bodyguards. Others have left it to God to decide their fate and carry on just as before.

"I know five of them on that list, including the most prominent imam in southern Yemen. Abdul Rahman Mara'i led the Dar al-Hadith Mosque in Al-Fayush north of Aden, and he was wiped-out in a terrorist attack. In spite of this, the Salafists are not looking for revenge. They do not have it in them, and it is not part of their culture," said Adel. I shuddered at the thought of the grim list and how it was being used in the very neighbourhood where we were sitting.

As time goes by, the imam list gets shorter and shorter, and they are said to be now turning their attention to non-religious Salafists.

"Now they go after anyone with great influence. It's awful. It's total overkill. As a result of this, people have now lost the little sympathy they had at some point for the Houthis."

It is, however, not the Houthis who have come up with this assassination plan, although most people blame them. Apparently, a wealthy businessman from the Emirates is behind it all. The attempt to create more division in the deadlocked civil war seems to have been successful to a degree. Concurrently, the alliance the Salafists have with the United Arab Emirates and the Yemeni authorities is not flourishing.

"The hatred goes far too deep. The Salafists will never follow the Emirates' lead, no matter what the government says. The long-term solution is for the different sides in Yemen to come together and negotiate a deal without foreign interference. The people here in the south cannot govern the country. The northerners are wiser, better organized and more able to govern the country. Both sides know this, and I hope they lay down their arms and come to a peaceful solution before this turns into a full-scale war, completely out of control. But with the current situation, we are a long way from peace," said Adel, sighing heavily. He pulled out another an American filter cigarette.

Ignoring the deadlocked conflict, then both Aden and the area around this large city are utterly fantastic. The city nestles among several mountains with houses that rise up the slopes, with an abundance of beaches and harbours. For instance, the fish market is close to an incredibly pretty little natural harbour, partly surrounded by two peaks and a beach. In the harbour, the fishing boats are tightly packed together, while the traditional rectangular brick houses have been built right next to the shoreline. Following the outbreak of the war, most large hotels closed, and it is not difficult to understand why. The walls are covered with bullet holes and major artillery damage. The entire mid-section of the Mercure hotel has collapsed, while there is only one section of damage to the Gold Mohur Hotel — on the top floor. It seems, however, to have been large-calibre ammunition that has been used. I would guess at a 1000-millimetre round.

We had a comfortable stay at a pretty anonymous apartment hotel and felt safe there. At least for the first two nights. The third night, both my photographer and I were woken up by machine gunfire just outside. Lexie stormed into my room. She was scared to death.

"What's going on?" she whispered, almost in hysterics.

The shooting had stopped, and she didn't want in any way to draw the attention of the shooters outside.

I got up, and we crept along to the window in the living room, carefully opening a small gap in the curtains. Hundreds of people stood outside. Had they heard that foreigners were staying here, and had plans to lynch us? Kidnap us? Or was it just a gathering, or a party?

The fireworks that went off hinted at the latter. Fortunately, the whole thing was a wedding, and in Yemen they celebrate by firing hundreds of times into the air with numerous Kalashnikovs. But bullets that go up, also have to come down and dozens of people die every year from being struck by celebratory ammunition.

The next day, we told Adel about the experience. He just smiled.

"Well, that's totally normal here. But since you have now experienced being scared here in Yemen, we must think about safety," he said, and signalled that we should get into the car. Half an hour later we had picked up a Kalashnikov and enough ammunition to get us through an average ambush. Then we drove out into an uninhabited desert area outside of Aden, and Adel showed us how to shoot. Lexie got to try it first. She pretty much mowed the top off of a two-inch metal pipe that was standing on the ground 30 metres away.

"Good shooting, Lexie!" shouted Adel. After shooting various rounds with the most common machine gun in the world, the AK-47, relaxing by the sea came as welcome respite. On the sandy beach of Gold Mohur, kids and teenagers were swimming. From there we could see the Elephant's Trunk, a distinctive cliff that forms a nose, thanks largely to a hole through the cliff. Adventurous and competent youngsters swam almost to the hole, but no water passed through it, so they couldn't swim to the other side. At the same time, the mothers seemed to relax on the beach in their black niqabs — if it is at all possible to really relax in Yemen, especially with so much clothing on. Lexie had a niqab on over her usual clothes and was just about dying from the heat.

"How on earth can the women here live with this? It's not even the hottest time of the year," she complained.

We were lucky with around 30 degrees in the shade, at the most. In July the thermometer can reach 50 and sometimes 55 degrees. Poor people. And poor, poor women. The fact that the niqab is black does not exactly help. The distinctive robe of the men in the Middle East are, if nothing else, made of white fabric, usually cotton. In the Middle East, such a garment is called thawb, dishdasha, jubbah, kandoorah, gandora, khaftaan, aselham, mudawwar, gamis, perahan, bekishe, cübbe or jelebeeya — except in Yemen where the robe is known as a zannah. The precious robe has many names, while the burqa has only one — clearly not as cherished.

With a few dozen people on the beach, Adel was of the opinion that the beach was a bit overcrowded.

"Let me take you to a better beach. Is it okay if we take a boat there?" asked Adel. The country is 50 percent larger than Norway and has a long coastline. I had nothing against exploring more parts of it. The promise of a boat on waveless, blue-green sea in the 30-degree heat was something very amenable indeed. We drove to the fishing village of Bassem Alwan. Adel asked us to stay seated in the Korean car, with blacked-out windows, as he opened the door and was about to go out.

"If the fishermen see your white faces, it will be double the price. At least!" he explained. Our fixer sorted transport with the fisherman Nasher Said, and we were on our way to the beach of our dreams just ten minutes later. The 44-year-old fisherman had four kids and his wife was pregnant with number five.

"How many wives does he have?" I asked Adel. Nasher did not speak English and had to have the question translated. Our skipper became noticeably a little self-conscious.

"Just one," he almost stuttered. "And you're not the only one who has asked. My mother is always on at me to have more wives and many children. 'They will take care of you when you get old,' she says."

So far, he had resisted. The fishing didn't amount to much, and his income was not particularly compatible with 8-10 kids. Child benefit does not exist in Yemen. The extra income from our journey was greatly welcomed, and he used the opportunity to take along two of his sons. There was no doubt that he knew his fishing trade. He spoke, with Adel translating, about the time a British fisherman had joined them on an evening trip. Even in the dark, Nasher was able to tell the Brit exactly what kind of fish were in the vicinity, based only on how the fish moved around and disturbed the surface.

The Brit thought it was quite incredible that people with echo sounders and other modern aids, on board large steel fishing boats, knew far less about how much and which fish were in the surrounding waters than Nasher did in his open wooden boat. I was impressed and applauded, and the shy fisherman was clearly embarrassed. He was hardly used to praise.

The beach was nestled between two cliffs, just beyond a steep 60-metre-high dune. It was hard going up the hill in the sand, almost like walking in deep snow. Each step was a workout, but the view was worth it! The yellow boat lay a few metres from the beach, with a grapnel on the sandy bed. To the left of the field of vision was a tiny island with a distinctive 12 metre high and very steep rocky area. The island is called The Rook, after the chess piece of the same name. To the right was a rounded cliff, and a few skerries. The tints of colour in the water across the shallow beach were remarkable. And on the beach were only Nasher, his youngest son and Lexie. She was not ready to race up the dune into her forced textile prison. None of the locals would have cared if she had taken off the black robe, but she felt that it was not quite right to do so. I rubbed her decision in after I ran down the dune, threw everything off apart from my boxer shorts, wading into Neptune's kingdom and began swimming. What a water temperature! I swam the 200 metres to the Rook and considered trying to climb all the way up, but barefoot it was a lost cause. I contented myself with walking around the top before I dived into the wonderful water. It felt completely surreal that this was actually in war-torn Yemen.

After lunch, Nasher took us back to the village, and from there we drove to an elderly camel farmer. 63-year-old Naib told us that he had been doing the same thing since he was half a metre tall. He used to have 5-6 times as many animals, and now in his twilight years he was content with 10 camels.

"That's enough for an old man like me," he said, laughing in his white 14-day beard until his whole big belly shook. Lexie was allowed to take a picture of him, and he asked if one of them could be sent to him. I suggested doing it digitally.

"Huh? What's Facebook? What's WhatsApp?" he asked in bewilderment. Adel promised to print out the picture and take it with him the next time he was going to buy camel milk. On this occasion we picked up two litres, waved goodbye and drove onwards. Camel milk tastes a little more bitter than cow's milk, but still quite sweet. I thought that it would make a good caffe latte. Unfortunately, Adel did not know any cafés with an espresso machine in the city, so it will have to be tested another time.

A forty-five-minute drive later we were standing outside a mango farm on the outskirts of the village of Al Makhshabah, with 80 houses. 50 large mango trees with thick branches and green leaves provided us with shade. The copious amount of fruit meant that some branches were heavily laden just above the ground. Around every tree they had dug small circular pits, so that the fruits would gather around the trunk when they fell down. Easy collection. On one side of the mango grove was a deep well. An old and well-used diesel engine was coupled to a pump which was sometimes used for essential watering. The farmer welcomed us and invited us to taste some small mangoes. You could say they were ripe, while the larger fruits were still green and hard. The samples melted in the mouth — they were the freshest and best mangoes I have ever tasted. I asked, once again through Adel, what the farmer was called.

Both grinned.

"Ali Abdullah Saleh," they said almost in unison, as if the name had an uncomfortable translation.

"Why are they laughing?" I wondered.

"He is called exactly the same as the former president of Yemen," the fixer explained. "And not many are."

The fact that the mango farmer was a supporter of the former president wasn't such a strange thing — he even had a picture of him inside his house. That was perhaps not very wise. "If it comes out, he'll be living dangerously," said Adel.

In Yemeni politics, one should never tempt fate, but neither should one be seen to support someone other than the sitting president at all times. Democratic, in a way.

"Wouldn't it be more lucrative to grow khat?" I asked the mango farmer, Ali Abdullah Saleh.

"Yes, a lot more lucrative. But there is not enough water here in the lowlands. If I had been able to grow khat, I would never have even left my farm, instead sat in the shade under a tree, relaxing and chewing on khat all day, every day, all my life," he smiled dreamily.

I asked Ali several questions, and he was impressed with my curiosity, and how much I wanted to know. In the end, he invited us to lunch. We had plans to visit a filthy-rich alcohol smuggler for lunch. I was curious about how the smuggler operated, and I tried politely to avoid lunch by agreeing to a quick coffee.

The strategy seemed to have worked. We were shown into the living room, where a small chunky 12-inch TV stood on a tiny chest of drawers. Otherwise, there was nothing else in the room, except for thin foam mattresses that were covered with colourful sheets. The floor was made of large beige and brown tiles a foot square, while the walls were pastel green and the ceiling pale pink. All the windows were wide open in their metal frames, and a fresh breeze made the temperature bearable. Except for poor Lexie in the niqab. On the outside of the windows there was a metal lattice, and one end of a clothesline was fastened to this lattice. The other end was tied to a slender tree a few metres from the house. On the line hung garments in widely varying colours.

Coffee soon arrived, served on the floor, and we savoured the jet black 90-degree hot drink. Yemen produces some of the best coffee in the world — the problem is that no one knows about it. Several attempts at export have been unsuccessful, and the current situation is not exactly inviting anyone to try again. After half an hour, while Ali was out for a walk, I tried to hint that we would have to be on our way.

"I swear on my grandmother's grave that you'll eat lunch here," said Hashed, one of Ali's five sons. The mango farmer had five daughters as well, but all were married off and no longer lived at home.

"This means we have no choice. It would be extremely offensive if we do not eat here," Adel explained. "We can meet the alcohol smuggler later."

After a while Hashed brought in the food. We sat in a circle around the food, which was placed on a large round metal tray — chicken soup, a kind of fish stew and freshly baked flat bread from the round stone oven that was out in the courtyard. It was Ali's wife who had done the cooking, but we never got to meet her. Men in Yemen are often protective of their wives when it comes to unknown men.

"It is an honour for me to offer lunch here on my farm. I am very proud that you have chosen to share this meal with us," said Ali. Chosen, in a way. We said nothing about the grandma's grave. But the meal was totally fantastic and the best we ate in Yemen, even when I include a lobster dinner in the city, where I was given one and a half steaming fresh lobsters for 11 dollars. There was no doubt that the chickens were free-range at Ali's home, completely without growth hormones or industrial feed. Several of the chicken's siblings were still running around the yard.

Ali told us about drought, and I asked if he noticed 'global warming' at all. The mango farmer knew nothing of the notion and had no complaints.

"It is Allah who decides, we have nothing to do with the weather, wind or climate."

But the farmer, who was in his sixties, had noticed a change. And he knew what he was talking about after having run the farm since 1964. In the beginning, he helped his father before he took over. Ali said that they had noticed a change in climate in 1994.

"I remember the year because the crops were noticeably smaller than the year before. It has never been the same again since. It is becoming increasingly drier with worse water conditions. We have to use more diesel now to run the pump, but in the driest periods of the year the well runs dry after an hour or two of use. Then we have to wait for the water to be replenished for a few hours before we can pump again."

He was clearly engrossed. Whether it was Allah or man to blame, there was at the very least a noticeable decline in his mango production.

"Worst of all was in 2016. Then it was really dry," he recalled, despite the painful unrest the year before. When the troops from the north had come through the area on their way to Aden, they had had to abandon the farm for a day.

"We dislike Houthis so much that we call them repulsive worms, after the worms that sometimes attack our tomatoes," smiled Hashed. The shy 16-year-old mango farmer's son definitely had a clear-cut opinion about one side in the war. "If we try to plant a new tomato bush from a tomato that has been attacked by worms, nothing grows. It's totally dead."

We thanked them wholeheartedly for the hospitality and went out into the hallway to put on our shoes. Before we left, I asked how many lived in the village of 80 houses. Ali grinned.

"In one of the houses lives a man with his 28 sons. And about 12 daughters."

Clearly it is a patriarchal society. The number of girls was not very important.

"Incredible! Can we visit him?" I wondered.

Ali and Hashed had a discussion in Arabic to clarify the situation.

"Sorry, he actually died last week," Ali replied quietly. "May peace be upon him."

For the first time, I hoped that a man had had more than one wife.

I never got an answer to how many people actually lived in Al Makhshabah, but it was guaranteed to be more than 2.2 people in every household, like in Norway.

I would not have swapped the outstanding dinner at Ali's home, but it meant that we never had the time to meet the busy alcohol smuggler who was about to pick up a new delivery in a secret location. If nothing else, I have an open invitation to learn about his methods on my next trip to Yemen.

Instead, I gave Adel the challenge of finding a local tourism expert. Finding someone who had seen even a single tourist in Aden was not easy, but no one could categorically deny that tourists came to the Aden region. In the end we found someone who knew at least something. Historian and writer Bilal Hussein has written four books about Aden, the most recent of which was published in 2018 and is currently on the bestseller lists in the country. His biggest problem is getting the books distributed to northern Yemen without a working postal service. The solution is to ask acquaintances who are on their way north to take a stack of books in their luggage, or to send them with a good-natured bus or lorry driver.

"In 2010, 400 tourists came to Aden and in the preceding years just as few. But in the 1950s and 60s, Aden was like Las Vegas. Then we had between 800,000 and 900,000 tourists every year, spread over almost 7,000 boats! The reason was largely due to the city being a free trade zone where people made a pilgrimage from many parts of the world, as well as the unique geography here with mountains and beaches all around the city," Bilal said enthusiastically. He had invited us to his home in the centre of Aden. We sat on plastic chairs in his shady backyard and were served incredibly good and fresh water from a local spring in the heat of the afternoon.

Bilal thought that something revolutionary had to happen if Aden was going to see such high tourist numbers once more, and he wasn't just talking about the war ending.

"Ideally, Aden should become a free trade zone again, putting the city on the map again and attracting foreign investors and businesses. Aden should be free from Yemen when it comes to business, similar to Hong Kong and China," he explained, making the point that tourists need to have something to do, or more importantly: something to spend money on.

"What good are tourists if they don't leave behind money?" he asked rhetorically. He had a good point, and he elaborated:

"I mean, what is the use of cruise tourists coming here and being ashore for just a few hours if they are then only driven to monument A, beach B and castle C? They are then only wearing out our infrastructure, polluting with their ships and buses as well as causing further traffic and delays, all without spending a single rial," he went on fervently.

He might as well have been talking about foreign cruise ships in Norwegian fjords.

"The very least we must do is to charge entrance fees, offer souvenirs and get them involved in activities such as diving or rock climbing. That will create jobs as guides or instructors for the people who live here, and it will provide employment for souvenir producers and vendors."

He had personally calculated that a maximum of 100 tourists visited Yemen each year, and Bilal was not far off. I received the decisive number in a conversation with a director in the Ministry of Immigration. He did not want to be quoted but claimed that there were on average five tourists a month. As mentioned, most go to Socotra, while the odd one strays to Aden or across the border from Oman. There are two border posts there, and as mentioned earlier, they are often used by country collectors who are in the country for just 30-ish minutes, or maybe a whole hour to secure the essential photographic evidence. Preferably geotagged.

The question then is just how many minutes one needs to be in a country to be able to call oneself a tourist. In any case, they did not manage to use very large sums of money. But five dozen tourists are not satisfactory for any Minister of Tourism. Yemen has a long way to go before the country can employ anyone at all in the tourism industry, let alone making good money from inquisitive foreigners with cameras, maps and cash.

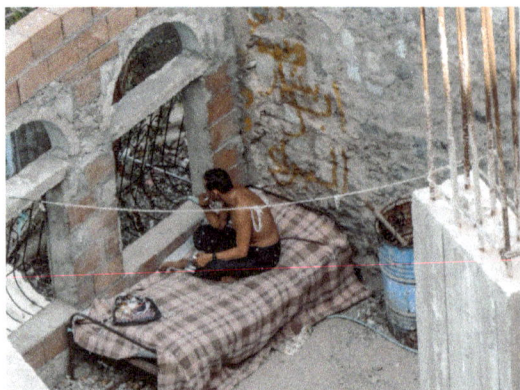

We saw this man from a ridge near Aden. The roof of his house had been damaged in the war.

90 per cent of Yemeni men use khat, a mild narcotic. Even soldiers don't go far without a khat bag.

The scarf makes squatting easier for the many fishermen in the Gulf of Aden.

It's late afternoon and the net fishermen on Goldmohr beach are cleaning their nets so that they are ready for use the next morning.

The son of a fisherman inspects the boats in the village of Bassem Alwan. We were later taken to a beach in one of them.

The elephant trunk in the Aden.

The old town in Sana resembles a gingerbread town.

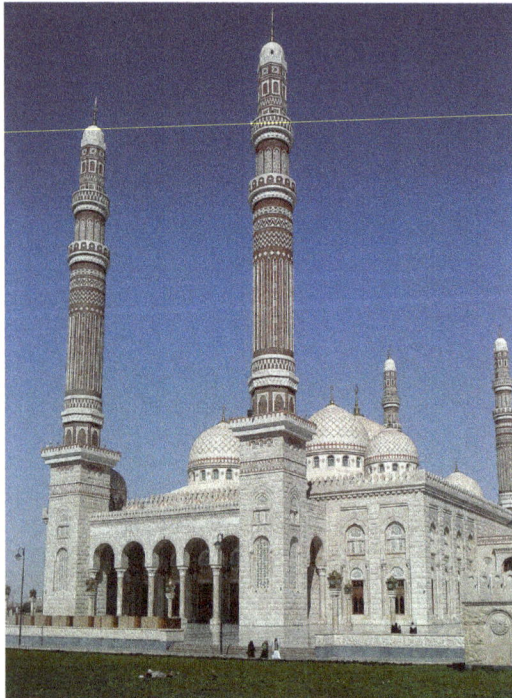
The modern mosque in the capital has room for over 40,000 people.

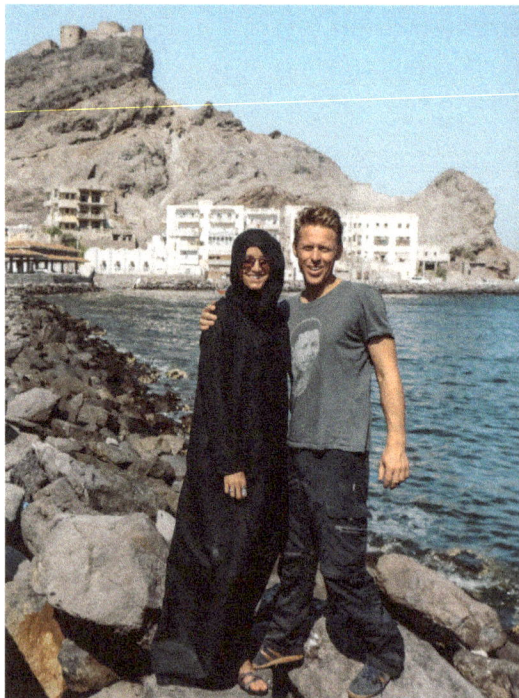
Lexie is usually behind the camera.

A camel driver outside the country. He uses the camel to transport goods for small businesses, and is cheaper than lorry drivers.

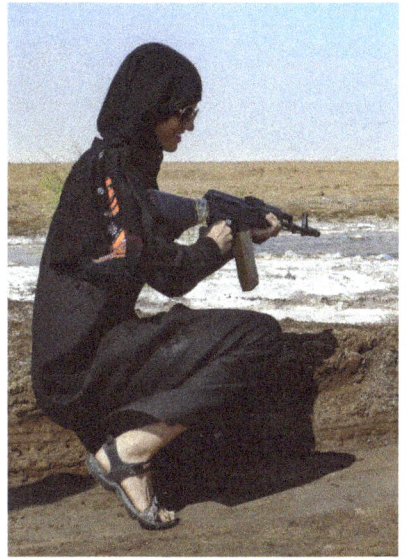

Shooting practice in the desert. Lexie had to learn to defend herself, later it was my turn.

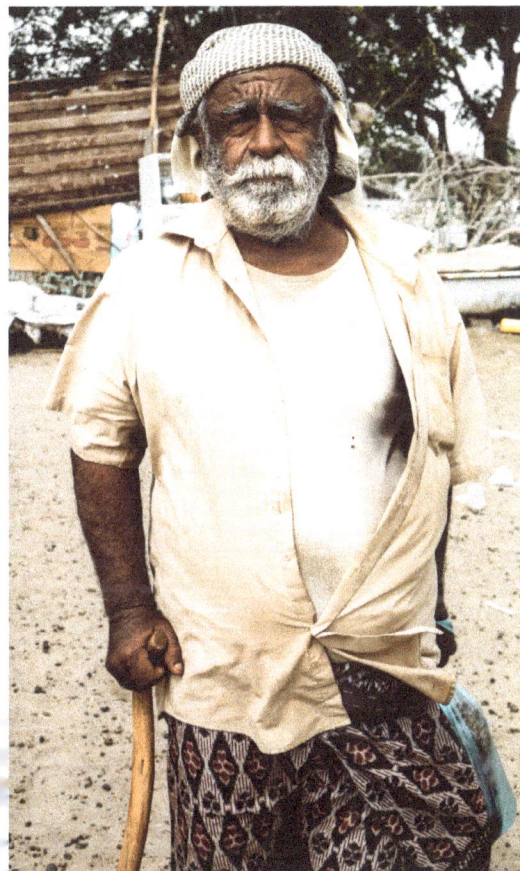

63-year-old Naib has been a camel farmer since he was half a metre tall.

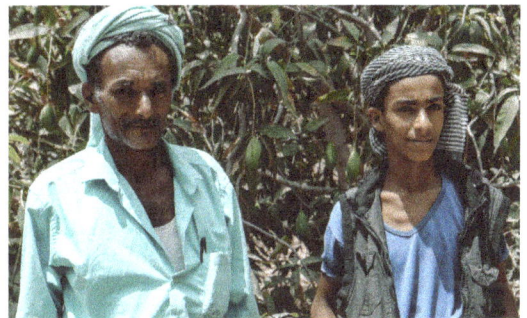

Mango farmer Ali Abdullah Saleh has the same name as the country's ex-president. Here he is with his son.

The market situation is far worse now.

As long as war is raging, the number of tourists, quite understandably, will not increase. But in contrast to Nauru, which has hardly a single tourist attraction, the potential for tourism is enormous in wild and beautiful Yemen. The only major stumbling block is the perception of the security situation. If residents feel safe, foreign investors will get on board quickly. After that it is a matter of weeks or months before the first above-average adventure-seekers arrive. The stories they will go on to tell and the pictures they go on to share, will almost certainly come back, and in a short time Yemen will no longer be on this list of the least visited countries in the world. There are too many attractions, too much fantastic food and such an excess of hospitable people for the war-torn country to look back at all.

The question is when it will happen. On behalf of all Yemenis and tourists all over the world, I hope it happens before the year ends.

If I only knew which year.

LAY OUT YOUR UNREST, GLOBALLY

Milton Keynes UK
Ingram Content Group UK Ltd.
UKHW051824090424
440885UK00006B/124

9 781916 938960